D0742497

The North, the South, and the Powers

1861–1865

The North, the South, and the Powers
1861–1865

D.P. Crook
University of Queensland
Australia

JOHN WILEY & SONS
New York London Sydney Toronto

In memory of my father,
and for
Lisa, Peter, Daniel and Gabrielle

Library of Congress Cataloging in Publication Data

Crook, David Paul.
The North, the South, and the powers, 1861-1865.
Bibliography: p.
1. United States—Foreign relations 1861-1865.
2. Confederate States of America—Foreign relations.
I. Title.
E469.C76 973.7'2 73-16355

ISBN 0-471-18855-7

10 9 8 7 6 5 4 3 2 1

Preface

Although more words have been written upon the American Civil War than upon most historical subjects, that upheaval has never been accorded its just place in the international history of our times. The Civil War threatened to break up the entire balance of power in the western hemisphere, and beyond. But it betrayed that promise and, in world history, was soon overshadowed by the drama of Germany's rise to power. Nevertheless, the American crisis contributed its legacy to the world that was being born in the later nineteenth century. The simplest, and most fundamental, outcome of events was that the United States was enabled to continue its headlong rush into super-powerdom. Men talked at the time of a world divided between American and Russian spheres of influence; and they knew that a battle in the Wilderness, or at Gettysburg, might hold the key to that future. Again, as this volume will suggest, the war marked a turning point in "Atlantic history," diverted the career of American imperialism, and bore upon the great debate on Democracy's future which rent the developed world. The most intimate phase in the Anglo-American association was ending before the 1860's. But the animosities which developed between the American contestants and the great powers during the Civil War hastened the process of economic and cultural disengagement. Thereafter, the relationship of Britain and the United States was more frankly a power relationship. Only the rhetoric of historians who wrote during the Great Rapprochement of 1895-1930, and the wishful thinking of apostles of Atlantic unity since, have obscured that fact. The War Between the States also put a stop, for a time, to American expansionist activity, so conspicuous a feature of the preceding generation. Secretary of State Seward's abiding achievement was to deflect that former energy into the Unionist war effort. In the south, it went into the struggle for survival. In retrospect what is truly surprising is how resilient the idea of American imperial mission proved to be, even during the national firestorm. Geo-political ambitions featured persistently in the foreign policy outlook of both sections. Those who view the "new imperialism" of 1898 as an aberration from American tradition would be well advised to look again at the neglected 1860's. Finally, that decade witnessed the ordeal and crisis of American democracy. The course of events seemed of epochal significance for the politics of Western Europe. There the American image had long been ideologically symbolic. It is not the least of history's ironies that victory for the north gave impetus abroad to militarism, centralist nationalism, and monolithic capitalism, as well as to the liberal ideals of Abraham Lincoln.

This book offers a narrative history of civil war diplomacy, incorporating the results of current scholarship. The central focus is, unrepentantly, upon the interplay which took place between the American contestants and the "great powers" of the day: Great Britain and France. Lesser powers, like Spain, Austria, Russia, merely flit across the stage. The decisions which counted were made in London and Washington, Paris and (perhaps to a diminished extent) Richmond. A narrative approach has its problems, as I am acutely aware. But it can offer a proper sense of context, an overall perspective of the range of historical forces operating at a given time. Even the classic works on the present subject fail, on important occasions, to provide that context, to gaze steadily at what Carlyle called the whole historical Transaction.

It is my pleasure to thank the following: for financial assistance, the Australian Research Grants Council; for library guidance, the Reference Section of the University of Queensland Library, and in particular Mr. Spencer Routh; for research assistance, at various times, David Denholm, Duncan Anderson, and Rex Wood; for information and comment, Marcus Cunliffe, Mary Louise Ellison, Norman Ferris, Thomas Keiser, Frank J. Merli, R. W. Van Alstyne, Gordon H. Warren, and Robin Winks. Harry C. Allen, Elliot Trommald, and Damodar Singhal gave me wise counsel and encouragement. Robert A. Divine has been a tolerant and helpful editor, and I am grateful to Wayne Anderson at Wiley for putting the manuscript to press.

David Paul Crook
Queensland, Australia

Contents

Maps

Abbreviations of Sources Cited in Text

AEJ	*Albany Evening Journal*
AHR	*American Historical Review*
B. M. Add. Mss.	*British Museum Additional Manuscripts*
BSP	*British Sessional Papers*
CWH	*Civil War History*
EDA	Ephraim Douglass Adams, *Great Britain and the American Civil War* (N.Y., 1926, repr. Gloucester, Mass., 1957)
EHR	*English Historical Review*
JMH	*Journal of Modern History*
JSH	*Journal of Southern History*
MHSP	*Massachusetts Historical Society Proceedings*
MVHR	*Mississippi Valley Historical Review*
NYDT	*New York Daily Tribune*
NYEP	*New York Evening Post*
NYH	*New York Herald*
NYT	*New York Times*
NYW	*New York World*
PRO	Public Records Office (London)
WDMC	*Washington Daily Morning Chronicle*
WNI	*Washington National Intelligencer*

Chapter I

The International Setting

As nineteenth century Americans elbowed their way to the Pacific coast, thrust south and southwest into the old domain of the Spanish empire, claimed the western hemisphere as their sphere of influence, whitened the seven seas with their sails and sought for control of trade routes vital to their commerce, they encountered the competitive interests of European powers. Recent historical writing has tended to set the expansion of the American republic in a wider context than was once fashionable: to portray it as part of the rise of Western nationalism and imperialism, denying any quintessential uniqueness to the American experience. Central to the revisionist historians is the view that American expansionism can only be understood as a struggle for mastery against imperialist rivals, a struggle not merely for territories but for resources, commercial leverage, and strategic advantage in the world at large.[1] The United States' most tenacious tussle took place with the British, firmly installed in Canada and the West Indies, strategically located in Central America, commercially strong in Latin America, almost impregnable in world trade because of their industrial power and maritime supremacy. Spain held Cuba and retained ambitions within the "American orbit" of the Caribbean area. France, jostled out of its eighteenth century American empire, tried in the new century to reassert itself in Texas and Mexico, competed with Britain and the United States in the

1. See William H. Goetzmann, *When the Eagle Screamed: The Romantic Horizon in American Diplomacy* (Wiley, New York, 1966). The major pioneering study is Richard W. Van Alstyne, *The Rising American Empire* (Oxford, 1960).

Isthmus of Panama, the Pacific, and Asia. Independent and chaotic Mexico, already partitioned by American forces during President Polk's momentous administration, seemed foreordained (with Cuba) to be the cockpit of the hemisphere.

By the mid-1850's an uneasy detente had been arrived at between the United States and the powers. At its most basic, the detente was a recognition of realities by all sides. Europe recognized that it was prudent, even profitable, to come to terms with American power in the hemisphere, a power likely to prove irresistable in any contest for hegemony. The United States recognised, morbidly, that the worsening sectional dispute threatened to disable its national effectiveness abroad. Whether that detente would survive the firestorm which broke out in 1861 was the central issue of civil war diplomacy.

The Clayton-Bulwer treaty, signed in 1850, was an appropriately shaky symbol of Anglo-American accommodation. It proposed that the two countries jointly renounce colonial ambitions in Central America, and promote in partnership an Isthmian canal route (which would give whoever controlled it a stranglehold over the lucrative trade between California, no longer Mexican, and places east.) The British doggedly pursued a lasting settlement of the "envenomed question" of the Isthmus, but they were frustrated until 1858 by American filibustering and partisan politics. For Whitehall a settlement would mena long-term benefits and relief from a number of imperial difficulties.[2] Stability in Latin America and free rights of transit between the Atlantic and Pacific oceans promised a commercial boom in the area, a thriving British market, and accorded well with the fashionable free trade doctrines of the Manchester school. The treaty would afford protection to Britain's West Indies colonies against American encirclement. Even more important, good relations with America would relieve pressure upon Canada, which was (in chess terms) a weak piece whose need for support tied up too many other men. Canada's border defenses were fallible against an American land thrust. They could be improved, according to the experts, only by massive expenditure on fortifications and armed forces. That was not likely from a parsimonious British Treasury, while the inhabitants of British North America were notoriously reluctant to shoulder their share of defense burdens. Preoccupied with their far-flung commercial and imperial interests, and determined above all to preserve a free hand for dealing with major European

2. R. W. Van Alstyne, "British Diplomacy and the Clayton–Bulwer Treaty, 1850–1860," *J. Mod. Hist.*, XI, No. 2. (June 1939), pp. 149–183. Lord Napier, the British minister to Washington, made the remark about an "envenomed question" in a long and able paper supporting the treaty in 1858.

questions, the British were willing to settle for the existing balance of power in the hemisphere. Although no English government proposed abandoning imperial obligations in Canada (or significant bases such as Halifax), many Englishmen privately expected—and some openly desired—that the colonies would voluntarily enter the American orbit. Nor did the ultimate absorption of Carribean countries such as Cuba, Santo Domingo, or Haiti into the American empire seem at all unlikely in the mid-nineteenth century. As Palmerston put it in a classical complaint:

> These Yankees are most disagreeable Fellows to have to do with about any American Question; They are on the Spot, strong, deeply interested in the matter, totally unscrupulous and dishonest and determined somehow or other to carry their Point; We are far away, weak from Distance, controlled by the Indifference of the Nation as to the Question discussed, and by its Strong commercial Interest in maintaining Peace with the United States. The Result of this State of Things has been that we have given way Step by Step to the North Americans on almost every disputed matter, and I fear that we shall have more or less to do so upon almost every other Question except the maintenance of our own Provinces and of our West Indian Islands —I have long felt inwardly convinced that the Anglo Saxon Race will in Process of Time become Masters of the whole American Continent North and South, by Reason of their superior Qualities as compared with the degenerate Spanish and Portuguese Americans; But whatever may be the Effects of such a Result upon the Interests of England, it is not for us to assist such a Consummation, but on the Contrary we ought to delay it as long as possible.[3]

Whether America's Civil War provided the heaven-sent opportunity not only to obtain this delay, but also by disintegration of the Union permanently to paralyze the American imperialist impulse, became an open speculation in 1861. Disruption of the United States had superficial attractions to Englishmen who wanted an arrogant rival pared to size. The radical Liberal *Leeds Times* doubted

> whether any people can be morally the better or the happier for cherishing those inordinate dreams of 'manifest destiny' and unapproachable imperial grandeur which used to inflate the American imagination, and which certainly gave a very disagreeable character to American diplomacy. It is probable that we will find it easier to live on amicable and pleasant terms with two or more American federations than with one . . .[4]

---

3. Palmerston to Lord Clarendon, December 31, 1857, q. Van Alstyne, "Anglo-American Relations, 1853–1857," Documents, *AHR*, XLII, No. 34 (1936–1937), p. 500.

4. *Leeds Times*, April 20, 1861, q. D. G. Wright, "English Opinion on Secession: a Note," *J. Am. Stud.*, V, No. 2 (August 1971), p. 153.

On the other hand, it would be rash to jump to the conclusion that the Civil War extinguished entirely the assessments of the 1850's, to assume that Britain necessarily welcomed a breakdown in the hemispheric power balance, or the onset of an era of instability and European meddling in North America. Even France's dictator Napoleon III, although driven toward Mexico by European diplomacy and colonial ambitions, was aware of the perils of dissolution of the old order in America. At the least it might deprive him of a counterweight to British seapower. Avidity may come easily to great powers, but the balance of advantage to be won in the obscure situation created by the south's rebellion could not be easily struck. The Union might fall apart without help from its enemies. Intervention, depending on its form, would have costs to be assessed as well as benefits to be reaped. Foreseeably, no power could afford to move on America without consulting its full range of international interests, inspecting its alliances and the security of its European standing. During the prelude of great changes in the European balance of power, that scrutiny produced precautionary views.

There are other considerations. While it is entirely proper of the realists to insist upon the element of power struggle in America's antebellum relations with the great powers, those relationships had other dimensions. Economic, cultural, and ideological ties bound Britain, and to a lesser extent France, to the new world. These forces were powerful but not always predictable. They bred intimacies, but also hostilities: Bernard Shaw's quip about Englishmen and Americans being divided by a common language is to the point. Certainly such forces created the imagery and national stereotypes which served, and shaped, diplomacy. The civil war, as an epochal world event, made its impact in turn upon the mind and politics of Western Europe.

Anglo-American relations were full of paradoxes in the early nineteenth century. Not the least of these was that, while the two countries engaged in imperial rivalry, they were yoked together in a uniquely complementary economic relationship. Although the British and Americans parted politically at the Revolution, America was to become an integral part in the genuinely international economic system upon which British prosperity was based. Britain's eighteenth century economic revolution depended, to some extent, on using her naval and trading capacity to capture the lion's share of overseas markets at a time when the international economy was expanding rapidly. Taking advantage of their early industrial start, and exploiting their privileged global position, the British created a "kind of planetary system circling round the economic sun of Britain."[5] An economy was constructed which relied upon exchanging manufactures—narrowly based on the cotton, coal, and iron industries—and highly developed supplies and services (banking, capital, shipping, insurance) for raw materials and food. In this system, cotton played a conspicuous role: it was the pacemaker of industrial change; upon it British shipping and exports for long depended; while the areas providing its raw materials (the American South) and its giant export markets (India and the Far East) became almost dependent economies of Lancashire. For forty years before the War Between the States British industry depended upon America's slave economy for well over three-quarters of its raw cotton supplies. For the same years, raw cotton was America's major export, often totalling over half the value of all exports. So great was the dependence of Britain on a single supplier, and the Republic upon a single export commodity, that spokesmen in both nations—particularly antislavery interests—clamoured for diversification.

Textiles, however, had lost their central importance in the British system by mid-century. England was saved from the slump of the "hungry forties" (induced, some thought, by over-reliance on cotton) by a staggering railway boom, which spurred the real revolution in the heavy industries, coal, iron, and later, steel. Iron rails, machinery, implements, and steamships from Britain flooded world markets, and particularly the industrializing areas of Western Europe and North America. A transformed capital market facilitated a spectacular rise in the export of capital abroad. The chronic British balance of payments deficit was more than offset by the return on overseas investment and by the colossal profits made by London as the world's financial center. American investments, the bulk of them in the north, made up an important component of British overseas earnings, going into American public securities, land and railroads. Such resources speeded American development at a critical period, when national income was rising too slowly of its own accord to provide for large scale internal investment. British involvement revived in the 1850's, when memories had faded of the Anglo-American commercial crash of 1837–1839. By 1854 British bondholders held between £50 million and £60 million sterling in publicly issued American securities—£5 million more than total British holdings in

5. E. J. Hobsbawm, *Industry and Empire: an Economic History of Britain since 1750* (London, 1968), p. 112 and *passim*.

French, Belgian, Dutch, and Russian government bonds.[6] The American railroad boom of the early 1850's created an insatiable appetite for foreign capital. By 1857, American railroad stock worth in the vicinity of £80 million was held in Britain, and British backing was important in lines such as the New York Central, the Erie, Pennsylvania, Michigan Central, and Illinois Central. (Richard Cobden, renowned as an admirer of America's free institutions and flexible economy, sunk money voted him by the Anti-Corn Law League in the Illinois Central.) The bonds of southern banks and authorities were freely marketed in London, which thus underwrote cotton growing. Northern industry attracted little British interest—it was competitive—but northern commerce was sustained by an intricate credit network. Anglo-American merchant banking houses, such as Barings, Peabody's, Brown-Shipley & Co., offerred capital at low interest and with long repayment terms, and had extensive entrepreneurial interests.

Britain, in short, was supplying capital, labor, tools, and technology essential for the development of America's huge natural resources. The United States stood in semi-colonial status to the sophisticated "metropolitan" center, and the ocean linked the two regions in what has been described as a single, Atlantic economy.[7] The trading figures testify to a degree of interdependence for the years 1815–1860 unattained in the period before or since. In that period, almost half of American exports went to the United Kingdom, and 40% by value of American imports came from the United Kingdom. About 25% of total British exports went to the United States, while imports from the United States ran at approximately 20% of all imports into the United Kingdom for most of the years from 1830–1860 (rising to one-quarter during the forties). In an era when both nations achieved remarkably high growth rates in foreign trade, each was the other's best customer.

If significant realignment was occurring within the Atlantic economy by the fifties because of American industrialization, it did not prevent Anglo-American trade reaching a climax in that decade.

---

6. L. H. Jenks, *The Migration of British Capital to 1875* (London, 1927), p. 413.

7. Frank Thistlethwaite, *The Anglo-American Connection in the Early Nineteenth Century* (Philadelphia, 1959), especially Chapter 1, a brilliant and original survey. See also J. Potter, "Atlantic Economy, 1815–1860: the U.S.A. and the Industrial Revolution in Britain," in A. W. Coats and R. M. Robertson, eds., *Essays in American Economic History* (London, 1969), pp. 14–48; P. S. Bagwell and G. E. Mingay, *Britain and America 1850–1939* (London, 1970), pp. 18–26; Brinley Thomas, *Migration and Economic Growth: A Study of Great Britain and the Atlantic Economy* (Cambridge, 1954).

Recent research has emphasized the dominant importance of the American component—American raw materials and markets—in British foreign trade across the period 1815-1860; and it is clear that the value of the American trade more than held up during the tremendous expansion of the mid-Victorian British economy.[8] (If the commerce within the "North Atlantic Triangle," Britain, Canada, and the United States, is considered as a unit, the figures are even more impressive.) The computed real value of British imports from the United States for the years 1854-1861 was £287.3 million sterling; the nearest competitors were the British East Indies (£126.7 m), France (£107.7 m), and Russia (£83.7 m). While cotton continued to dominate the trade statistics, being worth 65% of American imports by real value for 1854-1861, the fifties saw a massive expansion in British imports of grain and foodstuffs from the American prairies. In the sixteen years following repeal of the Corn Laws (1846), the United States was Britain's main supplier of grains and flour in no fewer than ten. In 1860, wheat, flour, and other grains supplied 15% by value of American imports into the United Kingdom. Bacon, salted and fresh port, lard, salted and fresh beef from America accounted for 55% of all imports of foodstuffs into Britain in the eight years before the Civil War.

While low American tariffs in the fifties ensured that the United States remained Britain's best national market, the balance of trade was strongly in America's favor. British imports from the United States in 1860 cost twice the value of exports to the United States (in real value terms, £44.7 million compared to £21.7 million). British exports, particularly of iron and steel, expanded impressively in the early fifties, but expansion tapered off later in the decade as the American railroad and textile industries acquired a separate dynamic. The United States continued, in comparative terms, to be a stable market for British goods, northern Europe as an area proving to be more elastic. The United States' share of British exports by value in fact declined from 21% in the early fifties to 16% for the last half of the decade. Altogether, although the strategic importance of British trade and investment in America was immense, with whole branches of industry closely implicated with the United States, the signs were there to see that the old phase in Atlantic relations was ending.

The trend to massive American industrialization predated the Civil War; this can be stated without venturing upon the contentious

---

8. Potter. The following statistics are from this source. Cotton and corn economics are discussed more fully in a later chapter.

issue whether the war retarded or stimulated that revolution.[9] During the fifties, northern cotton manufacturing produced three times as much manufactured cotton as was imported from Britain, absorbing 40% of the southern cotton crop. High production rates marked the domestic iron industry and railroad construction. Advanced methods of standardization and mass production of household goods enabled American industries to compete with European rivals. As the economy matured, local money markets such as that of New York developed, and American enterprises drew increasingly upon native resources and those of continental Europe rather than upon British sources. Migrants came increasingly from the continent of Europe. Moreover the aptness of Atlantic ties seemed less apparent as settlement expanded and American preoccupations became continental and internal.

Fearing the disappearance of what was a quasi-free trade area, British businessmen envisaged a difficult struggle to maintain position in American markets and enterprises. A number of Anglo-American concerns failed in the commercial crisis of 1857, marked by bank failures and falling railroad securities. Investor confidence was barely recovering in England when secession jolted the bank rate up to 8%. The conservative interests of British businessmen opposed the onset of civil disruption which threatened the maintenance and promotion of trade. Peace in America, and peace with America, would be preferred in the best of all worlds. "England and America," the youthful Cobden once wrote "are bound together in peaceful fetters, by the strongest of all ligatures that can bind two nations to each other, viz. commercial interests."[10] While geo-political rivalry contributed to jealousies between the two countries in the North American theatre, the entrenched interests within the Atlantic economy had successfully swung their influence behind the cause of peace during the bitter disputes over the Maine and Oregon borders in the thirties and forties. To them, war over empty tracts of forest and national prestige was senseless if it threatened the vast mutual interests and affinities of the two peoples.

Although the Civil War smashed the unity of the Atlantic economy, and raised a query over the future of cotton—still the most

---

9. Thomas Cochran, "Did the Civil War Retard Industrialization?," *MVHR*, XLVIII (1961), pp. 197-210. Discussion in D. T. Gilchrist and W. D. Lewis, eds., *Economic Change in the Civil War Era* (Greenville, Da., 1965).

10. Richard Cobden, *England, Ireland and America* (London, 1835), p. 105. Cobden wrote to Henry Ashworth in 1842, "Free Trade, by perfecting the intercourse and securing the dependence of countries one upon another, must inevitably smash the power from the governments to plunge their people into wars . . . ." April 18, 1842, q. Morley, *Cobden*, I., pp. 230–231.

valuable item supplied by Americans to Britain—it did not extinguish the ties of mutual self-interest which bound British business to largely northern partners. Secessionists were exceedingly rash in predicting that crude materialism would dictate British intervention to secure a cotton supply and cripple a rival maritime and commercial power. Such language had a quaintly mercantilist ring in a post-mercantilist age. In economic terms a vindictive British stance towards the north would jeopardize investments, and markets, invite commercial retaliation, and threaten to speed the development of a rival industrial system behind tariff walls. (If diplomacy were in fact determined by economic Machiavellianism, there is a case for arguing that Britain would most rationally have preserved her interests by helping the north to crush a rebellion which disrupted cotton exports.) On the other hand, prolongation of the American war struck at the foundations of the Atlantic economy, despite the bonanza which accrued to industries such as munitions and the merchant marine. Momentum was thus given to "stop the war" campaigns which embittered relations with Washington and threatened to embroil Britain willy-nilly in the conflict. As Walter Bagehot, the brilliant young editor of the *Economist*, saw clearly, economic forces in England were predominantly peace forces; but they had failed to stifle the Crimean and other wars.[11] Whether they would prove adequate to sway events in an Anglo-American crisis was yet to be tested. Other issues were at stake.

If intellectual warfare marked the 1860's in England—and some felt that the Victorian state of mind exhibited a sense of crisis—it was waged over science, religion, and the cosmos, not over political ideologies or social antagonisms. Britain's age of *Sturm und Drang*, of sharp class tensions and intense social questioning, had ended by the fifties: such was the general consensus. The change was variously explained: Britain was affected by a backwash from Europe, participating in a European-wide conservative reaction following the failure of the 1848 revolutions. Struck by the barrenness of European revolutionary ideology, Englishmen had taken new faith in their own liberal constitution which had remained impervious to the virus of 1848. Empiricism was strengthened, the principle of progress blended carefully with that of moderation. Again, the victory of free trade in 1846, and the demise of Chartism during the fiasco of 1848, had

11. Cf. Cobden's assertion: "We have been the most combative and aggressive community that has existed since the days of the Roman dominion .... It is displayed in our fondness for erecting monuments to warriors, even at the doors of our marts of commerce." *Political Writings* 4th edition, (London, 1903), II, p. 377.

removed the most controversial issues from the public arena and blurred the lines dividing parties. A transition from class conflict to collaboration was seen to be a side-benefit of the prosperity of the mid-Victorian high noon. The transport revolution, growth of heavy industry, and influx of gold from California and Australian mines, promised limitless new expansion and engrossed men in materialist pursuits. Labor ambitions were concentrated upon attaining improvements within the existing structure; the empiric "laborist" tradition, always strong in the movement, now dominated at the expense of militant, populist and utopian themes. Reformist energies were directed at infiltrating the establishment (and commonly to self-preferment in local office and business), using Jeremy Bentham's now honored weapons—the parliamentary committee of enquiry and the blue book. While the power of organized moral indignation against abuses and injustice was by no means dead, it commonly seemed in abeyance in the fifties, restrained by apathy and the dogmas of economic individualism. Antislavery zealots were only one class of improvers who railed against waning public support for their cause.

Profound indifference was met with in the country toward the succession of abortive bills proposed in the fifties for parliamentary reform. The Great Reform of 1832 had not shaken the grip of the landed aristocracy upon politics. Nor had increasing population or the convulsions of the forties significantly altered the electoral balance. The £10 householder franchise for British boroughs demanded a relatively high property qualification for voting: according to the 1866 returns the ratio of £10 voters to population was slightly less than 5%, although it had risen from 3.3% in 1832.[12] The local influence of the gentry predominated in the county vote, with 40 shilling freehold and leasehold franchises. Independent politics were possible only in certain large industrial and "open" boroughs, often with radical members, but the populous areas of the midlands and north were strikingly under-represented by comparison with the rural south and west. Half the House of Commons in 1865 either belonged to the peerage and baronetage, or were connected to it by marriage or descent, while Palmerston's second administration filled eleven of fifteen cabinet posts from the ranks of the great families. This situation was coming under mild challenge by 1860. Parliamentary support for reform proposals—being made from both sides of the house—was edging toward 50%. But democratic theory had little to do with members' conviction that something would have to be done in the

12. F. B. Smith, *The Making of the Second Reform Bill* (Melbourne Univer. Press, 1966), p. 20. See Chapter 2 for thorough analysis.

near future. Nobody proposed to enfranchise the turbulent and ignorant masses. Lord John Russell's bills aimed at giving voting privileges to a broader range of safe, responsible, and deferential electors, at preserving a constitutional balance between interests and classes without eroding traditional leadership. This was Whig theory adjusted to the realities of the steam age. Richard Cobden, John Bright, and the middle-class radicals wanted most urgently a redistribution which should give power to their class at the expense of hereditary privilege. Disraeli sponsored change which would give the Conservatives a parliamentary majority, and offer scope for his own ambition and talents. John Stuart Mill's *On Liberty* and his pamphlet *Thoughts on Parliamentary Reform* appeared in 1859 (so did Darwin's *Origin of Species*); but even Mill's attack on the existing system of bribery and oligarchy was blunted by an emphasis upon the illiberal and anti-individualist potentialities of mass society.

Party chaos and ministerial instability characterized politics in the wake of the crisis of 1846. By engineering Repeal of the Corn Laws, Peel rescued the nation from constitutional crisis and preserved power in the hands of the ruling landed elite. But in the process he broke his party, and failed in his program of modernizing Conservatism and broadening its electoral base. The Tory rump was condemned to almost perennial opposition for a generation. The Peelites formed a complicating factor in the political calculations of the day. The dominance of the Whig–Liberals (the Liberals as they became by 1859) was maintained by the formation of a series of uneasy coalitions involving Peelites—with a disproportionate share of administrative skill—reformist Radicals, and Irish Liberals. The divisions and conflicts between cliques prevented programmatic politics, and inhibited a trend to more efficient party organization; while alliance between center groups occurred across party lines to counter unpopular measures.[13] Lord Aberdeen had attacked party labels when he set up his Crimean coalition: "Those terms had ceased to have any definite meaning except as party cries and the country was sick of them."[14] The sentiment still persisted in 1860; nor was Palmerston ashamed to act in accord with it when necessary. His indifference to social reform was notorious: he once rebuked a young colleague who inquired about his legislative plans: "there is really nothing to be done. We cannot go on adding to the statute book *ad infinitum.*"

13. See Smith, Chapters 2, 3; J. B. Conacher, "Party Politics in the Age of Palmerston" and W. O. Ayedelotte, "Patterns of National Development," in P. Appleman, W. A. Madden, and M. Wolff, eds., *1859: Entering an Age of Crisis* (Indiana Univer. Press, 1959).

14. Speech, House of Lords, December 27, 1852, q. E. Halévy, *Victorian Years 1841–1895* (London, 1961, 1st ed. 1951), p. 335.

Palmerston and Lord Derby, the Tory leader, could cooperate on this basis, but weak government was the inevitable defect of loose party ties. Seven ministries held office between 1846 and 1868. Four times an independent House of Commons displaced a reigning executive and set up a government with only minority support in the legislature. Cabinet shuffling was a commonplace occurrence. Palmerston's last ministry, 1859–1865, was the stablest of the period, but it was a fact discovered in retrospect. Solidity was achieved when in 1859 the Peelite chiefs, Graham, Herbert, Cardwell, and Gladstone (the most important) resolved their quarrels with Palmerston, legacy of the Crimean war. They joined a ministry headed by Palmerston, with Russell at the Foreign Office, the two men subduing a rivalry which had riven the party for over ten years. But, revitalized or not, the Liberals enjoyed a tenuous majority of about 40 in parliament, Palmerston relying to some extent upon Derby's distaste for forming a minority government like that which he led briefly in 1858. Palmerston also relied upon skillful manipulation of the press, a device he favored to offset his own deficit of party connections. His mass appeal was extraordinary, especially to a public obsessed by foreign affairs, and only too often chauvinist, touchy, aggressive. Viewed in this light, Palmerston was not the antiprogressive anachronism from the Regency era, but distinctly a modern: his emphasis was upon maintaining national face, defence capability, and a competitive edge internationally; more realist ideas (he claimed) than Gladstone's budgetary parsimony or the Manchester School's faith in "peace by arbitration." "Diplomats and protocols are very good things [he once alleged] but there are no better peace-keepers than well-appointed three-deckers." Many Liberals shared his view. But Palmerston, despite his bluster, also shared the liberal faith in promotion of constitutional governments abroad (England's interests permitting a condition frequently absent). He prided himself that he had helped crush the slave trade. And he accepted the "Little England" argument against "crusades of conquest" which heaped expense and responsibilities upon Britain; better to raise up primitive peoples by "the general influence of our commerce."

In the anti-ideological context of the 1850's even the traditional radical admiration for American democracy began to falter. Not only was the American example less urgently needed as reformist propaganda in an age which was tired of the improvers; but it seemed less pertinent when America itself was riven by sectional forces. Anti-imperialists—and chauvinists—were alienated by American expansionism. Even Cobden, whose admiration for America's free political and economic system endured through thick and thin, recoiled at the aggressiveness of American policy in Texas and Mexico: "I am more jealous of *their* falling into the marauding and conquering propensities of the old world than anything besides."[15] Anticapitalists—from the depleted Chartist left or from the Tory right—deplored America's exploitative industrial system and ruthlessly competitive ethic. They compared the New England mills with plantation slavery, and pronounced a curse on both. Idealists could not admire the violence and corruption of American politics, or the crudities of transatlantic culture.

While America was politically stable and materially prosperous, these criticisms mattered less. Those who were kept out of the charmed circle of power and privilege, those who were alineated from the political and religious establishments, could still appeal to America as an argument against aristocracy, status, and establishments. A large spectrum, including professional and middle-class groups, Nonconformists, and politically conscious artisans, made up the friends of America. The American idea was to many British and continental radicals a universalist one, a world dream, not just an American one. Americans were not really unique, as they liked to claim, but were universal men freed from sin by environmental purification. Radicals claimed that the American condition was exportable; man's goodness would emerge from institutional corruptions if only he were allowed to embrace American liberties and enjoy universal suffrage. (Conservatives rejoiced in the uniqueness of the American experiment just because it then became nonexportable; it was irrelevant to an overcrowded, traditionalist, class-ridden Europe.) When the American republic began to break up, the naivetes within the radical analysis were shown up. Readjustments were required. For the more influential body of English opinion which had always opposed doctrinaire politics based on American comparison, the war had less political significance. Englishmen had constantly fitted the facts about America into their existing values. To Benthamites America vindicated utilitarianism; to Whigs, Whiggery; to free traders, the dogmas of the Manchester School. Conservatives could hail the underlying conservatism of American history, and grudgingly respect American power. Even during the heroic age of English reform before 1848, British ideas about America were accommodated into a long-standing pragmatic, gradualist tradition.[16] The effect was to reduce the threat

15. Cobden to Henry Richard (of the pacifist *Star*), March 23, 1852, *B. M. Add. MS.* 43,653, Part 2.

16. The use to which stereotypes about the United States were put in England is dealt with in detail in my *American Democracy in English Politics 1815–1850* (Clarendon Press, Oxford, 1965).

to tradition, or to the Victorian social balance. It was now to be seen whether the war would raise unsettling new issues which might disturb this pattern.

The sudden worsening of transatlantic affairs in 1860 took Englishmen unaware. They had become accustomed to the interminable sectional wranglings of the 1850's, and had come to respect "the singular facility which the Americans have shown themselves to possess for getting out of scrapes that threaten to be fatal."[17] As one would expect from a sophisticated industrial society, a complex reaction was to develop to the immense crises which struck the United States, euphemistically described in the British press as "the American difficulty." The enormous heterogeneity of economic, ideological, and group interests involved in the English response—together with the spectrum of issues raised by the breakdown of the Union—should enforce caution upon the historian who wishes to paint his civil war scene in bold and simple strokes. The search for convenient partisan categories has too often provided a distorting mirror through which events are viewed, or become a Procrustean device by which the data are chopped or stretched into the required form. The partisans existed, and were important. But a significant and intelligent part of British public opinion was created by men—especially of the "center"—who were not deeply committed, whose approach was essentially pragmatic. Either ambiguous about, or healthily sceptical of the war aims and propaganda of both sides, subjected to the conflicting pressures of humanitarian, liberal, and nationalist sentiments, such men molded their attitudes according to what was happening.

Across the channel, Napoleon III's authoritarian regime was entering a time of test. Elected President of the ephemeral second republic in December 1848, at a time of antirevolutionary reaction, Louis Napoleon took power by *coup* on December 2, 1851 and was proclaimed Emperor of the Second Empire exactly a year later. Liberal opponents of the regime were jailed, or exiled to Algeria, while Napoleon installed himself as master of the most powerful executive seen in France since 1815. He fully controlled the legislature—Senate and Legislative Body—through government deputies and a president appointed by the Emperor. Official candidates dominated the Legislative Body, the elections to which (despite universal suffrage) were skillfully managed by the prefects. A quarter of a million functionaires ran France: prefects, mayors, procureurs-generaux, gendarmerie,

17. *Fraser's Magazine*, LXIII (January, 1861), p. 133.

headed by the key ministers of the Interior and Justice. From 1852 the press was firmly controlled, republican and opposition opinion being tolerated at the pleasure of the Emperor. The system was authoritarian, if not particularly draconian, depending upon the support of the army, church, and business. The Catholic heirarchy overlooked Napoleon's "revolutionary" view of foreign affairs—he proclaimed his contempt for the treaties of 1815 and the Congress system which followed, and defended oppressed national minorities struggling for independence—in return for the restoration of the Church's role in education and French military support for the Pope in Rome, whose temporal power was endangered by Garibaldian nationalists.

The French economy flourished, along with those of its neighbors, during the years of mid-century expansion. Building on Saint-Simonian principles of easy credit, planning, and consumer benefits, Napoleon claimed credit for making Paris a financial center of Europe, for effecting a railroad and steamship revolution, for stimulating industrial production. If the empire was irredeemably vulgar and parvenu, French culture and science flowered within it: the age produced Flaubert, Baudelaire, Offenbach, Berlioz, Dumas, Manet, Bizet, Comte, Taine, Pasteur. While peasant farming remained little changed, and working class living standards rose almost imperceptibly, railways changed the face of France and Haussman that of Paris. So long as the bourgeoisie was profitably absorbed in business, Napoleon could count upon its effective abstention from politics. Opposition to the regime was splintered between monarchists, Orleanists, and republicans. The legitimists, on the advise of the Comte de Chambord, boycotted politics, and did so until 1863 when their leader Berryer became a deputy. Many Orleanists entered government service. Louis Phillipe's son (the Duc D'Aumale) preferred frosty retirement, and the Oleanist *Journal des Debats* offered generally sedate criticism. The only radical alternative came from the republicans, still with potentially dangerous areas of support from the urban poor, but discredited in the country at large.

By 1860, however, the brash confidence of the Second Empire was wearing thin at the edges. The recently concluded Italian war, hatched against Austria by Napoleon and Cavour, had evoked little enthusiasm from the mass of Frenchmen who wanted a respite from adventurism and uncertainty. (French troops had been engaged in Algeria, Syria, Egypt, Indo-China, and China in the late 1850's.) The war eroded church and conservative faith in the regime without winning Napoleon many laurels as the saviour of Italy from Austrian despotism. The catholic Foreign Minister Walewski resigned in Jaunary 1860. He was replaced by the pro-Italian Antoine Edouard Thouvenel. Republican joy over the campaign ended with the armistice of Villafranca, which kept Venetia under Austrian rule and was interpreted as a betrayal of the Italian patriots. The subsequent coalescence of much of northern Italy under the Piedmontese owed little to Napoleon, and threatened the creation of a greater Italy which might rival Bonapartist France, a denouement Napoleon had not had in mind. By annexing Nice and Savoy as the price of his alliance with Peidmont, Napoleon almost destroyed the foundation of his European policy: the accord with England reached by treaty in 1854. Buffetted by the storms accompanying the Crimean War and the Orsini affair of 1858, coolly regarded by the people of both countries, eyed askance by Palmerston, the Anglo-French alliance survived strictly through self-interest on both sides. Napoleon attempted to strengthen economic ties across the channel, and thus the alliance, by sponsoring the Cobden-Chevalier treaty of 1860, involving a reciprocal lowering of tariffs. The power of free traders in Palmerston's new government provided Napoleon with the opportunity of buying mass support at home through cheaper imports. But he underestimated the outrage of traditionally protectionist French industry and business, among his chief supporters. The textile millers of Normandy and iron interests protested vehemently. Their anger was to no avail. But it underlined the political difficulties facing the regime, and it put limits to the future liberties which Napoleon might take in major sectors of the economy.

In the latter respect, the American Civil War promised difficulties. France imported 93% of its raw cotton from the south. The French had been most inert in developing alternate sources of supply, as John Claiborne—sent by the Buchanan administration for the purpose—had reported to Congress in 1858. Aware of the industry's vulnerability, French experts had canvassed the prospects of cotton culture in regions as diverse as Central America, Italy, Haiti, Cambodia, Cyprus, and Aleppo. French Algeria offered fine conditions for cotton growing, but Napoleon's glowing promises of turning it into a New South petered out in bureaucratic incompetence.[18] The French cotton industry was localized in Normandy, Alsace, and the Nord. Although small-scale and backward in technique, it employed almost three-quarters of a million workers at the outset of the sixties. If their jobs were not in immediate jeopardy, because of an over-supply of cotton stored from 1860's crop, the same was not true of French export

18. Earl S. Pomeroy, "French Substitutes for American Cotton, 1861–1865," *JSH,* IX (1943), p. 555. See also A. L. Dunham, *The Anglo-French Treaty of Commerce* (Ann Arbor, 1930), Chapter 10.

industries dependent upon the American market. It was an unlucky portent for southern diplomacy that French economic ties with the north were stronger than comparable links with the south. A whole string of industries catered to northern markets and experienced a downturn in business from Lincoln's election outwards: Lyons silk, Limoges luxury goods (carpets, gloves, shoes), Rochechouart china. Also vulnerable were the clock and watch industry of Monbeliard and the Rouen, woollens of eastern Normandy, shipbuilding, wines, hatmaking, glass, lace, and embroidery trades.[19] An American civil war was deplored on all sides in late 1860. Not only would northern sea power seal off the south, and cotton, but rebel privateering was expected to disrupt trade carried in northern bottoms. Moreover, the North American markets for French luxuries would surely shrink as money was diverted to the war effort. The French economy would bear the reverbatory effects of declining incomes in key industries. The political repercussions of a recession were incalculable.

The events in America also had ideological significance. The fact that the American war coincided with a revival of liberal opposition in France had important ramifications. The revival was, in part, Napoleon's own creation. In 1860 he broadened the basis of government and mitigated press censorship. He explained to his ministers, who were dubious, that he wanted to improve his foreign image. Perhaps he desired to conciliate his critics, perhaps he believed in the unassailability of his position. The scope of parliamentary debate was extended, ministers defended bills in the Legislative Body, parliamentary control was extended over government expenditure, the trappings at least of a liberal system introduced. The five-man republican opposition who sat as deputies after the 1857 election demanded further liberties. Political journalism received an infusion of life, with voices of dissent emerging from liberal catholics, Saint Simonians, socialists and protestants as well as from republicans, Orleanists, and legitimists. The Emperor's grant of amnesty in 1859 to political exiles permitted the return of eloquent critics, including the Orleanist Adolphe Thiers. In this context the fragile growth of the antiauthoritarian movement needed hothouse conditions if it was to grow to maturity. It was not a time to abandon the inspiring ideals offered by the republican democratic experiment in America; not, as in England, an appropriate moment for liberal doubts and reappraisal concerning the relevance of the

19. Lynn M. Case and Warren F. Spencer, *The United States and France: Civil War Diplomacy* (Philadelphia, 1970), Chapters 4 and 5 (hereafter Case and Spencer).

American experience. Even Alexis de Tocqueville, America's most sophisticated observer, and a man with more than a fair measure of hesitations about American democracy, had proclaimed it to his countrymen as the system of the future.[20] Others had clung more uncritically to America as the French revolutionary impulse had been driven underground: ". . . for thirty years [sniped a critic] a universal and dogged conspiracy of adulation has surrounded the United States. Each publicist in turn has bowed to the fashion of presenting his homage and good wishes to this idol with feet of clay." For republicans now, only one response was possible: "Liberal Europe [said Eugene Forcade, political writer for the Orleanist periodical *Revue des Deux Monde*] cannot balance between these two sides: its wishes will accompany the cause of the North, the cause of human liberty and emancipation against the cynical and violent party of slavery." When the court and the enemies of democracy sympathized with the south, America became the touchstone of ideological struggle within France itself. Serge Gavronsky comments: "From Lincoln's election to his assassination, France watched with apprehension the trial of American democracy. Few failed to appreciate what was at stake: democracy itself, and the representative form of government, the abolition of slavery, and the future of republicanism in Europe."[21]

---

20. See Chapter 5 of my *American Democracy in English Politics.* The classic study of American influence in France during the early 19th century is René Rémond, *Les Etats-Unis devant L'Opinion Francaise, 1815-1852,* 2 vols. (Paris, 1962).

21. Serge Gavronsky, *The French Liberal Opposition and the American Civil War* (New York, 1968), p. 28 and *passim.* The preceding quotes are from Gavronsky, pp. 24, 28.

Chapter II

Portents of War

As the American nation endured the catastrophies which led from the Kansas-Nebraska Act, the Dred Scott case, John Brown's Raid, the division of the Democracy, and the election of Abraham Lincoln, to the secession of South Carolina from the Union, the prospect of an independent Confederacy assumed an international reality. Discussions of future Confederate diplomacy flitted in and out of the secession debates held throughout the south during the fateful winter of 1860-1861. They were duly relayed to the European capitals. The expansionist reputation which had been earned by southern filibusterers and politicians in the antebellum period bred a natural suspicion abroad. A separate southern nation was likely to be an aggressive force in the Caribbean and Central America. The south's leaders hoped to offset this fear by stressing the limited aims of their rebellion. They supposed, in any case, that greed would eclipse discretion, that the powers would regard as bait irresistible the chance to snap up spoils and reassert European power in the hemisphere. Quick recognition, or judicious intervention by Europe, would seal the rebellion's success. At one stroke the United States' continental power and commercial rivalry would be diminished. The south would gain its right to independence—all that it asked—while its friends would achieve a profitable eruption of the American power balance.

The other foundation of Confederate diplomacy was more stringently economic. Every American schoolboy knows the King Cotton dogma—that the south held Europe in thrall because of its monopoly of raw cotton—and knows that it proved delusory. But a bedrock of reality underlay the often ludicrous rhetoric of cotton theory. Cotton's dominating role in Atlantic trade has already been discussed. It continued to be cardinal on the eve of the war, although the Atlantic economy was diversifying and changing in ways not fully appreciated by the cotton planters. Of cotton landed at British ports during the 1850's, 72% was American; in 1860, with a bumper crop in Dixie, it was 85%. Lancashire was the world's largest cotton manufacturer, and cotton exports ran at between 40% and 55% of total British exports during the fifties. The home market for cotton clothes and fabrics was large, while between four and five million people were said to be dependent upon the industry and its subsidiary trades.[1] As we shall see, Britain's cotton economics were complex, and the industry was plagued by an over-production crisis in 1861; but there was no widespread awareness of these facts in the Atlantic world. The French seemed entirely dependent on the south for cotton.

The King Cotton doctrine began voluptuously to flourish from the mid-fifties, becoming sacred dogma to all classes of southerners. If it begat confidence in the south's capacity to "go it alone" in the family of nations, it started as sectional pride, and an expression of ire against the north's "imperial" exploitation of southern agriculture. Antitariff orators such as Robert Toombs (the Confederacy's first Secretary of State) speechified against the northern states' violation of the original federal compact, which set out to obtain economic justice for every section. The expanding north and northwest had instead joined in unholy alliance to force upon the cotton states the so-called "American system": its protectionism and restrictions benefited northern industry, but thrust high costs upon the planters. Trade, and profits, were channeled from the rural south into the entrepreneurial north. Natural outlets from Dixie to world markets were prohibited. Yet where would the north be without cotton? Pamphleteers, writers like David Christy (whose *Cotton is King* appeared in 1855), journals such as *De Bow's Review*, southern congressmen spelt out the answer, suggested by the country's trade statistics. The southern contribution to American trade was staggering, even by the somewhat inflated figures of the day: almost $200 million out of total exports of $278 million in 1859 were estimated to come from exports of southern origin (mostly cotton, also tobacco and rice). The new textile manufacturing trade in the north was almost entirely reliant on southern staple. Moreover cotton emerged unscathed from the 1857 panic which disrupted northern commerce.

1. Frank L. Owsley, *King Cotton Diplomacy: Foreign Relations of the Confederate States of America* (2nd ed. rev. by Harriet Chappell Owsley, 1959; 1st end. 1931, Chicago), p. 3 and *passim.*

Lobbying for a higher revenue tariff ensued, with cries for protection coming from special interests such as the Pennsylvania ironmakers. Angered, southern editors predicted secession of the cotton states. Grass would then be growing in the streets of New York and the seaboard ports. Cotton logic of this type nourished southern complacency: secession would not cause war, because war would dry up trade between north and south. If the Republicans attempted to coerce the rebels, there would be a revolt of the middlemen and merchants whose wealth was built upon the south's bulk exports. Nor would the world permit a war upon cotton. A cotton famine would raise the spectre of revolution over the aristocratic regimes of Europe. When war came, the south—or large sections of it—confidently expected the powers to intervene to wedge open their lines of supply to cotton. The *London Times* military correspondent, William H. Russell (famous for his eyewitness accounts of the charge of the Light Brigade and the fall of Sebastopol) was in the Carolinas a few days before Sumter, and encountered cocky buoyancy from farmers he met in full army regalia, complete with swords:

> I inquired of a fine, tall fair-haired young fellow whom they expected to fight. 'That's more than I can tell' quoth he 'The Yankees aint such cussed fools as to think they can come here and whip us, let alone the British.' 'Why, what have the British got to do with it?' 'They are bound to take our part: if they don't we'll just given them a hint about cotton, and that will set matters right'. This was said very much with the air of a man who knows what he is talking about, and who was quite satisfied 'he had you there' . . .[2]

Vainly Russell warned his southern hosts not to expect Britain to acknowledge the Confederacy readily, or the Royal Navy to disperse Lincoln's blockading fleet. Vainly he added that bluster and cotton blackmail were likely to turn England against the planters. The Richmond *Whig* thought otherwise: ". . . the Confederacy has its hand on the mane of the British lion, and that beast, so formidable to all the rest of the world, must crouch at her bidding."[3]

The south did not speak entirely in cotton imperatives. It also hoped to exploit British resentment at the Union's "new protectionism," symbolized by the Morrill tariff, and offered the lure of a free-trade south as a vital new market for British goods. Southern propaganda excoriated the Morrill tariff, passed in the last days of

2. W. H. Russell, *My Civil War Diary*, ed. Fletcher Pratt (London, 1954), p. 61 (Original *My Diary North and South*, London, 1863). See also Rupert Furneaux, *News of War: Stories and Adventures of the Great War Correspondents* (London, 1964), Chapter 2.

3. Richmond *Whig*, December 12, 1861.

Buchanan's administration, and branded it as a major cause of secession. This was misleading (one historian calls it a *ruse diplomatique.*)[4] The tariff was passed in Congress only because of the departure of cotton representatives: it was the result, not the cause, of secession. Not all secessionists shared the obsessive antitariff views of Toombs or Robert Barnwell Rhett. Alexander H. Stephens persuaded the Charleston convention, meeting to debate his state's secession, to say nothing on the tariff as a grievance: the south had controlled the administration for sixty out of seventy-two years, he noted, and had made the tariff and government what they were. Nor did the tariff figure prominently in the heated debates of the winter. It became useful as war propaganda mainly because it distracted world attention from the slavery issue, and was appealing to free trade opinion. Free trade seemed the way of the future, the new enlightenment. Fifteen years after the Repeal of the Corn Laws, the triumph of Cobden, Bright, and Peel, England's glowing prosperity was assigned to that event. When in 1860 Cobden and Louis Napoleon engineered the Anglo-French Treaty of Commerce, Western Europe seemed on the brink of becoming a free trade area. The Confederacy might well be added to that world, once it had detached itself from the monopolist grasp of the northerners.

Rebel overtures were made to Britain along such lines even before South Carolina had seceded. Robert Bunch, the British consul at Charleston, was visited in mid-December, 1860, by Robert Barnwell Rhett, stormy petrel of planter politics, ally of the slavetraders and head of a noisy faction which controlled the Charleston *Mercury*. Informing Bunch that a cotton federation was to be set up within sixty days, Rhett put his pet scheme before the consul:

> He stated that the wishes and hopes of the Southern States centered in England; that they would prefer an Alliance with Her to one with any other Power; that they would be Her best customer; that free trade would form an integral portion of their scheme of Government, with Import duties of nominal amount and direct communication, by steam, between the Southern and British Forts. Thus, he hoped, that with Great Britain dependent upon the South for Cotton, (upon which supposed axiom, I would remark, all their calculations are based) and the South upon her for manufactured goods and shipping, an interchange of commodities would ensue which would lead to an unrestricted intercourse of the most friendly character.[5]

---

4. James M. Callahan, *Diplomatic History of the Southern Confederacy* (Baltimore, 1901), p. 277.

5. Bunch to Russell, December 15, 1860, F. O., Ser. II, v. 745, printed in *AHR*, XVIII (July, 1913), pp. 784-787. See also Laura A. White, *Robert Barnwell Rhett: Father of Secession* (Gloucester, Mass., 1965).

Bunch indiscreetly encouraged the idea, but the two quarreled over the question of the slavetrade, which Britain had labored for generations to stamp out. Rhett blustered that British intransigence would be countered by offering France and other countries commercial advantages over England. Bunch was unmoved; his stand perhaps influenced the decision to insert in the Confederate constitution a clause prohibiting the slave traffic. Rhett persisted in urging upon the south a forceful and tangible foreign policy. At Montgomery, as chairman of the Committee on Foreign Relations, he wanted a mission sent to Europe to offer the powers treaties of commercial alliance. The signatories would enter "reciprocal obligations offensive and defensive for twenty years or more." In return the south would impose no import duty higher than 20% ad valorem, "and would permit European parties to the treaty to enjoy the privileges of the coasting trade free . . . ." A 10% discriminatory duty would be levied on all nations refusing to sign. Rhett tried too hard to impose the plan on the incoming administration. He merely alienated Jefferson Davis, and smoothed the path for a weaker strategy. The time for such measures had passed once Britain and France had proclaimed their neutrality and accepted the northern blockade. Foreign merchant energies were diverted to the booming neutral trade with the Union, or to illicit blockade running. The trader's Eldorado in the new south receded from view. Palmerston, and others, consoled themselves that it would return when, as was "in the highest Degree likely," the rebellion proved irreducible.[6] Meanwhile scepticism rose abroad when Davis, unwilling to impose direct taxation to finance the war, raised higher revenue tariffs. (The first rise was in May, 1861.) Then rumors mounted that the planters were withholding cotton from Europe by embargo, even burning millions of bales to hasten a cotton famine abroad. A more flagrant violation of the free operation of the forces of supply and demand could hardly be imagined.

During the early war months the newspapers of the cotton states confidently listed the reasons why Europe would take the infant Confederacy to its bosom. Motives of self-interest, economics and territorial ambition predominated.[7] But there were others. Genuine sympathy was anticipated for the underdog in a struggle between imperial sway and nationalist aspirations. The south's self-image had become fixed by the time of the war: it saw itself as a

6. Palmerston memo, October 20, 1861, Layard Papers, *B. M. Add. Mss.*, 38987, f. 301.

7. Schuyler Dean Hoslett, "Southern Expectation of British Intervention in the Civil War," *Tylers Quart. Hist. and Genealogical Mag.*, XXII (January, 1941), pp. 76–82.

coherent civilization whose values were distinct from those of the restless, moneygrubbing, hectoring, abolitionist north. It saw itself as a leisured and aristocratic culture; the slave-run plantation was the basic social unit, and upon it rose a social system which exhibited the benefits of heirarchy and paternalism. Leveling and utilitarian philosophies were rejected in favor of agrarian elitism. Parallels were drawn by the planters between their condition and that of the English manorial system. Cavalier origins were assigned to southern gentlemen, Puritan beginnings for the Yankee. Such a romantic and conservative image was expected to appeal to the aristocratic ruling classes of Britain and the continent. It was notorious that the latter despised the radical principles of Yankee democracy.

The Confederates counted confidently on ideological estrangement between aristocracy and democracy to precipitate unfriendly displays against the United States. Such views underrated the strength of the democrats in Western Europe, and assumed too readily that the governing classes wanted to risk a confrontation with reformist movements within their countries. The south's invocation of the rights of small nations was potent, but it ran counter to a deeply held, historic commitment of European liberals to the idea of the American democratic experiment. In fact neither north nor south foresaw that the war would evoke complex cross-currents in world opinion. The Civil War actually posed an extraordinary crisis of conscience for the "left," particularly in Britain. Friends of the international cause of liberal nationalities—men who rallied to the cause of the Greeks against the Turks, Hungarians and Italians against the Habsburgs, the Poles against the Tsar—could also be antislavery radicals, seeing malevolence in the south's conservative revolt; progressives who deplored heirarchic social theory and the archaism of chattel slavery. Humanitarian sentiment operated to the south's advantage when men considered mediation to end the unbelievable carnage; or when pressure mounted to relieve the distress of cotton operatives. But it also led to pacifism. Nor was southern free trade a magic key. Symptomatic of southern isolationism, no regard was taken of crucial facts such as the Manchester School's involvement in peace leagues designed to keep Britain out of impoverishing wars. The most illustrious free traders of the age, Cobden and Bright, had long been apologists of American democracy and its free enterprise economic system.

It cannot be gainsaid that early Confederate diplomacy was handicapped by misconceptions and wishful thinking which deterred the facing of reality.[8] And it was handicapped by fatal ignorance of

8. See Henry Blumenthal's brilliant indictment, "Confederate Diplomacy: Popular Notions and International Realities," *JSH*, XXXII (May, 1966), pp. 151–171.

European conditions, one result of the cultural isolation in which the south had sought redemption from sectional tensions. The defence of slavery, Cash tells us, "not only eventuated . . . in a taboo on criticism; in the same process it set up a ban on all analysis and inquiry."[9] Hence, perhaps, the ingredient of credulity so marked in the reports of southern diplomats, the hugging to comforting ideas, the spurning of unpleasant facts. A diplomatic offensive in the fluid early stages of the war, one exploiting the south's limited strengths and recognizing the odds facing the rebellion, might have clinched the trick. It never took place. Platitudes were mouthed about how the fate of America's first revolution had been sealed in London and Versailles. And contemporary history taught that small nations needed allies at the hour of their birth. Italy had needed French help against the Austrians in 1859, while diplomatic isolation explained a catalogue of failures: that of the nationalist revolutions of 1848, of Russia in the Crimea, and those other "lost causes" of the 1860's, the Poles and the Danes. But southern self-assurance proved a stumbling block to decisive action. Bred on states rights theory, southerners believed that their states were entitled to withdraw peaceably from a federal compact to which they had given only provisional allegiance. They hardly believed that the north would fight a war against brother-whites for abolitionism, or the chimera of republican unity. In any case the war would be short. The south's military leaders and statesmen were superior, Johnny Reb's military flair greater than that of Yankee townsmen. The Confederate armies would have the advantage of interior lines of defense (beloved by the Swiss strategist Antoine Jomini, whose *Summary of the Art of War* was a bible of West-pointers.) Its generals, like Lee, were masters of the tactical offensive, another Jominian principle. The people were determined in defense of their homeland, their war aim was simple and nonaggressive: the right of self-existence. These were compelling arguments which won many converts abroad. History provided few examples of imperial success over a rebellious people so well situated.

Less appreciated was the northern will to win, its willingness to launch an unprecedented mobilization of resources to keep the Union intact. Davis saw the trouble ahead. As Mary Chesnut diarized: "Mrs. Fitzpatrick says Mr. Davis is too gloomy for her. He says we must prepare for a long war and unmerciful reverses at first, because they are readier for war and so much stronger numerically. Men and money count so in war."[10] Indeed. In 1861 the north held over

---

9. W. J. Cash, *Mind of the South* (Vintage, 1960; 1st ed. 1941), p. 101.

10. Mary Boykin Chesnut, *A Diary from Dixie,* ed. I. D. Martin and M. L. Avary (London, 1905), p. 153 (May 9, 1861).

three times the south's value of real and personal property, four times the capital of incorporated banks, ten times the value of products manufactured annually. Disproving the cotton prophets, the northern economy survived the commercial crisis sparked by hostilities, and thereafter expanded, even financing the war without exorbitant inflation. Northern industry thrived on war demand, moving noticeably toward a condition of self-sufficiency. Overseas supplies were maintained by ships under neutral flag, offsetting the deadly blow struck by rebel commerce-raiders to the United States merchant marine. Meanwhile the southern economy was to waste away. Confederate credit eroded steadily and the government, desperately short of mobilizable capital, scraped to finance the army and buy a tiny navy.[11] Schemes were devised to ship cotton through the blockade to raise cash but died under the cannonades of King Cotton theorists. Instead an embargo was placed on cotton exports.

The blockade itself illustrated the tremendous disparity between the maritime resources of the two sections. The south hardly disposed of a notable ship, and had negligible naval facilities at the war's beginning. Brilliant improvisation by Navy Secretary Stephen R. Mallory, who launched a determined program to purchase a navy abroad, created a feared striking force. It was an example of using southern power to the limit, and might have been emulated in other arenas. But the odds remained strikingly in favor of the Union navy. There was more money to build ships, well-appointed yards for their construction, no foreign complications attached to shipbuilding, more trained officers to man ships. The north's ports were unblockaded, while southern raiders lacked bases or prize harbors, their movements constantly reported to the enemy by United States consuls and agents. The south's difficulties are sufficiently stated in the fact that by 1865, Navy Secretary Gideon Welles was administering the world's largest navy.

In 1861 the north had a flourishing diplomatic establishment; the Confederacy had to create a State Department. It had no diplomatic corps, archives, traditions, or status; nor at any time during the war was the south able to match the Union in the number of agents, spies, and special missions abroad.[12] Seward, Lincoln's Secretary of State, controlled foreign policy throughout the war. The south had three Secretaries of State (one ad interim) in the first year. The first, Robert Toombs of Georgia, was a signal failure, bored by

11. See R. N. Current, "God and the Strongest Battalions," in D. Donald, ed., *Why the North Won the Civil War* (La., 1960), pp. 3, 20.

12. For account of one of South's most successful propagandists abroad, the Swiss-born Henry Hotze, see Robert J. Smith, Jr., *The Confederate Index and the American Civil War* (MA Thesis, Univ. of Wash., 1961).

the inactivity of his office and resigning within months to become an unsuccessful brigadier general. The Virginian R. M. T. Hunter regarded the job as an "obscure place." A competent administrator, he transferred to the Senate within six months. The State Department was an illustrious post in name alone; ministers hankered after tasks more directly concerned with the fighting. Not until Judah P. Benjamin of Louisiana filled the post—after being pushed out of the War Department—was there a man of genuine stature in charge. Quite apart from the problems of erratic communications and defective intelligence caused by the blockade, Richmond's international position was weaker than it liked to admit. Its foe had vast commercial strength which could be applied at points of international pressure. Moreover the United States sought only to maintain the *status quo*; it asked merely to be left alone to quench a domestic conflagration. "A nation," Seward said "has a right and it is its duty, to live." Obviously states like Russia and Austria would agree, as they were ever-fearful of revolt from the subject peoples within their own ramshackle empires. But neither could the British or Napoleonic empires treat lightly the principle of legitimacy, despite their apparent sympathy for liberal and nationalist causes. The south needed to induce action from the powers, when as a proud nation it preferred to demand as a right recognition and acceptance among other states. (Both sections found it bitter to sue for favors from Europe, for Americans were accustomed to barter from a position of strength in the hemisphere.)

The Confederacy's first emissaries—William Lowndes Yancey, Ambrose D. Mann, and Pierre A. Rost—sailed for Europe in March, before the Civil War had erupted at Fort Sumter. They left a community still exhilarated by the escapade of secession. ("All was noise, dust, patriotism," reported W. H. Russell.[13]) The mission had been approved by the Confederate Convention which met in Montgomery, Alabama, in February, the self-appointed heir of the Continental Congress of 1776. President Davis named Yancey head of mission, a popular choice as Yancey was Alabama's leading politician and had been a strong aspirant for the Presidency. He had played a major role in splitting the Democratic party, and was noted for his flamboyant proslavery oratory. Bunch sent an unflattering portrait to London: Yancey was able but "impulsive, erratic and hot-headed; a rabid Secessionist, a favourer of a revival of the Slave-Trade, and a 'filibuster' of the extremist type of 'manifest destiny'."[14] Mann had been a

13. *My Civil War Diary*, pp. 52 and 64.

14. Bunch to Russell, March 21, 1861, *MHSP*, XLVIII (Jan. 1915), pp. 208–210.

member of the roving commission sent by Webster to Hungary in 1850; Bunch dismissed him as having "no special merit of any description." Rost, a planter and Supreme Court judge in Louisiana, was deemed, because of his French origins, a suitable choice to represent the Confederacy in Paris. The French court showed scant enthusiasm for Rost—"Has the South no sons capable of representing your country?" asked one nobleman—and he proved ineffectual.[15]

Toombs anticipated no troubles for the mission: it was to obtain recognition from London, then proceed to the courts of Napoleon III, Alexander II, and Leopold of Belgium. The commissioners' despatch bag carried a treatise on states rights, a lecture on King Cotton, and a prospectus on market opportunities. But Davis gave the envoys no powers to request foreign aid for the rebellion, or to negotiate treaties beyond the usual ones of reciprocal trade and amity with countries conceding Confederate independence. Rhett did not conceal his contempt for proceedings. He told Yancey: "You have no business in Europe, you carry no arguments that Europe cares to hear. My counsel is . . . to stay at home, or to go prepared to conciliate Europe by irresistible proffers of trade."[16]

Yancey and Rost reached London via New Orleans and Danish St. Thomas in the West Indies. Against Davis' advice, Mann determined to sail from New York. In Washington he secretly conferred with Senators James M. Mason, John C. Breckinridge, and former Attorney-General Caleb Cushing. Mann showed them the new Confederate constitution. "I remember [Cushing] saying as he laid it down, 'there is brains there, gentlemen, brains'."[17] Protective tariffs were outlawed, limited budgets praised, cabinet ministers allowed to sit in Congress to discuss departmental affairs (Acton later judged that this alone was worth a civil war.) The President was granted a six-year term but denied reelection. The African slavetrade was prohibited, but slavery was explicitly guaranteed. (The Confederacy would assume treaty obligations binding on the United States except for those requiring cooperation with other countries to stamp out the slave traffic.) Mann was convinced that the world would recognize the political sophistication being shown by the new republic.

---

15. Paul Pecquet Du Bellet, *Diplomacy of the Confederate Cabinet at Richmond and Its Agents Abroad . . . etc.*, ed. W. S. Hoole (Tuscaloosa, 1963), p. 30. Du Bellett was a New Orleans lawyer living in Paris and self-appointed southern agent.

16. J. S. Du Bose, *Life and Times of Yancey* (Birmingham, Ala., 1892), pp. 588-589.

17. J. Preston Moore, "Lincoln and the Escape of the Confederate Commissioner," *Illinois State Hist. Soc. J.*, LVII, pp. 23-27.

Meanwhile, the State Department planned to arrest the emissary as his steamer left dock in New York. Mann believed himself immune:

> . . . until I do something under [my] commision, I have done nothing that can be construed into treason . . . . If it arrested me, the administration would be forced to release me, and it would be damaged even in the North by its having committed so arbitrary an act.

Lincoln reasoned similarly, and allowed Mann to escape. Mann's New York Democrat friends still ridiculed the idea of war. The President of the Bank of the Republic "said he had heard that I was going to Europe to place a loan of $15,000,000.00 in London for the Confederate Government. If it was true his bank would take the loan and place it on the Northern market." Mann politely declined. On March 30 he sailed on the *Europa*, many of whose passengers were English cotton buyers obviously sympathetic to the south; he reached London a fortnight ahead of his colleagues. His escapade proved to be virtually his last success against the Yankees.

The conduct of United States diplomacy during its time of greatest trial lay in the hands of William Henry Seward. Seward's reputation as a Secretary of State, and even more as an imperialist, has skyrocketed in recent times. His political stature had been obscured by Lincoln hagiology; while those who wrote in the calmer days following the Civil War often expressed genteel distaste for Seward's wartime ruthlessness and expediency. John Jay, for instance, welcomed Seward's successor, and political opposite, Hamilton Fish, as a man who would restore

> the high-toned dignity and noble principle which marked the diplomacy of the Revolution, but which during our recent troubles . . . were exchanged for the low-toned and shuffling policy that for eight years has complicated our difficulties and compromised our honor.[18]

However, Seward knew, better than his critics, the well-springs of American nationalism, and he contributed a new understanding of the necessary connection between public opinion and foreign policy. It was Seward who began the systematic publication of State Department correspondence, skillfully edited to raise northern morale.[19] Some of the "aberrations" in Seward's diplomacy, deplored by

---

18. John Jay to Hamilton Fish, March 12, 1869, q. Allan Nevins, *Hamilton Fish* (New York, 1936, repr. 1957), I, p. 114.

19. Dexter Perkins, "William H. Seward as Secretary of State" in *Union Worthies No. 6* (Union College, Schenectady, N. Y., 1951), p. 12.

orthodox scholars of foreign policy, are explicable as domestic wartime measures, and by that test they were at times remarkably successful. Another dimension to Seward's career—and one essential to an understanding of his stance towards the powers—was his long-standing vision of America's world role. The controversies over foreign policy which racked American campuses during the 1960's have encouraged a reassessment of the republic's long-term aggrandizement, a preoccupation with the domestic conditions—and dilemmas—which forcefed the original search for empire. Seward has been rediscovered: not only because he was the most brillant and systematic articulator of the idea of imperial mission in the middle period, and thus a precursor of the so-called "new imperialism" of the 1890's, but also because he was aware of expansionism as a facet of America's nascent industrial-capitalism. Seward, says Richard Van Alstyne, "is the central figure of nineteenth-century American imperialism. He understood the nature and the directions which American expansionism historically strove to follow . . . ."[20] William Appleman Williams describes Seward's central vision as an "American empire embracing the world through the revolutionary power of its economy and ideas. His emotional nationalism was anchored in hard economic analysis."[21] Williams discerns two controlling assumptions in Seward's worldview. Disturbed by the economic stagnation which set in after the 1837 depression, he insisted that American manufactures and commercial agriculture had to have a constantly expanding market. Hence his emphasis, not on territorial expansion outside the continent, but on the control of bases and trade routes needed "for the projection, development, and protection of trade and investment." Secondly, Seward wanted peaceful expansion, as war consumed democracies; and he wanted above all to avoid a sectional war which would terminate the dream of national destiny. Thus, although Seward is remembered in the school books as the freesoil politician who spoke of antislavery principle as "higher law" and forecast the "irrepressible conflict," he "persistently preferred a compromise that would allow the rising industrial economy to subvert slavery in a peaceful process as it went on to greater victories throughout the world." It is possible

20. Van Alstyne, *Rising American Empire*, 176.

21. W. A. Williams, *The Contours of American History* (Chicago, 1966, 1st ed. 1961), pp. 292, 318. Walter LaFeber, a younger Wisconsin scholar, develops a similar view of Seward (whose "vision of empire dominated American policy for the next century") in his stimulating and controversial, *The New Empire: An Interpretation of American Expansion 1860–1898* (New York, 1963), pp. 24–39. For a splendidly researched biography from a more traditional stance, see Glyndon G. Van Deusen, *William Henry Seward* (New York, 1967).

to interpret the American imperial "frontier" of antebellum days, in Williams' radical analysis, as a means of evading outstanding economic and sectional problems within America. When the sectional crisis became unevadable (we may add), Seward and others naturally appealed for unity by reference to the nation's grander destiny. His threats of resorting to a foreign war, of welding north and south together in a swoop upon Cuba and other spoils, were thus not inexplicable gestures (as they are so often described), but the desperate extension of prevailing logic.

When Lincoln offerred the State Department to Seward (on December 8, 1860), he recognized the New Yorker's high eminence within the Republican party. Seward was far better known to Americans than Lincoln. He had entered Whig politics as a struggling young lawyer, a disciple of John Quincy Adams and something of an intellectual. Ability, amiability, and alliance with Thurlow Weed's party machine in New York, made him governor of New York (1838-1842) on an antimasonic, heavy-spending program. Thereafter he contended for internal improvements financed nationally by high tariffs, policies of cheap land and cheap labor, the expansion of seaboard trade and industry, and rapid development by means of transcontinental railroads. Antislavery votes put him in the Senate in 1848, but the reputation he acquired as a radical in the fifties belied his essential moderation on the issue. Seward accepted the Compromise of 1850 in an unsuccessful bid to save the Whig party. He played a vital role in bringing about a merger of the Whig rump and the newly formed Republican parties, after conciliating his old foes the Know-Nothings. He took care to disarm possible enemies among the "iron-back" founders of the new party—Charles Sumner, Joshua Giddings, Gerrit Smith—but he shunned radicalism, "always convinced the abolition had to be accommodated to national needs, even if this meant delay."[22] His trimming was to tarnish his historical reputation: he was a 'rawhead and bloody to the South' (although in fact he had many friends among southern Democrats, including Jefferson Davis); while he was suspected by the abolitionists of betraying sacred principle. ("It was evident of him," said Garrison, "that his moral nature is quite subordinate to his intellect.") Seward's uncertain image cost him the nomination for President at Chicago in May 1860, although he ran Lincoln hard. The press, which he always cultivated assiduously, gave him strong support, and he carried New York, New England, Michigan, Wisconsin, and Minnesota. But prominent

22. Frank Otto Gatell, review of Van Deusen, *Seward,* in *CWH,* XV, No. 1 (March, 1969), p. 58.

Republicans such as Horace Greeley, W. C. Bryant, Samuel Bowles, and the future Secretary of the Navy, Gideon Welles, opposed Seward, and he failed to swing the crucial states of Indiana, Pennsylvania, and Illinois. Hurt, Seward talked of quitting politics, but campaigned loyally for Lincoln. Although rumor gave the State Department to Sumner or Salmon P. Chase, antislavery stalwarts, Lincoln was convinced of the need for a cabinet of "all the talents"; he chose to risk the chance that Seward would prove an unruly subordinate, or that strong men would fall out.

Seward hesitated before accepting. Many thought of Lincoln as an "available" nonentity, and expected Seward to be the *éminence grise* in the new administration. On the other hand, Seward would be abandoning senatorial leadership and independence, and he expected to be outnumbered in the cabinet by his political opponents. (Chase and the ex-Democrats Gideon Welles and Montgomery Blair were already slated for portfolios.) In the end, his decision was probably influenced as much by a sense of national duty, occasioned by the perils of the "interregnum" period before Lincoln should accede, as by prospects of power and patronage in high office. Nobody quite knew with Seward. As young Henry Adams, who admired him, noted, Governor Seward was

> a type in one way simple because it was only double—political and personal; but complex because the political had become nature, and no one could tell which was the mask and which the features . . . he chose to appear as a free talker, who loathed pomposity and enjoyed a joke . . . . Underneath the surface he was conventional after the conventions of western New York and Albany. Politicians thought it unconventionality. Bostonians thought it provincial . . . [But] Mr. Seward was never petty or personal; his talk was large; he generalized; he never seemed to pose for statesmanship; he did not require an attitude of prayer.[23]

He was in his sixtieth year, slightly built but endlessly energetic, beak-nosed, a careless dresser, immoderately fond of cigars, brandy, good talk, keeping one of the best tables in Washington—a political salon for men of all camps. The genteel (like the historian George Bancroft) recoiled from his earthiness, vanity, cynicism; the idealists distrusted his practicality and taste for backstairs intrigue; others (like Charles Francis Adams) respected his goodwill, capacities and learning. (A voracious reader, he relished the spacious writings of the ancients, Bacon, Burke, Macaulay, Brougham, Carlyle, and Prescott; and had talents as a naturalist.) Superficially there was little in common

---

23. *The Education of Henry Adams: An Autobiography* (Boston, 1918), p. 104.

between Lincoln, the frontier lawyer, and the easterner, closely linked with New York financial interests. In fact both were superb politicians with fundamentally compatible views on the negro question—the conservative and mediating approach of the Whig party (of which both had been stalwarts) rather than that of the radical Republicans. Lincoln was not versed in foreign affairs, and permitted Seward to be a strong Secretary of State, occasionally curbing his impetuosity, and defending him from partisan critics. Ultimately the partnership proved to be highly fruitful for the Union, but it went through an uncertain apprenticeship during the appallingly tense "secession winter" of 1860–1861. As Union diplomacy was to be forged in the furnace of that situation, we shall afford it more than cursory attention.

The party over which Lincoln now presided was very nearly shattered in the crisis spawned by its electoral victory. The party had been conceived during the Kansas–Nebraska storm, and its *raison d'être* was exclusion of slavery from the territories. The founding coalition of antislavery Whigs, Democrats, and Freesoilers was, however, gradually outnumbered by newcomers sensing the existence of a new force in politics: old-line Whigs, Irish and German immigrants, Know–Nothings, place-hunters, and moderates of all kinds. The secession of South Carolina and sister states destroyed the temporary unity which had been achieved to ensure Lincoln's election. Outside a hard core of uncompromising "Black Republicans" favoring coercion, most at first accepted the necessity for compromise, but division was rife over its terms. Seward himself reflected common northern attitudes which underestimated the determination of the secessionists, believed that the dispute was negotiable, or trusted that delay would cool tempers and spur to action the inert Unionists in the south. Only a relatively few abolitionists, and then only momentarily, considered separation better than bloodshed, and harbored thoughts of a new freesoil confederation embracing Canada. But the party could not agree to accept the westward expansion of slavocracy into newly organized portions of the old Mexican empire. Such expansion was implicit in the Crittenden proposals and was demanded as a right by southerners, who pointed to the Dred Scott decision and interpreted Lincoln's intransigence on the point as marking a northern policy of containment of a rival society, and economy. Seward was more flexible than Lincoln, believing that the superority of the free labor system in noncotton areas spelt the practical elimination of slavery. He worked tirelessly for a settlement while Lincoln, wishing to dampen tensions, stayed in voluntary exile in Illinois as President-elect. Then, if ever, Seward earned the title "Wolsey of the new administration," sarcastically accorded him by Jeremiah Black, Buchanan's stopgap Secretary of State after Lewis Cass's resignation. (Cass was indignant at Buchanan's failure to reinforce the federal forts at Charleston.) Seward acted a strong role with Lincoln's consent, and out of deliberate policy. Although carried away by self-importance—he acted beyond Lincoln's strict terms in negotiations with southerners, and saw himself as savior of his party and country—Seward knew that the north must not only have, but be seen to have, effective leadership.

The failure of the peace schemes and the withdrawal from the Union of Mississippi, Florida, Alabama, Georgia, Louisiana, and Texas—soon members of the rebel government at Montgomery—foreshadowed the failure of Seward's maneuvers. The Texans' rejection of Sam Houston, who appealed to the old flag, was a particularly bitter blow. The last weeks before Lincoln's inauguration were spent by Seward in struggling to prevent the exodus of the border states and an outbreak of war before the new regime was firmly settled in power. Negotiations, ingenious and varied, were carried on to strengthen at all costs the position of southern loyalists, and to restrain northern hotheads. At the same time Washington was quietly strengthened against the possibility of a *coup*. Wherever feasible, federal authority was protected where it was subject to challenge. John J. Crittenden, Stephen A. Douglas, and Charles Francis Adams collaborated with Seward; but he was censured by Republican ultras for ambiguity on the issue of permitting slavery into areas of the southwest such as New Mexico. (He ensured that no mention was made of slavery when Dakota, Colorado, and Nevada were organized as territories: as a pragmatist he saw no point in wrangling over principle when areas were practically unsuited for slave labor.) When outmaneuvered in the contest for cabinet places by a powerful anti-Seward faction, led by Salmon P. Chase, Seward threatened on March 2 to withdraw from the State Department. Lincoln headed him off without displacing Chase from cabinet, Seward's real purpose. Nevertheless, the New Yorker's main aim had been achieved: the Republicans had taken office, and civil war might yet be staved off.

The first reaction of the British Foreign Office, like the French Quai d'Orsay, to American events was to regret change and fret for trading interests. A genuine rebellion threatened awkward entanglements. During the election of 1856, southern Congressmen at Sweet Sulphur Springs had sounded a British consul on the question of England supporting the south in the event of disunion. The consul warned home that many northern politicians considered that "a war with some European power—England of course—would be the only remedy for the internal dissentions of the States, by rallying all parties against the common enemy." He included Stephen A. Douglas, Caleb Cushing, Jefferson Davis, and Seward among those hostile to England.[24] Seward needed the Irish vote and had shown that he was capable of playing to the galleries with threats of war. When Pierce had tried to retrieve his popularity in the mid-fifties by picking a quarrel with Britain over the Isthmus, Seward outmatched him in Congress by advocating war and broadening the scene of action to include Canada.[25] This was domestic politics, designed to curb southern expansionism as well as to win votes; and Seward gleefully told the British minister: "I have made it *my* war, so don't be under the least apprehension of its success." Whitehall drew the lesson that he might prove to be an unscrupulous and dangerous foreign minister. During the secession winter Seward's speeches were aggressive toward the powers. At a celebrated Astor House meeting he declared the basic loyalty of southerners as Americans, and proclaimed their willingness to defend the Union from predators abroad. One remark was aimed directly at British North America: "There is no such thing in the book, no such thing in reason, no such thing in nature as any State existing in the continent of North America, outside of the U.S.A. . . . ."[26]

The British minister at Washington, Lord Lyons, worried fussily about Seward and the national debacle. A thorough professional, Lyons had been appointed to America in December 1858 by Derby's short-lived Conservative ministry, a welcome piece of patronage after years of slow advancement. A shy and earnest bachelor of forty-one, Lyons was perceptive, temperamentally cautious, and a dutiful defender of British interests. With London's concurrence, he pigeonholed the delicate legal problems raised by South Carolina's secession, maintained his consuls in the rebel states despite doubts concerning their status, and tried without success to tidy up the last boundary issue still in dispute between the U.S. and Britain. (This concerned claims to San Juan Island, the terminus to the northwest boundary with Canada. Lyons urged the British solution of arbitration upon Buchanan, hoping to deprive Seward of a pretext for aggression; but a recommendation by the Foreign Relations Committee favoring the

---

24. L. A. White, "The United States in the 1850's as seen by British Consuls," *MVHR*, XIX, No. 4 (March, 1933), pp. 531, 534.

25. Van Alstyne, "British Diplomacy and the Clayton–Bulwer Treaty," p. 173.

26. *NYH*, December 24, 1860.

proposal lapsed in a Senate whose last executive session was devoted to patronage matters.)

Lord John Russell ordered Lyons not to express opinions which events might contradict, not to favor one party above the other, and to: "Preach against force and civil war." They were hardly compatible objectives. Russell had jumped with characteristic impulsiveness to the conclusion that the United States could not be "cobbled together again by any compromise."[27] Russell, immensely experienced in high affairs, descended from the famous Whig martyr of Charles II's reign, was cold, uncharismatic, and too indecisive to be the material of great biography. Nor has he won plaudits for his handling of foreign affairs during the difficult years of Palmerston's last administration, when he coped with the American war, the Polish crisis, and Schleswig-Holstein. He was proudest of his Italian policy which paved the way for Italian unification. But as he said in one of Parliament's earliest debates on the Civil War:

> The joy which I felt at the overthrow of some of the despotisms of Italy is counterbalanced by the pain which I experience at the events which have lately taken place in America. I admit that I have thought, and I still think, that in this country we enjoy more real freedom than the U.S. has ever done . . . . Yet we cannot be blind to the fact that the Republic has been for many years a great and free State, exhibiting to the world the example of a people in the enjoyment of wealth, happiness, and freedom . . . . I do not think it just or seemly that there should be among us anything like exultation at their discord . . . .

But it was soon clear that Russell's standard Whig regard for foreign liberties and America would be subject to realism: and could be applied to the south's nationalist cause. Russell privately expected the rebel government to be in an "impregnable" position by March 4, "except by mutiny and rebellion of the slaves," and thought the north should accept separation and the right of secession. But England should stand clear of the affair. No important British politician preached intervention at this stage. The country was disenchanted over policies of interventionism, even in the guise of aid for Constitutionalism and foreign liberties. "No more Crimeas" was the feeling of the day. Crimea had seemed a liberal challenge to Russian oppression in Europe, as much a blow for the Poles as the Turks: but victory proved pyrrhic, demonstrating the hollowness of the war's propaganda. Italy had better claims to be waging a war of liberation in 1859, but English aid (apart from a strategic

27. Russell to Lyons, December 26, 1869; January 10, 1861; q. *Mass. Hist. Soc. Proc.* (hereafter *MHSP*) (January, 1915), pp. 202–203.

maneuver by the Royal Navy to bluff Spain) was largely verbal. Nor did Britain help the Poles in 1863 or the Danes in 1864—public opinion was unmistakably against meddling in these affairs, even if its sympathies were clear.[28]

The slaveholding rebellion at first evoked little public sympathy in Britain.[29] Few saw Lincoln's election as a victory for crude abolitionism, or an intolerable threat to southern institutions. Educated and propertied opinion was more inclined to view secession in Radical Republican terms as a "great conspiracy" by disaffected southerners: "The game went against them, so they threw up their cards and kicked over the table . . . . Beaten in argument and by the ballot-box, they 'descended into the streets'. . . ."[30] Walter Bagehot (who thought the south the "deeply ulcerated semblance of civilization") argued that the rebels were determined upon a new imperial career, untrammeled by restraints imposed within the Union by the northern states: ". . . their cupidity [is] excited at the prospect of a vast Slave Empire . . . stretching over all the magnificent lands which lie between Virginia on the North and the Isthmus of Panama on the South. . . ."[31]

Slavery encountered a solid phalanx of opposition in Britain. Its evils were luridly fictionalized (a reform technique invented by the Americans). Harriet Beecher Stowe's *Uncle Tom's Cabin* and *Dred* were colossal successes. Her tours of England in 1853, 1856, and 1859 were triumphal, and refired antislavery fervor, running down after the apparent victories of the slave power in the Texan and Mexican wars.[32] John Brown's execution aroused the writers of Europe. Carlyle and Ruskin were among the very few luminaries impressed by proslavery arguments. Tory philanthropists, like Lord Shaftesbury, were old supporters of abolition. Churchmen—the most zealous from the Dissenting sects, but including Anglican divines such as F. D. Maurice—disputed the concept of man as property, and asserted the worth of each individual soul. Liberals decried bondage as a denial of inalienable rights. Conservatives decried it as a surrender to mammon and the profit motive, an extreme form of the

---

28. See A. J. P. Taylor, *The Trouble Makers: Dissent over Foreign Policy 1792-1939* (London, 1957), Chapter 2.

29. The topic is more fully documented in my "Portents of War: English Opinion on Secession," *J. American Studies*, IV, No. 2 (February, 1971), pp. 163-179.

30. *National Review*, XIII (July, 1861), pp. 155–156.

31. *Economist* (March 2, 1861), p. 226.

32. Frank J. Klingberg, "Harriet Beecher Stowe and Social Reform in England," *AHR*, XLIII, No. 3 (April, 1938), pp. 542–552.

tendencies of the age. Economists, including James Stirling and John Elliott Cairnes, judged the slave system to be an economic error, a transgression of the laws of supply and demand. The founder of Marxism (eking out a bare existence from journalism in London at this time) pronounced the inevitable doom of the south's outmoded social system at the hands of a bourgeois republic waging a revolutionary war.[33]

The American abolitionists had influential English friends.[34] But the power of abolitionists to change the course of American history seemed, even to those friends, distinctly limited, their "fanaticism" likely to obliterate their political influence. Lincoln's victory at the polls in 1860 was attributed to the more responsible moderates in the north. To the Victorians it seemed not unlike their own reformist triumphs, the Great Reform of 1832 or the Corn Law Repeal of 1846. The defections which followed in the south were interpreted as the defiant gestures of a corrupt *ancien régime*. President Buchanan's refusal to garrison Federal forts in seceded areas, his efforts to avert a clash, were seen as capitulating: "aiding and fostering treason till he shrank from the menacing spectre he had raised; yielding and temporizing when firmness was required, firm when firmness could only exasperate; finally neutral, irresolute, vacillating . . . ."[35] Buchanan's War Secretary, the Virginian John B. Floyd, was believed to have deliberately weakened the Union army, stripped forts of their garrisons, and traitorously supplied the south with enormous stands of government arms. The Treasurer, Howell Cobb of Georgia, was accused of bankrupting the United States Treasury. When southern ministers resigned from Buchanan's cabinet, the existence of a rebellious faction within the government seemed to be confirmed.

The failure of the compromises tried before Lincoln's accession was, on the whole, attributed by Englishmen to southern intransigence. The general impression was that the Republicans had offered concessions verging on the point of shameful surrender. The Crittenden Plan permitted the protection of slavery south of 36° 30′ (the old Missouri Compromise line), and allowed the status of future states entering the Union to be decided upon the squatter-sovereignty principle. The *Saturday Review*, a moderate Tory journal, thought

---

33. Marx's articles on the war for the New York *Daily Tribune* and the Vienna *Presse* are collected in K. Marx and F. Engels, *The Civil War in the United States* (Citadel Press, New York, 3rd ed., 1961).

34. See Frank Thistlethwaite, *The Anglo-American Connection in the Early Nineteenth Century* (Philadelphia, 1959), Chapter 4.

35. *North British Review*, XXXIV (May, 1861), p. 563.

this "an entire surrender of all the objects for which the Republican party has contended." The Personal Liberty Laws in force in some northern states were to be repealed, another blow at humanitarian convictions. Nor did champions of parliamentary supremacy like the suggestion that Congress be deprived by a constitutional amendment of any future power to interfere with slavery in any state.

The establishment of the rebel government at Montgomery, and the failure of the Virginia Peace Congress, provoked liberal exasperation. Bagehot wrote of the rebels: "they never showed the first desire or intention of remaining in the Union; but . . . pushed forward their proceedings with a reckless and indecent haste . . . ." The Tory *Fraser's Magazine* drew parallels between the south's despotic spirit and the "dynastic usurpations of Europe;" it spoke of a combat between treacherous aggressors who were "avowed patrons and glorifiers of an accursed form of slavery" and men who, whatever their failings, were "champions of human freedom."[36]

Up to this point there seems to have been very little romantic admiration for the south. This was to come later with the gallantry of Confederate arms against greater odds, and as a product of Confederate propaganda, and was to be by no means a negligible factor in a country where flourished such cults as pre-Raphaelitism and worship of Gothic.[37] But before Sumter the overwhelming emphasis was upon the "radically vicious social condition" of the slavocracy. The planter class was as yet decidedly less than Cavalier; imperious, ambitious, cruel were the adjectives commonly applied to them, while the poor whites were "ignorant, squalid, and brutal . . . with the additional mischief that, owing to the institution of slavery, they are not the working classes of the country."[38]

What gradually eroded British patience with the northern cause was the disenchanting march of events rather than, as the textbooks tell us, disappointment at Lincoln's refusal to make war on slavery. Indeed there was a surprising degree of accord among Englishmen of all political colors that there should *not* be a war upon slavery, if that meant a barbaric war between the United States and the Confederacy. Nor is it true that there was no understanding in England of the perplexed position in which Lincoln found himself. A reading of the journals and periodicals of the time indicates that they

36. *Saturday Review*, February 16, 1861, 151; *Economist*, March 2, 1861; *Fraser's Magazine*, LXIII (April 1861), p. 404.

37. See Sheldon Van Auken, *English Sympathy for the Southern Confederacy: The Glittering Illusion* (Unpub. thesis, Oxford, 1957). Van Auken finds few examples of positive regard for the Confederacy before the secession of Virginia, pp. 29–30.

38. *National Review*, XIII (July, 1861), pp. 168–169.

were reasonably well-informed on the attitude of the major parties and factions toward the question of slavery in the south, and on the distinct issue of slavery in the territories. From the time of the 1860 election, writers canvassed the constitutional and political obstacles which ruled out a Republican onslaught on the "peculiar institution," and explained why the territories had become the main theatre of sectional battle. Discussed widely was the vital need of the north not to alienate the slaveholding Upper South by being insensitive to states rights, or too sympathetic to abolitionism. Moreover, such issues were widely discussed *before* Lincoln's inaugural, which seems to have been over-dramatized as a turning point in English opinion. It is true that many believed that slavery was the root cause which had brought the sections to the brink of war. But this was not the same as believing that the north was willing—or should be willing—to resort to arms to free the slaves. Lincoln's inaugural only labored the obvious, namely that the immediate struggle was to save the Union, and a great deal of disappointment was soon generated at what seemed the sheer ineptitude of the Federal government to cope with just this problem. It was only after hostilities had begun that Lincoln started to suffer the disabilities of not waging a holy war.

It was the long months of negotiations and tension before Sumter, the exasperating vacillation of Northern politicians, the cumulating fears of a futile war which would disrupt the comfortable commercial arrangements of the Atlantic world, which depressed observers. The passing of the Morrill tariff in particular was a disastrous blow to Federal diplomacy. It provided a nasty shock to the idealists, who had so far believed that the burden of sectional animosity rested upon the south, for the tariff seemed a deliberate piece of sectional vengeance as well as a ludicrous economic error. As time went on, reports flourished of growing vindictiveness on the part of the north, of schisms within the Republican ranks, and a strengthening of the coercionist abolitionist school at the expense of Seward and the conciliationists. Lincoln's inaugural was held by critics to proclaim his powerlessness to the world. One English liberal, Isabella Bird, spoke sadly of "the Union itself falling to pieces under the weight of its own institutions, the vaulted Federal tie no stronger in an emergency than a rope of sand, and the Federal Government a symbol of confusion, humiliation, and contempt, in the sight of the armed despotisms and constitutional monarchies of Europe."[39]

---

39. *North British Review*, XXXIV (May, 1961), p. 563. Some regarded the inaugural as statesmanlike. See "Portents of War."

Hopes that a course of vigor would replace indecision and suspense at Washington were soon disappointed. The scramble for places which marred Lincoln's first weeks of office seemed an indecent example of Nero fiddling, a confirmation of the venality of democratic parties, and a reminder of Tocqueville's warnings against the consequences of the "tyranny of the majority." More menacing, as war fever rose in the north, was the prospect of the government trapping itself in a situation where war might occur by miscalculation.

As the shadows darkened over America, Europe watched and waited. There seemed little else to do. Yankee power had not yet broken down, and rashness by the powers now might bring a terrible retribution. But the chances seemed high of a strikingly new future in the hemisphere, involving the creation of a new state or set of states, whether peacefully or by arms. The prevailing uncertainty and confusion infected politicians in London and Paris. In this time of flux, there was a good deal of muddling through. Decisions were taken from day to day, and governments were slow to take fixed positions.

Chapter III

Appeal to Arms

No American government had come to office in such grave circumstances as those facing Lincoln's Republican administration. According to the British Minister ". . . the house is on fire, and neither those who are fanning the flames nor those who are endeavoring to extinguish them, can think of anything but conflagration."[1] The Republicans had never been in executive federal office, Lincoln was harassed by office-seekers and was feeling his way. In an atmosphere of civil crisis and perplexity, northern politicians thought little of diplomacy or the international consequences of a war between the states. Nevertheless, there was talent in the government's foreign appointments. The Senate confirmed Charles Sumner as chairman of its Foreign Relations Committee. The country's most renowned scholar-politician, he was the abolitionist martyr who had been crippled in the halls of the Senate itself by a cane-wielding southerner, Preston Brooks. (Sumner had only resumed his seat in June 1860.) One of the south's most detested scourges, Sumner could only have won the office in a purged Congress. He proved to be a strong chairman, helped by his knowledge of international law (not Seward's strongest point) and his wide range of European friendships. His correspondence with Cobden was one of the more momentous of the war. Sumner was almost an idol to antislavery Britons, and he is a major figure in Atlantic history: a "carrier" of humanitarian, reformist ideas in a movement which embraced both continents, and one who helped associate the New England cultural elite with the British intelligentsia. But insofar as the war broke down Sumner's love for Britain, he also typified the ambivalence embedded in the

1. Lyons to W. S. Lindsay, M. P., January 21, 1861, *MHSP*, XLVIII (January, 1915), p. 215. The comment was still true in March.

Anglo-American connection. There was to be a good deal of ambiguity in Sumner's diplomatic wartime role.[2]

Charles Francis Adams went to London—a piece of Seward's patronage which historians have warmly endorsed: indeed one scholar speaks of the Adams' family's historical apotheosis, and suggests that it has tended to obscure Seward's role in wartime diplomacy.[3] Lincoln passed Adams over for the cabinet, preferring a man with Democratic antecedents for political balance, and relations between the two were never particularly cordial. Moreover, distrust existed between Adams and Sumner. Their old political alliance had broken down during the secession winter, Sumner protesting at Adams and Seward being cohorts in the cause of unprincipled compromise, and Adams deploring "stiff-necked" policies from Sumner and his followers. Sumner's own name had been mentioned for St. James, and in Adams' appointment he discerned the hand of Seward, whose appointment to the State Department Sumner had attempted to block. Seward, always amiable, and Sumner, always dutiful to the higher cause, subdued their antagonisms, although Lincoln's regard for Sumner's advice on foreign affairs sometimes embarrassed the Secretary of State. Almost against the probabilities of the spoils system, able appointees went to important places: Thomas Corwin to Mexico, Carl Schurz to Madrid, consuls Thomas H. Dudley to Liverpool and John Bigelow to Paris, Henry Sanford to Belgium. Joshua Giddings was a failure in Canada, and Cassius Clay proved "better suited to the meridian of Kentucky than of St. Petersburg."[4] Lincoln's inexperience resulted in a quota of eccentric postings: William Dayton, New Jersey's favorite for cabinet, went to France, although he spoke no French. (Outside that limitation he performed respectably.) A sympathizer of Kossuth, Anson Burlingame, was sent to the Hapsburg court at Vienna, to be declared *persona non grata* (he was sent on to China, where he excelled.) Lincoln was only with difficulty dissuaded from sending a former German revolutionist, Schurz, to the Sardinian court, which had exhausted its need to insult Austria.

Seward began by building a diplomatic house of cards on the precarious notion of the rebellion's impermanence. But to Adams he admitted the ravage caused by disaffection, which "lurked in every department, and in every bureau, in every regiment and in every ship

---

2. See David Donald, *Charles Sumner and the Rights of Man* (New York, 1970).

3. F. O. Gattell, *CWH*, XV, No. 1 (March, 1969), p. 58.

4. Bayard Taylor (First Secretary, Russian legation) to Horace Greeley, July 5, 1862, q. H. J. Carman and R. H. Luthin, *Lincoln and the Patronage* (1943), pp. 84-85. See generally Chapter 4.

of war, in the post office and in the custom-house, and in every legation and consulate from London to Calcutta . . . "[5] The former Assistant Secretary of State, William Henry Trescott, had defected to Confederate service, and Seward's first task was to purge his department. His first dispatches firmly asserted American sovereign rights, and demanded energetic action from his agents to frustrate the designs of Confederate emissaries invoking foreign intervention. Seward appealed to the conservative instincts of established authorities: any temporary advantage to be derived from connection with the south would be eclipsed by the evils states would suffer from disseverance of the Union. For it was the Union's manifest policy "to maintain peace, liberal commerce, and cordial amity with all other nations, and to favor the establishment of well-ordered government over the whole American continent."[6] Disaster to the Republic "might tend by its influence to disturb and unsettle the existing systems of government in other parts of the world." Seward's instructions paralleled in rhetoric and analysis the "conciliationist" views he was using, contentiously, at home. Disunion was the work of "misguided partisans," the result of "popular passions, excited under novel circumstances of very transient character." Lincoln was taking a "firm, yet just and liberal bearing" towards the insurrection. Before Sumter, Seward professed a republican distaste for coercing fellow-citizens: this would be expected of imperial or despotic governments, but within America's federal system there were "adequate, peaceful, conservative, and recuperative forces."[7] (Some of his remarks on the point approached absurdity, as when he charged Adams to indulge "in no expressions of harshness or disrespect, or even impatience, concerning the seceding States . . . .")

As yet Seward avoided threats on the vital issue of recognition of Confederate sovereignty by the powers, and said nothing of a blockade—the major worry of Washington's diplomatic corps. Cabinet had shelved as provocative the idea of blockading the cotton states, but had been canvassing ways and means of collecting federal customs revenues at sea now that state authorities in the south had usurped those rights. Cabinet divisions soon emerged between Seward, Treasurer Salmon Chase and Secretary of the Navy Gideon Welles. Welles recorded in his diary that Seward "was vigilantly attentive to

---

5. Seward to Adams, April 10, 1861, *Foreign Relations,* 1861, pp. 72-73.

6. Seward to all ministers, Circular, March 9, 1861, *Foreign Relations,* 1861, pp. 32-33.

7. Seward to Adams, April 10, 1861, *Foreign Relations,* 1861, p. 74.

every measure and movement in other Departments, however trivial. . . watched and scrutinized every appointment . . . but was not communicative in regard to the transactions of the State Department."[8] Seward complained that he was isolated in a cabinet dominated by his enemies. They in turn feared that Seward was establishing an ascendancy over the inexperienced Lincoln (always "patronizing and instructing him" Welles observed). Lincoln, however, was no cypher, and was preparing independently to shoulder the onus of dealing with the south. Drawn initially to Seward's solution of "voluntary and peaceful reconstruction," Lincoln cautiously gravitated to "no appeasement." Seward felt in danger of being stranded by events. He had continued to act his "Wolsey" role, playing the peacemaker with southern agents; but he was assailed for his policy of "drift" and his miscalculation of Lincoln's position eroded his own cradibility. His sure touch faltered, and he tried to retrieve his mistakes by desperate bluff and strategem.

Whether to relieve or evacuate Fort Sumter in Charleston harbor—key symbol of federal authority—was the issue which threatened to make or break the administration, and the nation. Lincoln's inaugural speech agreed not to assail the south to repossess federal property surrendered during Buchanan's tenure, but promised to maintain forts which had not yet fallen into southern hands. Retreat from this position could place an intolerable burden on loyalist northern opinion. And, as Lincoln knew acutely, retreat could threaten the very basis of the Presidency. On the other hand, the south swore resistance to Sumter's relief as an invasion of states rights. Sumter had hardly six weeks' supplies and was menaced by South Carolinian troops under General Beauregard. Its commandant, Major Anderson, reported that the fort was militarily indefensible: his arguments implied evacuation, and avoidance of conflict. Seward favored retreat: a clash at Charleston might satisfy the irreconcilables, but it would destroy the southern loyalists and alienate the upper south. So far Virginia resisted secession but opposed the use of force against the seven cotton states. Seward was unofficially treating with southern commissioners, in Washington to seek recognition of the Confederacy. In a characteristic gambler's throw, aimed at stalling the quest for recognition and warding off any precipitate move by the Carolinians against Sumter, Seward made known to the commissioners his conviction that Sumter would be evacuated. It must have seemed a safe move then: the military advised against

8. *Diary of Gideon Welles: Secretary of the Navy under Lincoln and Johnson* (New York, 1911), I, p. 7.

reinforcement; cabinet had voted on March 15 (with one dissenter) against the weaker course of merely provisioning the garrison; Lincoln was expected not to force the issue. But rumors of a "surrender" provoked a northern outcry. Secession had waxed fat upon appeasement, the long-awaited Unionist revival in rebel areas seemed a chimera, and men were tired of conceding to the south. Patriots were impatient for action and, brutally insensitive to the excruciating dilemmas facing Lincoln, accused the administration of "indecision, of inaction, of fatal indifference."[9] With an increasing number of northerners, there was a pervading desire to expunge irresolution through the exhilarating catharsis of war.

On March 29 the cabinet reversed its stand and Lincoln made the fateful decision to supply Sumter. Whether he expected war, and preferred it now, started by the south, is a moot point in civil war historiography. But Seward's program lay in ruins. If Sumter was relieved, his word would mean nothing in the south. Even if war was avoided, he would be finished as a negotiator, and possibly destroyed politically in the north. And all because of blundering leadership at Washington. Even Seward's buoyant spirits and sense of realities lapsed. During the weekend of March 30–31 he devised his celebrated last-ditch plan to defuse the Sumter crisis, and place himself at the head rather than at the spigot of affairs. Almost predictably, he intended to discharge explosive domestic emotions by directing their energies into foreign conflict. The idea has been dismissed as aberrant, but it has since become a recurrent theme in American history.

Friction with the British had grown worse during March. From the start, London anticipated trouble over possible blockade of the cotton states, and brought to bear pressure on Washington in order to protect British trade with the south. The Palmerston government veered between a threatening attitude, dictated (it was thought) by Lancashire's vital interest in keeping open a lifeline to Dixie—Charles Greville feared a war which should interfere with the cotton crops, "and this is what really affects us and what we care about"[10]—and wariness not to fall into a trap set by Seward. In February Seward

---

9. *New York Times* (hereafter NYT), April 3, 1861. On Sumter see Kenneth Stamp, *And the War Came: The North and the Secession Crisis* (La. U. P., 1950), Chapters 12, 13; W. A. Swanberg, *First Blood; the Story of Fort Sumter* (New York, 1957).

10. H. E. Maxwell, ed., *Life and Letters of . . . 4th Earl of Clarendon* (London, 1913), II, p. 237.

had blustered to Lyons that he could unite America by a war against interventionists who wanted to further foreign interests in the south.[11] The main villains of the piece reacted by reaching an Anglo-French accord to act together in the North American theatre.

Britain was subject to conflicting tugs on the matter of blockades. Apart from immediate economic interest, the view was strong that blockades were a barbarism contrary to modern trends. (Mid-nineteenth century man had a touching faith that war was steadily being civilized, a faith badly jarred by the Civil War.) But a contrary principle held sway at the Admiralty and elsewhere: Britain's long term naval interests lay in affirming and expanding the blockade practice. The Civil War, as we shall see, created paradox on paradox with respect to Anglo-American attitudes to maritime rights, an area of historic enmity between the two nations. The imperatives of war placed the United States in an unfamiliar role as a belligerent power at sea, and pushed into the background its traditional neutral's concern for "freedom of the seas." Clearly, British acquiescence in a strong naval role by the north would set the Admiralty convenient precedents, superceding temporary inconveniences to British shipping and abrasions to national pride. Britain itself groaned under the unaccustomed burdens of neutrality; and would bear the brunt of maritime clashes with the Union navy, given the Royal Navy's command of major sea-lanes and the predominance of the British merchant marine in wartime Atlantic trade. Before Sumter, however, Russell and his colleagues only dimly appreciated these complexities, and steered between shoals with indifferent skill. Lyons was told to deny Washington any excuse for insolence, while permitting no infringement of English dignity. Russell wanted cotton, but by March 9 was coming to accept that a blockade of the rebel coast could hardly be repudiated: that is if, according to "American doctrine," it was "an actual blockade kept up by an efficient force." Britain could hardly do otherwise, considering its harsh use of blockade during the Napoleonic wars. Britain, moreover, had been one of the victor powers which at the Crimean peace had signed the Declaration of Paris (1856) laying down a new code of maritime law. The fourth item accepted blockades if effective, "that is to say, maintained by a force sufficient really to prevent access to the coast of the enemy." That condition was sufficiently subjective to permit Britain ample scope for maneuver, once a blockade

11. Lyons to Russell, February 4, 1861, q. E. D. Adams (hereafter EDA), *Great Britain and the American Civil War* (New York and London, 1925; repr. 1957), I, p. 60.

was instituted, but it could hardly be used to block American intention to blockade.

As Adams was slow to arrive in London, Lyons negotiated on the blockade. His approach was tougher than Russell's, and he had affronted Seward before he received his superior's soft instruction of March 9. Lyons thought that an attitude of British weakness would merely tempt the violent party in the north into tweaking the lion's tail. Better for the lion to bare its teeth now. With scant regard for legal niceties, Lyons tied the issues of recognition of the Confederacy and blockade. Washington (he thought) might soft-pedal in the matter of sealing off trade with the south if it was convinced that London seriously considered a quick recognition of southern independence.

Plied by anxious English merchants, Lyons badgered Seward for clarification of the administration's thinking on the blockade. He had good arguments. International practice conferred an unambiguous right of blockade only upon belligerent powers. But the Lincoln government insisted upon denying the existence of a state of war. Consistent with its view of secession as a Great Conspiracy lacking popular support the government described the Confederates as insurgents and not as belligerents. Had the United States been dealing with a genuinely local and minor insurgency, it may have been possible for it to claim the right merely to close some of its own ports as a matter of police action outside the concern of international law. But this was a moot point, and as far as the powers cared an irrelevant one: in their eyes the extent, strength and political organization of the rebellion sufficiently refuted the north's contention. Lyons claimed, with justice, that measures short of a full-scale wartime blockade used to harass cotton ports would amount to an obnoxious "paper blockade." It was known that cabinet had debated one such measure, closure by proclamation alone, and was canvassing whether to station cruisers offshore to levy customs dues from foreign merchantmen. Traders were aghast at the prospect of paying double duty, to the Union navy and Confederate state authorities. Lyons willingly represented their grievances to the State Department. Interference with foreign commerce, he pointed out with uncharacteristic aggression, "would in all probability be a fatal step to the party which first adopted it, by bringing the Powers of Europe into the quarrel . . . ."[12] On March 20, Lyons lectured

12. Lyons to Russell (pvt), March 18, 1861, q. *MHSP*, XLVIII, p. 219. Lyons drew a black picture of the United Kingdom being excluded from northern trade by the Morrill tariff, and southern trade by blockade.

Seward, who had been putting out nervous feelers about Britain's likely position on recognition of the Davis government:

> I said . . . If a considerable rise were to take place in the price of cotton, and British ships were to be at the same time excluded from the Southern Ports, an immense pressure would be put upon Her Majesty's Government to use all the means in their power to open those ports. If Her Majesty's Government felt it their duty to do so, they would naturally endeavor to effect their object in a manner as consistent as possible, first with their friendly feelings towards both sections of this Country, and secondly with the recognized principles of International Law. As regarded the latter point in particular, it certainly appeared that the most simple, if not the only way, would be to recognize the Southern Confederacy.[13]

This was the gravest of menaces, and it is often forgotten in discussions of Seward's early aggressiveness to England. Within days the Secretary of State had worked himself into a high state of cantankerousness, becoming "violent and noisy" at a dinner party given by Lyons on March 25. He loudly declared before the British, French, and Russian ministers that he repudiated the *de facto* authority of Confederate officials at southern ports, and threatened to confiscate without compensation ships coming out of such ports without papers required by United States law. Confiscation of neutral ships in peacetime, without notification of blockade, horrified the diplomats. Lyons expostulated that Seward's plan seemed to amount to a paper blockade of the south's enormous coastline: "that the calling it an enforcement of the Revenue Laws appeared to me to increase the gravity of the measure, for it placed Foreign Powers in the Dilemma of recognizing the Southern Confederation or of submitting to the interruption of their Commerce."[14] Lyons was sticking to his strategy, but he was apprehensive that he might be playing Seward's game for him. So he sought extra insurance, advising Russell to strengthen the accord with France so as to deter rashness at Washington. He added that the Yancey mission, on its way to Europe from Dixie, "should not meet with too strong a rebuff in England or France. Such a rebuff would be a great encouragement to violent measures here."

There is not much to be said for Lyon's impulsiveness except that it typified the tense and confused emotions of the day. Britain had been traditionally conservative in extending recognition of sovereignty to states claiming independence from an imperial connection. Recognition required the existence of a viable political

13. Lyons to Russell, March 26, 1861, *Ibid.*, p. 221.
14. Lyons to Russell, *Ibid.*, p. 222.

organization, and *de facto* abandonment by the previous rulers of efforts to restore dominion. The latter condition was signally absent in the American affair. But it should be remembered on Lyons' behalf that the United States had not yet termed recognition an act of hostility to the Union. Until this was done, Englishmen were slow to foresee that northerners would react quite so violently to any hint of acceptance of the south. For a time it appeared almost as if players on both sides were making their moves on separate chess boards.

The French minister to Washington, Henri Mercier, was disposed to regard southern independence as virtually a *fait accompli.* On March 29, he advised Paris seriously to consider recognition. A career diplomat under the Orleanists and Napoleon III, friend of Thouvenel's, Mercier was intelligent, outwardly extrovert but, according to his biographer, disgruntled by "exile" to America and by nature intense and "apt to try the imprudent."[15] His reports to Thouvenel were unflattering to the north, but this may be attributed to his upper bourgeois scepticism about democracy rather than to ingrained sympathy for the rebels (many of whom he had mixed with socially in 1860). Mercier felt, along with many European scholars, that the American federal system could not reconcile "the needs, the interests, and the passions of a population which has not been able to develop so phenomenally without losing a great part of its homogeneity."[16] Both Lyons and Mercier tended to assume that foreign recognition of the south would come close on the heels of the creation of a Montgomery government. Mercier was quick to see the irony of Lincoln's austere inauguration in an ambitiously lavish, but symbolically half-built Capitol: "It's as if one wanted to inaugurate a Quaker in a basilica. It is true that the fate of this monument, a new Tower of Babel, may be only to witness to future generations the bold presumption of those who conceived its design . . . the impression which all these contrasts leaves is that of a greatness vainly sought, a diminished power which no more holds the place which befits it."

Mercier hoped that north and south might be prevailed upon to associate together as independent states within a customs union similar to the German *Zollverein*: an idea to be often canvassed during the next years by the Quai d'Orsay. Mercier was aware of the perils of premature recognition of the south; but he felt that they might be outweighed by other factors: he apparently hoped that

---

15. Daniel B. Carroll, *Henri Mercier and the American Civil War* (Princeton Univer. Press, 1971), p. 6 and *passim*.

16. Quoted, Carroll, p. 37. For following quote, p. 47.

joint recognition by the powers would force Washington to bow before the inevitable, thus averting a war disastrous to France's cotton trade, and to maritime order. If civil war still came, it would then be already established on a regular footing. (He confused recognition of belligerency with recognition of independence, and his arguments for delicately timing recognition just prior to a final breakdown between the sections were weak: defining a state of war was a pragmatic question.) More startling was Mercier's desire that he and Lyons have a discretionary power to recognize the south. Lyons warded this off: "I should feel a good deal embarrased by having such a power in my pocket, unless the contingency in which it was to be used should be most clearly stated." Mercier's views became known to the Davis government, which too eagerly accepted the certainty of prompt French acceptance. (Even the Russians, it was said, were advising their northern friends to recognize the south, as Europe would certainly do.[17]) The northern press was cool towards France. Americans liked to believe that the French people were loyal to the "ancient friendship." The official world of the Second Empire, however, was a different matter: it would welcome the birth of a southern confederation as a cuff at democracy. The French were rumored to be on the verge of intervention in Mexico, and renewing their old interest in Louisiana. Americans in Paris spread gossip that southern agents (including Dudley Mann and Bailey Peyton) had already obtained assurances of cooperation from the Tuileries. The French were angry at the Morrill tariff, and drawn to the south as a market. The *Moniteur*, the Emperor's official journal, was blunt in March: "If the Union is not re-established, the programme of Free Trade proclaimed by the South will open up to our agricultural and manufacturing industry a new field of profitable trade and of large compensation."[18]

Late March saw friction with the powers turn into something of a scare. News arrived that the French and British were fitting out a powerful fleet of war steamers destined for American waters. "We may surmise," mordantly wrote an American correspondent from Paris, ". . . that it is intended as an audience for the struggle which is soon to take place between brothers and friends in the United States—as a sort of escort of honour for the funeral of the Great Republic."[19] More sinister implications were soon being drawn. It

17. Carroll, p. 51.
18. For rumors on France, etc., *NYT*, March 15, 18, 29; 1861.
19. *NYT*, March 29, 1861 (Paris report, March 10).

was learned that Spain was independently sending a formidable force of ships, men, and materials to the Gulf of Mexico. Qualms that Spain was looking to reassert its old hegemony in the Americas acquired a new significance when reannexation of the island republic of San Domingo was revealed as the Spanish design.

Occupying the eastern two-thirds of the old Spanish colony of Hispaniola, and a mere fifty-odd miles southeast from Cuba, San Domingo had eked out an existence of turbulent instability since declaring its independence from Madrid in 1821. After only a year it was brought under the oppressive rule of its neighboring black republic Haiti, and did not regain its autonomy until 1844. The ensuing years of corrupt administration and successive military uprisings invited foreign intervention. Both of the rival dictators who in turn monopolized power, Pedro Santana and Buenaventura Baez, intrigued to place their country under foreign protection, and only the checks and balances of international politics frustrated their designs.

While Spain, under the spur of a nationalist revival, dreamed dreams of imperial restoration, Spanish ambitions in Hispaniola had small chance of success so long as a strong United States regarded reconquest as a violation of the Monroe Doctrine. British policy, moreover, frowned upon schemes which could lead to a Spanish-American war, with its inevitable disruption of international trade. From the mid-fifties Britain had veered away from its earlier strategy of welcoming the consolidation of Spanish power, as "a kind of Caribbean Ottoman Empire, to stand in the way of aggressive powers."[20] The Foreign Office had since come to regard as inevitable, even desirable, American penetration into the unstable lands of the south. A similarly acquiescent attitude was taken toward the expansionist tendencies of the French. But Spain was now discouraged from extending its sphere of influence from Cuba to Hispaniola, where a clash might occur with either French or American imperialism.

Spain's opportunity was provided by the sectional crisis in the United States. Spanish-Dominican negotiators discussed reannexation during 1860. But although plied with warnings from its commercial agents in the island, the listless Buchanan administration refused to

---

20. Charles C. Haunch, "Attitudes of Foreign Governments towards the Spanish Reoccupation of the Dominican Republic," *Hispanic American History Review*, XXVII (1947), p. 248. The following account draws upon information in this article.

act with vigor. Nor did discouragement come from Paris. The French had once harbored ideas of establishing a protectorate over the Dominicans, whose culture was French-oriented, but they had given up in the face of British disapproval. Although London no longer stood resolute against French colonization, Napoleon III had adjusted his sights upon Mexico. The evidence suggests that in 1861 the Emperor had in mind a Dominican sprat to catch a Mexican mackerel. The Spanish had also been intriguing in Mexico and would have to be bought off: they could be given a free hand in San Domingo in return for French freedom of action in Mexico. Some suggested that, as an additional reward for the Emperor, the adjoining French-speaking state of Haiti would pass under the French flag. Moreover, it seemed wise to Spain to act before the Confederates had a chance to do so: "To prevent them from stealing an island that has been lying loose in her neighborhood, Spain steals it herself."[21]

Secure in his knowledge of American weakness, President Santana on March 18 publicly announced San Domingo's wish to be once again ruled by Madrid. Any trepidations he felt about British interference were soon dispelled, even though Lord John Russell took care to read Madrid a lesson on the dangers of provoking even a sickly America. Assuming that the rebellion would succeed, Russell warned that north and south might later combine in the Caribbean. Spain was foolishly risking an eventual American takeover in Cuba and Puerto Rico. But Britain would not be disposed to act, provided (and this was an important proviso to an administration led by Palmerston, a dedicated foe of the slave trade) that the Spaniards guaranteed no restoration of slavery in San Domingo. With some difficulty the Spanish government was able to satisfy the suspicious Russell on this point, and British interest in the affair subsided.

Northern opinion was not so distracted as to ignore Spain's blatant affront to national honor. Seen in connection with British bluster on the blockade, intrigues in Mexico, and the hovering of foreign fleets on the American seaboard, it seemed part of a more general plot by the powers. The southern firebrands, the most ardent champions of Manifest Destiny, had by an irony become the destroyers of the Monroe Doctrine, had invited what the Boston *Daily Journal* called, in an editorial banner, "The Gathering of the Vultures."[22] "The terror of the American name is gone, and the Powers of the Old World are flocking to the feast from which the

---

21. *Daily Boston Traveller*, April 5, 1861.
22. *Boston Daily Journal*, April 3, 1861.

scream of our eagle has hitherto scared them."[23] News that the Spanish frigate *Blanca* had left Havana for San Domingo on March 23, carrying a thousand troops, reached New York on Saturday March 30. Spain had accepted Santana's offer. With her "young fleets of splendid steamers and her well-clad troops," with the "snug sum of 27 millions of dollars" in her treasury, Spain was marching to recapture her pristine greatness. Northerners warned that the Dominican Republic would speedily become a slave state. Haiti would be next to fall, and its free Negro citizens would suffer transportation to Cuba's sugar plantations. The *New York Times*, in cahoots with Seward, called for "vigorous and decisive measures . . . If Spain seizes St. Domingo, and makes an organized attempt to re-establish her authority over Mexico, we may speedily look for the advent of fresh fleets from Europe—and the intervention of other Powers in the affairs of this Continent."[24]

Unionists were virtually unanimous that, in order to preserve their national greatness, it was imperative to put their house in order. But which task to tackle first? The "intractables" argued cogently that the disunionists would only welcome foreign complications, would exult to see the North beset by enemies, its energies dispersed, obliged thereby to concede southern independence. The south, having focused its efforts for a generation on the project of disruption, would not now feel remorse at having struck in the dust the national flag and reduced to a petty state the once proud United States. The Confederacy's courtship of the powers did not cow northern resolve as intended, but stirred a deeper patriotism by threatening to terminate the "destined" spread of American civilization in the hemisphere.[25]

One school of activists favored using the mailed fist at once, but against the traitors within, and only later—undoubtedly threats alone would then suffice—against the despots of Europe. But some of the "conciliationists," Seward at their head, chose to ignore the abrasive realism of those who took the south at its word. By resurrecting the plan of a "foreign war panacea," they hoped to appeal to strong

---

23. *NYT*, March 30, 1861.

24. *NYT*, March 30, 1861.

25. See Stamp, pp. 240-246. In 1860 Henry Raymond had publicly warned the arch-secessionist William Lowndes Yancey: "Nine-tenths of our people in the Northern and Northwestern States would wage a war longer than the War of Independence before they will assent to any such surrender of their aspirations and their hopes. There is no nation in the world so ambitious of growth and of power—so thoroughly pervaded with the spirit of conquest—so filled with dreams of enlarged dominions, as ours." (*NYT*, Dec. 13, 1860).

sections of opinion which for one reason or another—out of interest, conscience or politics—balked at civil war. Men's preference for a relatively bloodless maritime war against one or other of the powers was understandable enough. (Those who argued for a British war had not seen the British Admiralty's blueprint for a crushing blow at the north's seaports and commerce.) But less convincing was the glib assumption that foreign war eliminated both civil war and Confederacy. The hope was that by meeting the emergency in San Domingo, by invoking the tattered flag and the sacred Monroe Doctrine, the government would dramatically highlight the perils facing the Union: loyal men in the border and seceded states would respond to their country's call and even the fire-eaters might be shocked, or shamed, back into their senses. The alternative was a career of humiliation for the south. James B. Swain, the *New York Times*' Washington correspondent, warned the people of the south that secession would prove to be a "deceitful harlot that has shorn them of their strength, and exposed them to the contempt and the insulting interference of the European Powers . . . ."[26]

During this confused time, all sorts of rumors flourished concerning foreign intentions. Spain was suspected of being in an unholy, slavers' alliance with its old foes, the filibustering southerners, with the aim of conquering and dividing Mexico:

> What would be the line of division [pondered a Boston editor] is not stated, or even hinted at, but we may guess that the Southrons [sic] would prefer to expand toward the Pacific and the Gulf of California, while Spain would be allowed to take the territories in the Mexican Gulf—for the present, and until they should have ripened into a condition to be 'reannexed' to their old country, when they would be made to 'secede' from the European nation. The Confederates have designs on our Pacific possessions, and mean to look out upon the old South Seas, over which Castilian seamen gazed so long ago . . .[27]

Again, England perhaps planned to draw around the southern slave power a *cordon sanitaire* of free negro islands and progressive European colonies. This could be achieved by giving free rein to the Spanish in Hispaniola, and probably also in Mexico, on condition that Madrid accept the extinction of slavery in Cuba and its other possessions. In actuality such a plan was too ambitious for the cautious men who headed Palmerston's cabinet. Another speculation had the Anglo-French fleet poised to exact from the new Confederacy a

---

26. *NYT,* April 3, 1861.
27. *Daily Boston Traveller,* April 5, 1861.

treaty guaranteeing free trade and an "amelioration of slavery" in return for European protection against the Yankees.[28] It now appears that the key role played by the Raymond press in broadcasting these alarmist rumors was part of a broader domestic intrigue, in which Seward was up to his neck.

When Charles Francis Adams hastened dutifully to Washington at Seward's request, he felt at the capital an "irrepressible sense of moral desolation." Seward gave him the impression that Lincoln was a disappointment: "No system, no relative ideas. No conception of his situation—much absorbed in the details of office dispensation, but little application to great ideas."[29] Adams could excite nobody's interest in his English mission, neither Lincoln's (he seemed to "have no ideas at all" about foreign affairs), Sumner's nor Seward's. Seward was cheerfully complacent: Adams might linger for his son's wedding before sailing; no insurmountable difficulties were expected from London; nor was the minister briefed on the blockade—a staggering omission, given the wrangles of the past weeks.

In deciding to reject Seward's advice, and to provision Fort Sumter, Lincoln incurred the opposition of the influential *New York Times*, controlled by Henry J. Raymond. Raymond had been one of Seward's campaign managers in 1860 and had become, like many, highly critical of Lincoln's handling of affairs. Evidence recently unearthed suggests that Raymond and Thurlow Weed, who owned the *Albany Evening Journal*, were privy to Seward's decision to present Lincoln with the famous memorandum of April 1: "Some Thoughts for the President's Consideration."[30] This pressed for the abandonment of Fort Sumter; urged an onslaught on the predatory European powers in order to revitalize southern Unionism; and plainly invited Lincoln to step down in favor of Seward, the man of the hour. A newspaper campaign was to be at once mounted by the press barons to win over public opinion to Seward's program. In answer to an urgent request from Seward, Raymond arrived *post haste* in Washington about midnight on Sunday March 31. He gave

---

28. *NYT*, April 2, 1861.

29. C. F. Adams, *Diary*, March 26-29, 1861; Microfilm Reel 76 (Adams Family Papers, mf. ed.); Seward to Adams, March 23, 1861, Reel 553; cited in Norman Ferris, *Tempestuous Mission, 1861-1862: The Early Diplomatic Career of Charles Francis Adams* (Emory University, Ph. D. thesis, 1962), pp. 24, 25, 29.

30. Patrick Sowle, "A Reappraisal of Seward's Memorandum of April 1, 1861, to Lincoln," *JSH*, XXXIII, No. 2 (May, 1967), pp. 234-239. For the document and Lincoln's draft reply, Basler, *Works of Lincoln*, IV, pp. 316-318.

instructions to Swain, his Washington man, to hold open the telegraph to New York as "Seward had something in mind—something that would be a marvellous revelation to the readers of the *Times*."[31] No such telegram was sent. (This is why the front page of the *New York Times* for April 1, reserved for the late news, contained only unimportant filler.) Monday, All Fools' Day, was expected to see the culmination of Seward's designs. Swain, over a bottle with Raymond, was further instructed:

> . . . the coming night I was to obtain from the Secretary of State that Memorandum and the reply of the President, which it was thought by Messrs. Seward and Weed, could not fail to be in accord with the suggestion of the Secretary.
>
> All this I was to obtain, and forward by telegraph, while Raymond in New York, (whence he was to return by the early morning train) was to prepare a vigorous pronunciamento that Seward alone could fill the measure which Seward had outlined . . .
>
> When Raymond reached New York, he telegraphed back that I 'need not go to Seward for that important despatch.' I presume Raymond had in New York received from Seward the substance of Lincoln's response, and had reached the conclusion that 'that cat wouldn't raise.'[32]

Seward's April 1 program has been regarded as inexplicable by historians. It becomes more explicable if it is seen in the light of the developing events in the Caribbean. A dispatch from the American consul-general at Havana arrived on Sunday morning and confirmed that several companies of artillery had set out from Cuba in a Spanish warship to take possession of the town of Santo Domingo. It is possible that Seward interpreted Spain's maneuvers as the first step in a joint Anglo-French-Spanish project designed to bring Mexico under Spanish dominion.[33] More than one dispatch prophesying just this had been filed during 1860 from the American Minister to Mexico. Buchanan's Secretary of State Lewis Cass had threatened armed action by the United States if the powers tried such a move. In any case the cumulative events of the last few days must have

---

31. Letter, Jas. B. Swain to John Hay, February 21, 1888 (Illinois State Historical Library), printed in Sowle, p. 236. This recently discovered letter shows that the episode of the memorandum was more than a private exchange between Lincoln and Seward. It was hardly a coincidence that on April 2 the *New York Times*' news from Washington highlighted Spanish aggression, and pushed Seward's plan for swooping upon Cuba—all part of the "conciliationist" program.

32. Sowle, pp. 236-237.

33. Henry W. Temple, "William H. Seward," in S. F. Bemis, ed., *The American Secretaries of State* (New York, 1928; reprint 1958), pp. 30-31.

seemed to Seward sufficient indication that something was brewing, and that a European conspiracy lay behind it.

What was obvious was that Spain had at last taken the rash step which would have delivered Cuba, in normal times, into American hands. Seward hoped to cause a return to normalcy by rekindling the torch of southern expansionism. Would not the cotton states support a war for Cuba, the long-coveted jewel of the Caribbean, and for the *lebensraum* it promised the slave power? Indeed could the cotton states afford to stand idly by while the abolitionists conquered Cuba, and freed her slaves or while Britain and France contrived the same end by diplomacy? Professor Nevins has suggested further elements in Seward's strategy:

> If the Confederacy did not forego its independence or share in the new conquest, then the U.S. would at least gain a great island base for operating against the Confederates, and for closing the Gulf. It would also gain other advantages: The ending of the slave trade to Cuba, a closer relationship with Great Britain, which had long tried to destroy that monstrous traffic, and the enhanced respect of other nations. If France entered the war, the U.S. would also seize the French islands.[34]

There was talk at this time of proposals to negotiate a slavetrade convention with Britain. Certainly it fitted Seward's strategy: a treaty would show to waverers the power of the federal government, and "impress upon the South the need to protect slavery within the Union, where the influence of the slave states would temper such negotiations."[35]

Seward's April 1 program was breathtakingly simple:

> I would demand explanations from *Spain* and *France*, categorically, at once. Iw ould seek explanations from Great Britain and Russia, and send agents into *Canada*, *Mexico*, and *Central America*, to rouse a vigorous continental *spirit of independence* on this continent

34. Allan Nevins, *War for the Union, I, The Improvised War 1861-1862* (New York, 1959), pp. 62-63. Nevins has used reports of conversations between Lyons and Seward which are in Foreign Office archives.

35. Sowle, p. 238. A month later Seward suggested to Lyons the signing of an Anglo-American convention for suppressing the Cuban slave trade, guaranteeing the independence of the Dominican Republic: "For his part [Seward told Lyons] he should have no objection to make an anti-African-Slave Trade demonstration against Spain; if she were rash enough to provoke it. Such a demonstration might have a good effect upon the Southern States. These States had always held that the maintenance of slavery in Cuba was essential to their own safety. It might not be a bad lesson to them to see how much they had put at hazard by attempting to withdraw from the protection of the United States." F. O. 4/1137, Lyons to Russell, May 11, 1861, q. Nevins, p. 63.

> against European intervention. And if satisfactory explanations are not received from Spain and France, would convene Congress and declare war against them. . . .[36]

Extended analysis of Seward's memorandum may well be wasted effort, for it is likely enough that the dominant purpose of the document was crudely political, to stampede a worried Lincoln. A victory against Spain was feasible, despite naval unpreparedness, and might well place some useful cards in northern hands. But finding a *casus belli* against France would be difficult, and if successful would nullify the absurd miscalculation by which Spain had managed to isolate itself in the Caribbean. As for the British, Seward presumably threatened retaliation for British high-handedness on the blockade-recognition issue, and offered a snub to any project of interference in Mexico. At the same time he was keeping open the option—pending southern reaction to his flag-waving—of collaboration with Britain in jointly guaranteeing Dominican independence and an end to the Cuban slavetrade. The quality of Seward's brinkmanship is difficult to ascertain. He may not have been serious in baiting Britain; but cavalierly to demand explanations of a great power, to send subversive agents into its dependencies, was warlike behavior. Lyons, in bewildered effort to penetrate the enigma that was Seward, more than once concluded that the New Yorker must be hell-bent on wrapping the world in flames. Either he hoped thus to forge a new national unity, or he was acting in sheer unreasoning madness. Almost as dangerous, Seward perhaps believed he could threaten without war, just as Polk had done over Oregon.[37]

Some of the puzzles in Seward's memorandum disappear when it is viewed as a solution to the Sumter crisis. Sumter, the focus of tension, must be given up; but northern loss of face must be retrieved by reasserting federal authority over the Union forts on the Gulf of Mexico. Seward hoped that a scare over war with Spain would at least enable an uncontroversial reinforcement of these places. This is what he meant by saying that his plan would divert public attention "from what would be regarded as a Party question [at Charleston]

---

36. Seward to Lincoln, April, 1861, in Basler, *Works of Lincoln*, IV, pp. 317-318 (Seward's emphasis).

37. For his threat against Russia, apparently thrown in for good measure, Seward had flimsy grounds: Stoeckl, Russian Minister at Washington had striven for reconciliation between the Lincoln and Davis administrations, and southern papers had inflated his efforts into signs of an impending Russian recognition of the Confederacy. The "explanation" Seward sought was to be merely a request for clarification of Russian intentions on this point. See Frederick W. Seward to Bancroft, June 2, 1894, in Bancroft, *Seward*, II, p. 135.

to one of *Patriotism* or *Union*," a remark which baffled Lincoln. Fort Taylor at Key West and Fort Jefferson in the Dry Tortugas were isolated outposts vulnerable to a Spanish thrust from Cuba. The south could not readily resist their reinforcement, but Fort Pickens was another matter. Pickens controlled Pensacola Bay, where Union troops carriers had been standing by since February but had refrained from landing in response to a southern pledge of non-aggression. Lincoln had already ordered the troops landed, but a confusion over orders had prevented the plan's execution. Seward secured permission for another naval expedition to Pickens on Sunday March 31, and his intentions may perhaps be deduced from its plan of operations. It would secure Pickens "against all attacks foreign and domestic," but then make its main base of operations Fort Jefferson, only a hundred miles from Havana. Cuba was obviously Seward's target. Pickens' reinforcement would presumably be accepted by the south in a deal with a more amenable northern leader, Seward, as security against Spanish aggression.

On April 1, however, Lincoln squashed Seward's proposal. He evinced scant interest in a Caribbean or any other war, affirmed his own intention to lead, and was immovable on the need to supply Sumter. Seward abandoned his takeover bid, but plunged on with his Pickens plan with what some historians have judged to be dubious fidelity to his chief.[38] On April 2 he delivered a stiff protest to the Spanish ambassador against armed intervention in the Dominican Republic. Perhaps a Spanish war might yet break out before the die had been cast over Sumter. Seward used all his influence—and perhaps some skullduggery—to obtain top priority for his Pickens expedition, and pressed for compromise over Sumter. There was still a chance that Lincoln might reverse himself on Sumter if that would keep Virginia in the Union. At the worst Seward thought his scheme would bring war at Pensacola and not at Sumter, over which he had made too many promises. The warship *Powhatan* was commandeered for the Pickens expedition without the knowledge of the Navy Department, creating immense confusion when Secretary of Navy Welles subsequently earmarked the same vessel for the role of flagship to the Sumter relief flotilla. Before the confusion could be straightened out—with Seward playing an unhelpfully obtuse part—the *Powhatan* was hastily sent as a troopship to the Gulf of

---

38. For contrasting treatments of the controversial events of these weeks: Nevins, pp. 65-74 (severe on Seward); Van Deusen, Chapter 19 (the excitement of the time, and devotion to the Union explain Seward's behavior).

Mexico. Seward was also behind an attempt made to have the United States home squadron under Commander Pendergast stationed at Vera Cruz, Mexico, a likely base for French or Spanish military operations against the ruling Juárez regime. The project had to be cancelled when, on the initiative of Welles, it was discovered that Lincoln had not read the orders which Seward had submitted for his signature. Welles, unaware of Seward's Caribbean plans, came to suspect that the Secretary of State was conniving with men of suspect loyalty to jeopardize the Sumter project. Rancor grew worse between the two ministers and was to persist for the rest of the war, one more divisive influence in the cabinet.

Union naval activities in New York served merely to alarm the Montgomery government. On april 4 their commissioners in Washington telegraphed that an expedition was being organized, supposedly headed for San Domingo; but they warned that "this fleet may now or hereafter be ordered to our coast."[39] By March 6 the southern government had concluded that Pickens was to be reinforced, and additional troops were ordered to join General Bragg's Confederate forces around Pensacola. Ironically, Seward's peace plot was building up to war, for the situation at Pickens was almost at flashpoint. Unknown to the other, each side had determined to break the uneasy "truce." The Davis government was unwilling to tolerate a "foreign garrison" at Pickens even in return for the evacuation of Sumter.[40] Bragg had orders to reduce the fort at first opportunity—he hesitated only because of military problems—and would have reacted to reinforcement as an act of war. So much for the "Spanish war panacea." On April 12 Bragg was unable to prevent federal troops taking Pickens. By then however Lincoln's relief expedition had been sent to Sumter, and the Civil War was duly triggered off.

Amidst the ensuing excitement, the northern press did not fail to observe that America was helpless to prevent a Spanish takeover in San Domingo. Despite protests from Washington, the Monroe Doctrine had been violated. The prophecies of the nationalists were vindicated, and the United States entered a humiliating phase in its history, forced to play from an unfamiliar posture of weakness in the hemisphere. Diplomatic relations were preserved with the Spanish; Lincoln forbade the issuing of any ultimatum, and Seward

---

39. *War of Rebellion . . . Official Records of the Union and Confederate Armies* (Washington, 1880-1901), Ser. 1, IV, p. 257; q. Ludwell H. Johnson, "Fort Sumter and Confed. Diplomacy," *JSH*, XXVI (Nov., 1960), No. 4, p. 469.

40. G. McWhiney, "The Confederacy's First Shot," *CWH*, XIV, No. 1, (March, 1968), pp. 8-11.

for the rest of the war refrained from specific references to the Monroe Doctrine. Meanwhile Spain reaped bitter fruits in a demoralizing struggle against the Dominican nationalists. The north, now fettered in the Caribbean, could only swear sympathy with the Dominican rebels and a terrible future vengeance for Spanish perfidy.

Beauregard's shelling of Fort Sumter caused war fever in the north and war jitters in Washington, set in hostile territory. The President's call for 75,000 volunteer militia (April 15) was swiftly followed by Virginia's secession and a desperate struggle to preserve Maryland, Kentucky, and Missouri for the Union. Riots in Baltimore cut off the capital from the north, while the rebels took possession of the federal naval yards at Norfolk and arsenal at Harper's Ferry. The Union's first crucial diplomatic steps were taken in this distraught atmosphere. Seward's policy before Bull Run has been variously described as a piece of irresponsible warmongering, aimed at triggering off a healing foreign war, or as skilled brinkmanship, designed to make foreign warhorses skittish. Seward's diplomacy was often baffling: indeed it might be argued that it was his unpredictability and emotionalism that deterred the powers, rather than any profundity of design. But the facts best fit the theory of brinkmanship. Sumter's fall, and the mobilization of the south, demonstrated clearly the fallibility of any "foreign war panacea." A slender hope remained that the south might be persuaded, or coerced by diplomatic isolation, into coming to terms with the north. Seward's behavior is consistent with the view that he strove, not for war with Britain or France, but to demoralize the rebels by depriving them of the hope of foreign intervention or sympathy. His priorities were to stave off recognition of rebel independence or even belligerency, to have the world treat the Confederates as men engaged in a limited insurrection, to insist upon the Union's sovereign rights.

By demanding that the powers turn a blind eye to the realities, Seward invited legal wrangles. The United States, for instance, proposed to crush the so-called gnat of rebellion with the full hammerforce of its military might—in the process employing a naval blockade over three thousand miles of southern coasts. Seward wanted international respect for the blockade, but denied the assumption upon which such respect must rest, namely, the existence of a state of war. Legal consistency was not in fact something he valued highly, a trait which pained men like Sumner and Welles. Seward blustered in order to stop Europe exploiting American weakness, to prevent a quick *fait accompli* (such as recognition) which might seal the Union's fate. But to push bluster to the point of war would have defeated his purpose. What is sometimes forgotten is that he took extraordinary care to avoid trouble over the blockade. A war with England was there for the picking. He held out rewards for a policy of friendship to the Union. He even offered—again in order to isolate the south—to give up the nation's valued right to use privateers. That would have been an odd way to prepare for a naval war with Britain or France.

The instructions which Seward drew up for Adams in the midst of the Sumter crisis illustrate his approach. Seward's penchant for viewing foreign policy in propaganda terms was revealed when he took the extraordinary step of reading the dispatch to W. H. Russell of the London *Times*, two days before it was officially filed and nineteen days before it reached Adams.[41] For the first time the United States warned that recognition of southern independence would be regarded as a *casus belli*:

> . . . if they [the powers] determine to recognize, they may at the same time prepare to enter into alliance with the enemies of this republic. You alone will represent your country at London, and you will represent the whole of it there. When you are asked to divide that duty with others, diplomatic relations between the government of Great Britain and this government will be suspended.

That attitude was to endure for the rest of the war. W. H. Russell thought Seward was playing to the northern gallery, and may not have excluded the idea of a British war as a means of "refusing the broken Union into a mass once more." But Seward was unprovocative on issues apart from recognition, or British reception of southern agents. San Juan was played down. Adams was to stress the ties of mutual self-interest which bound together the Atlantic economy and dictated peace. The Morrill tariff might be modified:

> British censors tell us that the new tariff is unwise for ourselves. If so, it will speedily be repealed. They say it is illiberal and injurious to Great Britain. It cannot be so upon her principles without being also injurious to ourselves, and in that case it will be promptly repealed.

Was it British interest to give comfort to a slaveholders' uprising, to encourage perpetual warfare in the hemisphere? The British empire

---

41. Seward to Adams, April 10, 1861, *Foreign Relations*, 1861, pp. 71-80. Russell heard the contents on April 8; W. H. Russell, *My Civil War Diary*, p. 26. Adams got the instructions, impatiently awaited, on April 27, four days before he sailed for London on the *Niagara*. Seward probably wanted London to know of his hard line on recognition as early as possible.

itself was "an aggregation of divers communities," tied by "bonds as fragile as the obligations of our own federal Union . . . Would it be wise for Her Majesty's government, on this occasion, to set a dangerous precedent, or provoke retaliation?" The West Indies and Canada were periously "exposed." Seward's peroration invoked the circumstances of common descent, language, customs, sentiments, and religion which recommended close sympathy between Britain and the United States.

Nor was Seward's caution over the northern blockade the act of a man seeking war. The development of maritime war against the Confederacy promised to create endless international difficulties. In retaliation for Lincoln's call for volunteers, Jefferson Davis invited privateers to sail under the Confederacy's commissions of marque and reprisal (April 17). The south would adopt a defensive strategy on land—this might impress Europe that aggression stemmed from the imperialistic north—but expected to take some offensives at sea. The south's inferior naval capacity and facilities might be offset by the use of privateers and specially built commerce destroyers. Both sides lived in the past with respect to privateering, remembering the American glories of 1812 and forgetting the vulnerability of small wooden vessels against the firepower of iron-armored steamers. Maritime interests in the northern seaboard took grotesquely exaggerated alarm at Davis' proclamation, and plied Washington with pleas for protection. On April 19 Lincoln proclaimed that the government would punish as pirates persons who molested northern vessels under the pretended authority of the rebels. These developments forced to a head the issue of the neutrality of the powers.

The major sea powers had renounced their right to privateering in the Paris agreement of 1856; but America was a nonsignatory, refusing to relinquish privateering unless general protection was given to all noncontraband private property at sea. The Paris declaration gave immunity to enemy goods on neutral ships, and neutral goods on enemy ships, if noncontraband; but none to enemy property on enemy ships. The American proposal would drastically have circumscribed warfare at sea, and was unacceptable to Britain. Nonsignatories to the Paris convention thus retained the right to issue letters of marque to private citizens. In international law privateers normally acquired a belligerent status which protected them from hanging as pirates. However the case of authorities whose sovereign rights were unrecognized, or who had not been granted belligerent rights, was confused. The United States now proposed to disregard letters of marque issued by the Confederacy, and even Lyons thought that English warships might seize privateers "which sail under a flag we do not recognize."[42] As we shall see, this dilemma was one major incentive which pushed England into a prompt—the north thought overprompt—recognition of southern belligerency.

The other incentive was the blockade. On April 19 Lincoln proclaimed his intention of setting up a blockade of the ports of South Carolina, Georgia, Alabama, Florida, Mississippi, Louisiana, and Texas; on April 27 it was extended to the ports of Virginia and North Carolina. The blockade was a preventive measure against rebel privateers, but it was more than that: it was a centerpiece in the north's grand strategy. The south was to be crushed, as the prey of an anaconda was crushed. The Union would constrict its rebellious subjects by the combined pressures of a naval blockade, an amphibious invasion of the Mississippi basin, and a steady military advance on a broad Virginian front. As the Confederacy lacked defensible natural frontiers, Union generals such as the veteran Winfield Scott expected its armies to be driven back and its resources devastated. The blockade would complete the process of attrition by denying the unindustrialized south the sinews of war and even the necessities of life. Bankruptcy would be forced upon the Davis government by stopping the export of its major staple and income earner, cotton. A tight blockade was obviously in the northern interest, both from a military point of view and as a way of allaying foreign complaints. A carelessly declared, or inadequately enforced, blockade would provide those who were testy about disruption of trade an excuse to "sweep Mr. Lincoln's navies away like dust." (The latter was a common prophecy in Dixie.) Seward successfully passed the first test of his statesmanship when he ensured that the blockade was punctiliously notified and set up according to the canons of international law. He did not know that Lyons had grudgingly retreated from his hawkish stand of brandishing recognition of the south in retaliation against a blockade. Lyons thought the blockade the work of the seaboard merchant interests ("of course they could not endure to see Foreign Trade diverted to the South"). But it must be endured if carried on "with reasonable consideration for Foreign Flags, and in strict conformity with the Law of Nations." In any case the season of high trade with the cotton states would be over before London could implement any decision to intervene.[43]

British acceptance of the blockade was by no means yet a fore-

42. Lyons to Russell, April 23, 1861, *MHSP*, XLVIII, p. 225.

43. Lyons to Russell, April 12, 23; May 2, 1861, *MHSP*, XLVIII, pp. 224-225; *Brit. Sessional Papers* (hereafter *BSP*), H. of C., LXV (2836), p. 586.

gone conclusion. It would depend upon Welles' success in coordinating a Union fleet which had been scattered to the four corners by the secessionists in Buchanan's cabinet, and whose peacetime strength was conspicuously inadequate to the task ahead. Seward had promised to close the coast from Chesapeake Bay to the Rio Grande. Lyons was skeptical:

> I observed to him that the extent of the coast between these two points was, I supposed, about 3000 miles. Surely the United States had not a naval force sufficient to establish an effective blockade of such a length of coast. Mr. Seward, however, maintained that the whole would be blockaded, and blockaded effectively.[44]

Throughout the tedious negotiations between Lyons, the State Department, and the Navy Department, which went on into May and June, Seward's prudence on the blockade was conspicuous. It is most instructive, for here the British were likely to be in deadly earnest.

On April 24 Seward instructed his agents abroad that the United States was now willing to become a signatory to the Declaration of Paris. The plan had logic, and offered advantages to the Union—too obvious, it turned out, for the powers to accept. The code of 1856 offered an advanced and civilized set of rules for maritime war. Under it the United States would renounce privateering, accept that blockades must be effective, and agree to the rules governing neutral and enemy noncontraband property at sea. Seward hoped for two gains: the powers would be obliged to indict southern privateering, and to accept his doctrine that southerners were internal rebels, not belligerents. The second goal was as important as the first. No nation had yet conceded southern belligerency, and Seward was determined to block the blow. By tendering his country's adherence to the Paris convention he was offering safety for neutral ships and property. In return they must acknowledge American unity, for he would insist that the agreement was "to be obligatory equally upon disloyal as upon loyal citizens."[45] The Union navy could then suppress southern privateering as piracy, for it would be executing domestic laws making privateering by disloyal subjects piracy. The plan was to be outpaced by events. It lost its point when the powers accepted southern

44. Lyons to Russell, May 2, 1861, *BSP*, LXV (2836), p. 587.

45. Seward to Dayton, July 6, 1861, *Foreign Relations*, 1861, p. 233. Lyons commented "The time at which the offer would be made renders the whole thing rather amusing. It would no doubt be very convenient if the Navies of Europe would put down the Privateers, and thus leave the whole Navy of the U.S. free to blockade the Ports against European Merchant Vessels." Lyons to Russell, April 27, 1861.

belligerency, and when they subsequently denied their ports to privateers, the effective death knell to privateering. Negotiations with Britain and France became prolonged and were clumsily handled, creating confusion and mutual suspicion between the British and Americans. They were called off in August when the powers insisted that the agreement should have no bearing on "the internal differences now prevailing in the United States."[46] The United States nevertheless adhered for the rest of the war to the code laid down in 1856.

April and May were months of intense uncertainty and frustration for Seward. His hopes of a last minute reconciliation between the sections evaporated with Virginia's secession, the ratification of the Confederate constitution, and obvious popular support for the new government in the south. Confederate war preparations went on apace. Vice-President Alexander H. Stephens flatly declared the futility of peace talks when he spoke with the Bremen minister, Rudolph Schleiden, who visited Richmond with Seward's blessing (April 24-27). Washington's relations with Canada turned sour at the same time. The colonial authorities early determined on strict neutrality: they wanted to keep intact the reciprocity trade treaty, and avoid entanglements which might give a pretext for American aggression. (James Gordon Bennett's *New York Herald* had been campaigning for seizure of Canada as compensation for the loss of the slavocracy, and many believed Seward to be an apostle of annexation.) Canadian emotions tugged in conflicting directions over the Civil War within their giant neighbor, but the question of Canadian survival overshadowed all other issues.[47] Victory for either section posed a perilous situation: Confederate independence would destroy the power equilibrium on the continent, and make Canada a tempting object of revanchist anger in the north. A Union triumph might spur annexationist designs on the part of an overweening and ambitious neighbor. The war, in any case, was bringing about the creation of mighty armies in North America, a prospect feared by the militarily insecure Canadians for half a century. Seward, perhaps through miscalculation as much as design, managed to inflame these raw nerves. His tactics were probably piecemeal: to probe at British

---

46. The subject has been discussed exhaustively in: C. F. Adams Jr., "Seward and the Declaration of Paris," *MHSP*, XLVI, pp. 23-81; E. D. A., I, Chapter 5 (revising the younger Adams' interpretation); Case and Spencer, Chapter 3; Ferris, Chapter 5.

47. See Robin W. Winks, *Canada and the United States: The Civil War Years* (Baltimore, Johns Hopkins Press, 1960), for definitive account of this subject. See Chapter 4 for this period.

weakness in North America, to keep the British worried about the consequences of rashness, to test the quality of Canadian neutrality, to squash any Confederate operations to the north. Lyons believed that Seward underestimated the perils of baiting the British. ("One of the great difficulties I have to contend with . . . is the persuasion, which prevails, even with sensible men, that no outrage will compel England to make war with the North.")[48]

Northern opinion was incensed when the Canadian authorities, adhering to the Militia Act, refused to sell arms to neighboring northern states Ohio, Illinois, New York, and Massachusetts, desperately mustering forces in answer to Lincoln's call to arms. Canada had been expected to prove a more reliable ally in the contest against slavery. Seward sent Lincoln's colleague, George Ashmun, a Republican stalwart, to Quebec as a special agent: he was to propagandize for the north, and to exchange views with Sir Edmund Head, Governor-General of British North America. When the *Herald* (whose news sources surpassed all competitors) leaked details of the mission, Seward was forced to annul Ashmun's appointment, and the trip was completed on an unofficial basis. Head was embarassed. Hereafter, Newcastle instructed him from the Colonial Office, Head was to "continue quietly to discourage all missions whether from the United States or from the Southern Confederacy."[49] Ashmun reported back to Seward that "erroneous views" were indeed flourishing in the provinces. The affair confirmed London's conviction that military reinforcements were required in Canada as a precautionary measure.

The *Peerless* affair illustrated how thin Seward's patience had worn. With communications only just restored between Washington and the north, the State Department received intelligence that a Canadian steamship, *Peerless*, then at Toronto, had been sold to the rebels, and would pass down the St. Lawrence with British papers to be delivered to a pirate commander on the open seas. Head feared a raid by New Englanders upon the ship or the canals. Lyons interviewed Seward on May 1, to be told bluntly that if the Canadians refused to move against the vessel, the United States would seize it, regardless of British flag or papers. The American government could not tolerate the fitting out of "piratical vessels" in Canadian waters. The affair had the makings of a first-class scrape, prefiguring the *Trent* and *Alabama* cases. Although Seward had ordered seizure with the proviso that evidence was found of southern ownership, he had acted

48. Lyons to Russell, May 21, 1861, q. Newton, *Lyons*, I, p. 41.
49. Newcastle to Head, June 1, 1861, q. Winks, p. 41.

on the flimsiest grounds. It later turned out that federal, not southern, agents had purchased the vessel.[50] Luckily for Anglo-American relations, the *Peerless* escaped interference. Seward's later accounts of the incident indicate that he underestimated the effrontery of his act. Lyons thought "he has a strong inclination to try to what extent he may make political capital by highhanded conduct and violent language towards us."[51] It seems just as likely that his mind was on pirates rather than on a Canadian war, or that he was distracted by developments in London. A dispatch from Adams' predecessor, G. M. Dallas, indicated that English opinion favored separation. Lord John Russell, charged by Dallas to abstain from recognition of the south, "seemed to think the matter not ripe for decision one way or the other." (Dallas added that Adams' coming "would doubtless be regarded as the appropriate and natural occasion" for determining the question, the seed of much trouble.) Seward exploded. Russell's remarks were "by no means satisfactory to this government." Adams was told to protest:

> Her Britannic Majesty's government is at liberty to choose whether it will retain the friendship of this government by refusing all aid and comfort to its enemies, . . . as we think the treaties existing between the two countries require, or whether the government of her Majesty will take the precarious benefits of a different course.[52]

Whether Palmerston's government was merely wavering, or really planning a hostile move in concert with France, Seward judged that a strong response was required.

---

50. Van Deusen, *Seward*, p. 296. It seems likely that southerners intended to buy the vessel but lacked funds and that a northern sympathizer privately purchased the ship (information from Robin Winks, 1972).

51. Lyons to Russell, private, May 6, 1861, *MHSP*, XLVIII, p. 229. See also Seward to Adams, July 1, 1861, *Foreign Relations*, 1861, p. 112; Winks, pp. 45-47.

52. Dallas to Seward, April 9, 1861; Seward to Adams, April 27, 1861; *Foreign Relations*, 1861, pp. 81-83.

Chapter IV

The Powers Go Neutral

In England, Sumter caused a sensation and a flurry of speculation. Gauging the military prospects of the sections had been a favorite occupation of the armchair strategists during the spring. While many thought that the south could not be subdued, that a militia defending its own territory held a decisive advantage, that the north's institutions were not adapted to a war by invasion, there was by no means unanimity on the score. The south lacked the resources for a prolonged campaign, according to others: "if . . . , as historians assure us, money be the sinews of war, a very brief campaign must settle the question in favour of the North."[1] Walter Bagehot swung to this view as the news arrived of the clashes at Baltimore and Harper's Ferry. He had been pleading for a negotiated separation, and now blamed "the presumptuous aggression of the seceders" for beginning the slaughter and ending the stability of the Atlantic world. He conceded that the Confederacy held some strong cards. It had been strengthened by the adherence of the upper south; it was led by a man "of prompter mind and more vigorous decision than President Lincoln;" while the rebel army was all but ready to march upon Washington. Yet, Bagehot held, "a wealthy and free population of twenty millions cannot but conquer in the long run in a contest

1. *Sixpenny Magazine* (July, 1861), pp. 13-14. Also *Saturday Review*, May 18, 1861, p. 489. Karl Marx shared this view, against the doubts of his friend Engels, who fancied himself as a military strategist. Marx wrote extensively on the war as European correspondent for the New York *Daily Tribune* (1861–1862), and as English correspondent of *Die Presse*, a leading Vienna newspaper (1861-1862).

with a poor free population, numbering at most seven millions . . . ." Early defeats would only animate the north to greater and greater exertion.[2]

From the northern point of view, however, there was a disheartening undercurrent to British thinking. Sympathy there was, and not ungenerous sympathy, for the cause of the north, widely interpreted as the cause of right against wrong. But there was a repellent quality in the idea of a war between kindred Anglo-Saxon peoples, a fratricidal ordeal likely to be of the bloodiest kind. Pacifist and humanitarian feeling is not to be dismissed in Britain of the 1860's merely because it had been so cavalierly thrust to one side in contests such as the Crimea and the Indian Mutiny, where to the heady excitement of the joust was added the sober consideration of national interest. By 1860, one is tempted to venture, the country could permit itself the indulgence of civilized standards, perhaps as some sort of penance for the horrors of Sebastopol and Calcutta. There was in reality a *mêlange* of motives which opposed a forcible reduction of the south: ultranationalism, which exulted at the division of a rival power and a rival political system, which feared the creation of a strong army and navy by the United States in the event of war (one notes, however, that these chords are strangely muted considering the long history of territorial rivalry between the two powers); economic alarms, or uncertainty, over a disruption to Anglo-American trade, and a severance of the cotton supply from Dixie; a reputable liberal sympathy for the claims even of disreputable freemen who wanted independence; and a reasonable liberal foreboding that militarism and repression of liberties would be the bitter fruits of war. But quite striking in the commentaries of the time is the overriding sense of the utter futility of a civil war which, no matter what the verdict of arms, would succeed only in increasing hatreds and divisions.

In the process of being "civilized," English opinion had hardly faced up to some of the cruel dilemmas which bedeviled the task of the American peacemakers. A minority had pinned their hopes to peaceful reconstruction, and like Seward awaited a Unionist revival in at least the upper south. Those who considered themselves to be realists more usually counseled the north to swallow the distasteful fact of southern independence; in doing so they very often ignored the problem of boundaries and the plight of the

---

2. *Economist,* March 2, 1861; May 4, 1861.

border states.[3] They conveniently assumed that only the poorer states of the deep south would separate, to form a miniature Confederacy whose future expansion would be southwards into the domain of the old Spanish Empire.

Few denied the abstract right of the north to use coercion. Imperial Britain was too constantly skirmishing, in Ireland, India, Africa, and farflung stations, to reject the right to repress sedition and rebellion; too ready when the need arose to fight for her own national interest, to deny that necessity to another. While not yet the age in Europe of blood and iron, it was an age of muscular patriotism. The contractual, federal arguments of the secessionists had a quaint ring to European ears. The language of revolutionary struggle was being more commonly employed by the oppressed peoples, nationalities and classes of Europe. The authority of brute force was the expected reply of the constituted, usually autocratic, governments of the period: "Kingdoms and Republics exist, partly by the voluntary consent of subjects or citizens, and also, in no small degree, by virtue of the certainty that seceders will be liable to the penalty of treason."[4]

Yet, if few denied the north's right to use force, most counseled against the perils of a war against no ordinary riot. Bagehot's was was one of the most influential voices in this respect. Convinced that the south was in deadly earnest, he resisted both the reconstructionist and warhawk solutions. The first would retain the rebels within the Union at the price of servility and dishonor. The second was self-defeating. How could coercion be permanently continued in a republican nation? "It is not for Americans to take a leaf out of the book of Austria." In any reconstruction of the Union, the north would be dealing with a conquered people, united against them with "a feeling of ferocious unanimity: Those States may be conquered, may be held in military possession, but they can scarcely again be expected to take a voluntary part in the political institutions of the U.S." Would even the slaves lose their shackles after the war? Unless they did so by means of an unforeseen slave insurrection, it was more than likely that the political system would

---

3. George Cornewall Lewis raised the problem without solving it when he pointed out the possibility of a Western Confederation also being formed if the process of separation were allowed to continue. Since the process had begun "there is a difficulty in assigning a limit to it, or in determining the new centres round which the wandering stars of the Union may cluster." *Edinburgh Review*, CXIII (April, 1861), p. 581.

4. *Saturday Review*, January 19, 1861, p. 597. Also *Dublin University Magazine*, March 1861, p. 378.

be restored more or less intact: "except that mutual animosities will be deeper, both parties will be poorer, and both parties more vindictive than at the outset."[5]

Echoes of abolitionist reasoning were to be found in the school of thought which abhorred the idea of pinning the Union together with bayonets. Northerners, ran the argument, were understandably bitter at the "wilful, dogged, rapid pertinacity" with which the south had wrenched down the national structure, but anger should not be permitted to obscure the nation's better judgement. "Bulk is not the measure of greatness . . . ," commiserated an Irish journal, "Athens was not larger than some of the cornfields in Illinois."[6] Secession had relieved the north of the moral incubus, the terrible embarrassment, the evergrowing danger of slavery: "Why . . . should they be so anxious to buy back the crying shame, to bind again upon their shoulders the crushing burden . . . ?" Slavery had involved the northern stateman's country in unrighteous wars: "It stained his country with wrongful acquisitions; it taught him to hector abroad, and dragged him through mean compliances at home."[7] So attractive to the English was the vision of an emancipated north achieving a moral renaissance by sloughing off the south, and then steadily growing in strength and excellence at the expense of an independent but decadent rival, that it became something of a cliché in the next year or so. Conveniently, separation would serve both to cure Americans of the moral spasticity which ideas of Manifest Destiny generated, and to reduce the nuisance of such doctrines to other powers:

> For generations they [the Americans] had revelled in the unwholesome and perverting contemplation of their own grandeur . . . they had grown aggressive, overbearing, and unjust; Truth and Right had become dim and feeble in their sight before the pagan worship of a gigantic strength and a Titanic will; external greatness had blinded them to the progress of domestic degeneracy . . . Henceforth . . . their lawless volitions will be compelled to a decent consideration of the claims of others; while, at the same time, their policy will be free from any necessity to obey other dictates than those of conscience.[8]

---

5. *Economist,* March 2, 1861; May 4, 1861.

6. *Dublin University Magazine,* June, 1861, p. 751. Centralized despotism, it claimed, would result from the bloated hope "that the American eagle should touch the Atlantic or Pacific oceans with her outstretched wing, and brood over the continent with her beak in Cuba and her claws in Canada."

7. *National Review,* XIII (July, 1861), p. 157, and generally pp. 150-169.

8. *National Review,* p. 158.

Englishmen liked to believe, at least in this instance, that distance lent objectivity: "The proportion of events, as of mountains, are better discerned by those who do not live in the midst of them."[9] And an objective appraisal seemed to reveal the essential incompatibility of the sections, the intransigence of the emotional and moral issues dividing them, and the inevitability of conflict within the present framework of the Union. Common sense dictated that groups whose way of life was so abrasively different should live apart.

The British proclamation of neutrality was gazetted on May 14, the day Adams arrived in London. It shook the north where it was denounced as maliciously premature; a deliberately unfriendly act which virtually amounted to recognition of the slave confederacy, an act which kept the breath of life in an otherwise transient mutiny. After the war an immense superstructure of hysteria was raised by angry Americans, including Charles Sumner, John L. Motley, and Bancroft Davis, on the foundation stone of the Queen's proclamation. It became the basis for astronomic claims for damages, demanded for loss of life and national expenses incurred because of Britain's "prolongation" of the war. It was a major item in Sumner's calculation of $2,125 million as the British bill for dereliction of its international obligations (about the going price for Canada in 1869). The American barrage included a great deal of confused law and warped facts. The British had a reasoned case for seeking the protection which neutrality afforded, but they handled it poorly. When the French, after prudent delay, produced a lucid and professional apologia for their own declaration of neutrality, they helped their cause in Washington. What embarrassed the English was the failure of their confident expectation that full-scale war was about to set in. The period of "phoney war" before Bull Run gave countenance to northern complaints that Britain had acted before a bloody battle had been fought or a southern fleet created. In this view, granting the south belligerent rights converted the fiction of a state of war into fact. Moreover, sinister implications were read into the timing of the proclamation, for Russell proclaimed neutrality before Lincoln's envoy had arrived at his post, and while rebel envoys were already in London.

Adams was still enduring an uncomfortable Atlantic crossing, during which he read Macaulay, when the crisis matured for the London legation. Two of the Confederacy's three-man mission

9. *Fraser's Magazine*, LXII (January, 1861), p. 403.

seeking recognition from the powers arrived in London on April 27, at the same time as news of Sumter, the northern call for volunteers and southern threat of privateering: a quick succession of events which alarmed merchant interests and stampeded Russell from his policy of "wait and see." The envoys—Yancey and Rost—were welcomed by the "southern lobby," friends of the south, including the M.P., W. H. Gregory, who had given notice of motion in Parliament for recognition of the Confederacy. Gregory arranged an interview for the mission with Russell on May 3. Russell was prepared to receive the envoys unofficially, a recognized diplomatic practice in such cases. As with other events in this hectic fortnight, Russell anticipated no hostile reaction from the north over proceedings he regarded as perfectly proper. He was to be astonished at the hornet's nest he had disturbed. The assistant secretary to the American legation, Benjamin Moran, was perturbed that the southern commissioners might gain their way with Palmerston and Russell. An acute, if waspish, observer of people and events, Moran had little faith in his superior: "Mr. Dallas has some of the secession virus in him & he is clearly strong on the States Rights folly." Moran saw where the news of Baltimore's uprising, the loss of Harper's Ferry arsenal, and Virginia's secession was leading the British, and reported the northern community in London "all very anxious. This is the first bloodshed and God knows where it will end."[10]

On May 1 Russell ordered the reinforcement of the North American fleet under Vice-Admiral Alexander Milne, and sounded Minister Dallas on the possibility of a blockade. Dallas, whom Seward had not bothered to brief on the topic, pooh-poohed the idea. Dallas understood that Russell "acquiesced in the expediency of disregarding mere rumour, and waiting the full knowledge to be brought by my successor."[11] Russell, it turned out, did not interpret this "understanding" as a firm commitment to abstain from major policy changes on America until Adams was afforded opportunity to present the views and purposes of the Lincoln administration. Seward was to claim a breach of faith by Russell. (He chose to forget that Adams was not in-point-of-fact instructed on the question of the blockade, was not even anticipating trouble on the matter.)

---

10. S. A. Wallace and F. E. Gillespie, *Journal of Benjamin Moran, 1857-1865* (Chicago, 1948), I, p. 806 (May 6, May 2, 1861).

11. Dallas to Seward, May 2, 1861, *Foreign Relations*, 1861, p. 84. At this interview Russell also disclosed that the British and French had agreed to act together on recognition.

The day after the interview (May 2) the London press reported Lincoln's blockade proclamation. Dallas was discredited, and Russell was "rather grumpy."[12] What now seemed inescapable was the prospect of the Union fleet exercizing what was tantamount to a right-of-war to search and seize foreign vessels testing the blockade. Russell fended off a Parliamentary question on Confederate privateering. ("Nothing but the imperative duty of protecting British interests in case they should be attacked justifies the Government in at all interfering."[13]). He sought the Attorney-General's advice on the propriety of recognizing southern belligerency. According to that advice, the south had the right to issue letters of marque. The Attorney-General (Sir Richard Bethell) suggested a deal: the south's belligerency might be recognized on condition that it promised to conduct the war "according to the rules of the Treaty of Paris." The privateering threat to Britain's commerce with the north would thus be diminished. (Ironically Seward was hoping to deprive the rebels of belligerent rights by negotiating on the Paris rules.) The idea was impractical, and poor law: negotiations with the south would draw out the affair, might well fail (as the south valued privateering), and would mortally offend the north. Moreover, the status of belligerency was in international law, a question of fact; not something to be traded for a price. Russell ignored the suggestion. But he accepted the view that the European nations should treat the American situation as a "regular war." The cabinet apparently approved a policy of neutrality during the weekend (May 4-5). On Monday May 6 Parliament was informed, Lyons was sent notice of the decision, and Paris was approached to concert with Britain on the issue. As the French had already agreed to follow the British lead, their concurrence was prompt. The powers hoped to salvage some of the benefits of the 1856 groundrules for war by extracting from north and south an acknowledgement of Articles 2 and 3 of the convention dealing with enemy and neutral noncontraband property.[14]

The cabinet had acted swiftly but not, as was later claimed, on inadequate information or provocation. The Confederacy had been

12. *Journal of Benjamin Moran*, May 3, 1861.

13. *Hansard*, CLXII, 3rd Ser. (May 2, 1861), pp. 1378-1379.

14. They soon afterwards included Article 4, on the effective use of blockades, in their proposal. Strictly speaking Britain and France breached the terms of the 1856 Paris agreement, which bound the signatories to make future negotiations with nations wishing to accede only on the basis that they accept the Declaration as a whole.

created, had adopted a constitution, federal legislature, executive, and judiciary, begun to raise an army of 100,000 men, appropriated over two million dollars for a navy, and commenced hostilities. The Union was raising an army of 75,000, and had admitted a *de facto* state of war by proclaiming a fullscale blockade which would be strictly enforced according to international usage. (America's Supreme Court later justified Lincoln's use of the war power in proclaiming the blockade by declaring that act conclusive evidence that a state of war existed.[15]) The cabinet had such facts before it. A copy of the blockade proclamation was received on May 5 from the British consul in New York. The paper itself was officially communicated by Dallas to Russell three days before the Queen's proclamation was gazetted. The need for regularization was shown promptly enough, when on May 21 the British schooner *Tropic Wind* was captured for breach of blockade.[16]

The French memorandum on the subject put the issue squarely:

> . . . to be called belligerent, it is enough that a portion of a people in revolt have possession of only enough force to create, in the eyes of neutrals, a doubt as to the final outcome. In such a case modern international law requires that foreign powers, without prejudice to the final results of the clash of forces, keep an attitude of impartiality toward the two contestants.[17]

Belligerency conferred upon the south a status within its own jurisdiction similar to that enjoyed by sovereign powers, but its rights were practical rights granted for purposes of war and not a formal recognition of sovereignty. The Confederacy was now entitled

> to solicit loans, contract for arms, and enlist men abroad, except when forbidden to do so by neutrality laws; to send commissioned cruisers to sea, exercise belligerent rights of search and seizure, and to make use of prize courts; and to have the Southern banner and commissioners recognized as representing a quasi-political community.[18]

---

15. The Supreme Court decision of March 1863 was made after the court had been strengthened with Republican nominees, and the decision was still only five to four.

16. See "*Case Presented on the Part of the Government of Her Brittanic Majesty to the Tribunal of Arbitration*" (Geneva), in *House of Representatives Documents*, 2nd sess., 42 Cong., 1871-1872 (Washington, 1872), I, pp. 11-18; and Nevins, *Hamilton Fish*, p. 144.

17. Thouvenel to Mercier, May 11, 1861; q. Case and Spencer, p. 55.

18. Stuart L. Bernath, *Squall Across the Atlantic: American Civil War Prize Cases and Diplomacy* (University of California Press, Berkeley and Los Angeles, 1970), pp. 19-20.

Neutrality conferred obligations as well as rights upon the powers. It was for that reason that friends of the north in England already accepted its inevitability. W. E. Forster, recently elected Liberal M.P. for Bradford, a successful manufacturer whose ideas were strongly moulded by Quaker antislavery views and classical radical regard for transatlantic democracy, had asked a series of questions on the war in the Commons on May 9. It was clear that Forster and his friends favored neutrality as a means of deterring Englishmen from enlisting in the Confederate cause or equipping rebel privateers.[19] Moreover, practical recognition had been given by the world's first naval power to the Union blockade, a fact to temper southern joy over their achievement of limited international status.

Whether Russell deliberately rushed the cabinet into neutrality before Adams should arrive to bear official weight against the move has been often debated. The documents throw no light upon the matter. (This may in itself seem suspicious, or it may indicate that Russell regarded the move as little more than routine.) The advantage of presenting Adams with a *fait accompli* was achieved by Britain—Adams considered but rejected an immediate withdrawal—but it was achieved at considerable cost: Adams was outraged, his mission begun on a disastrous note, while northern resentment outlasted the decade. Adams' New England conscience kept him at his post when hurt pride might have excused him asking for his passports. The signs pointed to an early recognition of the south as a desperately real possibility, and that must be prevented at all costs. The minister's son, and confidential secretary, the famed Henry Adams, thought a rupture would have been "the extreme of shallowness and folly:

> . . . it would have been a tremendous load for the country . . . it would have been a mere wanton, mad, windmill-hitting, for the sympathies and the policy of England are undoubtedly with us . . . [He was soon to change his mind] . . . it would have been ruin in a merely private point of view. Two such wars would grind us all into rags in America. One is already enough to cut down incomes to a dreadful extent.[20]

19. On Forster see D. G. Wright, "Bradford and the American Civil War," *Journal of British Studies*, VIII, No. 2 (May, 1969), pp. 69-85. Bradford worsteds had a large American market, and Bradford capital was invested in U.S. bonds and railroads.

20. H. D. Cater ed., *Henry Adams and His Friends: A Collection of his Unpublished Letters* (Boston, 1947), p. 92. For detailed account of Adams' first year in London see Norman Ferris, *Tempestuous Mission.* A briefer coverage is given in Martin B. Duberman, *Charles Francis Adams 1807-1886* (Boston, 1961), a competent biography. As scholars have pointed out, a delayed declaration of neutrality by Britain would have been no guarantee of less trouble with the north. Moreover Adams might have felt compelled to leave his post if his efforts to block neutrality had failed.

Russell soothed the new minister's ruffled feelings by arranging an early presentation at court; and Adams avoided offense to the Queen by appearing in stockings and lace, instead of in the republican black assumed by previous representatives. But at his first interview with Russell (May 18) Adams took the offensive. The press had reported that the cabinet had gone far enough and was unlikely to consider recognition of the south in the immediate future; also Gregory had postponed his motion on the matter until June 7. Neither southern nor northern "lobbies" wanted an early trial of strength until they had the numbers to win. Adams permitted himself some slight reassurance, and set about delivering the firm line ordered by Seward (the latter's heated April 27 dispatch had just arrived). Britain (Adams complained) was giving unnatural encouragement to the disaffected cause, and had rashly pronounced the insurgents to be belligerent "before they had ever shown their capacity to maintain any kind of warfare whatever, except within one of their own harbours, and under every possible advantage. It considered them a marine power before they had ever exhibited a single privateer on the ocean." Unless Russell denied the existence of a sinister design to prolong the struggle, Adams "had nothing further left to do in Great Britain."

Adams' accusations caught Russell off balance. Britain, he replied, had acted out of legal necessity, and merely recognized the fact of the war's existence. There were no political overtones to the cabinet's decision, and no opinion was proferred on the justice of either cause. "In many preceding cases, much less formidable demonstrations had been recognized." Britain merely desired to bring the management of the war "within the rules of modern civilized warfare." The exchange cleared the air, and the principals discovered respect for each other. Adams was stiffly correct, passionless in external pose, something of a worried introvert in reality, full of rectitude—the antithesis of the brash Yankee image—but also stubborn and industrious. Russell, with a reputation for cold punctiliousness (which degenerated at times into fussiness), had a similar temperament. Both men were unable to forget that they were legatees of an illustrious and highly political family tradition. The interview, however, left the major issues disturbingly open. Russell refused to bind the government on future recognition of southern independence: that must be a matter of circumstance. Adams agreed that America had recognized revolutionary governments in the past, provided they were self-sufficient militarily and could maintain binding relations with foreign nations. But the south failed these tests; and the United States would resent to the utmost foreign interference which preceded the south's practical attainment of nationhood. That would be to create a result by external agency probably unattainable by other means. Russell promised that Britain would consult with the north before taking the final step of recognition.[21] He was henceforth to keep the southern commissioners at prudent arms length. Adams came away pleased that a rupture had been avoided, but apprehensive of Seward's wrath over the Queen's proclamation. "The permanence of my stay" he wrote in his diary for May 18 "is by no means certain." It was the beginning of a period of purgatory for the fifty-three year old New Englander.

France followed the British lead within a month, proclaiming neutrality on June 10. Other governments later followed suit: events left no alternative, whatever the sympathies of the various regimes. Indeed, as a matter of safety, Britain and France were applying pressure on their neighbors to coordinate on any future recognition of southern independence. It would be a bold nation which should make an independent stroke on America when Europe was being transformed by the underground changes associated with unification movements in Italy and Germany. Napoleon had balked at the international dismay he had created by his Italian Intervention, and sought to prevent French isolation. He was offering to block the creation of a unified Italy as bait for an Austrian alliance and—he hoped vainly—as a bloodless way of obtaining the Venetian independence he had promised the Italians. As Britain and France had fallen apart over the Emperor's acquisition of Nice and Savoy, his efforts were now bent to repairing that accord. Mutual distrust, not harmony, dictated that the two powers move in harness in both European and American affairs.

The Emperor's nervousness perhaps accounts for his initial reaction to the rebellion, which was warmer to the Union than might have been anticipated from a dictator (albeit a plebiscitory one) and the prospective rapist of Mexico. But then, despite his revolutionary language and theory of nationalities, Napoleon's instincts veered to the conservative. Dayton's predecessor at Paris was Charles J. Faulkner, a Virginian who requested his own recall during the secession winter. Yet Faulkner's reports, based on interviews with the Emperor, indicate that Napoleon was unaffected by the pro-southern sympathies rampant at court early in 1861: "He looks

21. Adams to Seward, May 21, 1861, *Foreign Relations*, 1861, pp. 92-93.

upon the dismemberment of the American Confederation with no pleasure, but as a calamity to be deplored by every enlightened friend of human progress."[22] He promised that no hasty encouragement of separation would come from France so long as reasonable hope remained of the reassertion of federal authority.

However the failure of reconciliation efforts, and the prospect of forceful suppression of the revolt, gave cause for changed language. British anxieties concerning the blockade, and interruption to the cotton supply, infected the French cabinet. Thouvenel was harping on "the commercial question" a month before the Queen's proclamation, although still denouncing to Lincoln's agents "a deplorable separation, from which we can expect no advantage . . . ."[23] Seward later complained persistently that France had betrayed friendship by failing to declare for the Union, or to disabuse the rebels of their expectations of sympathy, thus feeding the fires of secession at a critical time. The charge was anachronistic and unfair. Seward himself had been the opposite of vigorous in ensuring that the Union was represented by a loyalist minister in Paris. (Dayton did not arrive until May 11.) No strong plea was made for the northern cause, or very strong opposition launched against the reception of a Confederate mission while Faulkner conducted negotiations. It was Thouvenel who took the initiative by assuring Washington that France would avoid precipitate action on recognition of the south. He gave notice (April 24) that he would receive the rebel commissioners "as respectable foreigners, as I have received Poles, Hungarians, and others," but he would advise them to peace and harmony. He kept the promise; and his tact went a long way in appeasing Seward's wrath at a time when the Secretary of State was breathing war with England for trucking with southerners. It was not a matter of Thouvenel being a northern sympathizer (which he was, within the limits defined by French interest). Caution was a natural policy in the confused circumstances of the day. Indeed France was still delaying recognition of the new Kingdom of Italy, even though Napoleon had helped to create it, and although its *de facto* authority was no longer seriously challenged by the Habsburgs.[24] The French, said Thouvenel, were not in the habit of

22. Faulkner to Black, March 19, 1861, q. Case and Spencer, p. 24.

23. Thouvenel to Mercier, April 25, 1861, q. Case and Spencer, p. 30. (Interview of Thouvenel and Sanford, April 24. Sanford preceded Dayton to Paris in order to put the northern case more strongly than Faulkner.)

24. Faulkner to Seward, April 15, 1861; Sanford to Seward, April 25, 1861, q. Case and Spencer, pp. 49-50. See also Dayton to Seward, June 20, 1861, q. Case and Spencer, p. 63.

acting hastily on such questions. Not long after Dayton's arrival at his post, Thouvenel assured him that the Confederacy would require to survive successfully "over a long period of perhaps three or four years" before France would consider recognition.

The French caution on recognition was vital. Napoleon had lost his best chance of acting, while Union weakness was most marked. He realized this later. The British and French declarations of neutrality, rather than heralding recognition of the south, in effect pronounced its remoteness: the powers were tied to fixed positions of "impartiality" in the war until emphatic military changes should occur. As Professor Blumenthal has pointed out, the Union gained the time it needed to mobilize its industrial and military capacities against the south, and against potential interventionists: "Also the legal basis for recognition of the South or for the refusal to recognize the blockade was apt to be weakened with the passing of time. For the longer that foreign powers waited to take these steps, the more they exposed themselves to the charge, in case of intervention, of violating legal principles they had heretofore respected."[25]

From Seward's viewpoint threats, even from weakness, might give France, and others, reason for pause before meddling. Whether he succeeded will probably continue to arouse debate. While he created fear and trepidation among the diplomatic corps at Washington, and caused Lyons and Mercier to think thrice before budging, London and Paris were noticeably less agitated by his antics. After all, they were not impressive when coming from a beleagured Washington. His warnings against intervention (those who yielded it would be regarded as America's enemies, and opposed even at the cost of a "world in arms"), and his promise of a "high, resolute,and vigorous defence of the Union," were timely. But Seward's obvious, and perhaps calculated, insensitivity to the susceptibilities of the French emperor is puzzling. To the ruler of Europe's most glittering empire, Seward read a lecture on the virtues of republicanism. To a rival imperialist, apprehensive of Manifest Destiny, Seward dilated on American grandeur. ("We have extended our jurisdiction from the St. Mary's river to the Rio Grande, on the Gulf of Mexico, and in a wide belt from the Mississippi to the Pacific ocean.") To the adventurer eyeing Mexico, he paraded the indivisibility of the Union as the *sine qua non* for Latin American security against foreign envy.

---

25. Henry Blumenthal, *A Reappraisal of Franco-American Relations 1830-1871* (Chapel Hill, 1959), p. 124.

On the other hand Seward offered *realpolitik* arguments against the balkanization of America. His instructions to Dayton contain a remarkable concession to European-style diplomacy in recognizing "to a certain extent, the European idea of the balance of power." Seward shrewdly asserted that hemispheric equilibrium was essential to great power interests, and depended on the continuing stability of the United States:

> It is not easy to see how France, Great Britain, Russia, or even reviving Spain, could hope to suppress wars of ambition which must inevitably break out if this continent of North America, now, after the exclusion of foreign interests for three-quarters of a century, is again to become a theatre for the ambition and cupidity of European nations.[26]

Already a northern strategy was emerging: Anglo-French jealousies might be played upon by stressing the divergent interests of the two countries in the hemisphere. The experienced Henry S. Sanford (trying to stall French neutrality in the interim before Dayton's arrival in Paris) cautioned Thouvenel that England wanted to weaken the Union as a rival power:

> But it is to be supposed that the very reasons which would be apt to influence her, would have a directly contrary effect in France, whose policy, it seems to me, is to encourage the growth and development of a commercial power, the rival of England.[27]

Britain, on the other hand, could be readily aroused by rumours that France intended to exploit events to supplant British influence in Central America. While Russell and Palmerston supported the accord with Paris as a European necessity, they had no intention of allowing Napoleon to use it as a catspaw to further his American ambitions. Neither country would be drawn into removing the other's chestnuts from the fire by an appeal to the alliance.

Seward's actions come closest to the textbook version of panic, overreaction, and warmongering when he learned of the impending neutrality of Britain and France. There can be no doubt about the intensity of his bitterness or the militancy of his diplomatic response. He raged "like a caged tiger" and swore to give the British hell (Sumner remembered in 1869). He confided to his wife that he feared Britain was "in great danger of sympathizing so much with

26. For this and above generally, Seward to Dayton, April 22, 1861, *Foreign Relations*, 1861, pp. 195-201.

27. Sanford to Seward, May 12, 1861, q. Case and Spencer, pp. 56-57.

the South, for the sake of peace and cotton, as to drive us to make war against her, as the ally of the traitors."[28] What seemed from the meridian of London or Paris to be a proper and sober response to an awkward situation seemed from the meridian of Washington and New York to be menacing persecution. There was loose war talk, even in business circles of the northeast. Seward's bellicosity reflected current anger, and was a political response to it. In fact, as Mercier reported home, "Mr. Seward was in an embarrassing situation." With a special session of Congress about to meet, and unlikely to spare the "conciliationist" of earlier months, Seward could not afford a humiliating backdown: especially in front of those powers towards which he had previously taken such "an excessively high tone."[29]

Seward himself edited a *New York Herald* report (May 22) which called for united counsels, and remarked how fortunate it was

> that the President and Cabinet put so high an estimate on the sagacity and firmness of the Secretary of State . . . . It cannot but fill with surprise all who may have followed the career of this able statesman to see his usual caution and moderation suddenly converted by the force of events into boldness and decision.

This was a sure sign that Seward was not getting entirely his own way with his colleagues. His program of "quarantine" for the south was in ruins, hence his emotion. By granting belligerency, Britain and France were aiding and comforting the rebels, and their emissaries were already entering European audience chambers. What security existed for the Union blockade when cotton scarcity and southern inducements counseled its annulment by the sea powers? Seward proposed salvaging Union interests and rights, rudely trampled upon, by counteraction.

His notorious dispatch No. 10 (May 21) proposed breaking off relations with Britain if it continued to communicate (officially or otherwise) with Davis' commissioners. It gave anticipatory protest to recognition of southern belligerency, and spoke in provocative terms of being forced into war with Britain if it recognized Confederate independence. (Seward's goal was presented for popular consumption in the *Herald* when it said that the government was resolved not to tolerate British aid to the south, but would "launch against her the thunderbolts of a war that would not cease till

28. See Winks, p. 48; Van Deusen, *Seward*, p. 198, and generally pp. 296-305.

29. Mercier to Thouvenel, June 18, 1861, q. Case and Spencer, p. 73.

every Power in Europe was involved.") Seward's rashness provoked Lincoln into one of his rare interventions into foreign policy. The President countermanded Seward's order that the dispatch be read to Russell, and blue-pencilled the secretary's more warlike phrases. (Some were reinserted, with Lincoln's consent, after Seward added a preface to Adams insisting upon the confidentiality of the note.) The dispatch still had teeth: the United States would regard as "hostile in spirit" (Adams' phrase) foreign intercourse with its rebellious subjects, or their recognition (this latter was an old threat). And it would insist upon international respect for its blockade, if properly maintained. A similarly grim warning was dispatched to Paris. Adams had the satisfaction of seeing Russell retreat when reproached with receiving the Yancey mission (June 12). Russell did not regard the two conversations he had had with them as serious or breaching convention, but he "had no expectation of seeing them any more." The resultant isolation of the southern agents, which persisted for the war, was a triumph for Seward's strategy. But Lincoln's prudence, and Adams' tact in presenting the kernel of Seward's policy without its offensive husk, played a key role in averting an unnecessary alienation of the English. (Seward stupidly undid some of this good work a year later when dispatch No. 10 appeared in print.)

Seward's subsequent maneuvers, some of them with a comic opera flavor, are explicable in two regards: he was determined to minimize the importance of the Anglo-French entente in the eyes of the American public, and insistent that his country would not lend its imprimatur to the unwarrantable "proto-recognition" which the powers had extended to the south. Lyons and Mercier, working in close harmony, had nervously avoided the wrought-up Secretary of State during May. Mercier judged Seward "one of those demagogues who can sail only on the sea of popular emotion and who always try to stir up passion in order to exploit it."[30] Lyons advised the Canadians to strengthen their border defenses. As a safety measure the two diplomats sought to interview Seward jointly on the subject of southern belligerency and American adherence to the Paris Declaration. When they arrived at Seward's office on June 15, Seward jokingly admonished them, refused a joint encounter and arranged separate interviews. The incident was blown up in the press, and Seward in later life spoke with excessive pride of his dexterity in

30. Carroll, *Mercier*, p. 74, also 79 and following. See also Case and Spencer, pp. 64-76.

this matter. In these, and later, discussions Seward refused to receive "officially" documents assuming the Confederacy's belligerent rights, or making justifications of belligerency. America's acceptance of Europe's action must not be presumed. By reading unofficially the British and French documents, but pretending official ignorance of them, Seward evaded confrontation. As talks on the Paris Declaration involved the prickly issue of belligerent rights, he transferred the negotiations to the European capitals: time would allow passions to cool in the north. Meanwhile he promised northern coöperation in observing the Paris rules respecting private property at sea. This was surprisingly moderate behavior. Lyons began to revise his harsh verdict on the New Yorker, and hoped that he had seen the error of his truculent ways. Neither he nor Mercier were impressed by Seward's transparent strivings to wedge their countries apart. (Until France's official edict of neutrality arrived on June 23, Seward was able to harp upon England's greater intransigence. He also hoped to separate them on the privateering issue.)

The French benefited noticeably at this stage from Thouvenel's cagey diplomacy, which took greater care than Russell's to soothe northern susceptibilities and to pave the way for the unpleasantness of neutrality. Nor was Count Mercier undermining relations between Paris and Washington, as he is sometimes depicted. Mercier's attitude was discerning. He was privately an advocate of partition, on realistic grounds: force could never restore the old nationalist dream of a giant, thirty-four state Republic. But French interest dictated the organization of a powerful state composed of the north and west, where the sources of American vitality were located. France should not needlessly offend the United States, for it would still be a great force without the south: like England it would continue to have "a huge merchant marine, iron like hers, coal and cotton, the same aptitudes, the same greed, the same bumptious roughness, . . . it will be her real rival in the world, and since its field of action will not be Europe, by the same token it will be our ally."[31] Naturally he did not convey these musings to Lyons.

A hairline fracture in the entente occurred in a postscript to the above events. The British had poorer luck, or were less adept, than the French in the ticklish matter of obtaining Confederate adherence to as much as was practicable of the Paris Declaration.

31. Mercier to Thouvenel, (date uncertain, but about this time), q. Carroll, p. 75. Carroll clears Mercier of the charge of being simplistically prosouthern.

The powers wanted the sea war conducted on modern, civilized lines, giving maximum security to neutral shipping and rights. In their view international law permitted states to communicate with *de facto* governments to protect the persons and property of their nationals. The north regarded such dealings as verging upon international acceptance of the south, dangerously raising the prestige and morale of the insurrectionists. Hints from Seward indicated that he might turn a blind eye if discreet conversations took place; however he gave ample warning that, if forced to take official notice of foreign intercourse with the Confederate government, he would brand it an unfriendly act.

The probability that Jefferson Davis would seize upon overtures as a propaganda coup multiplied the problems confronting Lyons and Mercier, who were charged with the negotiations. They attempted to reduce legal affronts to the Union by arranging talks between consuls Bunch and Belligny de Saint-Croix at Charleston and Governor Pickens of South Carolina. The consuls were still legally accredited to the Union (a matter of high offense to the south, but which they tolerated for the moment), while the governor's legal standing at least predated the rebellion.[32] A chapter of errors ensued. Belligny and Bunch decided instead to contact Jefferson Davis at Richmond through W. H. Trescott (the same Assistant Secretary of State who had defected during the winter, some said with secrets for the Confederacy). Trescott's efforts bore fruit in August when the Confederate Congress approved Articles 2 to 4 of the Paris Declaration. The south kept its privateering weapon, but Europe got its guarantee of immunity for noncontraband trade. The affirmation of item 4 gave notice that the south would step up pressure on the powers to crack down upon the Union's leaky blockade. Davis showed irritation over the irregularity of the "negotiations," and a not unnatural resentment at the closure of neutral ports to rebel privateers. Proclaimed by the British on June 1, and the French on June 10, this prohibition applied to both belligerents. It effectively achieved the abolition of privateering envisaged in article 1 of the Paris convention.

Bunch foolishly consigned his diplomatic pouch to a fellow-countryman, Robert Mure, now a Charleston merchant and naturalized American, who was arrested after shipping to New York. Among letters carried by Mure without diplomatic cover was one to

32. Carroll, p. 92. See Case and Spencer, pp. 100-121 for lucid narrative. Richmond was now the south's seat of government.

England betraying details of Bunch's negotiations, details which Bunch had unforgivably confided to a friend. Seward instructed Adams to demand Bunch's removal. Adams was to request that if Bunch's sealed bag—carefully respected by the Americans—contained matter treasonable to the United States government the documents be relinquished to Adams, and Bunch be appropriately punished. Russell denied that the documents were offensive. An acrimonious exchange developed between London and Washington. The British denied that they had any intention to recognize the south as a "separate and independent State" and refused to recall Bunch. Seward revoked Bunch's exequatur. Russell advised Lyons on September 13 that if Seward used the occasion to break relations, Lyons should retire to Canada until the storm blew over. No such crisis was reached. Seward toned down his protests, skirting the complaint that Bunch had treated with Richmond but declaring him *persona non grata* because of his partisanship. (He did not in fact leave Charleston until February 1863.) France's role in the affair was rather obviously unprotested. The French, happy to be let alone, remained unresponsive to British urgings for support.

The Union army's humiliation at Bull Run in July occasioned sarcasm and sneers throughout Western Europe, and raised to dizzy heights southern hopes of recognition. But the fall months witnessed a mountain of diplomatic labors—the negotiations on the Paris Declaration and the blockade fill volumes—which brought forth a mouse. For the time being Britain and France accepted the effectiveness of the blockade, and avoided collision with Washington over Congress' hotheaded Ports Bill. Favored by Sumner and Welles, the bill passed in July, and gave Lincoln discretionary power to close southern ports by proclamation. It was protested by the maritime powers as a "paper" blockade, but they quietened down when Seward unobtrusively obtained an executive shelving for the bill.

Naval policy underlay British reluctance to make a demonstration against a less than watertight blockade, but Napoleon's coldness to ideas of interference sprang from complex motives. It was to take major distress in the textile industry, and the development of his Mexican ambitions, to stir him to more adventurous disposition. The Emperor followed the British lead on the blockade essentially because his European strategy dictated a strengthening of the British alliance: joint action on America would presumably lessen the distrust which marred the European relations of the two nations. Nor did the British stance contradict an older French policy which still exerted residual influence: the desire to maintain American unity as a counterweight to the British empire. Yankee friendship was worth having on three assumptions: that America desired no European role; that American naval power did not threaten to exceed parity with the British, thus creating a new disequilibrium; and that the geopolitical interests of France and the United States were compatible in the hemisphere. The crisis had temporarily eliminated the first two perils. (However European enmity to the north might cause the Americans to take a retaliatory role in Europe at some future date, while the war promised to create a massive Union navy within years.) The last was the sorest point: France resented the Monroe Doctrine and intended to challenge it. But the Mexican affair was still a stormcloud on the horizon in late 1861, and it suited neither Napoleon nor Lincoln to have a headlong clash about it.

Napoleon's motives in embarking upon the Mexican Intervention, disastrous to the empire in every way, have been minutely dissected by scholars. There can be no doubt of his genuine fascination with the idea of Mexico as the center of a Catholic, Latin-cultured empire rivalling the creations of the Anglo-Saxons to the north. Napoleon's propaganda on the topic was an almost Gaullist mixture. It pandered to French chauvinism, insisting on France's right to play a global role commensurate with her glory. It accused the Anglo-Saxon powers—Britain and the United States—of denying France that role, of trying to corner markets, control international commerce, and leech upon the untapped resources of undeveloped areas. France could provide a more civilized, humane, less racist, benevolent paternalism over unstable polities such as Mexico.

Characteristically, Napoleon deluded himself that he could achieve these grandiose goals by less than grandiose methods. He acted in 1861 because he thought he could get an empire on the cheap. Tangible strategic and economic gains seemed on offer at minimum cost. As a political prisoner in 1846 Louis Napoleon had written a pamphlet on Nicaragua, and had thought of going there to head the construction of the Canale Napoleone, a new axis of communication linking the Gulf of Mexico and the Pacific, the East and the West. His interest in the region persisted, as did his confidence that France could profitably exploit transit routes across Mexico or Panama, and tap the mineral resources of northern Mexico. The fabled gold mines of Sonora might become France's

California.[33] Powerful speculative interests with investments in Mexico pressed for the Emperor's protection. They included the Duke de Morny and his business partner Jean-Baptiste Jecker, a Swiss banker who held $15 million in bonds obtained from Miramón's regime.[34] Mexican emigres assured the court that the French army would be wildly acclaimed by a populace yearning for liberation. The emigre cause was ably espoused by José Hidalgo, who had the ear of Empress Eugénie. (Hidalgo had served as a diplomat for Santa Anna, when in 1853 the latter had approached the powers to install a foreign prince in Mexico.) But it was the Marquis de Radepont who most plausibly outlined for Napoleon plans for making Mexico a buffer against American expansion. Radepont had been an observer during the American invasion of Mexico, stayed on to seek his fortune, and since 1856 preached the doctrine of Mexican regeneration through French control.[35] One of his memorials to Napoleon was titled Mexico "the Turkey of America." Mid-nineteenth century minds were much swayed by Alexis de Tocqueville's forecast that the future belonged to the superpowers, Russia and the United States. As Turkey was being used to contain Russia, so Mexico might be used to check the rise of an American empire.

The War between the States provided the obvious opportunity for a French *coup.* It would however be attended by high risks unless executed with swift precision. A restored Union would inevitably wreak vengeance for violation of the Monroe Doctrine. ("Imperialism preached in the grand manner," Van Alstyne says of the latter "for the only restrictions placed upon the directing power are those which it imposes upon itself.") Alternatively, a southern success would create two nuclei tending to swell to more impressive

---

33. France was on a bimetallic standard, but in 1861 demands for silver by the U.S. to finance the war led to a financial crisis. Again in 1864 there was another, caused by the export of silver to India and Egypt in payment for cotton. Pressure grew for France to go on a single gold standard and might well have succeeded had France had more colonial gold resources. At the close of the war the franc-using countries—France, Belgium, Switzerland—attempted a modified bi-metallic system, the Latin Monetary Union.

34. See Egon C. C. Corti, *Maximilian and Charlotte of Mexico* (Archon books, 1968, orig. ed. 1928), Chapters 1, 2. Also Blumenthal, Chapter 6. The French minister in Mexico, Saligny, was a protégé of Morny's.

35. Kathryn A. Hanna, "Roles of the South in the French Intervention in Mexico," *JSH*, XX, No. 1 (February, 1954), p. 5, and generally on this topic. Subsequent to the preparation of the present volume has appeared A. J. Hanna and K. A. Hanna, *Napoleon III and Mexico: American Triumph Over Monarchy* (Chapel Hill, N. C., 1971). Hidalgo's claims to have master-minded the French intervention have been shown to be quite unreliable; see *ibid.*, p. 335.

dimensions by encroaching upon their neighbors. The British might expect trouble in Canada, while a tottering Napoleonic creation in Mexico would be helpless before a triumphant Confederate army. Napoleon hardly grappled with these challenges. He was reluctant to wage war at vast distance from France, reluctant to send more than a few thousand troops, or to incur unpopular expense. He preferred to believe that the Mexicans only awaited their deliverance to set up a stable and popular monarchy under French tutelage. With respect to awkward complications, he trusted to luck and his destiny.

The American conquest and partitioning of Mexico in the 1840's had left an aftermath of civil division and chaos which defied internal political solution. The latest to wrest power at Mexico City was Benito Juárez, Indian-born leader of a liberal-republican coalition of anticlerical and antiforeign bent. Juárez, a man of intelligence and ruthless vigour, was resisted by the church, conservatives, and independent local warlords. Unluckily his efforts to restore some solvency to his country brought the wrath of the powers upon his head at a time when the American shield had disappeared from Latin America. Confiscation of church lands—regarded as a necessary reform even by liberal Catholics—alarmed French and British investors, who trembled for their own interests. Mexico's foreign debts totalled over $65 million in 1861, $15 million contracted by Juárez' predecessor and rival Miguel Miramón. In July the national congress forced the President to suspend interest payment on the foreign debt for two years. The French and British ministers immediately broke off relations with Mexico's "faithless government." Napoleon's representative, Count Dubois de Saligny, pressed for a punitive stroke by France, Britain and Spain against the Mexican ports of Tampico and Vera Cruz, to be held hostage until reparation was paid.

Autumn negotiations between London, Paris and Madrid resulted in the adoption of Saligny's plan. A swift Mexican capitulation was anticipated. At British insistence the Tripartite Treaty of London (October, 1861) approved a joint expedition on two conditions, neither very palatable to the other signatories. The treaty included a self-denial clause which prohibited the powers from acquiring territorial advantage by forceful intervention in Mexico's internal affairs, and banned the use of force to prejudice the right of the Mexican people to choose freely their form of government. From the beginning France chose to interpret this clause freely, reserving its right to exert "moral" influence to gain a change of constitution. Indeed the treaty was signed by the French ambassador to London, Count Flahault, with knowledge of Napoleon's secret design to favor the Austrian Archduke Maximilian as prospective emperor of Mexico—a move which would give him leverage for an Austrian alliance as well as gaining glory for France in the new world. Britain's second condition was that the United States should be invited to participate in the project. As Russell explained to his ambassador in Paris, Lord Cowley, this did not signify any yielding to "the extravagant pretensions implied by what is called the Monroe Doctrine." Nevertheless it would be unwise, "as a matter of expediency," to provoke American ill-will "unless some paramount object were in prospect, and tolerably easy of attainment."[36]

Seward declined the offer on December 4. He accepted the formal right of the powers to coerce Mexico into observance of its international duties—the United States had more than once proposed to protect its Mexican interests in the same way. But he reiterated the nation's pre-war policy forbidding foreign dismemberment of Mexico, adding the reminder that the United States stood behind the principles of republicanism and self-determination in the hemisphere. However the fevered appeals of the Mexican minister at Washington, Matías Romero, for American resistance against subversion of Mexican republicanism met with polite inaction. As Seward knew, the Union was impotent to forestall imperialist aggression to the south, the signs and portents of which were swiftly discerned by northern opinion. Mixed with much loud remorse over the perils facing a sister American republic were sentiments of disappointed expansionism, and resentment that Mexico might pass into rival French, Spanish or even a Confederate sphere of influence.

Seward ingeniously proposed to sidetrack foreign intervention while improving his country's grip over vital transit routes and rich mineral lands in northern Mexico: the United States would assume the interest on Mexico's foreign debts for five years, security being pledged by public lands and mineral rights in Sonora, Chihuahua, Sinaloa, and Lower California. But Seward neglected to wean Congressional support, and the loan-treaty plan expired

36. Russell to Cowley, September 30, 1861, F. O. 146/978, q. W. S. Robertson, "Tripartite Treaty of London," *Hispan. A.H.R.*, XX, No. 2 (May, 1940), p. 173. Generally see: P. H. Reuter, "United States-French Relations regarding French Intervention in Mexico: from the Tripartite Treaty to Queretaro" *Sth. Quart.*, VI, No. 4 (July, 1968), pp. 469-489; K. A. Hanna, "Roles of the South in the French Intervention in Mexico," *JSH*, XX, No. 1 (Feb., 1954), pp. 3-21; Carl H. Bock, *Prelude to Tragedy: the Negotiation and Breakdown of the Tripartite Convention of London* (Philadelphia, 1966).

in the Senate. This outcome was hardly an expression of complacency concerning the intentions of the powers. Quite the opposite. The northern state of mind was apprehensive as Britain reinforced Canada and the powers closed in to gather pieces of a disintegrating continent. Editorial speculation attributed various motives for European aggression. They ranged from designs to restore lost imperial splendor (the most common explanation of Spanish ambition) to a modern desire for geopolitical supremacy in one of the world's most rapidly developing regions. Humiliation of the United States would reduce its charismatic appeal as a democratic model for Latin American peoples, opening the way for European-sponsored monarchies, and at the same time remove a disturbing revolutionary influence upon the downtrodden masses of old Europe. Some comfort was derived in the north from predictions that the allies would fall apart. Should France oust the others in Mexico, at least a barrier would be placed in the way of slavery's extension into Central America, whether sponsored by the Confederacy or by Spain. Endless intrigues for empire between the south and the European powers seemed a likely pattern for the future, should Jefferson Davis establish his nation.

During November the tripartite invasion was prepared, and the first troops—three thousand Spaniards under General Prim—landed at Vera Cruz on December 17. French and British contingents followed. It did not take great prescience to doubt the expedition's protestations of limited objectives. The powers, proclaimed the *New York Times*,

> are determined to make experiment in Mexico; but, should they succeed there, it must not be concluded that they will then rest from their labors. Ambition grows by what it feeds on, and success in Mexico will not improbably encourage them to repeat the operation in the other Spanish-American Republics.[37]

As it turned out, it was not the smell of success but the unexpected resistance of the Mexicans, and the prospect of military dishonor, which was to force Napoleon into the heavy commitment he dreaded. Before too long his daydreams of easy victory would be replaced by anxiety to disengage with honor.

Domestic pressure was as likely as global strategy to push Napoleon into making a strong *demarche* on America, such as breaking the blockade to get cotton. Almost phobic about the

37. *NYT*, March 3, 1862.

security of his regime, Napoleon was not the man to ignore an overwhelming popular clamor for intervention. It did not materialize in 1861. The emperor's agents reported an unwarlike spirit among the people, tired of a decade of escapades and scrapes. The Civil War caused significant, and worrisome, repercussions upon the French economy, but they were manageable for the first year of conflict. The much vaunted specter of cotton scarcity proved to be a prospective and psychological problem rather than an immediate physical one in 1861. Not until the autumn and winter did cotton imports fall dramatically, while reserves held over from the previous year's bumper crop had a cushioning effect. From interested commercial and manufacturing groups—cotton millers in Alsace, Normandy, Vosges, businessmen in Nancy and Bordeaux, chambers of commerce in Lyons, Rouen, and Mulhouse—came howls for help. But demands for recognition of the south, or French intervention, were outnumbered by appeals for nonintervention and neutrality.[38] The division reflected the complexity of the economic situation. The real damage inflicted by the American crisis was upon French export industries, dependent upon transatlantic markets, or vulnerable to the war's reverbatory economic effects which were dampening down activity generally in western Europe. Industries affected included Montbéliard and Rouen watchmaking, Lyons silk, Limoges chinaware, while exports fell generally in the glass, lace, ship-building, hat-making, leather goods and wine industries. Peace was the only cure for these troubles. Areas dependent on northern markets might support mediation, but they opposed policies which risked war with the Union. An attack on the blockade might bring relief to a narrow sector of the economy, textiles—that is, provided that sufficient cotton had escaped the ravages of war and the effects of the southern embargo. But it was likely to be at the cost of a wider war and wider depression of the French economy. Particular cotton interests and speculators saw opportunities for profiteering if scarcity conditions continued. Mercantile interests, as in Douai, regarded the American navy as auxiliary to the French, and opposed its destruction as playing into the hands of the British. Finally, the French wheat crop failed in 1861, causing high bread prices (the anathema of all European governments for bread riots were the commonest form of popular insurrection), and underlining the utility of cheap grain shipped from the American prairies.

38. See Case and Spencer, 164, and generally Chapter 5, a valuable pioneering survey, on which I have relied for this discussion.

Seward fully exploited such "peace factors" in the Anglo-French-American world. He showed to best advantage when taking such roles, displaying his imaginative awareness of the international dynamics of the time. His agents were instructed to wage their diplomatic campaigns on the broadest economic and political fronts. He himself schooled his opposite numbers on such subjects. With acuity worthy of Cobden, Seward described to Thouvenel how America, France and Britain formed one economic community, exchanging raw materials, food and manufactured goods. Though politically divided, the three nations "constitute only one great society or commonwealth . . . Civil War in either country . . . retards the accustomed operating of industries in the other two countries."[39] The powers' interests lay, not in America's partition—that would only distort the warp and woof of an intricate trade pattern—but in ending the war quickly. Cease your covert help for the south, he said, grant the United States its full sovereign rights, and normality would soon prevail.

Meanwhile Thouvenel had been exploring the prospect of obtaining cotton, and silencing his critics, by making a deal with Seward: French leniency to the north in return for some relaxation of the blockade. The idea began with Mercier, who detected latent defeatism in the north despite the frenzied war drive which followed the defeat at Manassas. In August and September Mercier toured the north with Prince Napoleon, cousin and liberal critic of Louis Napoleon. One of their distinguished hosts (probably Lewis Cass) was convinced that several important politicians regarded European intervention as the north's only salvation: they

> sighed for some pretext for an arrangement, and they could hardly wait for the time to come when France and England, pushed by their interest, would recognise the South and take a firm stand to obtain cotton come what may. Then, they said, the North could consider all chance of fighting as lost and could give up without shame.[40]

This was intriguing. The French were not yet ready to take a steep risk on intervention, but it was worth testing Washington's price for buying security from a carefully implied threat. Thouvenel made an

39. Seward to Dayton, October 30, 1861 (read to Thouvenel, November 25), q. Case and Spencer, pp. 184-185.

40. Mercier to Thouvenel, September 9, 1861, q. Case and Spencer, p. 167. Thouvenel's request for easing the blockade was sent on October 3, Seward's response dated October 30.

overture for access to southern ports. Seward gave it top priority: he conveyed his reply to Paris by special mission headed by the Catholic Archbishop of New York, John Hughes. In the mission was included Thurlow Weed, who was to do sterling work for the Union in Europe in the crisis months to follow. But Seward's offerings were tantalizingly vague, and his tone anything but defeatist. He prophesied success for amphibious operations being mounted by the Union navy to establish beachheads on rebel coasts (Welles was planning his Port Royal onslaught), and talked of funneling cotton through such outlets. But difficulties beset the question: which powers should have access? How much cotton could the Union afford to let go? For how long? How would rebel owners be paid? Would this compromise the Union's sovereign rights? The blockade was legal, and an essential war weapon for the north. Why should the north weaken itself? It was clear that Seward was playing for higher stakes: he might give France special access to cotton if it renounced its recognition of southern belligerency; and he hoped, no doubt, to split the allies if Napoleon accepted the deal, leaving England in the cold. On the other hand he warned Mercier that allied intervention on the blockade meant war. Whatever the result France would be mauled, and Franco-American trade and amity irreparably harmed. Thouvenel did not wedge ajar the door which Seward had left open, for in the last days of November all was swallowed up in the furor created by the war's most serious international incident.

Chapter V

"Wilkes and Unpardonable Liberty"

It was becoming obvious to the Richmond government by autumn 1861 that the Yancey-Mann-Rost commission, which visited the courts of Europe "like Methodist circuit-riders," was a limited instrument of Confederate diplomacy.[1] The time seemed ripe for launching a more massive diplomatic offensive abroad. Yancey resigned in early September, but it was not an act of despair, or a protest at the British decision of August 24 declining to recognize the south. Yancey, it emerged, was optimistic: the approaching cotton famine, he reported home, gave brighter hopes for forcing the powers into recognition than had existed since the war's start. After joining Rost in Paris, Yancey saw Thouvenel and gained the impression that the Emperor and his ministers were pro-Confederate. Interventionist rumors flew in Paris. The response of the new Confederate Secretary of State, R. M. T. Hunter, was to wind up the old mission. On September 23 he appointed James M. Mason of Virginia and John Slidell of Louisiana as special commissioners to London and Paris respectively. An ex-chairman of the Senate Foreign Relations Committee under Buchanan, Mason was an anathema to antislavery men as principal concocter of the Fugitive Slave Bill and sponsor of the Kansas-Nebraska Bill. Slidell, remarkably successful at the New Orleans bar, had been Polk's minister-plenipotentiary to Mexico in 1845 on the abortive mission to resolve

1. Owsley, p. 76. The chapter title is taken from London *Punch*, December 7, 1861.

the disputes which led to the Mexican war. He later acquired reputation as one of the more adroit and unscrupulous secessionists in Congress.

Hunter's instructions to the new men emphasized the Confederacy's military success, and its future as a lucrative market for Europe and supplier of raw materials. Mason and Slidell were to press for recognition. But the strategy thought most likely to contrive European intervention was one of gaining European repudiation of the blockade. Richmond considered the mission so important that it purchased and crewed a fast steamer, the ex-mail packet *Nashville*, to run the blockade at Charleston with the ministers. This plan being vetoed by naval officers as too risky, the government chartered a light, very swift side-wheeler river steamer, the *Gordon*, renamed *Theodora*, to put the envoys in Nassau or Havana, where passage could be made to England under the neutral flag of a British mail-steamer. The charter cost the impoverished administration $5,000, while it was prepared to guarantee the *Theodora* at the value of $60,000 out and back. "So you see how valuable we are considered," Mason wrote to his wife.[2]

The evaluation was shared in the north. The activities of rebel agents and sympathizers abroad were widely feared. A combination of factors alarmed northern imaginations: the danger of a war with Spain over the mooted tripartite Mexican intervention; the British reinforcement of Canada; the presence of Vice-Admiral Milne's naval force off the eastern seaboard; the fallibility of the blockade and the inglorious military record of recent months. What better time for foreign meddling? Suspicion grew that an Anglo-Confederate accord was being forged when it became known that a British M.P., Sir James Ferguson, had visited Richmond shortly before the departure of Mason and Slidell. The New York *Herald* warned that, if the envoys were permitted to present themselves at the courts of St. James and Versailles, "they have a much better chance of a friendly reception than at any previous period."[3]

The Union Navy had extra motives for wanting the envoys captured. Naval prestige had sunk disastrously as blockade-runners, and commerce-destroyers such as the C.S.S. *Sumter*, flaunted their

---

2. Mason to his wife, October 11, 1861, in Virginia Mason, *The Public Life and Diplomatic Correspondence of James M. Mason* (New York, 1906), p. 199; also pp. 209-210. Mason's detailed account of his experiences from his Charleston departure dispels many misconceptions concerning the *Trent* affair.

3. *NYH*, October 17, 1861.

successes. In October McKean's gulf squadron had been scattered by a rebel force off the southwest pass of the Mississippi, causing a bitter outcry in the press. Then came the false information, leaked by southern newspapers on October 14, that Mason and Slidell had eluded the blockade on the *Nashville*, and were enroute to Europe. The Navy Department immediately sent three cruisers on wild goose chases to intercept the *Nashville*, even though Welles was desperately pressed for ships for an amphibious onslaught on Port Royal. (Planned since June the raid aimed to create a Federal base midway between Charleston and Savannah.) One cruiser, the *James Adger*, crossed the Atlantic, and alarmed the Foreign Office by seeking the *Nashville* in the English Channel.

Mason and Slidell had in fact run the Charleston blockade in the *Theodora* on the dark and rainy night of October 12. Off the coast of Cuba they met a small Spanish steamer which hospitably (but irregularly by international law) gave them safe convoy to Cardenas, some 100 miles east of Havana. Disembarking there on October 16, they made a leisurely overland trip to Havana which they reached on October 22.

On October 16 the United States consulate in Havana learnt of the envoys' arrival at Cardenas, but was unable to convey the news to Key West until October 19 and it did not reach New York until the evening of October 24. The published government records are strangely silent on Washington's reaction. Clearly, however, the southerners were beyond the navy's reach and would complete their voyage under a neutral flag, unless exceptional steps were taken. Whether such steps were ordered by United States officials was much debated in 1861, but has been curiously ignored by historians since. It is sobering to remember that the Navy Department created a considerable wartime reputation for aggressiveness, for obeying the imperatives of conflict rather than legal niceties. War forced the navy to take a high belligerent stand on maritime issues, contrary to American tradition, and it was well aware of British practice permitting seizure of neutral ships suspected of unneutral behavior. Nor was the State Department unaware of the case for a capture. Adam Gurowski, a translator in the department appointed specifically as an adviser on international law (he taught the subject at Harvard), made this entry in his diary not long after Washington heard of the voyage of the *Theodora*:

> Mason and Slidell escaped to Havana on their way to Europe, as commissioners of the rebels. According to all international definitions, we have the full right to seize them in any neutral vessel,

> they being political contrabands of war going on a publicly avowed errand hostile to their true government. Mason and Slidell are not common passengers, nor are they political refugees invoking the protection of any neutral flag. They are travelling commissioners of war, of bloodshed and rebellion; and it is all the same in whatever seaport they embark. And if the vessel conveying them goes from America to Europe, or vice versa, Mr. Seward can let them be seized when they have left Havana, provided he finds it expedient.[4]

There is some evidence, fragmentary and unreliable, to suggest that Seward endeavored so to act. It includes a diary entry made by Attorney-General Bates (but a month later) which said that Seward had sent orders to the United States consul at Havana to make the seizure. Lyons repeated a similar story.[5] Telling against this view, no telltale dispatch has survived in the Havana consulate records; and other contemporaries denied government implication.

On October 30 the mail-steamer *Columbia* arrived in New York with two pieces of vital information: that Mason and Slidell were to embark for the Danish island of St. Thomas on November 7 aboard the British mail-packet *Trent*; and that the U.S. frigate *San Jacinto*, commander Charles Wilkes, was expected in Havana around October 28. A series of activities in New York and Washington on October 29 and 30 have inspired the conjectures, firstly, that the State Department attempted to send despatches to Wilkes by means of a special agent sailing on the Havana-bound mail-packet *Cosmopolitan*; and, secondly, that Welles—probably acting in conjunction with Seward—also tried to send orders via the U.S.S. *Bienville*.[6] However a hurricane prevented the *Bienville* reaching Havana altogether, and caused the *Cosmopolitan* to arrive too late to contact the *San Jacinto*. According to this theory, the plan to capture the *Trent* was not originally, if ever, known to Lincoln, and it was subsequently hushed up in order not to damage American interests.

Whatever the truth of such speculations, events forced Wilkes to act without orders, as he always claimed. Now aged 62, he was famous as a naval scientist and explorer, and well known within

4. Adam Gurowski, *Diary: From March 4, 1861 to November 12, 1862* (Boston, 1862), I, p. 109.

5. H. K. Beale, ed., *Diary of Edward Bates, 1859-1866* (Washington, 1933), p. 206 (entry for November 28, 1861). Lyons wrote privately to Russell on November 19: "I am told confidentially that orders were given at Washington which led to the capture on board the 'Trent', and that they were signed by Mr. Seward without the knowledge of the President." Newton, *Lyons*, p. 55. Winfield Scott's "revelations" on the episode are discussed later.

6. See D. Anderson, "A Question of Orders: the Arrest of Mason and Slidell Reconsidered," (Unpub. paper, University of Queensland).

the service for his turbulent and independent temperament. (Secretary Welles was among those he had managed to alienate.) Ordered in May to bring back the steam-sloop *San Jacinto* (1446 tons, 13 guns) from its West African station, Wilkes was inclined to season this unpleasing task with a dash of glory-hunting.[7] While cruising the Caribbean in search of the Confederate raider *Sumter*, he touched at Cienfuegos, on the south Cuban coast (October 23). There he learnt that Mason and Slidell had arrived in Havana, and he received a telegram from the United States Consul-General in Havana, Robert W. Shufeldt, to come post haste to that city. Shufeldt wanted to strengthen the American watch over blockade-runners, and to show the flag against the rebel arrivals. Wilkes arrived in Havana on October 31, to find that the city had welcomed the southerners with open arms. The story went around—it was later officially denied—that the British consul had received them in full ceremonial uniform. He certainly introduced them to His Excellency the Captain-General of Cuba, although "as private gentlemen from the 'Confederate States of America' . . . [and] no mention was made of political matters during the interview."[8] It was common knowledge that Mason and Slidell had booked passage on the *Trent*, sailing for St. Thomas on November 7, there to embark on the British packet *La Plata* to Southampton. (The fact that the British consul had apparently arranged the booking in the knowledge of the southerner's accreditation later inflamed northern opinion.)

Before sailing for Key West on November 2, too early to receive any orders from Washington, Wilkes had made the decision to capture the commissioners.[9] He consulted with Shufeldt who was initially dubious but offered no strong opposition:

> None of the authorities upon international law in my possession make mention of a case similar in its character . . . and at first, such a measure would seem to be a violation of the rights of neutrals upon the ocean. Yet upon reflection it is one, which admits perhaps of a more favorable consideration and Captain Wilkes after much thought upon the subject in view of the great

7. John Sherman Long, "Glory-hunting off Havana: Wilkes and the *Trent* Affair," *CWH*, XIX, No. 2 (June, 1963), pp. 133-144; Daniel Henderson, *Hidden Coasts: A Biography of Admiral Charles Wilkes* (New York, 1953).

8. Shufeldt to Seward, October 25, 1861, Despatch 74, *U.S. National Archives and Records Service—Despatches from U.S. Consuls in Havana,* Microcopy T20, Roll 42, Vol. 42, Supplement.

9. Shufeldt to Seward, November 9, 1861, Despatch 79, T20, Roll 41, Vol. 41, *U.S. National Archives, etc.*

> importance of the capture of these persons with their dispatches came to the decision of intercepting this steamer . . . and taking them from her by force if necessary.[10]

However, as Shufeldt conceded, it was an open question "whether Captain Wilkes will meet with the approbation of our Government or not in the responsibility which he has assumed."

Wilkes later explained in his official report that he had examined all the authorities on international law to which he had access, ". . . viz, Kent, Wheaton, and Vattel, besides various decisions of Sir William Scott, and other judges of the admiralty court of Great Britain . . . There was no doubt I had the right to capture vessels with *written* despatches; they were expressly referred to in all authorities, subjecting the vessel to seizure and condemnation if the captain of the vessel had the knowledge of their being on board." The lawbooks were reticent however on the issue of arresting ambassadors, and Wilkes, oblivious to the legal eccentricity of his decision, considered the gentlemen "as the embodiment of despatches."[11]

Wilkes broached his scheme to his first officer, Lieutenant D. MacNiell Fairfax. Fairfax objected to it as likely to goad a prosouthern Britain into war with the north, and tried to persuade Wilkes to consult Judge Marvin, an authority on maritime law stationed at Key West. Wilkes refused. His journal indicates that he was primarily interested in patriotically seizing dangerous enemies of his country: ". . . I trust we may make them prisoners for I know of no act that would so effectually [despoil] their diabolical scheme."[12]

Wilkes arrived at Key West on November 4, but found no ships to add to the expedition. He provisioned his ship to cater for a large party of passengers, and set off eastwards to await the English steamer (Map 1). The encounter took place in the Old Bahama Channel, some 300 miles east of Havana, soon after noon on November 8. The *Trent*, flying the English colors, was stopped by a round shot across the bows. Fairfax, placed in charge of the boarding party, had orders not only to arrest Mason, Slidell and their two secretaries, but also to take possession of their baggage and any

---

10. Shufeldt to Seward, November 9, 1861. See also F. C. Drake, "The Cuban Background of the Trent Affair," *CWH*, XIX, No. 1 (March, 1973), pp. 29-49. Drake places greater emphasis on Shufeldt's role, in an effort to show that Wilkes did not alone conceive the capture.

11. *Senate Executive Documents*, 1, 37 Cong., 2 Session, Vol. 3, p. 123.

12. Quoted Long, p. 136.

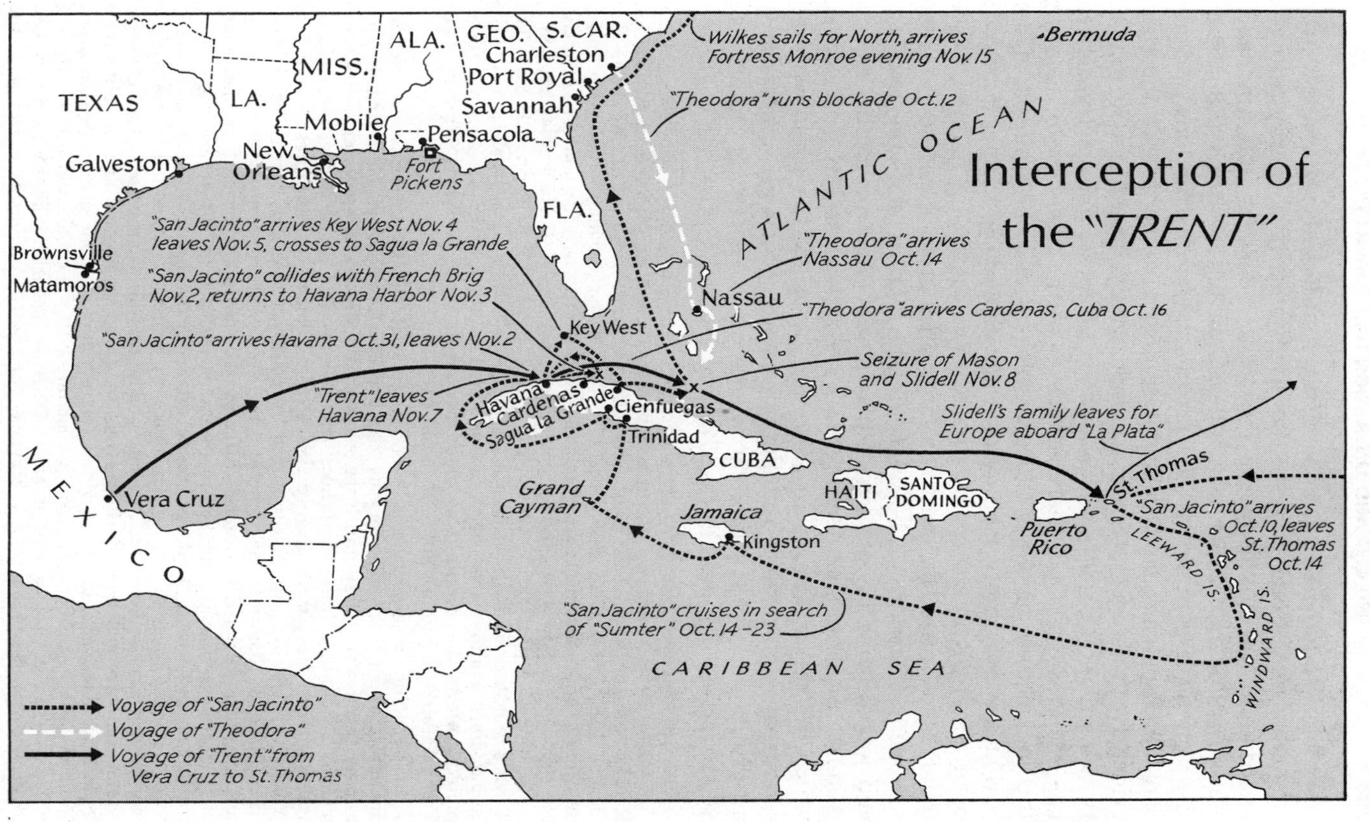
Interception of the "TRENT"
TEXAS
LA.
MISS.
ALA.
GEO.
S. CAR.
FLA.
Charleston
Port Royal
Savannah
Mobile
Pensacola
Fort Pickens
New Orleans
Galveston
Brownsville
Matamoros
MEXICO
Vera Cruz
ATLANTIC OCEAN
Bermuda
Wilkes sails for North, arrives Fortress Monroe evening Nov. 15
"Theodora" runs blockade Oct. 12
"Theodora" arrives Nassau Oct. 14
Nassau
"Theodora" arrives Cardenas, Cuba Oct. 16
Seizure of Mason and Slidell Nov. 8
Slidell's family leaves for Europe aboard "La Plata"
"San Jacinto" arrives Key West Nov. 4 leaves Nov. 5, crosses to Sagua la Grande
"San Jacinto" collides with French Brig Nov. 2, returns to Havana Harbor Nov. 3
"San Jacinto" arrives Havana Oct. 31, leaves Nov. 2
"Trent" leaves Havana Nov. 7
Key West
Havana
Cardenas
Sagua la Grande
Cienfuegas
Trinidad
CUBA
Grand Cayman
Jamaica
Kingston
HAITI
SANTO DOMINGO
Puerto Rico
St. Thomas
"San Jacinto" arrives Oct. 10, leaves St. Thomas Oct. 14
LEEWARD IS.
WINDWARD IS.
"San Jacinto" cruises in search of "Sumter" Oct. 14–23
CARIBBEAN SEA
Voyage of "San Jacinto"
Voyage of "Theodora"
Voyage of "Trent" from Vera Cruz to St. Thomas

dispatches found aboard, and, highly significantly, to make a prize of the *Trent*. Force was to be used only if necessary and the assignment was to be carried out with "delicacy and kindness." Fulfilment of these orders would have gone far towards legitimatizing the American action. But Fairfax disobeyed instructions, did not capture dispatches, and deliberately failed to confiscate the ship, evidently thinking that such a course would be a lesser affront to British pride.[13] Using a token display of force, Fairfax transferred the commissioners and their secretaries to the *San Jacinto*, ignoring the indignation of the *Trent*'s passengers and the protests of her master and Admiralty mail agent. Back aboard the frigate, Fairfax at once paraded some forceful arguments to justify his failure to take the *Trent* as prize. By putting a large prize crew upon the *Trent*, he reasoned, Wilkes would be weakening his battery and crew numbers and jeopardizing his chance of playing an effective combat role in Admiral du Pont's impending fleet operations against Port Royal, which Wilkes was eager to join. Furthermore, the capture would seriously inconvenience numerous passengers, and unnecessarily interrupt the *Trent*'s trading operations. Apparently convinced, Wilkes agreed to permit the *Trent* to proceed upon its voyage.[14]

---

13. D. M. Fairfax, "Captain Wilkes's Seizure of Mason and Slidell," in R. U. Johnson and C. C. Buel, eds., *Battles and Leaders of the Civil War* (N.Y., 1887-1889), II, pp. 136-137. The *Trent* incident has been much described (and romanticized). For the *San Jacinto*'s voyage, and the incident, see report by a Newport *Herald* reporter aboard, in *NYT*, November 26, 1861, p. 3. Wilkes' report and orders are in *ORN*, Ser. 1, Vol. 1, pp. 129-132. The *Trent*'s master refused to produce his ship's papers, a violation of the *San Jacinto*'s undeniable right of search. The account in the text was completed before the author was able to consult Gordon Harris Warren, "The Trent Affair" (unpublished Ph.D. thesis, Indiana, 1969).

14. The suggestion has been made that the Confederate government deliberately tried to engineer the capture of their envoys on a British ship, hoping for a war. (Case and Spencer, pp. 190-194.) The argument relies upon hearsay, including London rumors that Wilkes had made a deal with Mason and Slidell in Havana to arrange the capture. This accusation presupposes that Wilkes was a traitor, and is supported by no direct evidence. Nor is it consistent with Mason's account: his reaction to the actual interception was one of surprise, and he hastily secreted his dispatch bag with the British mail agent on the packet—hardly the action of one in on a plot. There are other difficulties in the theory that Richmond planned the capture in advance. It is hardly consistent with the original plan to cross to England in the *Nashville* (whose capture would of course have been entirely legitimate). Again, it was circumstance which caused the envoys to come to Havana and to stay quite so long, for the *Theodora*'s original program included the alternatives of going from Nassau to St. Thomas or another island, with the clear intention of catching a transatlantic packet as soon as possible. Any deal with Wilkes would have had to be spontaneously devised in Havana, for the *San Jacinto*'s presence in the area was not known until it touched at Cienfuegos.

Since the "great rapprochement" which took place between England and the United States in the first decades of the twentieth century, American historians have leant over backwards to see the British viewpoint in civil war wrangles. In the case of the *Trent*, probably the most perilous issue between the nations since the War of 1812, they have almost to a man accepted Wilkes' action as a simple infraction of international law. Yet the legal issues were by no means clear cut.

The right of belligerent vessels to visit and search neutral vessels to ascertain identity, to discover contraband of war or other evidence of unneutral activity, was well established in the law of nations. Britain had exercized that right arrogantly in past wars and could least of all complain of its use by the *San Jacinto*. These arguments applied, of course, only if a state of war existed, and during the crisis serious argument was conducted on the premise that the rebels were belligerents. The British were obliged to do so by their neutrality decree, the Americans by the fact that if they did not their case was lost at once. As Sumner was to contend in the Senate, if the envoys were not belligerents, Wilkes' proceedings were "indubitably illegal and void," as the men became political offenders and entitled to the asylum of foreign jurisdiction.[15]

More tendentious was the question of contraband. The United States, like all nations at war, could obviously restrict neutral commerce with the enemy in materials of war. Difficulties arose rather over the ill-defined category sometimes known as "conditional contraband," articles not normally contraband but capable in certain circumstances of sustaining an enemy's war effort. If demonstrably destined for hostile use such articles were subject to confiscation, although habitually neutral powers like the United States favored a narrow rather than a broad interpretation of goods. Legal disputes classically occurred over the nature of articles subject to capture, the possibility of a hostile use for articles, the existence of a hostile destination (either immediately or ultimately) for goods, and the degree of partisanship attributable to neutral shipowners and their agents. Confiscation usually implied confiscation of the neutral ship and its contents (including passengers), and its submission before a prize court for adjudication.

The long years of maritime peace following the War of 1812 had led to milder conventions of sea warfare. During the Crimean War Britain and France had exercized novel self-restraint in their

15. *Cong. Globe.*, 37 Cong., 2 Sess. (January 9, 1862), p. 245.

handling of neutral commerce with Russia. The Paris agreements made at the close of hostilities seemed to presage an era of enlightenment compatible with the pacifist views of the international free-traders. But opposing trends were at work, connected with the development of military science and the increasingly close relationship between commerce and the conduct of war. The idea of war being confined to a fixed arena was being made irrelevant by the expansion of railroads and general communications, which made possible the provisioning and arming of belligerent countries from adjoining neutral territory. As the distinctions between neutral and belligerent theaters dissolved, and war tended to become total, the narrow definitions of contraband became increasingly inconvenient to warring powers. The Civil War forced the United States to take a leading role in eroding neutralist conventions it had previously championed, particularly as it tried to devise solutions to two problems: by extending the old British doctrine of "continuous voyage" it sought to prevent neutrals from sending goods indirectly to the enemy via neutral ports; while in the case of the *Trent* it attempted to expand the doctrine of contraband to encompass enemy agents, even envoys, travelling on missions essentially hostile in character.

The *Trent* affair raised two important legal issues: (a) whether despatches were contraband, and whether Wilkes' act could be justified as interception and capture of dispatches; and (b) whether the carriage of persons in the diplomatic service of the enemy was analogous to the carriage of contraband or an example of unneutral service.

On British precedents, but not on American, dispatches could be contraband. Lord Stowell (Sir William Scott) had ruled in various cases during the Napoleonic wars that ships carrying enemy dispatches were liable to capture and adjudication; and that doctrine was still cherished at the Admiralty. The Queen's proclamation of neutrality moreover enumerated dispatches among contraband articles. The British Foreign Secretary eventually chose to argue that the dispatches carried by the *Trent* could not be contraband as the voyage was to neutral territory, Danish St. Thomas. But a strong view of belligerent rights might hold that a ship carrying dispatches relating to the war's conduct, likely to give succor to the enemy or likely to foment foreign conspiracies against the integrity of the United States, might fairly be confiscated despite a neutral destination. Indeed the late American jurist Henry Wheaton had argued this case.[16] Wilkes' contention that men could be "the embodiment of despatches" was more amateurish (Henry Reeve declared that it "either originated in an astounding ignorance of the first principles of maritime law, or it was the last resort of a desperate case"[17]); but a variant on the theme was later argued by at least one American authority, Francis Wharton. If diplomatic agents knowingly acted as couriers of dispatches promoting belligerent designs, he claimed, then the dispatches became contraband and the agent was exposed to the "same taint and . . . contingencies."[18]

Much heated debate centered around the proposition that diplomats forfeited claims to inviolability, and could be classed as a type of contraband, if it could be shown that their passage on a neutral ship was of material aid to a belligerent's war operations. Confiscation of the *Trent* might conceivably have been in order if the role of the emissaries could be assimilated to that of military or naval persons in enemy service, for no dispute existed that carriage of such personnel exposed a ship to condemnation. More than this, it was realistic to argue that such ships might be captured even without enemy destination, for it was absurd to limit the scope of war operations to enemy-held territory.

Inconveniently for the north the erosion of the idea of diplomatic inviolability had only been intimated, not established, judicially and the precedents did not exactly fit. Scott in the case of the *Orozembo* (1806) had suggested that civil functionaries of a warring power "if sent for a purpose intimately connected with the hostile operations" might fall under the same rule as military persons, but this was *obiter dicta* only. In the case of the *Caroline* (1808) he had declared that "you may stop the ambassador of your enemy on his passage." This was widely quoted in the north, and used officially by Seward, but out of context: Scott had relied upon the authority of the Swiss jurist Vattel who had applied the rule only in the instance of an ambassador who chanced to pass through an enemy's territory. To go further than this seemed an enormity to the nineteenth century mind. The trend of civilized practice had been rather to treat military personnel as an exception to a general rule giving protection to belligerent citizens sailing under a neutral

16. *Elements of International Law* (6th ed., 1855), p. 570. Later writers even claimed that such noxious dispatches might be removed without bringing in the vessel for adjudication. See Charles Cheney Hyde, *International Law, Chiefly as Interpreted and Applied by the U.S.* (Boston, 1922), II, p. 644.

17. *Edinburgh Rev.*, CXV, p. 275.

18. Wharton, *International Law Digest* (Washington, 1886), III, pp. 451-453.

flag. It was widely held that special protection should be afforded ambassadors on the high seas on the presumption that diplomatic missions were peaceful until the contrary was proved. Jefferson Davis was quick to accuse the United States of violating the rights of embassy "for the most part held sacred even amongst barbarians by seizing our ministers while under the protection and within the dominions of a neutral nation."[19] The new American doctrine, although logical, raised scarifying vistas of ruthless wartime interference with commerce which really require a twentieth century mind to accept.

It is possible to theorize that sufficient grounds existed, from a vantage point of high belligerent rights, to permit the confiscation of the *Trent* and the adjudication of the issues before a competent tribunal. However Wilkes, by heeding his first lieutenant's advice, had prevented the decision of such contentious questions by the proper authority, the prize court of the captors. America's strongest case, based on seizure of contraband dispatches (in fact concealed on the packet), was at once destroyed. Wilkes' justification for allowing the ship to proceed was cogent and humane, but seemed hardly to mitigate the assumption of arbitrary powers of arrest by a naval officer. Sumner, in a senate speech, later compared Wilkes' act with the outrage of impressment, which he described as the arrogant process by which men under the protection of the neutral American flag, "without any form of trial, and at the mere mandate of a navy officer, who for the moment acted as a judicial tribunal, were dragged away from the deck which should have been to them a sacred altar."[20] Ironically Britain, having since abandoned the right of impressment, was to protest against the *San Jacinto* in terms which closely resembled the persistent complaints of America against British pretensions during the Napoleonic wars. And on that issue of national honor the Americans finally had no alternative but to wage war in 1812.

After extracting Mason and Slidell from the *Trent*, Wilkes cruised north, was too late to participate in the fall of Beaufort, and berthed at Fortress Monroe on Friday November 15. There he

---

19. "Message to Confederate Congress," Richmond, November 18, 1861.

20. See *Cong. Globe*, 37 Cong., 2 Sess. (January 9, 1862), pp. 242-243. There were important differences between the impressment of seamen by British cruisers which claimed them as citizens, and the American seizure of enemy emissaries. But the right of a naval officer to be summary judge and jury was at stake in both cases.

told reporters that he had acted on his own initiative: ". . . he had done right, and said that, right or wrong these men had to be secured, and if he had done wrong, he could do no more than be cashiered for it."[21] His dispatches were forwarded by special train to Washington where Welles took them at once to the President. The *San Jacinto* subsequently took its prisoners to Fort Warren at Boston, and its captain to a Roman triumph in the north.

The traditional version of the *Trent* affair emphasizes the uncritical jubilation with which the north met the news of the exploit, and gives the impression that public opinion unanimously discountenanced ideas of reparation. The truth is rather more complicated. It is true that New York, and other places, exhibited the most extravagant joy at the arrest of the "arch-traitors." Experienced lawyers such as Richard A. Dana were swept off their feet by Wilkes' "noble act," and the sober *New York Times* spoke (with a hint of irony) of consecrating another Fourth of July to him. This was explicable enough. There was simple joy at discomforting the south, and also satisfaction at cheeking America's old arch-rival. The north was hungry for victories: the army's humiliation at Bull Run in July and Ball's Bluff in October had been followed by naval reverses. Rebel activities on the Potomac even threatened to cut Washington's communications. Then came in quick succession the Port Royal success (the papers minimizing the fact that the rebels had perhaps needlessly abandoned the fort after only a skirmish) and the "nabbing" of Mason and Slidell. Exaggerated hopes were raised of foiling southern diplomacy. It was expected that vital papers supposedly taken in the commissioners' baggage would expose Confederate plotting abroad, might reveal that Richmond was offering advantageous treaties to the powers in return for armed intervention. There was speculation that Davis had offered to place a European prince on a Confederate throne, with English backing. Wilkes' coup was viewed in the light of new naval pressures against enemy coastal defences, and of McClellan's pending offensive on the rebel lines in Virginia: ". . . the intelligence about their Commissioners will spread dismay throughout the insurgent States, and go far to break up the whole rotten fabric of the rebellion."[22]

But right from the start there was nervousness over Britain's reaction and a confusion of voices concerning compensation. Ex-senator Robert C. Winthrop of Massachusetts hoped that Seward

21. *NYT*, November 17, 1861.
22. *NYH*, November 17, 1861.

would be prudent in his management of the arrest case: "It gives undoubted cause for complaint, and the complaint ought not to be met with defiance."[23] The stock exchange did not reflect the bravado of New York's Irish-Americans. Even the *Herald*, notoriously anti-British, was subdued in its initial reaction. It saw that Wilkes' act could be construed as a violation of America's long-standing position on right of search. While opposing return of the prisoners, the *Herald* stressed that Wilkes had not been authorized to make the capture:

> . . . it is more than probable that the government will disavow the proceeding, apologise for it, promising never to do it again, and perhaps reprimand the naval officer for permitting his zeal to outstrip his discretion.[24]

Horace Greeley's *Tribune* conceded: "If Great Britain demands the liberation of these gentlemen, and reparation for their capture, we propose to sustain such response as our Government shall see fit to make." And Greeley spoke of dealing "wisely and generously" with the "venerable penitent," England.[25]

American attitudes are better understood if we remember that American jurists largely followed British precedents, and supported an expanded view of belligerent rights. Northerners concluded that England could remonstrate only by repudiating policies she had always stoutly defended: ". . . the chalice, which the government of Great Britain has so freely, during the present century, proferred to others, is, for once, commended to her own lips . . . ."[26] Intensive public discussion took place over the legal issues at stake: ". . . in the streets even Grotius, Puffendorf, Vattel and Wheaton are learnedly appealed to for justification."[27] It was widely believed that the *Trent* had unneutrally carried contraband of war, and that the British themselves upheld the right to arrest ambassadors of a hostile power on their way to a neutral country. The failure to take the packet in for adjudication was noticed, but at first hardly recognized as the Achilles heel of the northern case. Allowing the *Trent* to proceed was regarded as an act of forbearance, relinquishing a right rather than providing England with a grievance. Public

---

23. Winthrop to John P. Kennedy, November 18, 1861, *MHSP*, XLV, p. 82.

24. *NYH*, November 17, 1861.

25. *NYDT*, November 18, 1861.

26. *NYH*, November 19, 1861.

27. *NYT*, November 17, 1861.

confusion also arose between peacetime and wartime rights of search, practices of impressment and the right of visit claimed by Britain in suppression of the slave trade.

Domestic politics soon intruded into the debate. The country's Copperhead and Peace Democrat press assumed, with suspicious rapidity, an excitedly anti-British posture. Baltimore seethed with rumors, spread by rebel sympathizers, that the United States' "violation" of international law would issue in a fight with England. The secessionists clearly wanted to pitch the north into a war on many fronts. They were exploiting over-zealous patriotism to discredit the Atlantic peace apostles. The effect was to throng the peace camp with Radical Republicans and loyalist Unionists.

The angriest war of words was fought in New York. The *World*, *Tribune*, and *Times* accused Bennett's *Herald* of treasonable designs. (Writing from Washington, the London *Times*' correspondent W. H. Russell thought that the *Herald* was "playing the game of the confederates" by inflaming the masses against England.[28]) Bennett riposted with a withering attack upon "the quaking of timid and interested abolition croakers."[29] The heat in the conflict can be partly attributed to the political dogfight then raging over the New York mayoralty elections.

The *Herald*, together with the New York *Express*, *Journal of Commerce*, and many of the old Seward Republicans, supported the Peace Democrat mayor Fernando Wood. Greeley's *Tribune* and W. C. Bryant's *Evening Post* sponsored the millionaire Republican, and eventual victor, George Opdyke. Wood was an old friend of Buchanan's and had been a financial backer of Stephen A. Douglas. He had pleased prosouthern New Yorkers in January by slighting Lincoln when the President-elect passed through the city on his way to Washington. The *Tribune* now gleefully printed correspondence between Wood and Robert Toombs of Georgia to show the mayor's Copperhead sympathies. The *Trent* affair enabled Greeley to argue that Wood's domestic policies and Bennett's overseas designs were of a piece: "They hope either by creating internal divisions among ourselves, or else by involving us in a foreign war, to compel us to submit to the demands of the South, and to acknowledge the Southern Confederacy."[30] Were not the *Herald*'s reporters paid to write editorial articles for Jeff Davis?

---

28. London *Times*, December 10, 1861.
29. *NYH*, November 21, 1861.
30. *NYDT*, November 26, 1861.

The *Herald* had for a decade blamed "our abolition stock-jobbing organs" for inflaming the slavery issue, and thus serving as the handtool of an England which wanted the Union split asunder. Bennett now skilfully linked the Opdyke supporters in an unholy alliance with unpopular groups in the north—with antislavery fanatics, war profiteers and Wall Street speculators, Tammany Hall and the seaboard Brahmin class. These groups were backing down before Britain either because, like Sumner, they fawned upon the English, or because they had vested interests in the present war. The *Tribune*, *Times*, and *World* he accused of having heavy investments in stocks and shares which the war scare was devaluing. Proclaiming a second American Revolution about to begin, Bennett called for the hanging of abolitionists and appeasers. England was a "toothless old lion," and the United States never so well prepared for a foreign war. Less than a year after Sumter, "we shall have arisen to a position of . . . military and naval might, which has no parallel in history." Super-optimistically, the *Herald* saw the rebellion about to cave in, when there would be a million men in arms "left free to settle the question of Mason and Slidell and all old scores with England . . . ."[31]

This was dangerous nonsense to the "one war at a time" school. By November 21 Greeley was declaring return of the prisoners consistent with American honor: "If Great Britain is ready for a broad acceptance of the principle that free ships make free goods, it does not become us to object."[32] "Our neglect to seize the ship [the *World* admitted] was our own fault."[33] Both the *World* and *Times* put in a good word for Britain's neutrality policy, which well comported with northern interests. Britain had denied shipping bases to both belligerents, which greater hurt the south. Britain accepted the legality of the blockade, and respected the belligerent right of search. Ironically, the north was relying in the *Trent* affair upon a wartime right of search, yet it denied the basis upon which that right rested, namely, the south's belligerent status. Wilkes' act in peacetime would have been a purely municipal one and "outrageous trespass" upon another nation's rights.

Conflicting evidence exists concerning Lincoln's reaction to the seizure. To Edward Everett he expressed satisfaction, to Welles

31. *NYH*, November 21-26, 1861.
32. *NYDT*, November 21, 1861.
33. *NYW*, November 21, 1861.

fear that the prisoners "would be elephants in our hands."[34] Contemporaries recollected in later tranquillity, helped perhaps by hindsight, that Lincoln was sleepless over the affair, and spoke of restoring the men and of sticking to American principles.[35] An "inside" newspaper account, suppressed for a short time by the government, held that Lincoln had argued for restoration (if demanded) at a cabinet held soon after news of the seizure: "He said it was doubtful if the course of Captain Wilkes could be justified by international law; and that at all events, he could not afford to have two wars upon his hands at the same time."[36] But if Lincoln ever considered a spectacular conciliatory gesture, his resolve did not survive cabinet and public opposition. Of the ministers only Montgomery Blair, Postmaster-General, denounced Wilkes' act (it was "unauthorised, irregular and illegal," he said, and wanted the men shipped back to England on the *San Jacinto*.[37]). Seward was noncommittal (a becoming role if he had really been implicated in plans to have the *Trent* stopped). England, he said, was not going to fight over "a couple of slave envoys."[38] Instructively, he did not bother to write to his London embassy on developments until November 30, an omission which infuriated Adams, who did not know until December 16 if the seizure was authorized. In that dispatch Seward advised mollifying the British, who were to be told that Wilkes had acted without orders. But only a week earlier Shufeldt in Havana was officially congratulated by Frederick Seward, the assistant Secretary of State, and assured that

> the course adopted by Captain Wilkes in his late proceedings after consultation with you was entirely in accordance with the principles of international law laid down by the best and most authoritative writers on the subject . . . It gives the Department pleasure to acknowledge the great importance of the service which has been rendered by Captain Wilkes to his country.[39]

---

34. Lincoln to Everett November 18, 1861, in Basler, ed., *Collected Works of Lincoln,* V, 26; Gideon Welles, "Capture and Release of Mason and Slidell," *Galaxy* (1873), p. 647.

35. See Carl Sandburg, *Abraham Lincoln: The War Years* (N.Y., 1939), I, p. 364; B. J. Hendrick, *Lincoln's War Cabinet* (Boston, 1946), pp. 204-205.

36. *NYDT*, December 31, 1861 (Washington correspondent).

37. Gideon Welles, *Lincoln and Seward* (New York, 1874), p. 186.

38. *NYW*, November 20, 1861.

39. F. W. Seward to R. W. Shufeldt, November 22, 1861, *U.S. National Archives: Consular Records Havana,* Record Group 84; Instructions from State Dept., 1858-1863.

Tradition has it that Charles Sumner, head of the Senate Foreign Relations Committee, was one of the few not swept away by emotionalism and at once condemned America's departure from historic principles; but at least one scholar is sceptical on the point.[40] At any rate by the time Sumner had returned from Boston to Washington on November 30 for the opening of Congress, he discovered that the government was set upon a policy of masterly inaction, of awaiting events, avoiding commitment, and hoping for the best. The best in this case was expressed in the current optimistic hope that Britain would permit the Americans to keep their prey. It was a policy without teeth. Both Lincoln and Seward were disposed to peace, but seem scarcely to have considered what should happen if the British proved intransigent. Only feeble gestures were made toward fortifying the border with Canada. Lincoln revealed his true purpose to Galt, the Canadian financial minister, who on a White House visit (December 4) asked the meaning of fortifications and arms depots appearing on the Great Lakes. Lincoln answered: "We must do something to satisfy the people."[41] Asked about the *Trent* affair, he added, "Oh, that'll be got along with."[42] Seen in conjunction with the government's failure to advance even an elementary contingency plan for war, this frame of mind virtually ensured that no realistic alternative existed to capitulation should the British send an ultimatum backed by an armed threat.

Inconveniently for those who might have to propose a policy of surrender, there were signs that the period of waiting for the British was producing a stiffening of northern attitudes. A string of impressive experts and notaries had declared Wilkes' act justifiable, including the former Secretary of State Edward Everett, William Beach Lawrence (the accomplished editor of Wheaton's *Law of Nations*), the Harvard law professor Theophilus Parsons, the Bostonian jurist George Ticknor Curtis, Charles B. Goodrich, Charles A. Dana, and George Sumner (brother to the senator, whom the London *Times* immediately cast as the real author of the opinion.) On November 30 Welles—no doubt stomaching some pride—publicly congratulated Wilkes. But the secretary was careful to add a rider which was almost

---

40. V. H. Cohen, "Charles Sumner and the Trent Affair," *JSH*, XXII, No. 2 (May, 1956), pp. 205-219.

41. The text of Galt's conversation is in O. D. Skelton, *Life and Times of Sir Alexander Tilloch Galt* (Toronto, 1920), p. 315. See also Sandburg, *Lincoln: War Years*, I, p. 364; Newton, *Lyons*, I, p. 60.

42. Sandburg, p. 364. This phrase however is not in the memorandum as printed by Skelton.

a reprimand: Wilkes' failure to ensure adjudication must not be permitted to constitute a precedent for infractions of neutral obligations. Welles was hedging his bets.[43]

Wilkes, publicly feted at Boston's Faneuil Hall on 26 November (Governor John A. Andrew gave a laudatory speech), received the accolade of the House of Representatives on December 2. The chorus was impressive, but W. H. Russell reported home that "there are many people who in private hold very different language":

> The quiet little tongues of the Stock Exchange are hinting their doubts very unmistakeably, and I venture to assert that if the opinions of the judges of the land were sought privately they would pronounce against 'the bold and patriotic act of Commodore Wilkes.' The best legal authorities in this city [Washington] are against it. But with the moral cowardice which is the result of submission—habitual prostration to the force of the majority—men will neither publish, nor write, nor speak openly what they are free to confess in the study or the conversation corner . . . .[44]

In fact there were public dissenters, including the Washington *National Intelligencer.* Intriguingly, it now and then floated official balloons. We ask, it said, "not whether the arrest is justifiable according to British rulings and precedents, but whether our Government can afford to endorse those precedents and rulings as constituting sound national law, good for all time to come as well as for present emergencies."[45]

Lincoln's annual message, by ignoring altogether the *Trent*, avoided any impression of panic from the administration. It seemed sound judgment not to take high ground in advance of the long diplomatic exchanges expected to ensue. The message was accompanied by the State Department's carefully edited version of the country's diplomatic correspondence for 1861. Critics such as Robert C. Winthrop privately objected to Seward's pugnacity in threatening war against nations recognizing the south. He thought the collection of documents an "extraordinary" one, "of which not more than a dozen pages ought ever to have been published, and not more than two dozen pages ought ever to have been written."[46]

---

43. For his perplexity over the situation Wilkes had placed him in, see Welles, "Capture and Release of Mason and Slidell," *Galaxy* (May, 1873), p. 648.

44. Report from Washington, November 25, 1861, in London *Times,* December 10, 1861.

45. *WNI*, December 14, 1861; also December 9, 1861.

46. R. C. Winthrop to John P. Kennedy, January 2, 1862, *MHSP*, XLV, p. 139. Lincoln's message was dated December 3.

It was a minority view. Northern patriotism was stirred by documents which seemed to reveal an harassed republic, asking nothing but common justice from the powers, meeting with frigid indifference to its plight.

Anti-British feeling was inflamed when, on December 7, news came of the burning of the U.S. merchantman *Harvey Birch* by the rebel steamer *Nashville*, which had subsequently entered Southampton to refit and revictual before resuming her depredations. The *Nashville*, as a public ship of war commissioned by a belligerent power, was permitted by English neutrality laws to enter British ports for provisioning. (There was no time limit on the stay at this time.) The Queen's proclamation only interdicted armed ships and privateers of both sides from carrying prizes into home or colonial ports. The *Nashville* had not violated this provision, as it had burned the *Harvey Birch* to the water and carried only her crew as prisoners. In the English view the *Nashville* was enjoying the same limited hospitality which had been accorded to northern warships, including only a week earlier the *James Adger.* There was confusion on the facts in America, however, and the incident had all the earmarks of becoming a full-blown international squall had it not been overshadowed by the *Trent.* The government's refusal to concede belligerent rights to the south left unresolved the status of Confederate warships. The *Herald*, and many northerners, condemned the *Nashville*'s act as piracy, and accused England of acting in "palpable violation" of the spirit of the neutrality proclamation.[47] Anger over this "outrage" served to assuage the sense of guilt which some undoubtedly felt over Wilkes' aggressiveness, and there was talk in terms of one wrong justifying another and of the need for mutual forgiveness.

Counseling caution at this stage was Caleb Cushing, diplomat and Attorney-General under Pierce and old apostle of manifest destiny. Cushing's role during the *Trent* crisis has not been fully explored, but seems to have been a substantial one. Despite an unsavory reputation with abolitionists as sponsor of the Dred Scott decision and high priest in the old Democrat hierarchy, Cushing offered his legal services to Lincoln who entrusted him with important government affairs. His advice, and that of Sumner's, was to give considerable intellectual authority to the peace cause. Cushing's view was that the United States, although born of

---

47. *NYH*, December 17, 1861.

revolution and accustomed to applaud rebellions abroad without undue discrimination, might now learn to regard more charitably the problems of governments faced by insurgency. Cast by fate in the past as a neutral in the world's wars and accustomed to exaggerate neutral rights, the United States must now learn "that belligerency has its domain of rights":

> God forbid, at all events, that we should tread in that fatal path which other great Governments have trod in modern times, when visited by civil war and threatened with disruption; that is, to plunge wantonly into conflict with neutral Governments on minor and incidental questions, as Great Britain and Spain did, in like circumstances . . . .[48]

It is notorious that, when news arrived in Britain of the "outrage" on the *Trent*, the country rose in patriotic uproar. John Bright, remembering how the frenzy of public opinion had dragged England into the expensive and futile Crimean War, openly castigated the mob fury as "much more the conduct of savages than of Christian and civilized men." In a celebrated speech at Rochdale he accused men of ignoring the complexity of international law, and of forgetting Britain's naval pugnacity in the past. (". . . fifty or sixty years ago, during the wars of that time, there were scores of cases that were at least as bad as this, and some infinitely worse.") What could be more monstrous, he asked, than that Englishmen ". . . at a moment when an accident of this kind occurs, before we have made a representation to the American Government, before we have heard a word from it in reply—should be all up in arms, every sword leaping from its scabbard, and every man looking about for his pistols and his blunderbusses?"[49] The hysteria was indeed extraordinary, matched in the mid-Victorian period perhaps only by the emotion over the Papal Aggression of 1851 and the Indian mutiny of 1857.

There were various precipitants of anger. Wilkes, by his affront to the Union Jack, the mystic symbol of national virility, had touched a raw nerve. Naval histories, and books like Kingsley's *Westward Ho* (1855), had glorified England's seadogs and maritime vigor, providing heroic legend to counteract what Baldwin Brown was to call the

---

48. Letter to *WNI*, December 16, 1861.

49. Rochdale speech, December 12, 1861, in J. E. Thorald Rogers, ed., *Speeches on Questions of Public Policy by John Bright, M.P.* (London, 1868) I, p. 191.

"miserable huckstering spirit of the day."[50] The nation's military image had been tarnished by the fiascos of the Crimea and the near-disaster of the mutiny in India, creating hawkish desire to retrieve reputation (mixed with a saving grace of caution). It was an age when politicians were admonished to stop lick-spittling to bullying powers. In this regard, Prime Minister Palmerston's Tory opponents had fastened upon him a reputation for mercilessly smashing feeble adversaries, while bending low and speaking "in a bondsman's key" to lusty young powers like the United States.

British patriotism had historically favored belligerent naval operations. However, during the Civil War, that patriotism became newly focused upon the protection of British trade and neutral rights against American encroachments. Trade between neutral ports was now "sacred," and alarmists spoke of British commerce being exposed to mortal threat.[51] Wilkes' act personified that threat, against which even retaliatory war seemed justified. Perversely, the most dogged enemies of British adventurism abroad, the Manchester School, now found their international pacifism at odds with their worship of free commerce.

Unfortunately for Anglo-American relations, rumor, suspicion and mutual ill-will had poisoned the atmosphere before the incident. The irritations created in England by the blockade and the "wonderful folly" of the Morrill tariff,[52] were matched by northern resentment at Britain's "premature" declaration of neutrality, its dispatch of troops to Canada, and its participation in the Mexican expedition. Seward had appeared in a menacing role by his revocation of Consul Bunch's exequatur. Unluckily the British were to link Seward's October 14 circular—requesting governors of the seaboard states to reenforce coastal defenses—with the later seizure of Mason and Slidell, although in fact the circular predated by a day the first American news of the envoys' escape through the blockade. The *New York Times* observed: "the London journals persist in ascribing to the administration of President Lincoln . . . (a) wanton craving for a foreign war," while "Mr. Seward figures in the British imagination as a Giant Blunderbore, thirsting day and night for the blood of

---

50. W. E. Houghton, *Victorian Frame of Mind 1830-1870* (New Haven, 1957), pp. 324-325.

51. S. L. Bernath, *Squall Across the Atlantic* (Los Angeles, 1970), p. 151.

52. Bright to Sumner, September 6, 1861, *MHSP*, XLVI, p. 95.

Englishmen."[53] The depredations of rebel cruisers had both inflamed the north and brought the war uncomfortably close to English shores; while the mysterious activities of northern warships on British coasts seemed to foreshadow a deliberate attack upon neutral rights by the U.S. Navy. Englishmen were ready to place the worst possible construction upon the *Trent* affair. Anger blossomed under the assumptions that the act had been deliberately planned by Washington, and that the American government was irrevocably committed to approval of its wisdom and legality.

Britain's *Trent* policy was conditioned by a set of curious circumstances occurring in early November, and subsequently clouded in considerable mystery. Narrative exactness becomes obligatory. Rumors that Mason and Slidell were blockade-running in the West Indies had made the Foreign Office distinctly nervous that the north might try naval interference with neutral shipping in a bid for their capture. Suspense was created by the activities of the U.S.S. *James Adger*, sent by Welles as we have seen across the Atlantic to intercept the *Nashville*—wrongly thought to be carrying the envoys. After fruitless cruising in Channel waters, the *James Adger* berthed in London on November 6, the day that the London *Times* reported the arrival of Mason and Slidell in Cuba. The ship's captain, J. B. Marchand, thus determined to obey orders and return to Chesapeake Bay. But, during the week that elapsed before his departure, his crew apparently boasted that Marchand's real object was to stop the British mail-packet which plied the St. Thomas-Southampton run and was due in England about 11 November.[54] This packet, the *Seine*, had left St. Thomas on October 29, thirteen days after Mason and Slidell had arrived at Cardenas and time enough for them, with ingenuity, to be aboard. The prospect of an American warship intercepting the mailsteamer "with a view of getting possession of the persons of Messrs. Mason and Slidell, or of their credentials or instructions" was so alarming that Hammond, the permanent Under-Secretary for Foreign Affairs, on November 9 asked the crown law officers for an opinion on the legality of such interference. (According to the published naval records Marchand had no such orders, and the time sequence makes it unlikely that

53. *NYT*, December 19, 24, 1861. It complained: "In France we inspired a Tocqueville; in England we but provoked a [Mrs.] Trollope," November 17, 1861.

54. See a somewhat garbled report in Edinburgh *Scotsman*, November 21, 1861.

they would have been issued.) The officers sent their reply to Russell at the Foreign Office on Tuesday November 12. In it they cautiously recognized that the northern man-of-war might stop the steamer, "might board her, examine her papers, open the general mail-bags, and examine the contents thereof . . . ." In their opinion:

> The United States ship of war may put a prize-crew on board the West India steamer, and carry her off to a port of the United States for adjudication by a Prize Court there; but she would have no right to remove Messrs. Mason and Slidell, and carry them off as prisoners, leaving the ship to pursue her voyage.[55]

The officers' decision that the cruiser would "in strictness" be entitled to carry the packet "and all and everything in her" to America hinged on the assumption that the steamer carried enemy dispatches. But adjudication was essential, for as the experts carefully put it:

> The questions, whether any of the documents on board the mail-vessel are despatches contraband of war; and if so, whether they are protected either by the nature of the conveyance, or by the character of the persons to whom they are addressed, or otherwise, are all questions which may admit of doubt and controversy, and do not appear to us to be concluded by authority; but we think the decision of them, in the first instance at all events, belongs to the Prize Court of the captors.

The day before this opinion was delivered, Palmerston received intelligence that Marchand had got "gloriously drunk on brandy" with a Royal Navy officer on Sunday November 10, and had created the impression that he might have orders to take Mason and Slidell out of the *Seine.*[56] Palmerston at once called a high level conference which included Somerset, the first Lord of the Admiralty, Grey, the Home Secretary, Hammond, and five legal bigwigs: Westbury, the Chancellor, Lushington, judge of the High Court of Admiralty, and the three crown law officers, Atherton, Roundell Palmer, and Harding. Palmerston reported the result of their deliberations to the Queen:

---

55. Crown law officers to Russell, November 12, 1861, Adm. 1/5768, in J. P. Baxter 3rd., "The British Govt. and Neutral Rights, 1861-1865," *AHR*, XXXIV, No. 1 (October 1928), Documents Sec. pp. 84-86. Hammond was under the misimpression that the *Nashville* had conveyed the men to Cuba, and that they had probably embarked on the *Seine* at Havana. Cf., Montague Bernard, *The Neutrality of Great Britain during the American Civil War* (London, 1870), p. 225; and his *Two Lectures on the Present American War* (Oxford, 1861).

56. C. F. Adams Jr., "The *Trent* Affair," *MHSP*, XLV, pp. 54-55, citing his father's diary of November 12. Cf. slightly variant version in Ferris, 348.

> . . . the Northern Union being a belligerent is entitled by its ships of war to stop and search any neutral Merchantmen, and the West India Packet is such; to search her if there is reasonable suspicion that she is carrying enemy's despatches, and if such are found on board to take her to a port of the belligerent, and there to proceed against her for condemnation. Such being ruled to be the law, the only thing that could be done was to order the *Phaeton* frigate to drop down to Yarmouth Roads from Portsmouth, and to watch the American steamer, and to see that she did not exercise this belligerent right within the three-mile limit of British jurisdiction, and this was done.[57]

Strangely, Palmerston did not mention that the warship would have no right to take the commissioners out of the packet, although the law officers made it a crucial point when their opinion was written out next day (November 12) for the Foreign Office. Stranger still, the ageing Prime Minister took a meaning the diametric opposite of his law officers in a letter to Delane (editor of the *Times*) describing the meeting:

> . . . much to my regret, it appeared that, . . . this American cruiser might, by our own principles of international law, stop the West Indian packet, search her, and if the Southern men and their despatches and credentials were found on board, either take them out, or seize the packet and carry her back to New York for trial.[58]

Palmerston's version of the legal issues soon got about, and later heartened northerners worried by the *Trent*. (The *World* yelped with glee on December 9 that the news "settles the question that there will be no war with England."[59])

Palmerston, apparently believing that England had a worse case than it did, saw Adams on November 12, to forestall a senseless wrangle,

> . . . to represent to him how unwise it would be to create irritations in this country merely for the sake of preventing the landing of Mr. Slidell, whose presence here would have no more effect on the

---

57. Palmerston to Queen Victoria, November 13, 1861, in A. C. Benson and Viscount Esher, eds., *Letters of Queen Victoria* (London, 1907), III, p. 593.

58. Palmerston to Delane, November 11, 1861, in A. I. Dasent, *Life of John T. Delane* (London, 1908), II, p. 36. This letter caused endless difficulty for historians before Baxter's publication of the law officers' opinion in 1928, for it seemed to suggest that the Crown Law Office changed its mind after news arrived of the actual *Trent* incident. What seems most likely is that Palmerston misunderstood the oral opinions given at the conference on November 11—such aberrations were to become more common in his last years.

59. *NYW*, December 9, 1861. Confused accounts of the decision leaked to the U.S. via the *Scotsman*.

> policy of your Majesty with regard to America than the presence of the three other Southern Deputies who have been here for many months.[60]

Adams hastened to assure Palmerston that Marchand's orders merely directed him to capture the *Nashville*, with the envoys supposedly on her.[61] Adams, according to his diary and report, was careful not to go beyond this. He apparently did not make the remark (attributed to him by Palmerston in a dispatch to the Queen) that "the American steamer had orders not to meddle with any vessel under any foreign flag." Irritation later arose on this point. The interview, at any rate, calmed British fears. The *Seine* arrived safely on November 13, without the envoys, the *James Adger* having sailed for home the day before. Its quarry, the *Nashville*, soon distracted men's attentions by burning the *Harvey Birch*.

The packet *La Plata* arrived at Southampton on November 27, carrying the *Trent*'s passengers, and tidings of Wilkes' perfidy. Commander Williams (retired) the *Trent*'s Royal Mail agent, reported immediately to the Admiralty and was interviewed that afternoon at the Foreign Office. Williams made much of the fact that the outward-bound *Trent* had encountered the *San Jacinto* in St. Thomas between October 10 and 14 in company with some other American warships. This led him to believe that Wilkes had received orders from New York to seize the commissioners.[62] It was an improbable theory (Washington could not have learned of the escape of the men to Cuba before October 25); but it was reinforced by confidential information sent from the British embassy in Paris. General Winfield Scott (recently arrived in Paris after retiring as Union general-in-chief to make way for McClellan), was reported as saying to friends "that the seizure of these envoys was discussed in Cabinet at Washington, he being present, and was deliberately determined upon and ordered; [and] that the Washington Cabinet fully foresaw it might lead to war with England."[63] At this stage, the only evidence on the other side came from Slidell's wife and daughter, passengers on the

---

60. *Letters of Queen Victoria*, III, p. 594.

61. See *ORN*, ser. 1, Vol. 1, pp. 114, 129.

62. Sec. to Admiralty to Hammond, Encl. No. 1, Recd. November 27, 1861, in "corresp. resp. the Seizure of Messrs. Mason and Slidell . . . ," *Br. Parlt. Papers*, LXII (1862), p. 613.

63. Palmerston to Queen Victoria, November 29, 1861, in *Letters of Queen Victoria*, III, pp. 595-596.

La Plata; they told reporters that Lieutenant Fairfax, on boarding the *Trent*, had declared that Wilkes was acting on his own initiative. Wilkes' own Fort Monroe declaration to the same end was not made public in England until American newspapers brought by the *Persia* were published on Monday December 2. By then the British government's deliberations were completed. This timing also meant that the British decision—contrary to common assertion—was unaffected by tidings of northern excitement, the first extensive reportage of which came in the *Persia*.

Palmerston's first reaction was to ask Russell what the government should do. "I answered shortly quoting what Grattan said with reference to another Power, and on another occasion 'the United States Government are very dangerous people to run away from.' "[64] The situation thrust the veteran Prime Minister into a vile mood. He still seemed to labor under the impression that Adams had given an assurance that the American fleet had orders not to molest neutral ships. He now suspected that Adams had deliberately misled him, and Russell was instructed to extract urgently from Adams any information he had on the seizure. The *La Plata's* news had quickly created a sensation. Bright wrote to Sumner from the refuge of the Reform Club that ". . . the ignorant and passionate and 'Rule Brittania' class are angry and insolent as usual."[65] It was clear that irresistible pressure would soon be mounted to force government action. However a strong diplomatic response might seem awkward to Palmerston if he still falsely assumed that the crown law officers had condoned in advance the American action. This difficulty was disposed of on November 28, when the law officers reiterated their opinion of the 12th, declared the *San Jacinto*'s action illegal, and justified a British claim for reparation.[66] Individuals, not officers in the military and naval service of the Confederacy, had been taken by force from a neutral merchantman pursuing a lawful and innocent voyage. The *Trent*, they concluded, had not been carried into an American port for adjudication as a prize and could not, under the circumstances, be considered as having breached international law.

---

64. Russell reports this conversation on the evening of November 27 in his *Recollections and Suggestions 1813-1873* (London, 1875), p. 275.

65. Bright to Sumner, November 29, 1861, *MHSP*, XLV (November, 1911), p. 148.

66. Crown law officers to Russell (printed for cabinet), November 28, 1861, in Baxter, *AHR*, XXXIV, No. 1 (October, 1928), pp. 86-87.

Panic spread on the London Stock Exchange and Liverpool cotton market. Consols declined, Lloyds demanded war risks of five guineas on vessels from New York, and rumors spread that Adams had been given his passports. In Liverpool's Cotton Salesroom an indignation meeting was chaired by James M. Spence, Confederate propagandist and author of the best-selling *American Union* (1861). Turbulently patriotic, the meeting brushed aside legal quibbles. *Reynolds' Newspaper*, of Chartist sympathies, called for an immediate declaration of war because of a lawless and premeditated act by the American executive, unless "the most ample and submissive apology" be received and the men released.[67] Before the law officers' opinion became known, however, legal uncertainties tempered the national debate. The *Times*' city reporter believed that ". . . the Cabinet will be fully supported even in tolerating the act, provided it can be shown to be in conformity with the reciprocal law between the two nations, or the nations of the world generally."[68] The New York *Tribune*'s London correspondent wrote home that the administration papers—including the *Times*, *Morning Post*, *Daily Telegraph*, *Morning Advertiser*, and *Sun*—had received orders "to calm down rather than to exasperate."[69] Certainly the *Times*' editorials preceding the government's weekend decision-making were uncharacteristically mild, the "Thunderer" attempting to restrain emotion by presenting a balanced legal analysis.

Ten minutes before the Cabinet met on November 29, Russell saw Adams, whom the crisis had brought scurrying back to London from a country trip. Adams was obliged to admit ignorance of the affair, but he was able to correct Palmerston's version of their interview about the *James Adger*: he had said that there was nothing in Marchand's instructions to justify him interfering with any foreign ship bringing Mason and Slidell to Europe. This left open the question of orders being sent to other ships. Moran noted in his diary that Adams returned from the interview apprehensive that "we would not be here a month." Only a miracle, Moran thought, could prevent Palmerston from "getting up a war."[70] Henry Adams agreed, not doubting that Palmerston "would be rather glad than otherwise of

---

67. *Reynolds' Newspaper*, December 1, 1861.

68. *Times*, November 28, 1861.

69. *NYDT*, December 19, 1861. Outright support for the north came only from Bright's *Morning Star*, which judged the act lawful but impolitic. Even the normally friendly *Daily News* attacked Wilkes.

70. *Journal of Benjamin Moran*, II, pp. 914-915.

this opportunity to recover his waning popular strength . . . all the American party were cast down and anxious."[71]

The only absentee from the fourteen man cabinet was the pronorthern Privy Seal, the Duke of Argyll, who was in France. But even he was "all against submitting to any clean breach of International Law, such as I hardly doubt this has been."[72] Also attending were the three law officers and Robert Phillimore, admiralty advocate and writer on maritime law. Agreement was soon reached on two propositions: that a demand should be made for American disavowal of Wilkes' action, together with restoration of the prisoners and an apology; and that armed preparations must be set in train to back up this strong stand. There was less agreement over the language of the note, and the nature of the military strategy to be adopted. It was rumored that opposition to the "technical" legal view taken by the Admiralty and law officers came from "the highest legal sages in and out of the Cabinet. Several names of very imposing legal authority are mentioned as of opinion that a higher and larger issue should have been taken."[73] However Russell and a majority of ministers apparently feared that to take a more modern and generous view of neutral rights would not serve permanent British interests. Also, it would almost certainly lead to an interminable paper controversy with the State Department. As the *Manchester Guardian* warned:

> Mr. Seward . . . is probably at this moment preparing, in anticipation of such a despatch one of those long-winded state papers which U.S. ministers more than all statesman love to expand in . . . It is better that a decision should be speedily come to.[74]

Also overriden were the objections of Gladstone, who later told Argyll that at the meetings

> I thought and urged that we should hear what the Americans had to say before withdrawing Lyons, for I could not feel sure that we were at the bottom of the law of the case, or could judge here and now what form it would assume.[75]

71. Anonymous article (by Adams) in *NYT*, December 19, 1861, q. C. I. Glicksberg, "Henry Adams and the English and American Press in 1861," *Journalism Q.*, XVI (1939), p. 251.

72. Argyll to W. E. Gladstone, November 29, 1861, q. E.D.A., I, p. 212.

73. *Manchester Guardian*, December 6, q. *NYW*, December 25, 1861.

74. *Guardian*, December 6.

75. Gladstone to Argyll, December 3, 1861, q. Morley, *Gladstone*, pp. 73-74.

With the aplomb appropriate to the world's most powerful executive, the cabinet determined to preclude the Americans from arguing any countercase. They skirted legal potholes by simply declaring that "a gross outrage and violation of international law has been committed." Cabinet resolved to meet next day, when it would consider a dispatch to be drafted by Russell. This would demand the withdrawal of Lyons if the Americans refused to make the reparations.[76] Russell suggested an embargo on arms and war materials to the United States and was supported by Palmerston who felt that "this measure would not only diminish the Union's fighting power but might deter it from risking war at all."[77] According to participants, Palmerston was in a most bellicose mood, at one stage advocating that the Channel fleet be dispatched immediately to American waters.[78] Decision was postponed on these matters, perhaps because of pressure from Cobden, who called in twice at Downing Street while the meeting was in progress. Through Cornewall Lewis, Cobden apparently prevailed upon the Prime Minister not to make a provocative fleet movement.[79]

The British government had one compelling difficulty to dispose of before it could begin sword-rattling in earnest. It must make sure of France, must ensure at least French neutrality, so as to get a free hand in America if there was war. Despite the agreement reached by the two powers to act together on America's civil war problems, suspicion of French ambition had remained a controlling assumption of Palmerston's foreign policy. The Queen considered France the "one danger in Europe," and more likely than any other power to profit from unsettled world conditions.[80] Only a fortnight before the *Trent*, Palmerston had informed Windsor Castle that Napoleon regarded the English alliance as "precarious."[81] Foreign Office intelligence now suggested that the Americans were attempting,

---

76. Palmerston to Queen Victoria, November 29, 1861, in *Letters of Queen Victoria*, III, pp. 595-596.

77. Palmerston to Granville, November 29, 1861, in Lord Edmond Fitzmaurice, *Life of . . . Second Earl Granville* (London, 1905), I, p. 401.

78. Cf. account of his private secretary, Evelyn Ashley, in Sir Horace Rumbold, *Recollections of a Diplomatist* (London, 1902), II, p. 83.

79. Rumbold, 84. See also Bright to Sumner, November 30, 1861 in *MHSP*, XLV, p. 149. Forster also deplored an Anglo-American war in a speech at Bradford on November 30.

80. Queen Victoria to Palmerston, January 3, 1861, in *Regina v. Palmerston*, p. 297.

81. Palmerston to Queen Victoria, November 13, 1861, in *Letters to Queen Victoria*, III, p. 594.

clumsily, to exploit this rift. General Scott was rumored to be claiming that Washington had sent him to seek a French alliance in case of an Anglo-American war, using as bait the restoration of the French province of Canada. Palmerston ridiculed the idea: ". . . the French Government is more disposed towards the South than the North, and is probably thinking more about Cotton than about Canada . . . ."[82] But Scott's move might fit a pattern. Palmerston agreed with Clarendon in regarding the seizure of the envoys as "a deliberate and premeditated insult."[83] They feared that Seward was trying to fix a quarrel upon England. In such a war, with France an ally or neutral, lay the north's best opportunity for creating a face-saving peace settlement with the south. Lyons had smelt this trap, and so did Ambassador Cowley in Paris. Cowley wrote: "I wish I could divest myself of the idea that the North and South will not shake hands over a war with us."[84]

London's *sine qua non* of benevolent French neutrality was soon assured. France and the United States had in the past signed treaties of friendship and commerce which stood as a monument to the cause of neutral rights. These nations had agreed on minimal lists of contraband, the immunity of enemy persons covered by neutral flag unless they were combatants in enemy service, and the safety of cargo and passengers carried between neutral ports. America's violation of these principles was shocking to French opinion, and fears were voiced that similar assaults might be launched by the Federals against French shipping. The situation, moreover, offered some intriguing opportunities for French diplomacy. There is little evidence that Napoleon seriously considered the riskiest move, that of angling for war so that France might obtain cotton and a chance to make some Machiavellian gains in Europe. On the contrary, French policy was consistent with a conscientious desire for peace, preferably with the conspicuous aid of French good

---

82. Palmerston to Queen Victoria, November 29, 1861, *ibid.*, p. 596. The *Opinion Nationale*, influenced by Prince Napoleon, published a letter about this time, ostensibly from Canada, urging incorporation of the Canadian provinces into the USA. *Manchester Guardian*, December 6, 1861.

83. Palmerston to Russell, November 29, 1861, *PRO, G & D*, 22:21, q. Bell, *Palmerston*, II, p. 294.

84. Cowley to Russell, December 2, 1861, q. EDA, I, p. 214. The *Morning Post*, no doubt inspired by Palmerston, reflected this view. But the conservative *Standard* commented: "Mr. Seward counts on a broken reed if he reckons on assistance from the Slaveholding States in the struggle to which he foolishly and wickedly challenges the might of Great Britain," November 30, 1861.

offices. France would attempt to persuade the north to retreat, thus emerging once more as the champion of the rights of smaller neutrals, while Britain for the present would have to abide Gallic sermonising against "the vexatious practices of earlier days." Conceivably Britain might even be maneuvered into accepting French principles of maritime law. French support for the British position would help to recement the alliance. As a *quid pro quo* Napoleon surely hoped for a free hand in Mexico or at least more cordial cooperation by its ally in the tripartite mission just started.[85] Thouvenel raised the *Trent* issue at a cabinet meeting at Compiègne on November 28. A rapid decision was made to back up the British in any protest, while maintaining neutrality. The Emperor and his ministers were apparently incensed and ready to recognize the Confederacy if Britain did. Mercier would be instructed to place a bold expression of French opinion before the Union government. This gratifying information was in Russell's hands within days.

The English commercial world meantime prayed that peace with honor was attainable, and was heartened by the antinorthern reaction of France and other neutrals. Washington would surely realize its international isolation, and all might be well provided the mob was resisted by Yankees of the respectable trading classes. Amidst the general tumult in the British Isles, some voices called for calm. Bright's *Morning Star* predicted American capitulation as the north "would be mad to add to its troubles by a European war."[86] Dublin's *Freeman's Journal* accused the British of provoking violence by gun-running to the south.[87] The Manchester *Examiner* put the case for free trade liberalism by asserting that England's mercantile position forbade the luxury of "reckless politics." War would wreck the new formed Liberal party, "and a Tory Administration will once more ride rough-shod over all matters of domestic and foreign policy." The privilege of the strong was "to be magnanimous and even forgiving."[88] Palmerston's own disposition was, however, better expressed by the *Morning Post* which forecast American submission in the face of superior might: "In one month we could sweep all the *San Jacintos* from the seas, blockade the Northern ports, and turn to a direct and speedy issue the tide of the war now raging."[89]

---

85. L. M. Case and W. F. Spencer, *The U.S. and France: Civil War Diplomacy* (Phil., 1970), p. 196 and following.

86. *Morning Star*, November 27, 30, 1861.

87. Quoted *NYDT*, December 19, 1861.

88. Manchester *Examiner*, November 30, 1861, q. *NYDT*, December 19, 1861.

89. *Morning Post*, November 30, 1861.

It was scarcely the case that the Tories were crowding the Liberals into a foray upon the north, as Americans charged. The private papers of the Conservative leaders do not sustain the conventional view that party officials deeply sympathized with the south in the Civil War. The leadership tended to align against the Palmerstonian mode of meddling in other nations' affairs, and supported strict neutrality. During the *Trent* emergency, the Tory chiefs united behind the government. But in doing so, they were simply sharing current mores, nor did they capitalize on the situation for party benefit.[90]

Clarendon put the quintessential British view in a letter to Cowley. Tame submission before northern power would dangerously erode British prestige, none too high after the bungles of the fifties:

> . . . what additional proof it will be of the universal . . . belief that we have two sets of weights and measures to be used according to the power or weakness of our adversary. I have a horror of war and of all wars one with the U.S. because none would be so prejudicial to our interests, but peace like other good things may be bought too dearly and it never can be worth the price of national honour.[91]

On the morning of the cabinet's vital second meeting, the *Times* avoided sabre-rattling and opened a loophole for the State Department by raising the possibility that the seizure "was the act of the American commander, and was not expressly directed by his Government." Nonetheless it clearly stated its opinion that Washington had "secretly planned the outrage for which we are now asking reparation." It spoke of upholding "our strict rights," and plainly warned Americans that their two nations were on the verge of war.[92]

Cabinet, minus its legal advisers, met at 2:00 p.m. on Saturday, November 30. Russell's draft dispatch for Lyons was watered down with "the help of fourteen people . . . each proposing verbal alterations;"[93] but it was still, in the Prince Consort's opinion, "somewhat meagre." It flatly declared Wilkes' conduct "not justified

---

90. Wilbur Devereaux Jones, "The British Conservatives and the American Civil War," *AHR*, LVIII, No. 3 (April 1953), pp. 529-531.

91. Clarendon to Cowley, November 29, 1861, F.O. 519/178, q. Bourne, p. 247.

92. *Times*, November 30, 1861. Cf. N. Ferris, "The Prince Consort, the 'Times' and the 'Trent' Affair," CWH, VI (1960), pp. 152-156. Ferris first drew attention to the *Times'* moderation.

93. Palmerston to Russell, December 1, 1861, q. Bell, *Palmerston*, p. 295.

by international law" and the *Trent*'s voyage "lawful and innocent." English magnanimity was not overstretched in the key statement:

> Her Majesty's Government are unwilling to imagine that the United States Government will not of their own accord be anxious to afford ample reparation for this act of violence committed by an officer of the United States Navy against a neutral and friendly nation.

Lyons was to propose to Seward as reparation the liberation of the captives and their return to British protection, with an apology "for the insult offered to the British flag."[94] An accompanying letter from Russell instructed Lyons to withdraw the embassy should the Americans refuse compliance. The drafts were immediately sent to Windsor for the Queen's approval.

Gladstone had dined at Windsor on November 28, and recorded that the Queen and Prince Albert spoke much of the American news. Having undertaken to explain to Her Majesty what had occurred at the cabinet that day, Gladstone dined again at the palace on the twenty-ninth; on these visits he may well have sowed some conciliationist seeds.

During the night of Saturday and the early hours of Sunday, the Prince Consort painfully devised a draft which he thought less likely to offend the Americans while still exacting due atonement. He was suffering from heavy catarrh and insomnia, symptoms of typhoid, from which he was to collapse on December 2, and to die on December 14. While it cannot be determined whether his amendments ensured a bloodless victory for British diplomacy,[95] historical folklore is substantially sound in praising his dying effort to preserve Atlantic peace, which he justified as essential to British interests. The phraseology of the Prince's memorandum—the last that he wrote—paralleled that used in recent editorials of the *Times*, which he read conscientiously, although he carefully avoided that paper's asperity of tone.[96] The Queen, he wrote, would like to see a hope expressed that Wilkes did not act under instructions "or, if he did, that he misapprehended them." The U.S. government should be reminded that Britain could not allow its flag to be insulted or its mail communications jeopardized. It should be said that:

---

94. One of the few published versions of this draft is in J. Wheeler-Bennett, "The Trent Affair: How the Prince Consort Saved the U.S.," *Hist. Today*, XI, No. 12 (December 1961), p. 811, from PRO.

95. Cf. Wheeler-Bennett, pp. 813-816.

96. See Ferris, *CWH*, VI (1960), pp. 152-156.

> . . . Her Majesty's Government are unwilling to believe, that the United States Government intended wantonly to put an insult upon this country, and to add to their many distressing complications by forcing a question of dispute upon us, and that we are therefore glad to believe that upon a full consideration of the circumstances of the undoubted breach of International Law committed, they would spontaneously offer such redress as alone could satisfy this country, viz. the restoration of the unfortunate passengers and a suitable apology.[97]

Palmerston and Granville thought the Prince's suggestions "excellent" and cabinet on December 1 modeled a new dispatch upon them. It made reference to the friendly relations long subsisting between the two countries; professed a willingness to believe that the act was unauthorized or the result of a misunderstanding of orders; and hoped that the Americans of their own accord would make the redress required:

> For the Government of the United States must be fully aware that the British Government could not allow such an affront to the national honour to pass without full reparation; and Her Majesty's Government are unwilling to believe that it could be the deliberate intention of the Government of the United States unnecessarily to force into discussion between the two Governments a question of so grave a character, and with regard to which the whole British Nation would be sure to entertain such unanimity of feeling.[98]

In separate instructions Lyons was empowered to offer the Americans time to consider, "not exceeding seven days:"

> If at the end of that time [wrote Russell] no answer is given, or if any other answer is given except that of a compliance with the demands of Her Majesty's Government, your lordship is instructed to leave Washington with all the members of your legation, bringing with you the archives of the legation, and to repair immediately to London.[99]

Influenced no doubt by the spirit of conciliation at Windsor, Russell privately requested Lyons to prepare the ground tactfully before reading the dispatch to Seward, and "to abstain from anything like menace." Lyons was not openly to threaten withdrawal of the legation. If Seward asked the results of an American refusal, "I think

---

97. Theodore Martin, *Life of . . . the Prince Consort* (London, 1880), V, p. 422.

98. Russell to Lyons, November 30, 1861, *ORN*, Ser. 1, Vol. 1, pp. 159-160.

99. Russell to Lyons, *ibid.*, p. 161.

you should say that you wish to leave him and the President quite free to take their own course . . . ." The cabinet, concluded Russell, was disposed "to be rather easy about the apology" but were immovable on restoration. "The feeling here is very quiet but very decided. There is no party about it: all are unanimous."[100] A special messenger carried the dispatches by packet to Queenstown, where on December 2 he embarked on the *Europa* for America.

While the ultimatum was on the high seas, developments began in Britain which should have sobered the warhawks. They are telling clues to later wartime diplomacy. Britain mobilized for an American war, but found it could not dispose of the inherent difficulties of waging it. At the same time there was a swelling of peace opinion as the tragic dimensions of the crisis dawned upon men's minds.

Cabinet promptly acted according to the precepts long recommended by Lord Lyons: negotiate from strength, and prepare for war through Yankee miscalculation. But the military experts favored a quick strike against the unprepared north, and their thinking allowed no scope for prolonged negotiations. On December 3, Secretary of War Lewis submitted to Palmerston a design for a snap expedition against Maine. Launched at the onset of war, a land-sea operation would divert Union soldiers from an attack on Canada and provide desperately needed cover for Canada's vulnerable road links with Nova Scotia. The plan presumed cooperation from the Maine population, hopefully dissatisfied with Lincoln. Probably because of Admiralty scepticism, it was quietly shelved.[101] The cabinet extended the export ban on saltpeter to guns and ammunition, and authorized the dispatch of reinforcements to Canada. Arms for the colonial militia, together with a battery of regular artillery, two infantry battalions and a company of engineers, had been already ordered out. By December 8, this had been increased to four battalions of infantry, three batteries of field artillery and two companies of engineers. Blueprints for a comprehensive defense of Canada were drawn up by the War Office and on December 9 submitted to a war committee consisting of Palmerston, Somerset, Lewis, Newcastle, Granville, and Cambridge.

One of the ministry's first acts had been to alert Vice-Admiral Milne. He was told to keep in touch with Lyons, and advised not to

---

100. Russell to Lyons (pvt), December 1, 1861, in Newton, *Lyons*, I, pp. 62-63.

101. Bourne, 235.

weaken his North American squadron by sending more than a battleship and two corvettes to participate in the tripartite Mexican intervention. Reinforcements were ordered to Milne's fleet, giving him the capacity to implement a tight blockade of the northern coast. The Brazil and Good Hope squadrons were instructed to destroy northern shipping immediately on news of war. The menace of American privateering bulked large in British imaginations, but it was to be minimized by taking defensive precautions in British harbors combined with a decisive naval offensive. The time limit of seven days imposed upon the Americans was in fact designed to give them minimal time to fit out predators. Strategic needs accounted for Russell's determination to extract a plain yes or no from Washington without procrastination. He was despondent about protecting Canada against the Union legions, but reasoned that "An early resort to hostilities will enable us at once to raise the blockade of the South, to blockade the North, and to prevent the egress of numerous ships, commissioned as privateers . . . ."[102]

Told of American complacency, Lewis at the War Office retorted that "we shall soon *iron the smile* out of their face."[103] Palmerston appeared genuinely untroubled at the outcome of events:

> If the Federal Government comply with the demands [he reported to the palace] it will be honourable for England and humiliating for the United States. If the Federal Government refuse compliance, Great Britain is in a better state than at any former time to inflict a severe blow upon, and read a lesson to the United States which will not soon be forgotten.[104]

His philosophy was fatalist and cynical of human nature. Who could predict the actions of a government "not guided by reasonable men?" He would have none of the fashionable Manchester doctrine "that Commercial Intercourse is the best Security for Peace, because it creates Interests which would be damaged by War." Passion, he lectured Russell, "sways the Masses, while Interest acts comparatively on the few." In any case there was no telling whether New York might not fancy its interests furthered by a victorious campaign; and American vanity was only too likely to conjure up deluded expectations of success "if we are not wide awake."[105]

---

102. Russell to Palmerston, December 11, 1861, q. *EDA*, I, p. 224; Russell to Lyons, December 7, 1861, q. Newton, *Lyons*, I, p. 224.

103. Lewis to Twistleton, December 5, 1861, q. Bourne, p. 246.

104. Palmerston to Queen Victoria, December 5, 1861, q. *Regina v. Palmerston*, p. 311.

105. Palmerston to Russell, December 6, 1861, *PRO., G and D*, 22:21; q. Bell, p. 295.

To peace devotees such as Gladstone, the war preparations were "a very sad and heart sickening business . . . ."[106] For Motley in Vienna, the thought of Boston bombarded, the Federal Navy destroyed, occupation of Washington and New York by the Confederates and their English allies was "too much to bear."[107] Adams, who feared that Seward would be truculent and that the ending of his mission was imminent, wrote back to Motley with the morbid consolation that England would be more severely mauled by war in the long run than the United States. England would get her cotton, but at the cost of her present war-profiteering. American ports would be harassed, but the country could not be militarily subdued (a proposition which the War Office already recognized). England in return would earn the bitter enmity of Americans, and world-shaking trading and political realignments would be forged. In Adams' mind, an English alliance with the slave power "must be made only as that of Faust was made, exchanging present enjoyment for eternal condemnation."[108]

Meanwhile John Bright had made his lonely stand against an infuriated people. Supplied with ammunition by Adams, Bright gave his Rochdale speech on December 4. The Union's enterprising consul at Liverpool, Thomas H. Dudley, was at the banquet, and there struck up what was to be a lifelong friendship with Bright. Before the speech Bright told the consul "that he felt the weight of responsibility resting upon him that night heavier than he had ever felt it before." He was depressed that his friend Cobden had declined to come out and sustain him in his stand. Cobden was by now persuaded that north and south could never again lie in the same bed. He knew the future of America lay with the north and antislavery, but thought the Union lacked the power to carry an invasion into the south, or to inflict a crushing defeat. Stalemate would be enough to ensure southern survival. Cobden dared aspire to nothing more ambitious than British nonintervention. "How long" he asked Bright, "will foreign powers look on if nothing decisive be done? I doubt

---

106. W. E. Gladstone to Robertson Gladstone, December 7, 1861, q. *EDA*, I, p. 215. For Gladstone's letters to various clerics on the crisis, see *B.M. Add. Mss.*, 44277 and following.

107. Motley to Adams, in John Lothrop Motley, *Correspondence*, II, pp. 218-219, quoted Ferris, p. 472.

108. Adams to Motley, December 4, 1861, q. Ferris, p. 473.

whether another year's blockade will be borne by the world."[109] Privately he grumbled that Bright would hear nothing against the north.

Bright, predictably, preached on the text of Atlantic kinship, international peace, and the American experiment in freedom. Rashness now would drive a wedge between the two great English-speaking peoples. A populous and free north was a future certainty:

> I pray that it may not be said amongst [this people], that, in the darkest hour of their country's trials, England, the land of their fathers, looked on with icy coldness and saw unmoved the perils and calamities of their children.

To his mind international law was "very unsettled, and, for the most part . . . exceedingly bad." Wilkes' act, whether legal or not, was impolitic. It would almost certainly turn out to be unauthorised. The Americans would make reparation if they believed the act illegal, "for there is no Government in the world that has . . . been so anxious to be guided always by the most moderate and merciful interpretation" of international law.[110] Dudley considered Bright's an act of rare moral courage: "To me it seemed almost like another Curtius, who was willing to plunge into the chasm to save Rome." The Rochdale speech rallied friends of the north, many of whom, like William Forster, had become despondent. But it was roughly handled by the patriots. The *Times* accused Bright of riding in blood up to his saddle-girths to put down the rebellious south: "it seems a pity [his] energy and unscrupulous determination do not rule in the White House, instead of amusing a sixth-rate provincial town in England."[111]

Also on December 4, the Paris press carried a letter from Winfield Scott, denying his alleged confession that Washington had ordered the *Trent*'s seizure. Scott signed the letter (the composition of Bigelow) under advice from Bigelow and Thurlow Weed. Weed, sent to Europe by Seward before the upheaval, came on to London. "Such prompt and gigantic [war] preparations were never known,"

---

109. Thomas H. Dudley, "Three Critical Periods in our Diplomatic Relations with England during the Late War: Personal Recollections," *Penn. Mag. Hist. and Biog.*, XVII, No. 1 (1893), p. 41; Cobden to Bright, December 6, 1861, in Morley, *Cobden*, p. 384; Donald Read, *Cobden and Bright: a Victorian Political Partnership* (London, 1967), pp. 219-221.

110. Rochdale speech, December 4, 1861, by Bright, in Rogers, *Speeches*, I, pp. 167-195.

111. *Times*, December 12, 1861.

he reported to Seward. Even the Anglo-American banking houses were unsympathetic. Baring "is against us 'flat-footed.' Peabody tries to see both sides—ours dimly." With characteristic vigor, Weed set out to right matters, urging Seward to release the men, writing letters to the press, dispersing money to create friendly journalists, making a wide range of personal contacts and interviewing ministers.[112]

The mobilization accentuated scruples about war, although it would be an exaggeration to describe Britain as polarized over the issue. Arbitration grew popular as an acceptable solution. Bright pressed Milner Gibson, president of the Board of Trade and an old free trade colleague, to withdraw from the government if it intended war. He begged Gibson to insist upon arbitration and magnanimity.[113] Simultaneously, through Charles Sumner, he urged the north to arbitrate.

The first church move came from the Quakers. Having maintained strong links with their American brethren for nearly two centuries, and being unyielding in the cause of antislavery, they were tender towards the north.[114] A memorial, drafted by John Hodgkin, was approved by the London Meeting for Sufferings on December 9 for presentation to the Prime Minister and Foreign Secretary. It referred to "the combined ties of blood, of language, of religion, of constitutional freedom, and of commercial interest" which united Britain and the United States. It advocated arbitration, a principle recommended by the powers in the Paris treaty of 1856. How could old friends of antislavery like Palmerston and Russell bring England into cooperation with the south and slavery against the north and freedom? The signatories promised to ask influential American Friends to press their state legislatures for peace. Palmerston refused to see a Quaker deputation from London; and Hodgkin was left to hope that the memorial, promptly printed, "may in some directions and especially with men of Christian feeling, have a sedative effect . . . ."[115] Jonathan Pim, a Dublin Quaker, continued to proselytize the idea of turning over to a congress of the maritime

---

112. Weed to Seward, December 7, 1861, q. Ferris, p. 465; Weed to Bigelow, December 5, 1861, in Bigelow, *Retrospections*, p. 402; and see Van Deusen, *Thurlow Weed: Wizard of the Lobby* (Boston, 1947), Chapter 17.

113. Bright to Milner Gibson, December 7, 1861, Bright *MSS, B.M.*, 43,388, q. Ausubel, *Bright*, p. 124. The London *Dial* denied that England had any real interest at stake; it was not worth war to avenge "a petty insult," December 6, 1861.

114. David Large, "Friends and the American Civil War: The Trent Affair," *Friends Hist. Soc., London J.*, XLVIII (Autumn 1957), pp. 163-167.

115. Hodgkin to J. Pim, December 20, 1861, Pim Mss., q. Large, p. 167.

powers the whole question of neutral rights and limitations to the right of search. Prayers for peace began to stream from nonconformist pulpits, and were made at large religious meetings held in London, Liverpool, and Edinburgh. The Peace Society asked Palmerston to refer the quarrel to an impartial arbitrator.

Whether public opinion could be wrenched round to peace was not clear. The Prince Consort's death chastened the national mood. Cobden assured Sumner that "there is a powerful moderate party."[116] But how powerful? The strength of the peace movement must not be inflated, although it enjoyed strategic advantages. Of thirty-three political meetings reported in the press to the close of December only six favored a strong peace line or arbitration. Contrary to tradition, working class opinion seemed to run strongly against the north. Dudley reported from Liverpool: "The great mass of the people did not seem to care what we said or did. We had insulted their flag and they wanted to fight us."[117] *Reynolds' Newspaper* judged the time apt for breaking the blockade, and saving Lancashire from starvation. The Lancashire press, with some exceptions in Rochdale, Preston and West Lancashire, demanded a retributive war, although concern that war might precipitate a cotton glut and falling prices softened merchant opinion.[118] Working men packed into meetings held at Ashton-under-Lyne and Oldham, there to hear vitriolic anti-Yankee speeches from Joseph Howe, the Prime Minister of Nova Scotia, and S. T. Lilley, Cabinet Minister from New Brunswick.[119] At Tunstall a hostile crowd shouted down the northern publicist George Francis Train when he attempted to defend Wilkes. Train told his audience what he would have done with the envoys: ". . . he would have convicted them of high treason; he would have hanged them—[hisses];—and then sent them to England, if England insisted on their being given up—[Confusion]."[120]

Peace opinion, however, was making an impact at the official level. The first sign of a softening attitude came on December 13. Weed, in interview with Russell, received an intimation that war would not necessarily follow automatically from American rejection of the British terms.[121] That same day, Russell told Gladstone he

116. Cobden to Sumner, December 12, 1861, q. Morley, *Cobden*, p. 388.

117. Quoted Ellison, p. 264.

118. *Reynolds' Newspaper*, December 8, 1861; Ellison, Chapter 7.

119. *Manchester Guardian*, December 4, 7, 1861.

120. *Guardian*, December 13, 1861.

121. Weed, *Autobiography*, p. 634.

was willing to make a treaty with the United States in return for release of the commissioners. England would give up its 1812 pretensions, securing immunity to persons not in arms on board neutral vessels, or to individuals going bona fide from one neutral port to another. "This would be a triumph to the U.S. in principle while the particular case would be decided in our favour."[122] On December 16, Russell wrote to Palmerston:

> I incline more and more to the opinion that if the [American] answer is a reasoning, and not a blunt offensive answer, we should send once more across the Atlantic to ask compliance . . . I do not think the country would approve an immediate declaration of war.[123]

As Freeman Morse, at the London consulate, put it to Seward, Atlantic peace factors were beginning to operate, if belatedly:

> . . . men of the 'middling classes', men of Republican proclivities, of the Bright and Cobden school, and many religious persons, are looking at the matter seriously and temperately and are unquestionably having some influence on the public mind of England.[124]

Meanwhile Britain was facing up to the legacy of more than a generation of torpidity on Canadian defense. From the start of the war, Palmerston had wanted a fortress Canada at his back, with 10,000 regulars safely installed before the St. Lawrence iced up. His advice had been rejected for reasons which reflected an odd mixture of national complacency and timidity. Complacency urged that a divided United States would be imbecile to incur the wrath of the world's greatest power; or else held that Canada was safe from an incompetent northern army during winter. Timidity suggested that it was unwise needlessly to antagonize the Americans; and expressed itself in fears that Negro West Indian, or Irish, regulars might desert *en masse* to the north. Overriding all else was governmental fear of expense, and confidence in an aggressive and mobile naval strategy.[125]

The War Office experts placed little reliance upon Confederate military assistance in any war. Nineteenth century military thought

---

122. Russell to Gladstone, December 13, 1861, q. EDA, I, p. 224.

123. Russell to Palmerston, December 16, 1861, q. EDA, I, p. 215.

124. Morse to Seward, December 18, 1861, q. Ferris, p. 491.

125. In what follows I have drawn heavily on Kenneth Bourne, "British Preparations for War with the North, 1861-1862," *EHR*, LXXVI (October, 1961), pp. 600-632 (cited Bourne, *EHR*).

was sceptical of the effectiveness of combined operations between armies of different countries. Nor, in any case, could Britain dismiss the possibility "that the Northern Government, driven to their wits end for money, and foreseeing no success in their present hopeless undertaking" might be driven to make peace with the south.[126] An undergarrisoned Canada would then face an army 200,000 strong. Whatever happened, the United States would hold a central position with good internal lines of communication, plus excellent rail and canal links with the lakes. Canada was open to even a modest offensive. Canadian settlement was strung along a 1500 mile line of river and lakes "less an obstacle" as Kenneth Bourne says "than an invitation to attack."[127] The most likely threat from the Americans was an assault launched from Lake Champlain, under cover from the Union fort at Rouse's Point. This would endanger Montreal (a mere forty miles away) and Quebec (Map 2). Northerners might also cut the St. Lawrence by expedition from Ogdensburg, or attack Hamilton or Toronto from Niagara. Historic strategy envisaged three main defenses against such invasions: a system of extensive and fixed fortifications, British naval control over the lakes, and a large defensive army (the minimum estimated was 100,000 militia and 10,000 regulars). The British lacked all three in November 1861. Nothing practical could be done to restore the fortifications system of earlier years, now decayed or anachronistic against the enemy's rifled cannon; nor did modern military theory any longer have confidence in fixed systems. Again, quite insuperable problems prevented the British rapidly gaining command of the lakes. They had no warships on the lakes, while the Americans had the *Michigan*, carrying eight-inch guns, and there was virtually no chance of introducing large ships from the Atlantic before winter ice or war should close the St. Lawrence. (Even in summer large ships were able to get no more than forty miles above Quebec, while the Americans could easily cut the St. Lawrence by destroying some of the numerous canals along which vessels must pass.) Recognizing the futility of doing anything at once about these problems, the Admiralty virtually surrendered the lakes.

All that could be done quickly was to strengthen the army, and upon this objective the War Office concentrated its efforts in

---

126. Memo Colonel Macdougall to Lewis, December 3, 1861 (basis of War Office strategy), q. Bourne, *EHR*, p. 607. Lewis also received appreciations from General Burgoyne, Inspector-General of fortifications, and the ageing Lord Seaton, Commander-in-Chief in Canada during the rebellion.

127. Bourne, *EHR*, p. 609.

Great Lakes - St. Lawrence Frontier
Canals
Railroads
Montreal
Ft. St. John
Ft. Lennox
Rouse's Point
St. Albans
Lake Champlain
Plattsburg
Ft. Ethan Allen
Burlington
LAKE SUPERIOR
CAN.
U.S.
ONTARIO
QUEBEC
Quebec
St. Lawrence
R.
MICHIGAN
Ft. Brady
Ft. Mackinac
LAKE HURON
LAKE MICHIGAN
WIS.
Montreal
Ottawa
Ft. Lennox
CAN.
U.S.
Rouse's Point
Lake Champlain
(DETAIL ABOVE)
Ogdensburg
Kingston
VT.
N.H.
NEW YORK
Toronto
LAKE ONTARIO
Oswego
Ft. Niagara
Hamilton
Ft. Gratiot
Ft. St. Clair
Ft. Erie
Buffalo
Albany
MASS.
Detroit
Ft. Malden
LAKE ERIE
CAN.
U.S.
ILL.
Chicago
CONN.
PENNSYLVANIA
INDIANA
OHIO
Cleveland
N.J.
New York

what was, by the lights of the time, a very respectable performance. Whether it would have achieved the goal of saving British North America is another matter. One of the better British generals of the day, Wolseley, thought it would have been "toughish work."[128] The war committee acting on the advice of Cambridge and de Grey, increased reinforcements to provide for a total addition to Canada of over 10,500 men. This would bring the number of regulars to 12,500 in Canada and over 5,000 in the Maritime Provinces. Further forces, including cavalry, were held ready to embark.

The problem of placing British troops where they could be of use to the Canadians was not, however, a simple one. Should the St. Lawrence prove unnavigable, troops would have to move from St. Andrews in New Brunswick by rail to Woodstock, from there to Riviere du Loup by road, finishing the trip by rail to Quebec (Map 3). This route, using the Temiscouata road, was the most negotiable for the purpose, but for over 100 miles it ran perilously close to the American border and was highly vulnerable to ambush. Military experts had long demanded its fortification, or the development of the more northerly but primitive Matapedia road to Metis on the St. Lawrence; but nothing had been done. In an awkward situation, the War Office gambled upon conveying almost its whole force up the St. Lawrence before it froze. With luck this might not occur before the end of December. In what has been described as "a miracle of despatch," a hired fleet of miscellaneous vessels, some hardly seaworthy and packed with soldiers, arms and stores, set out for Halifax during December. Only one, the *Persia*, managed to get as far as Bic Island, 150 miles below Quebec, and even it was forced back to Halifax by gales and ice after unloading only part of its cargo and men. Bad weather and mismanagement resulted in the headquarters planning staff not arriving at Halifax until January 5, at the tailend of the main force, although they had left Woolich on December 7. The crisis had by then passed, and in a bizarre touch, the officers took a mailsteamer to Boston where they travelled in civilian clothes to Montreal by the Grand Trunk Railway. The major force (including the Guards) disembarked at Halifax and moved into Canada by sleigh. If war had broken out they would have been separated from their headquarters staff, and forced to use the Temiscouata road to reach Quebec—even though the Chief-of-Staff in Canada and Generals Paulet and Wolseley regarded the road as unusable in war. The War Office gamble had failed and placed the entire operation in jeopardy.

---

128. Wolseley to Biddulph, December 10, 1861, q. Bourne, *EHR*, p. 631.

Matapēdia Road
Temiscouata Road
St. Lawrence River
Metis
Matapēdia River
Riviere du Loup
Matapédia
QUEBEC
Edmundston
Grand Falls
Quebec
NEW BRUNSWICK
MAINE
Woodstock
Fredericton
CAN.
U.S.
St.John
CAN.
U.S.
St.Andrews
Bay of Fundy
NOVA SCOTIA
Halifax
VT.
Augusta
N. H.
Portland
Concord
North-Eastern Frontier
MASS.
Boston

With the small force already in North America, little could be done to delay any American advance. There was brave talk of the irreducibility of Montreal and Quebec in winter conditions. (Newcastle spoke of a Yankee campaign ending in another Moscow.) Plans existed for surprise attacks on Rouse's Point and Maine, rather reckless schemes depending upon northern unpreparedness. But the Colonial and War Offices advised the wisdom of adopting nothing more ambitious than a holding operation against Union offensives for the duration of the winter, with stress laid upon retaining Quebec, Montreal, and Kingston. Guerrilla warfare by settlers and local resistance by militia might offer minor annoyance to Union troops, but American occupation of large parts of the Canadian countryside seemed inevitable in the new year.

The documents show that the British government recognized these brutal facts. Although hopeful of retrieving something in North America and satisfied that it had done its best in difficult circumstances, the cabinet did not expect to secure victory in Canada, nor did it regard Canada as vital. In the last analysis, the British were prepared to tolerate the loss of Canada, and to rely upon a massive naval offensive to win the war and recoup lost possessions.

The British fleet was technically superior to the American although not so large. The Union navy had over 260 ships, but they were mostly wooden sailing ships, ex-merchantmen, and far inferior in firepower to the wooden British steamships. By the end of December Milne's squadron, reinforced from the Mediterranean and Channel fleets and the steam reserve, numbered forty steamships, including eight battleships and thirteen frigates and corvettes, while reserves could quickly be sent out from Gibraltar, Lisbon, or the U.K. British naval confidence was much improved in 1861, for the Admiralty had recently established a slender lead over the French in naval technology by building the *Warrior*, over 9000 tons screw-driven, and with the world's most advanced iron armoring. (She was built to supersede Dupuy de Lôme's steam battleship *La Gloire*, Napoleon's pride.) Certainly Britain had the industrial capacity to construct an ironclad navy in shorter time than any rival power, and would no doubt have done so in any American war. However, deep draught ironclads were of severely limited use for blockading and bombarding operations in the shallow waters of the American coast. The United States, for its part, also enjoyed the industrial capacity to build ironclads, and was already building turretships—heavily armored floating citadels capable of mounting revolving casemates—which were to become of revolutionary importance in coastal defense.

Milne's blueprint for war called for quick aggression. Ignoring the bleatings of alarm from merchantmen and undergarrisoned imperial stations, quite reasonably fearful of attack from American marauders, Milne planned to concentrate his forces into two main squadrons based on Bermuda and Havana. From there rapid strikes would be made against the Union blockading fleets. From Havana (where the Spanish were permitting the fitting out of the joint Mexican expedition) Dunlop was to destroy McKean's Pensacola Bay squadron. From Bermuda, Milne would descend upon the North Carolina and Virginia fleets. At a stroke, it was hoped to lift the blockade and annihilate any possibility of northern retaliation against exposed British bases in the West Indies. Orders were also given to destroy enemy shipping in the main sealanes at the outset of war. Washington would then be harassed by warships brought into Chesapeake Bay and the Potomac, cutting off communications with Fort Monroe. (The latter was one of the few operations where liaison with southern forces, already investing Chesapeake Bay, would be necessary.)

In London there was a good deal of talk about the regrettable necessity of burning America's seaboard cities, of ending the war quickly, for instance, by threatening to bombard New York, the country's commercial heart. The Admiralty, however, was dubious. In the first place such behavior was uncivilized. "Modern views," as Milne said, "deprecate any damage to a town. If ships are fired upon in a Port the town must suffer; therefore the shipping cannot be fired on."[129] In the second place, the Lords of the Admiralty had a healthy respect for heavily defended positions, and had no intention of risking the destruction of their fleets by sending them in against cities like Boston and New York, unless they were almost completely unprepared to repel an assault.

Primarily the British intended to rely upon the imposition of an unbreakable blockade upon the north. Encircled by foes it would presumably capitulate. The outcome in practice might well depend upon whether the Navy Department could speed up its production of turret ships, whose effectiveness against the type of wooden warships used in any blockade was to be amply demonstrated in 1862 in the clash of the *Monitor* and *Merrimac.* More generally, of course, the outcome would depend on the strength of northern

129. Memo in Milne papers, 1862, q. Bourne, *EHR*, p. 625.

morale. The issue would turn on the willingness or otherwise of northerners to mobilize their continental resources and latent industrial power in a bid to achieve self-sufficiency against British mastery at sea. British military optimism was carefully sustained during the crisis, but it was by no means necessarily well-founded. Nervousness kept edging into press comment, even from the *Times.* On Christmas Day it admitted that

> . . . the Americans possess maritime resources of no ordinary kind . . . our adversaries will lose not a moment after the declaration of war in pressing forward the construction and equipment of cruisers, and it must be expected that many of these vessels will, as in the last war, elude the blockade and prowl about the ocean in quest of prey . . . It is quite possible that while England is ruling undisputed mistress of the waves a Yankee frigate may appear some fine morning off one of our ports and inflict no slight damage upon us.

Canada's continuing military weakness, the impossibility of British territorial conquest of the United States, the exposure of British shipping to American privateering, the potential threat of the monitors—all made an Anglo-American war something less than a foregone conclusion.

Chapter VI

The Path to Settlement

News of the storm created in Britain by the *Trent* affair began to arrive in America from December 13. It led to the most anxious Christmas season in living memory. Every edition of the newspapers carried details of British troops, arms, and supplies on their way to Canada before the winter ice. Nervous articles appeared in the New York press on the vulnerability of seaboard defenses against naval and land assaults. The New York exchange reflected an obvious feeling of suspense. The prices of imports and war materials took an astonishing upward turn, while the sale of cotton goods was abruptly suspended. Businessmen and grain merchants received instructions from their overseas agents not to ship goods on American vessels in case of war.

To many northerners it appeared that Britain was set upon war; not least because it rested its case upon irregularities in the form of arrest used in the *Trent* incident rather than on the question of principle on which the British record was so imperfect; namely, the rights of individuals to protection of the neutral flag. Horace Greeley described Britain's "quibble" over Wilkes' failure to capture the *Trent* as degrading "a great and grave question of international law by interposing the arts of the special pleader and the tricks of Quirk, Gammon and Snap employed for the defence of a desperate felon at the Old Bailey."[1] Common sense argued that diversion of the mail packet's passengers, mails, cargo, and specie would have amounted to a much

1. *NYDT*, December 17, 1861.

more serious deprivation of neutral rights. Since Wilkes only took four men out of the *Trent*, England was outraged: "This is the single fine point upon which the whole question burns, and for a point so minute a great country threatens war."[2] More than one American ironically suggested that Mason and Slidell be restored, with ample apologies, to the decks of the *Trent*, which should then be promptly captured and brought into New York.

Torn between national pride and awareness of the need for peace, the northeastern press swung with surprising speed to the side of compromise: " . . . to plunge into a war with England now, would be simply to give the army and the navy of England to the support of the rebel cause," warned the *New York Times* as it called for the "highest and steadiest" statesmanship from the administration.[3] Close to officialdom, the *Washington National Intelligencer* urged that the case might be so managed by the United States "as to result in a valuable acquisition to the law of nations," by settling the "vague and undetermined" definitions of belligerent and neutral rights.[4] It called for a grand international commission to revise the rules of world intercourse. Mediation by Napoleon III or King Leopold of Belgium was widely canvassed as a solution to the crisis. Resistance to surrender of the envoys was still, however, widespread.

The task of the peacemakers was considerably lightened by the Peace Democrats. Congress on December 16 laid aside by 106 to 16 a resolution by the Democratic Congressman for Ohio, Clement L. Vallandigham, urging Lincoln to strike a defiant attitude to England. Here, accused the *World*, was "a man of doubtful loyalty, who would perhaps court a war with Great Britain in the interests of the rebels. . . . This fact should teach loyal men to practice circumspection."[5] On December 17 Samuel A. Cox, a member of the Committee on Foreign Affairs, gave a speech in Congress vindicating Wilkes. It was also received sceptically: "Every traitor among us was instantly converted into a flaming patriot, . . . eager to defend the act of Capt. Wilkes with the last drop of his blood."[6] Richmond unwittingly undid its cause, when editorials in the *Examiner* and *Inquirer* exulted at the north's "incredible follies" over the *Trent*. Excerpts were promptly splashed in the north. The effect was to weaken the influence of the

2. *NYDT*, December 19, 1861; see also R. H. Dana to C. F. Adams, December 17, 1861, *MHSP* (November, 1911), p. 98.

3. *NYT*, December 14-16, 1861.

4. December 17, 1861.

5. *NYW*, December 17, 1861.

6. *NYT*, December 19, 1861.

hawkish *Herald*, and to present the government with a convenient escape route should the British demand retreat. The day before the British terms were presented, the *New York Times'* Washington correspondent reported that the administration was "probably satisfied" that the war clamor originated with southern sympathizers.[7]

Historians have insufficiently emphasized the fact that, on the eve of the cabinet's final grappling with the crisis, most of the north's major newspapers were foreshadowing the ultimate settlement. Raymond and Seward were closely associated; and by December 18 Raymond's paper held that the government regarded the issue of the envoy's return as "a most inadequate one on which to base a great international struggle." According to one of Charles Francis Adams' New York friends, writing on December 21, the American public now viewed "the Wilkes affair unfavourably, and would much prefer it had not occurred at all."[8] Wilkes' action was more widely admitted to have been irregular. The Boston jurist George Ticknor Curtis weightily adjudged the omission to bring in the *Trent* for trial "not a mere matter of form, but . . . of very serious and important substance." Wilkes had deprived his country of the means of showing the lawfulness of the capture when he prevented judicial determination of the issue. Now England's protest would range all Europe on her side.[9] Some orators and journalists still mouthed words of war. Others skirted the unpalatable prospect of returning the rebels by vague but clamorous talk of a "diplomatic settlement." What that might mean it was up to the politicians to decide.

The *Europa* arrived at Boston on December 17 carrying a special messenger, Captain C. C. Seymour, with the fateful British demand. It also carried dispatches from Adams which an anxious Washington hoped would shed inner light on London's intentions. Seymour was delayed by a railway accident between Boston and New York, and hastily chartered a special train to take him to Washington, a fact which hardly lessened American blood pressures. He delivered Russell's dispatch to Lyons at 11:30 P.M. on Wednesday December 18. The next morning's train brought 100 pounds of Adams' reports, none of them very helpful to the government. Adams had no knowledge of the British cabinet's reaction, was indeed ponderously resentful at being kept in the dark by both London and Washington.

7. *NYT*, December 18, 1861.

8. Charles Augustus Davis to C. F. Adams, December 21, 1861, q. C. F. Adams, II, "The Trent Affair," *MHSP*, XLV, p. 107.

9. G. T. Curtis to *Boston Journal*, December 18, 1861, q. *WNI*, December 23, 1861.

Rumors of all kinds were flying in Washington, among them the recurring suggestion that Lincoln had hardened his attitude against any truckling to the British. On December 18 the *Herald*'s reporter in the capital wrote on "the highest authority"—in flat contradiction to the inside information of the *New York Times*—that there was now no possibility of surrendering the envoys: "The President is firm and immovable on this point."[10]

The Senate meantime had blocked a House of Representatives move for a Christmas adjournment. A respectable number of Congressmen were willing to give the administration a free hand over the *Trent*, but a majority preferred that Congress should not abdicate its high functions during a war crisis. For his part Lincoln did not welcome a contentious debate in Congress which might embarrass negotiations, and Sumner labored successfully to stall discussion in the Senate. Nor did the President desire unnecessary cabinet deliberations. Cabinet meetings were adjourned from the receipt of the British note until Christmas Day, in order as it was thought, "to avoid the risk of a general and premature discussion which might establish a policy."[11]

While at a brief noonday cabinet held on Thursday December 19, Seward learned that Lyons awaited him with Britain's terms. They confirmed American fears. Immediate delivery of the prisoners into British custody was demanded, together with a suitable apology for the aggression committed. Failure to comply within seven days of the note being formally presented would result in closure of the British legation. The Americans, however, were granted a breathing space, the result of the British cabinet's and Prince Consort's obvious concern not to humiliate the Lincoln administration. Lyons had been carefully briefed. He was not to present the formal demand at his first interview, but to "prepare" Seward unofficially, and to ask him to settle with the President and his cabinet what course they would pursue. At first Lyons took care not to mention any time limit. It was not until Seward pressed for this information "privately and confidentially" that Lyons told him of the seven days and gave the Secretary "unofficially and informally" a copy of the dispatch. No one but Seward and Lincoln was to know of it. Lyons readily agreed to Seward's request to delay formal presentation of the note for two days while the Secretary consulted with the President. Lyons hoped that this would allow Seward, "who is now on the peace side

---

10. *NYH*, December 19, 1861.
11. *NYDT*, December 24, 1861.

of the Cabinet," time to convert his colleagues. It would also permit the arrival of a dispatch from Paris to Mercier, adding French pressure on the United States to conciliate. So far Lyons had admirably fulfilled his instructions to "abstain from anything like menace," a policy which appealed to his prudent nature. Since the crisis had blown up he had acted with almost superhuman tact in maintaining the discreetest of silences; for this and for his subsequent skill in negotiations, he was to be decorated by the Queen. At this stage his concern was that the Americans should not mistake British courtesies for weakness. Again confidentially, he made it quite plain to Seward that no evasions, no failure to surrender the men, would be tolerated. On this, he said, his instructions were positive and left him no discretion.[12] It was to prove a timely caution. Seward for his part failed to live up to his reputation as a warmonger. He had received Lyons "without any manifestation of dissatisfaction," declaring that he was very sensible of the ambassador's "friendly and conciliatory manner." That same day he told Mercier that there would be no war, and that he could so inform Paris.[13]

Such easy confidence received a check from Lincoln who still balked at restoring the captives. Seward, according to one version of events, insisted that there was no other safe course than to bow to the demand; if Lincoln refused to yield the men, he would have to write the reply to the British government himself, for Seward would not do it.[14] Lincoln's compromise was that Seward should draft the case for, and he the case against, immediate release; and that the documents be compared before cabinet was consulted. When Seward and Lyons met as arranged on Saturday December 21, the Secretary asked for a further postponement of the formal interview until Monday 23. He had, he confessed, not yet completely mastered the question. Lyons graciously granted the favor. He could well afford to do so. As he explained to Russell, no time was practically lost, "for whether the seven days expired on Saturday next or Monday next, I should have been equally unable to announce the result to you sooner than by the packet which will sail from New York on Wednesday, the 1st January."[15] However, suspicious of American vacillation and

12. Russell to Lyons (Private), December 1, 1861; Lyons to Russell, December 19, 1861, in *ORN*, Vol. I, Ser. I, p. 174; Lyons to Russell, December 12, 1861, in Newton, *Lyons*, pp. 65-66.

13. Van Deusen, *Seward*, p. 312.

14. N. B. Ferris, "Lincoln and the Trent Affair," *Lincoln Herald*, LXIX (1967), p. 132.

15. Lyons to Russell, December 23, 1861, in Newton, *Lyons*, I, p. 67.

anxious to send a progress report to Russell on the Monday 23 mail packet, Lyons insisted upon no further delays. At 10:00 A.M. on Monday, Lyons officially read Seward the dispatch and received the promise of a prompt reply. That evening Lyons reassuringly sent out his normal invitations for Christmas dinner, although a week previously he had indicated that "the necessities of his position" might force him to postpone it.[16]

Intense pressures were now building up in favor of conciliation. Most obvious, Britain had prepared for war with great seriousness, the United States had not. There was no abnormal activity in northern naval yards, there were no extraordinary military preparations to meet a foreign invader. Such laxity would have amounted to an inconceivable dereliction of duty on Lincoln's part if he had had the slightest intention of risking a war. The danger was of war by miscalculation, by misjudgment of British intentions. On this crucial issue intelligence from overseas confirmed Lyon's plain talking. Minor gratification may have been possible over John Bright's oratorical efforts for peace, and over the occurrence of antiwar meetings in Ireland which seemed likely to rise in arms at the outbreak of hostilities. But the biggest headlines cited Britain's immense war preparations, the weakening of the world's money markets, and the onset of a disastrous crisis in the American shipping industry. British vessels had been notified that war was probable, a course of action which had been publicly called for by Lord Derby, the leader of the Tory opposition, after consultation with the Palmerston administration. Derby, it was clear, had given his party's blessing to the government's American policy. The hasty cancellation by General Winfield Scott of his visit to France and Italy, and his return to America in the *Arago*, seemed to indicate that the aged warrior shared Derby's gloom. Rumors spread that Scott brought advices, an offer of mediation, or even an ultimatum, from Napoleon III, a prospect which seems to have alarmed the British embassy in Washington almost as much as the American public. From Europe took place a stampede of loyal Americans anxious to regain their homeland before being stranded by hostilities. The opinion of neutral nations was depressingly unsympathetic towards America's untraditional championing of belligerent rights.

Peace pressures from banking and investment interests were brought to bear on the Union government. Throughout 1861 there had been jangled nerves on the northern money market over any

16. *NYDT*, December 24, 1861.

rumor of Anglo-American discord. Such rumors threatened to sabotage efforts to raise the huge loans required for the war. Lyons for one believed that Wall Street constraints lay behind Seward's trek from a policy of bluster to comparative moderation. But investor confidence had waned with the scarcity of Federal battle victories, and promised to collapse completely with the *Trent* scare. The banker Jay Cooke, the man upon whom Lincoln most heavily depended for the financing of Union loans, apparently played a critical role in urging upon Seward, Treasurer Chase, and old political associates in Ohio, the overriding need for peace abroad. Seward later explained to Adams that "troubles about Currency and finance" had been paramount in Congress and the public eye.[17] Conciliatory editorials were becoming the order of the day. Restitution of the men would not disgrace the United States, if Britain could be maneuvered into renouncing the arrogant pretensions which had led to Anglo-American warfare in the past. Even the *Herald* bowed to this logic. On December 21, Bennett made a spectacular about-face (not the last of the war). He predicted and justified the return of the southerners. Perhaps he was embarrassed by the charges of treason being plentifully bruited against him; more likely he had been recruited by Seward. But Bennett promised future revenge against England once the "absorbing and paramount issue"—suppression of the rebellion—had been disposed of: " . . . as Rome remembered Carthage from the invasion of Hannibal . . . so will the people of the United States remember and treasure up for the future this little affair." Bennett's vision was of a restored Union, with a million men in the field and an iron-plated navy, enjoying the power "to prescribe the extent and limitations of European authority on this continent." This was the nightmare haunting British civil war strategy. Charles Sumner was taken aback that Bennett should so openly invoke it: "If England sees that war is inevitable [he wrote to Francis Lieber] she will accept it now."[18]

Sumner's letters at this period indicate his anguish, and the uncertainty of the situation. "Does England mean war?" he asked Bright:

> The impression here is that she does; and two foreign ministers have given today the opinion that she does. If this be so, then must

17. See M. P. Claussen, *The U. S. and Great Britain: Peace Factors in International Relations* (Unpub. Ph. D. thesis, Illinois, 1937), pp. 99-104. Seward to Adams, January 11, 1862, q. Claussen, p. 103.

18. Sumner to Lieber, December 24, 1861, in Pierce, *Sumner*, IV, p. 58.

> I despair. It is said that if the 'Trent' question is adjusted, even on English terms, another pretext will soon be found. Can this be so? All this is to me inexpressibly painful; for I am almost a Quaker in principle. Besides my sympathies have always been thoroughly English,—so much as to expose me to frequent criticism. Thus on every account I protest against such a contest; but I fear that it is coming.[19]

The Massachusetts Senator's waxing Anglophobia, climaxed in his later role over the Geneva claims, may be traced back at least to this time of trauma. There had been on the part of the British government, Sumner felt, no want of courtesy, but "there had been want of candor and fairness." However, on the whole, the news that the British had left open the door to negotiation was met with relief. The *New York Times* rejoiced that the British note had avoided "all hurtful expressions," and welcomed the general lowering of temperature on both sides of the ocean.[20] "People talk cooly of surrendering the Rebel emissaries, if it can be done without a sacrifice of honor," reported the *Tribune.*[21] Only Bryant's *Evening Post* of the largest eastern papers still rejected outright any idea of restitution.

By an historical irony the apostles of Atlantic amity—the men who have gone into legend as averting the war—were laboring during these crisis days on an impractical and risky peace program to which they almost converted Lincoln; while it was left to the "warmonger" Seward to engineer an effective settlement. Sumner, Cobden, and Bright were the moving spirits of the peace party, but they were momentarily led away from the power realities by their crusading zeal for the idea of international arbitration. Sumner had several times pressed upon Lincoln a solution by arbitration—proposing Prussia, "or better still, three learned publicists of the Continent," to sit in judgment.[22] Such a scheme was consonant with the agreement made by the powers during the Paris Conference of 1856 to put points of international difficulty to arbitration before resorting to arms. It also seemed a way of postponing the whole trouble, although this was a dangerous delusion.

Sumner almost certainly showed to Lincoln a peace plan sent recently to him by John Bright, for Lincoln was shortly to produce a draft reply to the British note which incorporated Bright's ideas and even reproduced his language.[23] Bright's letter offered "a courageous

19. Sumner to Bright, December 23, 1861, q. Pierce, *Sumner,* IV, p. 57.
20. *NYT*, December 17, 24, 1861.
21. *NYDT*, December 20, 18, 1861.
22. Sumner to Bright, December 30, 1861, q. Pierce, *Sumner*, IV, p. 59.
23. Ferris, "Lincoln and Trent Affair," p. 133.

stroke, not of arms, but of moral action":

> If I were Minister or President in your country, I would write the most complete answer the case is capable of, and in a friendly and courteous tone, send it to this country. I would say that if after this, your view of the case is not accepted, you are ready to refer the matter to any sovereign, or two sovereigns, or Governments of Europe, or to any other eligible tribunal, and to abide by their decision, and you will rejoice to join with the leading European Governments in amendments and modifications of international law in respect to the powers of belligerents and the rights of neutrals . . . .

Bright suggested an apt line to take with the British:

> You would not have authorized such an act against a friendly nation, calculated to rouse hostile feelings against you; you repudiate any infraction of international law; the capture of the Commissioners is of no value when set against the loss of that character for justice and courtesy which you have always sustained; and you are willing to abide by the law as declared by impartial arbitration . . . Any moderate course you may take will meet with great support here, and in the English Cabinet there are, as I certainly know, some who will gladly accept any fair proposition for friendly arrangement from your side . . . Be courteous and conceding to the last possible degree, now in your time of trial . . . .[24]

Lincoln experimented with these suggestions. In his draft answer to England, preserved in his papers, the President emphasized that the United States had intended no affront to the British flag; Wilkes had acted "without orders from, or expectation of, the government." On the other hand a government dedicated to guarding American rights "could undo the act complained of, only upon a fair showing that it was wrong, or, at least, very questionable." Was not the British government unreasonable in pressing for a categorical answer, when their information upon the affair was "only a partial record?" London should hear the United States upon the matter. He suggested two possible plans. The first proposed arbitration, but with such wide terms of reference as to confirm Lord Russell's worst fears about the litigiousness of the Americans in international affairs. The precedents in law were to be exhaustively examined, and issues such as the object of the southerners' mission, and the complicity of the *Trent*'s master in it, would be raised. Worse still, Lincoln intended to reventilate the whole vexed issue of the justice of the British proclamation of neutrality. His second proposal was that the British government, after duly considering both sides of the dispute, might alone

24. Bright to Sumner, December 5, 1861, in *MHSP*, XLV (November, 1911), pp. 150-153.

determine "whether any, and if any, what reparation is due from the United States." The Union would be willing to make reparation, provided that it did not exceed that already demanded by Russell, and provided "that the determination thus made shall be the law for all future analogous cases. . . ."[25]

Press rumors in the days before Christmas gave considerable publicity to "the Lincoln plan," but its fatal defects were becoming increasingly obvious. It proposed a policy of procrastination which would, at the least, have caused high exasperation in England. Russell, who had been going over in his mind "the possible evasive answers of Mr. Seward," had written to Lyons on December 7 to emphasize that: "What we want is a plain Yes, or a plain No to our very simple demands, and we want that plain Yes or No within seven days of the despatch." Lyons must not be trapped by American legal ingenuity into "endless arguments on Vattel, Wheaton, and Scott."[26] Should the Confederates not be restored within the time limit, Lyons was ordered to obey his instructions and withdraw. Seward, and presumably Lincoln, already knew these plain alternatives. What they did not know was that Russell had not entirely ruled out further negotiations with the Americans had they tried delaying tactics. Nevertheless the Lincoln plan would certainly have caused the withdrawal of the British legation and the creation of a tinderbox situation. By Christmas Eve, Sumner realized that Britain was in no mood to arbitrate, and he advised Lincoln ("who is essentially pacific") to make a "complete" settlement "without mental reservations which shall hereafter be forged into thunder-bolts."[27]

The perils in an arbitration scheme must have dawned upon Lincoln for he did not present it to the cabinet on December 25, when it met to consider its reply to the British demand. Sumner attended the first meeting and read to the ministers his collection of letters from Cobden and Bright. Their latest intelligence was desperately gloomy and much astonished Lincoln. The warlike excitement in Britain had convinced Bright "that this government believes that you intend war with England," or else "that itself intends war with you." Cobden cautioned that plenty of Englishmen were content to unleash upon the United States "a fleet surpassing in destructive force any naval armament the world ever saw."[28] Meantime,

25. Basler, *Works of Lincoln*, V., pp. 62-64.

26. Russell to Lyons, December 7, 1861, q. Newton, *Lyons*, I, p. 64.

27. Sumner to Lieber, December 24, 1861, q. Pierce, *Sumner*, p. 58.

28. Sumner to Bright, December 23, 1861, q. Pierce, p. 57; Bright to Sumner, December 14, 1861, Cobden to Sumner, January 12, 1862, q. Cohen, *JSH*, p. 211.

Seward, who had been preparing his draft reply at the State Department, had received compelling advice from abroad—in particular from Adams, Dayton, Bigelow, and Weed, trusted advisers—to give up the prisoners. The State Department was under pressure from merchant interests to avoid a ruinous naval war, and under pressure from men determined to vanquish the south to avoid a fatal foreign war. The *Tribune*'s Washington correspondent reported: "Surrender, in preference to war, is without doubt the choice of many influential persons here, and it is pressed upon Mr. Lincoln by both civilians and military men, high in position."[29]

There remained a glimmer of hope for the pugnacious, a diversion by France, perhaps an offer of mediation. Lyons, on tenterhooks for the American answer, feared complications stemming from such daydreams.[30] London and Paris had in fact concerted their policies over the *Trent*, but despite promptings from the Foreign Office, the French were slow to convey their official position to the Americans. Mercier had unofficially intimated to Seward the futility of expecting French support. He had approached Seward on Saturday December 21, and expressed strongly his conviction that the Americans had no choice but compliance or war. Many northerners indeed were suspicious that Napoleon's Mexican intrigues led him to wish for an Anglo-American war which should give him a free hand in the Caribbean theatre. The Senate Foreign Relations Committee was already alarmed at the hovering of the joint Anglo-Spanish-French fleet off the Gulf of Mexico. Combined amphibious operations against the northern seaboard seemed by no means impossible in the event of war. The French, it was true, appeared to be working for a settlement, and the French press seemed to accept that Napoleon would be neutral in any war; but the situation was by no means clear-cut. An Anglo-American war might weaken the vital Anglo-French accord in Europe; by embroiling Britain in America, it would immobilize her in Europe, leaving Napoleon with an impotent ally. Such a war might also destroy American seapower, which France traditionally regarded as a desirable counterweight to that of Britain. But Napoleon III was notoriously fascinated by immediate gains and prestigious coups, and there were some in the offing. Seward knew of London rumors that France would join England as an ally, provided it would be given a "free swing in taking Syria."[31]

---

29. *NYDT*, December 24, 1861; and Van Deusen, *Seward*, pp. 312-313.

30. Lyons to Russell, December 23, 1861, in Newton, *Lyons*, pp. 67-68.

31. James Leslie to Seward, London, December 4, 1861, in Blumenthal, *Franco-American Relations*, p. 129.

Certainly Napoleon's enemies in Europe feared that he would welcome an American distraction for England in order to pursue without opposition his own European designs. Bigelow wrote to Seward from Paris: "The idea is prevalent here that a war between England and America would occupy the British navy to such an extent as to enable France to occupy the Rhine, which is the dream of all imperialists."[32] Mercier begged Seward to dismiss such an interpretation as a "vulgar notion."[33]

The official French attitude, expressed in a dispatch from Thouvenel to Mercier, arrived only just in time to be read at the Christmas Day cabinet. According to the *Tribune*, it "convinced the opponents of the policy of surrender that the public opinion of Europe would sustain England."[34] In a powerful appeal to Franco-American maritime traditions, as expressed in treaties between the two countries, Thouvenel concluded that the neutral flag protected all passengers, except military men actually in the service of the enemy. The right asserted by the *San Jacinto* to arrest persons as contraband on a neutral vessel bound between neutral ports would render neutral immunities vain; and "would inflict restrictions upon the liberty of commerce and navigation which modern international law refuses to acknowledge as legitimate." Thouvenel urged the Federal cabinet to yield to the British demands.

Seward had already devised a face-saving way out of the American dilemma. With much spirited language, and in the garb of a defense of historic American principles, his draft reply for the cabinet ended with the promise that the prisoners would be "cheerfully liberated." Hardly an argument the Secretary employed had not been canvassed in the press during the crisis, a fact which must be recognized in explaining the favorable political impact of the document. Seward contended that the capture of the *Trent* might have been validly made, but he condemned Wilkes' needless failure to permit judicial examination of the vessel. In effect he had capitulated to a high British view of belligerent prerogatives, contrary to American tradition, on virtually every issue at stake except that of adjudication. He attempted to expand the doctrine of contraband to encompass enemy agents, including envoys, travelling on missions essentially hostile in character:

---

32. Bigelow to Seward, December 5, 1861, q. Blumenthal, p. 130.

33. Lyons to Russell, December 23, 1861, in Newton, *Lyons*, p. 68.

34. *NYDT*, December 31, 1861. Case and Spencer remedy earlier historical neglect of the Thouvenel dispatch; pp. 246-249.

> All writers and judges pronounce naval or military persons in the service of the enemy contraband. Vattel says war allows us to cut off from an enemy all his resources, and to hinder him from sending ministers to solicit assistance. And Sir William Scott says you may stop the ambassador of your enemy on his passage. Despatches are not less clearly contraband, and the bearers or couriers who undertake to carry them fall under the same condemnation.[35]

Wilkes, in this view, had acted legally in exercising the right of search and would have been justified in undertaking "as a simple, legal and customary belligerent proceeding" the arrest and capture of "a neutral vessel engaged in carrying contraband of war for the use and benefit of the insurgents." But this had not occurred, leaving the capture unfinished. Seward returned belatedly to the defense of the "old, honoured and cherished American cause" on this point. He cited the principle laid down by Madison in 1804:

> Whenever property found in a neutral vessel is supposed to be liable on any ground to capture and condemnation, the rule in all cases is, that the question shall not be decided by the captor, but be carried before a legal tribunal, where a regular trial may be had, and where the captor himself is liable to damages for an abuse of his power.

A patriotic peroration declared: "If I decide this case in favour of my own Government, I must disallow its most cherished principles," a vague generality which adroitly obscured the lengths to which he had gone in breaking with tradition. Seward had, moreover, been forced to concede the south's belligerent status, against which the government had so long contended; otherwise his arguments fell to ground. But he was more realistic than some of his later critics, for the north's civil war interests were by no means damaged by the assumption of a strong posture on belligerent rights; and, like it or not, the world was to move in the same direction in the next half century and more. To please the patriots, Seward added some truculence. The "waning proportions" of the insurrection, he said, justified the return of the comparatively unimportant captives. But "if the safety of this Union required the detention of the captured persons, it would be the right and duty of this Government to detain them."

---

35. Seward to Lyons, December 26, 1861, *ORN*, Vol. I, Serial I, pp. 177-187 for dispatch. Wilkes, according to the Secretary of State, had acted without instructions.

It took two days' discussion, perhaps "the most fateful held in the course of the civil war,"[36] before the cabinet united behind Seward. (He was later to confide to Lyons that he had been "through the fires of Tophet" to get the men released.[37]) In the course of the debate Lincoln quietly dropped his own plan as he, and the other ministers, bowed to necessity. Sumner had been urging an immediate decision on the case. "Its pendency" he told Bright, "caused a paralysis upon all our naval and military movements against the rebellion, which gave us a foretaste of the certain effect of a British war."[38] Chase, whose inclination had been to disoblige the British, now opposed vacillation, which would unsettle the public mind, seriously harm commerce, and hobble the military campaign.[39] Bates agreed: "Our trade would be utterly ruined, and our treasury bankrupt." As Attorney-General he was prepared to waive the question of legal right, "upon which all Europe is against us, and also many of our own best jurists."[40] Although the ministers still worried about displeasing their own people, certain facts could not be brooked: the north was unprepared for a British, and possible French, war; it lacked allies, and by impetuousity would create them for the rebels. In short the country could not afford the blunder of bringing about what all the efforts of southern diplomacy had so far failed to achieve, a steel encirclement of the north. Mason and Slidell were accordingly conveyed in an American tug from Fort Warren to Provincetown, and in a British warship, the *Rinaldo*, to St. Thomas, whence they sailed under the British flag to Southampton.

The Senate, sitting on Boxing Day, heard an hysterical war speech from the chairman of the naval affairs committee, John P. Hale of New Hampshire. One of the impeccably loyal New England Republicans who now dominated the Senate committees, Hale had been cold-shouldered by the administration over the *Trent* affair, and was obviously irked. He denounced the rumored surrender of the

---

36. Hendrick, *Lincoln's War Cabinet*, p. 206.

37. Lyons to Russell, December 27, 1861, q. Newton, *Lyons*, I, p. 72.

38. Sumner to Bright, December 30, 1861, q. Pierce, *Sumner*, p. 59. He warned Lieber that war would mean instant acknowledgement of the south, rupture of the blockade, a British blockade of the northern seacoast, and "the sponging of our ships from the ocean." Sumner to Lieber, December 24, 1861, q. Pierce, *Sumner*, p. 58.

39. D. Donald, ed., *Inside Lincoln's Cabinet: The Civil War Diaries of Salmon P. Chase* (N.Y., 1954), p. 55.

40. Bates, *Diary*, p. 216 (December 25, 1861). H. K. Beale, ed., *The Diary of Edward Bates, 1859-1866* (Washington, 1933).

men as a national humiliation, "worse than war," and reducing the United States to a second rate power. "Let our cities and villages be pillaged and burned" he raged, "but let our National honor be preserved." He threatened that an appeasing administration "would meet with such a fire in the rear that it would be harried from power."[41] Hale was at once rebuked by Sumner, who assured the House that the matter was in "safe hands," and it quickly became clear that the country would sustain no fire-eating. Seward's dispatch releasing the prisoners was promptly published and received numerous tributes from the press, while even those who demurred at his reasoning, or disliked his tone, breathed relief at the pacific outcome of events. The New York *Commercial Advertiser*'s opinion that Seward's reply was "a masterly production" was widely echoed. Richard Henry Dana, the lawyer, thought Seward "not only right but sublime," although he was critical of the document as "a little too sublimated, dephlegmated and defecated for common mortals."[42]

Far from being harried from office, Lincoln's administration seemed as a result of the affray to have consolidated itself in the public estimation. Certainly it was able to exploit the swelling demand which emerged for the delivery of a smashing blow at the south, now that foreign complications had been avoided. The apparently Machiavellian attitudes of the powers lent urgency to such a policy. Many Americans felt as if their eyes had become unglued, that no longer could they rely upon the friendly disposition of the mother country or other nations. The north must move for itself in a world of harsh realities. "For the first time since we became a nation" the *World* grieved, "the bitter cup of national humiliation is presented to our lips . . . . " The nation no longer manifestly controlled its destiny; internal division tied it to "the dictates of an imbecile prudence."[43] Horace Greeley warned of external dangers to the Union:

> The ostentatious and reiterated protestations of neutrality which reach us from over the water do not deceive even the utterers. Hereditary Aristocracy yearns toward Hereditary Slavery, and plans its rescue from impending ruin. If one pretext for interference will not serve, another will be trumped up.[44]

---

41. *NYT*, December 27, 1861. Lovejoy of Illinois was to make a bitterly anti-British speech in the House of Representatives on January 7 when the correspondence between the two countries on the *Trent* was laid before the House.

42. q. Van Deusen, *Seward*, p. 316.

43. *NYW*, December 28, 1861.

44. *NYDT*, January 3, 1862.

The Union must be saved soon or never. In a stirring appeal to arms, Greeley called on Congress to spare no effort "to the end that the next Fourth of July shall see us once more a nation united, triumphant, and at peace."

While there is no doubt that a great sigh of Anglo-American relief went up after the return of Mason and Slidell, a legacy of bitterness remained. Sumner feared that the north had obtained "a truce only," and asked his English friends to publicize the pacific intentions of Lincoln and his cabinet.[45] Sumner even "puffed" Seward, his rival, who had been assuring all and sundry that he "had no memory for injuries, and that in surrendering Mason and Slidell he did it in good faith—laying up nothing for future account or recollection . . . Seward may be careless or hasty; he is not vindictive."[46] One long-term result of the *Trent* crisis was to stimulate northern propaganda campaigns abroad. Efforts were made in particular to counteract the enmity of the upper classes in England by appeals to middle and working class opinion. The affair also lent weight to the emancipation program of the Radical Republicans. The war must have a clearer character, that of an antislavery crusade, if overseas opinion was to support it. But a yawning psychological gulf appeared to separate the two peoples. Englishmen, in being self-righteous about the fairness of their nation's neutrality, failed to appreciate the mentality of a people in arms and under ordeal. The north, with over half a million men in the army, divided politically, and plagued by complex problems of finance and administration, longed for international sympathy. It got, it seemed, distrust and chill neutrality from Britain and France. "It is hard," complained Sumner, "that with complications such as history has scarcely ever recorded, our position should be embarrassed by foreign nations."[47] In a remarkable prayer in the Senate, God was asked to help the American people "in this hour of our trial, when domestic treason stabs at the nation's heart, and foreign arrogance is emboldened to defeat the public justice of the world."[48]

In less pessimistic mood northerners hoped that their sacrifice over the *Trent* would earn neutral goodwill, and convince even Englishmen of the responsibility of transatlantic democracy. The

---

45. Sumner to Bright, January 9, 1862, in Pierce, *Sumner*, p. 61.

46. Sumner to Cobden, December 31, 1861, Pierce, p. 59.

47. Pierce, p. 61. Winthrop spoke of England unleashing the Dogs of War "when we were crippled." Winthrop to John P. Kennedy, January 1, 1862, *MHSP* (November, 1911), p. 123.

48. December 30, 1861, q. Newton, *Lyons*, I, p. 76.

accusations of mobocracy freely leveled by the British press had nettled Americans. Now, as the *Utica Daily Herald* countered, "The mouth of England is shut." The Republican government had risen above popular passion, and survived. Events had shown that the United States was "as well governed as the most rigid monarchy of Europe." *(New York Sun)* Indeed, the *Sun* added with justice, "for mob fury and excitement we must turn to England herself, for nothing on [America's] part can approach her recent demonstration of this character."[49]

Seward's concession was for a moment magnified into a wholesale victory for neutral rights: "We fix the English so they cannot back out hereafter as to the rights of neutral nations," claimed the *Hartford Courier.* The *Herald* rashly talked of England being debarred from future intervention in the Civil War, of the insurrection collapsing within ninety days. It unblushingly described itself and Seward as the saviors of the country, which raised guffaws from Bennett's rivals.[50] Politics and propaganda obscured the true proportions of the question; but a perceptive minority realized that, in their eagerness to defend Wilkes, Americans had been on the brink of seriously weakening their historic commitment to neutral rights. W. C. Bryant now thought that disavowal of Wilkes' act would have been appropriate, and should have been associated with an outright denial of the right of search even in wartime—a policy once advocated by Madison. Greeley was generous to Seward, but insisted that in future "our flag shall be unfurled . . . in accordance with all our National instincts and traditions, on the side of the recognition, the establishment, or even the enlargement of [neutral] rights—never on the other."[51] Hamilton Fish, a future Secretary of State, wrote privately to Sumner that Seward had abandoned national principles. Fish thought his dispatch "verbose and egotistical; in argument flimsy."[52]

On January 9, 1862, Sumner made a brilliant Senate speech, which was remarkable for reaffirming pure American doctrine. "The seizure of the rebel emissaries on board a neutral ship" he stated candidly, "cannot be justified according to our best American

---

49. See editorials in *Utica Daily Herald, Boston Post, New York Sun, Providence Journal,* from *AEJ,* December 31, 1861.

50. See *NYT,* December 31, 1861, "How it was done—Splendid Zampillaerostation."

51. *NYEP,* December 30, 1861; *NYDT,* December 30, 1861.

52. Fish to Sumner, December 29, 1861, in Pierce, *Sumner,* IV, p. 54; Van Deusen, *Seward,* p. 316.

precedents and practice. There seems to be no single point where the seizure is not questionable, unless we choose to invoke British precedents and practice, which beyond doubt led Captain Wilkes into the mistake which he committed." He clearly implied, without mentioning the Secretary of State, that Seward's whole rationale of events was ill-founded.

Sumner described the "two old men" taken from the *Trent* as wicked enemies of their country, engaged in a hostile venture to array England and France against the United States; and he sympathized with Wilkes' patriotic desire to frustrate their designs. But he refused to sanction the extreme and novel belligerent doctrines which would justify their seizure. The only persons liable to capture according to American practice were military or naval personnel, strictly and narrowly defined. Diplomats were immune. Dispatches were immune. Contraband must have a hostile destination. Adjudication was absolutely indispensable once capture occurred. This was his case in a nutshell, but it was defended in the speech by elaborate reference to American diplomacy and solemn treaty provisions.[53] The basic American posture had been struck by Madison in 1804, during the impressment wrangle, when he stated that, with the exception of soldiers, "we consider a neutral flag on the high seas as a safeguard to those sailing under it."[54] In its treaties the U.S. had consistently adhered to a narrow concept of contraband; and its enumerated lists had excluded dispatches. France and other Continental countries followed this practice and, during the *Trent* crisis, remonstrated with Washington against any departure from established neutral traditions. Jay's and other treaties, moreover, had declared contraband articles to be detainable only when being carried "to an enemy." Foreshadowing Lord Russell, Sumner warned:

> If a neutral voyage between two neutral ports is rendered illegal . . . , then the postal facilities of the world, and the costly enterprise by which they are conducted, will be exposed to interruptions under which they must at times be crushed, to the infinite damage of universal commerce.[55]

Sumner preferred to hail the release of the prisoners, not as a surrender under duress, nor as a recompense for a capture which was

---

53. *Cong. Globe,* 37 Cong., 2 Sess., January 10, 1862, pp. 241-245. See also V. H. Cohen, "Charles Sumner and the Trent Affair" *JSH*, XXII, No. 2, (May, 1956), pp. 205-219. Sumner's use of treaty provisions was dismissed as irrelevant by certain jurists.

54. Quoted *Cong. Globe,* p. 243.

55. *Cong. Globe,* p. 244.

technically imperfect, but as a vindication of historic American principle. The *Trent* affair, he said, had had at least one happy outcome: it had achieved the epochal effect of committing Britain belatedly to the side of neutral rights at sea, and "to a certain extent this cause is now under her tutelary care."

> If the immunities of passengers, not in the military or naval service, as well as of sailors, are not directly recognized, they are at least implied; while the whole pretension of impressment, so long the pest of neutral commerce, and operating only through the lawless adjudication of a quarter-deck, is made absolutely impossible . . . . There are victories of force. Here is a victory of truth.

Meanwhile in Britain, tension fell when it became known that the American government has disowned any complicity in Wilkes' action. On December 19 Adams conveyed Seward's official assurance on this point to Russell, who at once instructed Lyons to accept such an explanation in place of an apology. Seward's initiative in this respect seemed highly encouraging: "Could anything show more clearly that they desired to avoid collision, to keep open a door for their own retreat?" Argyll asked of Gladstone.[56] In Lancashire interventionish sentiment fell off markedly although pro-southern sympathies continued to be strong. Liverpool's *Weekly Mercury* was soon condemning physical intrusion by England as likely to prolong the cotton famine; peaceful mediation was now seen as the best means of solving America's, and Lancashire's, problems.[57]

England now waited on tenterhooks for the north's reply. Adams and his countrymen abroad wavered neurotically between buoyancy and anguish. Strong rumors insisted that the ministry believed war now out of the question, but Bright's assessment varied: "I *suspect* there is a section of our Government disposed for war; but I *know* there is another section disposed for peace. . . ."[58] The growing strength of the "peace and arbitration" school, and the setback to the reinforcement program in Canada, were indeed creating a headache for the government: would it be possible to rekindle the country's war-spirit, should the Americans confound the optimists and reject the British terms? The plan to launch a mid-nineteenth century equivalent of a *Blitzkrieg* on the outbreak of war was fast

---

56. Argyll to Gladstone, December 20, 1861, in Argyll, *Autobiography and Memoirs*, II, p. 180.

57. Liverpool *Weekly Mercury*, January 25, 1862, q. Ellison, p. 261.

58. Bright to Sumner, December 21, 1861, *MHSP*, XLV, pp. 155–156.

crumbling at each delay and sign of national division. Russell now felt that an American refusal would need to be referred to Parliament, not due to meet until February 6. Significantly, such qualms were to be forgotten in the welter of self-congratulation which followed the settlement. A discouraging dispatch from Lyons created a last-minute panic in London, but on the afternoon of January 8 telegraphic news arrived confirming that Mason and Slidell were to be released. Moran declared: "This lifted a load of lead from our hearts."[59] "Thank God," wrote Lady Russell to a friend, "I rejoice with all my heart and soul. John was delighted. He was *very* anxious up to the last moment . . . it has been a surprise to us to hear of the . . . ill-concealed disappointment of *London Society*; but John says London society is always wrong."[60] General rejoicing followed.

It is usual to emphasize that England's response to the settlement was one of relief at narrowly escaping a damaging war with a kindred people, a relief soon translated into reaction against any policy of truckling too closely with the Confederates or of needlessly courting further trouble with the Union. In other words, the Atlantic idea, the concept that the vested interests of the Atlantic world lay in peace, had survived this its severest threat and was to continue to be one of the underlying predeterminants of civil war diplomacy. Such a view is persuasive—it is even partly true—but it is also dangerous because it masks the subtle realities of the developing situation. It is undeniable that the settlement stimulated relief. It fulfilled the requirement of peace without dishonor; it encouraged Bright and the Manchester school and all who hoped that reason would prevail in international affairs; it even convinced some people that the north, including Seward, was conciliatory to England. A man like John Stuart Mill found it impossible to think "without something like a shudder, from what we have escaped"—the emancipators of the slave collaborating with, and thus helping to set up in a commanding world position, "a powerful republic, devoted not only to slavery, but to pro-slavery propaganda. . . ."[61]

Viewed in another light, however, the affair augured less well for Anglo-northern relations. Offsetting the efforts for peace of "the

59. *Journal of Benjamin Moran*, II (January 8, 1862), p. 939.

60. D. MacCarthy and Lady M. A. Russell, *Lady John Russell, A Memoir . . . etc.* (London, 1910), p. 195. In Liverpool the news of the settlement was met with mingled cheers and hisses. *Weekly Mercury*, January 11, 1862, q. Ellison, p. 265.

61. Mill in *Frasers' Magazine*, LXII (February, 1862), q. EDA, I, p. 240.

quiet and religious citizens of the middle classes"—the archytpal "U.S. lobby"—was the ominous alienation from the north of proletarian opinion, particularly in Lancashire where prosouthern and mediationist sentiment was tenaciously to persist. Economic interest (in a restoration of the cotton supply), a liberal regard for oppressed nationalities, and an emerging anticapitalism seem to have motivated working-class rejection of the Cobden-Bright view of the Civil War: a capitalist, racialist, and centralist north tended to supplant the laboring man's democratic utopia of earlier mythology.

More ominous for the State Department, members of the official and military elite in England commonly drew the moral from the *Trent* that a hard line was the most profitable way of dealing with the Americans. Britain's muscle-flexing produced a sense of exhilaration and self-confidence which obscured the real uncertainties which had existed in the military situation. Cambridge did not at all regret the demonstration:

> It will be a valuable lesson to the Americans, and to the world at large, and will prove to all what England can and will do, when the necessity for so doing arises. It also establishes the fact that we are not that insignificant *military Power*, which some people are disposed to make out, and that the military organisation of our departments is now such, that at any moment we can be, and are prepared for war, should it suddenly arise.[62]

The fact was that the British now had a ready-made blueprint for war with America; and this placed them in an insuperably stronger military and diplomatic position *vis-a-vis* the United States than at any time prior to the *Trent.* A case could be put that the outcome of the settlement—far from smoothing Anglo-American relations and reinforcing a policy of British neutrality—encouraged a more truculent British disposition in 1862 toward joining in projects for mediation of the war or recognition of the south than would have been the case if the *Trent* had not occurred. During December Adams was perturbed that, because the English people had been so lashed into hostility, " . . . if we get over this, it will only be to fall into the next trap."[63] It is noticeable that the relief with which Americans in London received the news of peace, and the government's cold-shouldering of Mason and Slidell, soon gave way to misgivings about the future. Adams (realizing that he must now "remain in this purgatory a while longer") expected the "gale" of opinion now blowing in

62. Cambridge to Doyle, February 27, 1862, q. Bourne, *EHR*, p. 630.
63. Adams to Motley, December 26, 1861, *MHSP*, XLV, p. 109.

the north's favor to be as fickle as that which previously ran against them.[64] He was pessimistic that it would last out the oncoming parliamentary session, from which he feared some antinorthern moves. Cobden still believed that three-fourths of the Commons would gladly vote the dismemberment of the republic.[65] Bright exulted that "the war-mongers here are baffled for a time." But he warned Sumner that he had received information that Palmerston and Napoleon "do intend at an early period to recognize the independence of the South, and to repudiate or break the blockade."[66]

The *Trent* affair is too often treated as an isolated incident. In fact it was only a more spectacular symptom of a basic antagonism created by the maritime war. As Sumner said to Bright: " . . . in this mighty war, with so many points of contact and of question between the two countries, there is constant danger of collision."[67] The history of the next years was to show the strength and persistence of such frictions. Seward's inclination towards a high belligerent stand, as revealed in his dispatch releasing the prisoners, was symptomatic of the way in which the pressures of war forced the United States further away from its historic position on neutral rights. British pride was galled, and British economic interests bruised, by America's high-handedness at sea—by its flexible interpretation of blockade, its extending concept of contraband, and development of doctrines such as "continuous voyage." But for the immense restraint imposed by Britain's long term naval interests, which favored strong belligerent rights, the British response would have been much more bellicose. As it was, tempers became badly frayed on both sides of the Atlantic, as the Americans interfered with neutral shipping, and the English gave "unneutral" encouragement to Confederate shipbuilding plans and commerce-raiding. Two perils emerged for the north: a war by miscalculation might be precipitated after a series of incidents had stretched British patience too far, just as the War of 1812 had "happened" after too many affronts to American honor. Or, perhaps more likely, an embittered public opinion in England might give irresistible support to one or other of the schemes for foreign intervention or mediation which flourished in 1862.

---

64. Adams, *Diary*, February 8, 1862, q. Ferris, p. 523.

65. Morley, *Cobden*, p. 156 and following.

66. Bright to Sumner, January 11, 1862, *MHSP*, XLV, p. 156 and following.

67. Sumner to Bright, December 30, 1861, in Pierce, *Sumner*, p. 59.

Chapter VII

Prelude to Intervention

The south was less disappointed at the outcome of the *Trent* affair than its enemies expected. Isolation from the center of affairs, together with suspicion that the British would act with perfidy and the north with craven submissiveness, had discouraged exaggerated hopes of a quick end to the war. Cassandras abounded. The *Richmond Examiner* expressed pale hopes that national pride and scarcity of cotton would sting Britain into war, but its longstanding anti-British fervor prevented it welcoming Albion wholeheartedly in the role of deliverer; and in the period of waiting for an outcome its optimism quite evaporated.[1] The *Charleston Mercury* was more perverse. In its first editorial it regarded the seizure with "mortification:" it was legal and would not produce war. ". . . disagreeable as it is we cannot resist the inference that the English government will decline any interference on behalf of our captured Commissioners."[2] Later on the *Mercury* still preferred to put its faith in King Cotton, military successes, and southern self-reliance. The *Times Picayune*, in still Confederate New Orleans, admonished that "much harm has been done to the cause of the Southern Confederacy by relying, with absorbing confidence, on the relief in our struggle . . . by the early interposition of foreign powers."[3]

1. *Richmond Examiner*, November 18-December 27, 1861.
2. *Charleston Mercury*, November 19, 1861. Also November 20, 23, 1861.
3. *New Orleans Times Picayune*, January 3, 1862.

France, because of its traditional hatred of "paper" blockades, seemed the best theater for Richmond's new year offensive. The ground seemed ready enough, despite the cynics who said that nothing was quite what it appeared in the second empire. Distress was worsening in the French cotton industry, partly because of imperial inefficiency in exploring alternative sources of supply. Plebian satisfaction being essential to the Bonapartist system of plebiscitary democracy, Napoleon must make some gesture on the issue. (He was to make gestures for the rest of the war.) The recent imbroglio had left an aftermath of anti-Yankeeism in official circles, and encouraged ideas of wringing concessions from a weakened Union. Unfortunately for Seward the "stone fleet" episode gave the gladiatorial an opportunity simultaneously to beat the drums of neutral rights and Americophobia. The Union navy had tried, ineptly, to ease the task of the blockaders by sinking stone-laden whalers in the great ship channels to Charleston harbor. This provoked a British protest during the *Trent* crisis, and French opinion generally sided with Lord Russell when he spoke of "a project worthy only of times of barbarism. . . . It is a plot against the commerce of nations."[4] It also seemed an admission that a regular blockade could not be maintained. Thouvenel carefully refrained from overreaction, lodging only an informal explanation of opposition with Seward. His position was strengthened when information arrived that the damage done to Charleston harbor was mild and impermanent.[5] (New channels were rapidly formed by the currents; as Melville said:

> A failure, and complete
> Was your Old Stone Fleet.)

The efforts of Dayton, Bigelow and Weed in Paris had been devoted to lowering the temperature, in particular by citing numerous European precedents for blocking ports. (Britain was hardly fitted to complain as she had closed Dunkirk in 1713, and justified high-handed naval actions such as the bombardment of Copenhagen and seizure of the Danish fleet in 1807 as necessitated by the exigencies of a power situation. The Confederates themselves had blocked the Charleston channel during the *Star of the West* incident in January

---

4. Russell to Lyons, December 20, 1861, *BSP* (1862) [2909], LXII, No. 127, p. 114. Russell was denouncing the plan in advance, the actual operation taking place on the same day (December 20). He thought it indicated "utter despair at the restoration of the Union."

5. John E. Woodman, "The Stone Fleet," *Am. Neptune* (October, 1961), pp. 234-259.

1861.) The Emperor's annual speech to the assembly (January 27) proved to be innocuous on America. In it there was no suggestion that his recent recognition of Italy (June, 1861) presaged a similar move towards the Confederacy: " . . . as long as the rights of neutrals are respected, we ought to limit ourselves to praying ardently that these dissentions may soon come to an end."[6]

Slidell arrived in Paris at the end of January. He found ministers Persigny (interior), Baroche (justice), Fould (finance), together with Count Morny (President of the lower house) cordial to the south. The belief was current that financial difficulties would soon force the Union to consider mediation of some sort. Confederate victories were lacking, however, and Thouvenel was cool, making it clear that the question of recognition of the south was not at present on the government's agenda. "Nor," Thouvenel added "am I prepared even to suggest the lapse of time or any circumstances which might hereafter render it a subject of conference with agents or representatives."[7] Practical considerations left Slidell no alternative but to focus upon the blockade. In that respect his plans were to be sadly handicapped by the efforts of his colleagues across the channel.

The real effectiveness of the Union blockade during the Civil War is still a matter of dispute. Marcus Price, in a painstaking study of Confederate and Union customs, naval and court records, and other sources, has compiled lists of ships known to have tested the blockade.[8] Although these are minimum and confirmed figures, they are impressive: There were 2960 runs attempted through the blockade of the Gulf ports, 2054 at Carolina ports, 1302 at Georgia and East Florida ports. Of a total of 6316 runs attempted during the war, 5389 were successful, an 85% success rate. Steam blockaders achieved a 92% success rate (2525 out of 2742 runs attempted). The ships best fitted for blockade-running were light-draft, preferably speedy, with necessarily limited tonnage; at night, by hugging the shoreline, they could elude the vigilance of the heavier Union cruisers, which were usually forced by coastal shallows and other hazards to anchor four or five miles offshore. Small, fast paddle and screw steamers were

---

6. Quoted Case and Spencer, p. 257.

7. Slidell to Hunter, 11.2.62, q. Case and Spencer, p. 258.

8. Marcus W. Price, "Ships that Tested the Blockade of the Carolina Ports, 1861-1865," *Am. Neptune*, VIII (1948), pp. 196-241; "Ships that tested . . . Gulf Ports, 1861-1865," XI (1951), pp. 262-290; XII (1952), pp. 52-59, 154-161, 229-238; "Ships that tested . . . Georgia and East Florida Ports, 1861-1865," XV (1955), pp. 97-132.

popular, many being built especially for the trade on the Mersey or Clyde, where from 1862 they sold like hot cakes. Blockade-running became a highly organized and flourishing industry, paying high wages for skippers and crews (mostly foreigners, many British), and returning astronomic profits. Ports such as Nassau in British New Providence, St. George's in Bermuda, and Matamoros in Mexico became thriving entrepôts for the illicit trade. Cotton and other southern exports made their way to these centers, and thence to Europe, while goods destined for the Confederacy were here transshipped from large neutral traders to flotillas of small blockade-runners.

These facts may also be construed as demonstrating the dislocative effects of the blockade. Modern naval opinion is inclined to the broad view that the blockade achieved its major objective by scaring off a potentially massive trade with the south. Risk of capture deterred huge numbers of regular merchantmen from making even a token attempt to enter the southern ports—the chances of heavy draft steamers or sailing vessels negotiating the major channels to the relatively few big ports such as Charleston, Wilmington, Savannah, or New Orleans were minimal. Even the more intrepid were forced to confine their trade to the intermediate ports such as Nassau. The statistics of blockade-running are less impressive when the light tonnages of runners are remembered, and also the fact that a substantial proportion of successful runs occurred in the first year of the war, when Union blockaders were few and crews were unfamiliar with the demanding routine of blockade duty. As an extreme indication, 1123 out of a total of 1302 runs attempted through the Georgia and East Florida ports occurred between April 20 and December 31, 1861, before the cordon tightened. Furthermore, most of these runs were made by coastwise traders, very few by ships engaged in foreign trade. Price concludes that blockade-running to these particular ports "may be written off as an insignificant effort . . . insofar as its contribution to the war effort of the south and the material needs of its far-flung civilian populace are concerned."[9] More realistic would be an attempt to compare wartime clearances with prewar figures. Projections based on clearance rates for Carolina ports during May, 1861, while the blockade was still innocuous, would suggest a rate of over 1400 attempted runs between May and the end of December, whereas the actual figure is 733 attempts.[10] Comparable

9. Price, *Am. Neptune,* XV (1955), p. 97. Foreign trade was more extensive from other ports.

10. Price, "Blockade-running as a Business in S. Carolina, 1861–1865," *Am. Neptune,* IX (1949), pp. 31–62. Cf. Benjamin's claim in 1863 that Charleston's foreign trade had risen over its 1858 level.

figures for 1862-1865 fluctuate, but never rise above 515, while a steady decrease is noticeable in the number of vessels engaged in the trade as the war continued. The blockade forced the Confederacy to breathe through a constricted windpipe, and the effort became more debilitating with time. Runners brought in large quantities of essential arms and supplies, but greed for maximum profits caused many shippers to waste space on luxury items. By paying low prices for cotton, speculators made profits at the expense of the southern consumer and government, while the blockade accelerated inflation, perhaps discouraged rapid industrialization, and bred war fatigue. The profiteering of shippers created bitterness, and in itself demonstrated clearly the existence of scarcity and the fall-off in volume and regularity of prewar commerce.[11] Not least, the cordon deprived the southern navy of needed bases.

Such considerations exerted little force in Europe in 1861, when the blockade was at its leakiest. Southern sympathizers peddled statistics on blockade-running, pointing out that the north was attempting to close by proclamation over three thousand miles of coastline while it was capable of stationing cruisers off only a few major ports. Disputes over such definitions of blockade had been particularly contentious during the Napoleonic wars. France and the United States had striven for restricted definition, arguing that a blockade only existed at a particular port if enforced by a cordon of ships placed in front of it and strong enough to prevent ships entering or leaving. Britain embraced a mobile concept, demanding the right to blockade an entire coast, provided it was properly notified and effective. The question "What was effective?" was carefully maintained by the British to be a pragmatic issue. The imperatives of war now forced the Confederacy to assume the old American stance, the United States the old British one.

The Palmerston government, with one eye on Britain's future interests as mistress of the seas, had no desire to erode the nation's historic claims on blockades. The Declaration of Paris had left open the matter of definition—an effective, and thus binding, blockade was one maintained by a force sufficient "really" to prevent access to an enemy port—and the government was intent on keeping the definition open. The Admiralty, acutely aware of the lurking embarrassments in the situation, resisted pressures from mercantile and shipping interests—and from neutral nations—to denounce the Union

---

11. John B. Heffernan, "The Blockade of the Sth. Confederacy," *Smithsonian J. Hist.*, II, No. 4 (1967-1968), p. 38.

blockade. Meanwhile it carefully recorded for future use every extension of belligerent claims made by the north. Because it suited naval interests, and because trade was less seriously bruised by an ineffective blockade, the Royal Navy displayed noticeable forbearance concerning the enforcement of Lincoln's blockade proclamation of April 1861. Examples of ineffective blockade were met at first merely by the practice of British warships representing the facts (courteously but precisely) to the commander of the blockading squadron. Even this was abandoned in November, after Russell had consulted his law advisers, and directed the Admiralty that the communications were unnecessary "and may possibly be attended with evil effects."[12]

During early 1861 Lyons had exceeded London in his zeal for discovering lapses in the blockade, and made myriad representations to Seward on behalf of British subjects who claimed to have suffered losses because of its uneven application.[13] In June, the crown law office advised Russell that it was "highly desirable at present to avoid discussions upon abstract principles of International Law" with the Union, which appeared "upon the whole to have acted liberally in regard to this blockade." Lyons was accordingly told in August to restrict formal protests which would only increase the vigilance of the blockaders, and make life difficult for English merchantmen. By the year's close, Russell was well informed of the inadequacy of the blockade from consular reports and Liverpool Harbour Board records (the latter revealing that over 1200 ships had violated the blockade in 1861). But angry Confederate protests against British "laxity" made no dent upon official policy. The *Trent* affair had shown only too well that "a blockade is by far the most formidable weapon of offence. Surely we ought not to be over-ready to blunt its edge or injure its temper?"[14]

Mason finally arrived in London in late January, having barely survived a nightmarish voyage through icy gales in HMS *Rinaldo*. He set himself to make a blitz upon the blockade. The ministry, he thought, "may hang back," but he hoped that the new parliament would demand action. Russell, in an unofficial interview on February 10, "seemed utterly disinclined to enter into conversation at all as to the policy of his Government, and only said, in substance, they

---

12. Adm.1/5768, Hammond to Admiralty, October 5, November 5, 1861; q. Baxter, p. 78.

13. M. R. Pitt, *Gt. Britain and Belligerent Maritime Rights from the Declaration of Paris, 1856, to the Declaration of London, 1909* (Unpub. Ph.D. Thesis, Univ. of London, 1964), p. 33 and following.

14. *Times*, February 10, 1862.

must await events."[15] Russell had in fact already consulted his legal and naval advisers, and had determined to resist the southern lobby if they tried to force his hand. Indeed from the discussions emerged a new willingness to safeguard British interests, if necessary by an expanded concept of blockade. Russell explained the government's opinion in a dispatch to Lyons, which soon obtained public notoriety:

> . . . assuming that the blockade is duly notified, and also that a number of ships is stationed and remains at the entrance of a port, sufficient really to prevent access to it or to create an evident danger of entering or leaving it, and that these ships do not voluntarily permit ingress or egress, the fact that various ships may have successfully escaped through it . . . will not of itself prevent the blockade from being an effective one by international law.[16]

Russell's "evident danger" doctrine harked back to the Anglo-Russian Convention of 1801, was considerably more flexible than the Declaration of Paris formula, and was to alarm neutrals and southerners as a resurrection of paper blockades.

Mason, unaware of the intricacies of the political situation, welcomed the Commons debate on W. G. Gregory's motion declaring the blockade ineffective, set down for March 7. Gregory had wanted to propose southern recognition, but, apparently after consulting Disraeli, redirected his attention to the blockade issue.[17] The effect of the motion was to force the administration's hand. It tabled twenty-six pages of papers on the blockade, maximum publicity thus being attracted to Russell's "evident danger" dispatch. In debate Gregory aired the south's protests, borrowing neutralist arguments from the French jurist d'Hautefeuille, who had accused England of selfishly conniving at an illegal blockade to justify future arrogant pretensions. Britain was risking a continental response of armed neutrality once again. It was also unjustly allowing the people of Lancashire to suffer privations illegally thrust upon them. Gregory's

---

15. Mason to Hunter, February 22, 1862, q. EDA, I, p. 266.

16. Russell to Lyons, February 15, 1862, *Br. Sess. Papers,* LXII (1862), pp. 119-120.

17. Disraeli's friend and adviser on foreign affairs, Ralph Earle, had been against discussion of recognition, writing of Gregory's original project:

> Now this, it appears to me, will do mischief. What we ought to avoid is a debate *without an issue*, for the Govt. are doing all in their power to ascertain which way the wind is likely to blow . . . . If it should appear to you that G. [Gregory] should be stopped, or receive another direction, you might send for him. . . .

Earle to Disraeli, Feb. 2, 1862, q. W. D. Jones, p. 530.

speech abounded with severe definitions of blockade, taken from continental and American authorities repudiated by England in the past. His own interpretations of the Paris declaration was that a blockade "shall be thoroughly effective and unintermittent, and of such a character that vessels shall, except in very rare contingencies, be unable to get in." The speech was cogent, the statistics of blockade violations impressive, but the tone—of casting unpatriotic aspersions and of southern partiality—was unfortunate. Gregory had affirmed "that secession was a right, that separation is a fact, and that reconstruction is an impossibility."[18]

The occasion evoked a forceful speech from Roundell Palmer, the Solicitor-General, which drew wide applause. Roundell Palmer denied that one could be at once an advocate of recognition and strict impartiality. If the question of recognition "were prematurely and precipitately decided before the course of events has justified such a policy, it would be an act wholly inconsistent with the neutrality which we profess to observe." Gregory had swallowed the views of continental writers whose minds were inflamed against England, which was doing nothing inconsistent with her previous practices and principles or the settled principles of international law. It was legitimate for Britain to resist "new fangled notions and interpretations of international law which might make it impossible for us effectively at some future day to institute any blockade, and so destroy our naval authority—that great arm of our independence and safety." Blockades had never been entirely airtight, and probably never would be; and with improvements in warfare and the introduction of steam, it was becoming increasingly impractical to have an exact technical definition of blockade. In the British view, the absence of blockading forces at particular points along a coast did not render the whole blockade invalid. Nor did occasional violations or remissness in enforcement invalidate an otherwise vigilant investment. The law officers' opinion was that the blockade was effective at major ports, and it was not willing to maintain that an efficient blockade must cut off access to small coasters using shallow inner channels to evade capture. Britain could not dictate to the United States the manner of carrying on belligerent operations without risking war: "You will have to send armed cruisers as convoy with your merchant vessels, and you will break through . . . it would be war."

> . . . how would it have been if, for the purpose of consulting and considering our own interests, we had been the first to break the

18. This and following speeches from *Hansard*, 3rd Ser., Vol. 165, Commons, pp. 1158-1231.

> recognised usages of established law—the first to say that the United States as a belligerent Power should not exercise all belligerent rights in the ordinary manner, because we wanted cotton? . . . we should not have been able to look in the face Europe or the world . . .

Russell confirmed this stand in the Lords on March 10, when he asserted that the Federal government had made great efforts to render the blockade efficient; their success was illustrated by the interruption to the world cotton supply, and by the failure of British and French manufactures to arrive freely at southern ports. British interference would mean war, he prophesied, and war would only provoke an emancipation proclamation from the north—causing "the horrors, murders, and pillage" of a slave insurrection by four million negroes. Blandly he suggested the prospect of the war ending within months by northern consent to peaceful separation.[19]

Much mention was made of Lancashire on the floor of the Commons. The pronortherners, such as Forster and Monckton Milnes, cited the "famine" as evidence of the blockade's effectiveness, knowing that no southern lobbyist dared admit the operation of a deliberate embargo. The stoicism of the cotton operatives was highly vaunted. Its existence was assumed by all speakers—the southerners had done no homework in the north, and found later that the idea of "silent Lancashire" had become ineradicable in the public mind—and was more convenient to the government than agitation for intervention. Roundell Palmer drew a pretty parallel between the high idealism of suffering Lancashire and that of the government: both esteemed a spirit of "justice and virtue, honour and patience" rather than "any objects of personal interest which they could gain from provoking an unjust and unnecessary war." (The *Manchester Guardian* promptly accepted Palmer's "high eulogium as a fair description of the mind of Lancashire."[20] *Reynolds'* thought the people "too beaten down to hold indignation meetings . . . five millions of our countrymen are now hovering on the verge of starvation . . . and all because of the existence of this illegal and immoral blockade, which our rulers have the means of terminating."[21]) Forster, representing Bradford (whose worsted trade was benefitting from Lancashire's discomfiture), claimed that both workers and capitalists in the north were putting the principles of international law above self-interest;

---

19. *Hansard,* 3rd ser., Vol. 165, Lords, pp. 1238-1243.
20. *Manchester Guardian,* March 10, 1862.
21. *Reynolds' Newspaper,* February 9, 1862.

but he added, more practically, that intervention was also thought likely to embitter and prolong war and was thus not a realistic means to achieve cotton quickly.

There seems to have been, as a matter of cold fact, no unanimity in Lancashire on the blockade. If anything, resentment outweighed stoicism or apathy, with reactions varying according to region, material interest, and political alignment. The Liberal *Manchester Guardian* made it a party issue and strongly supported the Palmerston government against Tory criticism. Lancashire, it volunteered, was "pretty equally divided" on the Civil War. But the blockade issue should be raised above partisanship. England had an obligation to be impartial between the combatants and to take "a comprehensive view of our national interests." Russell and Roundell Palmer had "got hold of the right end of the stick" in opposing severe definitions of blockade: " . . . a great naval power best consults its own interests by leaving the matter in as vague a condition as possible."[22]

Even James Spence, who at first condemned the blockade as an act of arbitrary power, came to take a nationalist attitude, contending against any weakening of the state's major maritime weapon: "We have maintained the right of blockade when in our favour; it becomes us to uphold it as rigidly when against us."[23]

Recent research has indicated considerable pockets of opposition to the blockade in Lancashire, although indignation did not run at a high level by March 1862.[24] Contempt for the blockade, and the Queen's indictment of its unneutral violation, was rife in Liverpool. In order to recoup losses resulting from the disruption of normal trade with the south, Liverpool shipping interests built blockade-runners, financed and participated in smuggling enterprises and ultimately turned to the construction of Confederate warships. "In Liverpool" reminisced a contemporary, "was awakened a spirit the like of which had not been known since the palmy days of the slave trade."[25] Tory organs like the *Courier* took the chance to cuff away at their old Whig enemies, Russell and Palmerston. By May the *Albion* felt that the Brights and Forsters were losing proletariat support: "We can only observe, that so far as those classes who are

---

22. *Manchester Guardian*, March 10, 1862.

23. *American Union*, 4th ed., pp. vii-viii.

24. Ellison, Chapter 8.

25. Thomas E. Taylor, *Running the Blockade: A Personal Narrative of Adventures, Risks and Escapes during the American Civil War* (London, 1896), pp. 9-10, q. Ellison, p. 282.

suffering most from this war have yet expressed themselves, their cry has been rather in favour of breaking the blockade than of countenancing the North."[26]

Such emotions were milder in the weaving towns of the northeast, and nonexistent in West Lancashire. Preston and Burnley, responding to the pressure of spinning firms which needed supplies more urgently than the weavers, echoed Liverpool, whereas Blackburn's press denounced blockade-running as likely to involve England in the war and perpetuate the scarcity of raw cotton. The southeast, with the exception of Rochdale, was sympathetic to projects for opening southern ports. Public attacks on the blockade were made at Oldham in December 1861, and there were signs of public impatience with government policy at Wigan, Bury and Manchester in the new year. The multifarious interests in Manchester affected by the war prevented clearcut alignments, and there was consistent opposition to any move likely to embroil the country wantonly in war.

Mason's first exercise in diplomacy had unexpected and disastrous repercussions for his entire mission. The debate in parliament compelled a premature stand by the government in recognition of the blockade, one from which retreat was difficult, and which severely limited the south's room for maneuver for long time to come. Moreover it forced a change of strategy upon Slidell in Paris. Contact with the Emperor and his advisers soon convinced Slidell of the falsity of his first assumption that Napoleon was capable of forcing his initiatives upon the English. Rather, Napoleon was extravagantly nervous of eroding English goodwill: "he will make any sacrifice of his own opinions and policy to retain it."[27] The allies were already in danger of falling out over Napoleonic designs in Mexico, and France was unlikely to risk further squabbling by making a suspicious lone move on the blockade. While England was uncommitted on the matter, the south's obvious tactic was to seek joint action. Now England had accepted the blockade. Slidell's only diplomatic resource was to fight the long odds, and to encourage separate French action by emphasizing the differing national interests of France and England on the question. He outlined persuasively Britain's expedient naval interest in popularizing paper blockades (used before, and probably to be used in future, against France); Britain's relatively thicker insulation against the effects of a cotton famine; and the

---

26. Liverpool *Albion*, May 12, 1862, q. Ellison, p. 285.
27. Slidell to Hunter, March 26, 1862; q. EDA, I, p. 273.

vested interests of her merchants in blockade-running. If Britain would not act, France must, thereby striking a blow for neutral rights, preserving her future defense interests, and getting cotton for aggrieved workers.

Slidell's was a desperate hope, fated to be annihilated on the rocks of European realities, although his appreciation of the fact was dim enough. Unilateral action had abstract appeal for the romantic Napoleon, but pragmatics won out. Balance of power considerations dramatized the dangers of playing solitaire in overseas adventures to the neglect of French security in Europe. It was not just a question of offending England, although the Anglo-French accord continued to be regarded as vital. Napoleon wavered between fear of alienating England by unilateral action on the blockade, and suspicion that by so doing he was being cleverly maneuvered into drawing England's chestnuts out of the fire. Vulnerable in Europe, overcommitted on Mexico, the emperor could not take the additional risk and expense of war with America. Friends and enemies, no doubt, would stand on the sidelines, ready to swoop upon any pickings. By persisting in his policy, Slidell managed only to stir suspicion between London and Paris and render less likely the prospect of joint intervention. This played into Seward's hands, for by a mixture of bluff and promises he was confident of forestalling independent action by individual nations.

Seward's policy in 1862 was to hold out hopes that friendly negotiations with the north would issue in limited access to cotton through captured ports. A string of northern victories in the first six months of the year, together with the development of a Union ironclad navy, were exploited to soften European nerve for interventionism. Union and Confederate foreign policies began to display ironic parallels, with Seward also intent on wedging apart the big powers. But his reasoning was more realistic than Slidell's, his axiom being that the United States had little to fear from France or the lesser powers unless they joined in a grand alliance with British might. Differing British and French interests over maritime rights and Mexico provided Seward the opportunity to create dissention. However his first efforts, focussed upon the law of the sea, were ill-timed and unsuccessful.

Seward's "capitulation" on the *Trent* had been widely justified in the north as an altruistic stroke on behalf of more civilized maritime practices. Much was said in the press and Congress about Britain being now committed to a milder view of neutral rights. In fact, of course, neither Britain nor the United States were committed to anything very much as a result of the *Trent*—technically perhaps only to the necessity of adjudication of prizes. But a considerable public opinion in France, America and Britain thought the time opportune for a general reform of international law. Seward, in a note delivered to Thouvenel on January 24, called for French sponsorship of a conference of maritime powers which would endorse the strongly neutralist principles enshrined in Franco-American treaties (narrow concepts of contraband, circumscribed rights of search and seizure, inviolability of neutral ships sailing between neutral ports), and perhaps even endorse the cherished American claim of safety for all noncontraband private property at sea. In return the United States would raise its blockade as part of a general abolition of blockades.[28] These were immensely tempting gains for neutral nations, and a good deal of pleasure was evinced in European capitals at the prospect of leashing England's seadogs. Seward's move, however, did not look well, coming so soon after his blatant espousal of high belligerent arguments in his dispatch on the *Trent.* France might seem to be cooperating in a tawdry attempt at vindictiveness against the English. Russell, meanwhile, had taken a milder stand on neutral rights than the Admiralty when he formally replied to Seward's Christmas Day disputation on January 23: Contraband must have a hostile, not a neutral, destination, hence the *Trent*'s voyage could not have involved a violation of neutrality; nor could ambassadors proceeding to a bona fide neutral terminus on one of its merchant ships be considered contraband.[29] This was as far as Britain might realistically be expected to go. The government fended off any idea of a conference, and Thouvenel quietly shelved the project.

One reason for French quiescence was fear of aggravating English relations made bad enough over Mexico. The surface unity which had marked the joint occupation of Vera Cruz by the French, Spanish and British quickly fragmented in the new year. Ostensibly acting according to the Treaty of London, the French army advanced on Mexico City to restore order and "seek our guarantees." It was arranged that General Juan Almonte accept the Mexican regency, pending discovery of the wishes of the Mexican people concerning their future government. In April, after wranglings among the

---

28. Case and Spencer, pp. 244-245.

29. Russell to Lyons, January 23, 1862, *Foreign Relations*, 1862, pp. 248-253. Russell complained: "According to Mr. Seward's doctrine, any packet ship carrying a Confederate agent from Dover to Calais . . . might be captured and carried to New York."

allies, General Prim, the Spanish commander, and Sir Charles Wyke, the English minister to Mexico, branded the French action contrary to treaty stipulations. After making separate bargains for reparations with the Juárez government, the British and Spanish pulled out. England and France regarded the treaty as no longer in force, the Spanish held it to be "suspended." But the French professed to be loyally pursuing the objects of the original convention. Spain's withdrawal perhaps recognized Napoleon's unbeatable headstart in Mexico, but was more probably payment for French abstention from the San Domingo affair. British motives were clouded in a smokescreen of self-righteous declamation. The Foreign Office had long suspected French duplicity, and it recoiled from the folly of baiting the Americans. Russell reminded Paris that "there was a sort of understanding that so long as European powers did not interfere in America, the United States might abstain from European alliances." But, in the event, the British played the French game: they joined the combined expedition, disregarding Wyke's advice that Juárez could establish order and collect duties; and it was only after the French had become inextricably involved that the British ostentatiously washed their hands of the affair.[30] They reaped both goodwill in the north, and distractions for Napoleon. Palmerston no doubt relished Napoleon's exposure as a faithless adventurer. Yet he wanted the Mexicans punished (among other offenses they had broken into the British legation), and he had only cynical approval for the principle of European rule in Mexico:

> As to the monarchy scheme if it could be carried out it would be a great blessing for Mexico and a godsend to all countries having anything to do with Mexico . . . It would also stop the North Americans . . . in their absorption of Mexico. [Palmerston strongly feared Seward's treaty-loan idea as laying the ground for foreclosure by a new creditor]. If the North and South are definitely disunited and if at the same time Mexico could be turned into a prosperous monarchy I do not know any arrangement that would be more advantageous for us. We cannot with our seven hundred marines take part in such an enterprize, but if France and Spain can manage it and the Arch Duke Max. could become king, I do not see that we need complain.[31]

---

30. Russell to Cowley, September 27, 1861, q. Blumenthal, p. 167. See Chapter 6 generally.

31. Palmerston to Russell, January 19, 1862, *PRO, G. and D.*, 22:22, q. Bell, *Palmerston*, II, pp. 313-314. Russell later wanted to discourage Maximilian (whom Napoleon favored as ruler of Mexico), but Palmerston demurred on the grounds that what France was doing in Mexico "will have a tendency to fetter her action in Europe . . . ." Palmerston to Russell, September 26, 1863, q. Bell, pp. 352-353.

In 1862 the world watched the early success of the Union's western campaign under Grant's vigorous leadership. Coordinated land-and-river operations enabled the reduction in February of the strategic Forts Henry and Donelsen on the Tennessee and Cumberland rivers. This gave Grant a stranglehold over northern Tennessee, and forced the Confederates (under Albert Sidney Johnston) to retreat from unprotected Nashville. These setbacks damaged the southern cause in the English blockade debate, but worse was to follow. A regrouping of rebel forces in southern Tennessee was foiled at Shiloh, despite early Federal disorder and bloody casualties on both sides. Johnston's death in battle, and a further southern retreat to Corinth, underlined the weakness of the rebels in the west. On the Mississippi, Pope (Halleck directing) pushed south from Columbus with naval support, overwhelming enemy positions at New Madrid on March 14 and Island No. 10 on April 7; while at the end of May Beauregard was forced to evacuate Corinth. On the Virginia front, McClellan's massive Peninsular campaign got ponderously under way, threatening Richmond from Chesapeake Bay and seeming to promise a speedy end to the war.

Projects for recognition of the south, or direct intervention by the powers, languished under such conditions. The French senate, a weak body habitually echoing the Emperor's opinions (or what it hoped were his opinions), endorsed his policy of neutrality on February 17, piously declaring that the American struggle "would be shorter to the extent that it is not complicated by foreign interference." So quiescent were the French on the blockade that Mason in London suspected Thouvenel and Russell to be in league over the latter's doctrine of "evident danger;" and Slidell was to write home in March counseling the southern people to rely exclusively on their own resources.[32] However according to one school of thought, the north would lose face if it negotiated separation with the Confederacy after military reverses, but might be prepared to talk peace after prestigious victories. The axiom in the theory was the ultimate irreducibility of the south. European good offices would become necessary, according to the pundits, after further Union triumphs. The British were cautious about exploring this line with a prickly State Department, but Thouvenel in March instructed a reluctant Mercier to canvass mediation prospects in Washington. An early peace, achieved through French good offices, would have been vastly pleasing to Thouvenel, whose whole American policy turned on the

32. Case and Spencer, p. 262.

need to localize troubles likely to engulf his country, while diminishing the economic effects of the war on the French people.[33]

Meanwhile a spectacular development in the seawar gave a portent of man's swiftly improving capacity for destruction, and a sign of the impending industrialization of warfare. The historic contest in Hampton Roads between Ericsson's *Monitor* and the Confederate *Merrimac* coincided with the English debate on the blockade, and forcibly illustrated the novel dangers attendant on any European attempts to break the blockade. Mallory, the Confederate naval chief, had had the *Merrimac* urgently fitted out in Norfolk navy yard as a visible sign of his dogged faith in an ironclad navy.[34] A captured Federal frigate, it was clad in four inches of iron over twenty-two inches of wood, and was armed with a formidable ram and rather less formidable smoothbore guns. Essentially a fixed floating turret, the *Merrimac* had low freeboard and negligible seaworthiness. (An observer of events from Fort Monroe described it as "looking like a submerged house, with the roof only above water."[35]) Southern reverses determined Mallory to launch his "iron-shelled turtle" upon enemy squadrons in Hampton Roads. Its destructiveness caused a sensation in the north, and discredited British advocates of fixed fortifications and wooden ships of the line. Impervious to fire from the forts, the *Merrimac* on March 8 rammed and sank the wooden *Cumberland* (losing her ram in the process), and forced the wooden *Congress* to strike her colors (she was later fired with hot shot). Broadsides from Union warships struck the ironclad but "glanced off having no more effect than peas from a popgun."[36] Early press reports in London and Paris gave the impression that the northern blockade was doomed, and that Washington and New York were about to be bombarded and burned. (An impossible task for the unseaworthy *Merrimac*, but one which even Mallory considered.) The indecisive encounter on March 9 between the *Merrimac* and *Monitor* quenched these prospects, but graphically indicated the significance of advanced naval architecture. Ericsson's design employed the modern "turret" principle developed in England by Captain Cowper Coles—the *Monitor* was a floating ramp, with only two-foot freeboard, carrying a heavily

---

33. Blumenthal, *Reappraisal*, p. 138.

34. Joseph T. Durkin, *Stephen R. Mallory: Confederate Navy Chief* (Chapel Hill, 1954), Chapter 9.

35. Dispatch from Ft. Monroe, March 8, 1862, in *Manchester Guardian*, March 26.

36. *Manchester Guardian*, March 26, 1862.

armored, revolving chamber of two eleven-inch smoothbore guns. It was clad in eight inch iron armor, and the contest was a triumph for the defensive capabilities of armor. Mutual withdrawal occurred after four hours of pointblank broadsides, neither vessel being seriously damaged.

The action stimulated the French, always more logical than the British about iron ships, to hasten their naval modernization program. In England the Admiralty spurned a panic reaction but quietly pushed ahead with new ships. In a Commons debate on March 31, the government found itself under pressure to build a massive iron steam navy, and advised to scrap planned fortifications of naval dockyards such as Portsmouth. While Bright happily supported retrenchment on Gladstonian principles of economy, the patriots wanted lavish spending on a fleet of monitors for home defense. Lewis spoke derisively of their projects requiring a supplementary naval estimate of 12 to 15 millions. Government speakers dampened down "groundless alarm" by reasserting the Defence Commissioners' confidence in a combined system of forts and ironplated auxiliary vessels. Lewis, reasonably, claimed that the recent action threw little new light upon the qualities of iron ships, adding that artillery advances were the answer to monitors. He promised a policy of careful vigilance. Palmerston neatly parried a move by Bentinck on April 4, to divert the fortifications vote to iron-sheathed ships, by referring it to a revived Royal Commission on National Defences.

The Hampton Roads duel had provided a neat enough object lesson, seen in context, but public opinion in Europe vastly exaggerated its implications. France had demonstrated the efficacy of ironclad floating batteries against Russian shell at the bombardment of Kilburn in 1855, and Britain had followed with armored wooden and iron floating batteries of the *Trusty* and *Erebus* class. A French armoring program, starting in the late 1850's, had forced Britain to lay down the *Warrior* in 1859 and to make extensive trials with sheathing and new offensive guns. It was true that wooden hulls, as the foundation for armor, retained favor with many experts; and that during the *Trent* crisis the *Warrior* was the only ocean-going, iron-hulled, armored ship in the Royal Navy. But its sister ship, the *Black Prince*, was almost complete, and the smaller iron-hulls *Defence* and *Resistance* had been launched. Only the center portion of these vessels was protected by iron plate, and critics claimed that under fire bow and stern would be shot away. However the decision to rectify this defect was made well before the monitors appeared. On September 2, 1861, the Admiralty was given its first vote to builda series of iron-hulled frigates, with end-to-end armor on the waterline. (These ships, *Hector*, *Valiant*, *Achilles*, *Minotaur*, and *Agincourt* were launched between 1862 and 1865.) Also in 1861 the navy began an extensive, if slow, program of converting older wooden battleships to ironclads.

Professional opinion was thus less carried away by the lessons of Hampton Roads, and counseled against the panic measures shoved forward by amateurs. The monitors themselves were useless at sea, and their role was likely to be confined to harbor service and local defense. Hampton Roads strengthened the case for turreted warships and all-round fire—a crucial development, but already pioneered by Coles with the *Prince Albert.* (Coles' armored "cupola" had been extensively tested against heavy artillery in 1861, and so impressed the experts that they proposed to build a ship with six turrets, designed for coastal defense.) The *Merrimac* helped create a fashion for rams, but it proved to be temporary and unproductive. Finally, the clash showed the superiority of heavy and complete armoring, but only against traditional weaponry. Rifled guns and armor-piercing shells were the inevitable response. Whitworth reacted by proclaiming the superiority of rifled guns firing hardmetal projectiles designed to penetrate wrought-iron hulls and plate. On April 8, at Shoeburyness, he was vindicated in an Admiralty experiment. Targets covered with iron plates of the same thickness as the *Warrior*'s (four and a half inches) were fired on by a new 300-pounder Armstrong gun. They were pierced and smashed (in Palmerston's phrase) like "pats of butter."[37] Heavier powder charges and higher shot velocity would clearly do the same to thicker armor. Nervousness about the monitors dropped noticeably with this demonstration of British armaments development. A week earlier the navy had ordered the conversion of the battleship *Royal Sovereign* to an armored turret-ship carrying five inch muzzle-loaders.

Reassurance was aided by the consideration that the world's largest industrial power was splendidly placed, with its coal and iron resources and dockyard facilities, to build the world's most powerful iron fleet. The *Manchester Guardian* provided perspective:

> There may be a certain sort of truth in saying that our whole navy consists of but two men of war [*Warrior* and *Black Prince*]; but it is to be observed that, in the same sense, the French have but one, the Americans have only a gunboat, and no other nation has any navy at all . . .[38]

---

37. *Manchester Guardian*, April 10, 1862.
38. *Manchester Guardian*, April 3, 1862.

Although the momentary alarm of politicians like Russell over the monitors soon subsided—"Only think of our position [he had written to Palmerston] if in case of the Yankees turning upon us they should by means of iron ships renew the triumphs they achieved in 1812–13 by means of superior size and weight of metal"—the Union's stocks rose.[39] With a strong ironclad navy within its capacities, the north seemed to have established an irresistable maritime advantage over the less industrialized south. In Paris, Bigelow felt that the *Monitor*'s performance " . . . had done more to re-establish us as a national power in Europe and inspire respect for our military resources than anything that has occurred since the rebellion."[40]

Meanwhile an attempt by the southern zealot, William S. Lindsay, to harness London and Paris in a move on the blockade only succeeded in highlighting the abiding discord between the capitals. Lindsay, a self-made millionaire shipowner—the largest in England—was radical M.P. for Sunderland, a committed freetrader and close friend of Cobden. Welcomed in Paris as an architect of the Chevalier treaty, Lindsay denounced the blockade in interviews with Napoleon (April 11, 13, and 18). The Emperor agreed that, although notoriously inadequate, the blockade was damaging Europe's maritime and cotton trade. He claimed that England was at fault, that he had proposed some form of joint action to London in the summer of 1861 and in March 1862, but without response. Neither the British minister, Cowley, nor Thouvenel knew officially of such initiatives, and they became incensed at the whole display of amateur intrigue which followed. Reports from the *procureurs general*, and an alarming number of petitions reaching Paris from the provinces, indicated a politically unsafe degree of distress. Napoleon conveyed to Lindsay that he favored joint recognition of the south. (Slidell was exultant, assuring Mason that he had "positive and authentic evidence that France only waits the assent of England for recognition and other cogent measures."[41]) Napoleon called the war futile, and spoke of sending a fleet to open New Orleans—if England cooperated. Sounded by Lindsay, Cowley firmly discouraged any such expectation, and echoed the Admiralty: the blockade was improving and must be acquiesced in. But Napoleon seemed set upon making a characteristically unorthodox stroke behind the backs of his advisers.

---

39. Russell to Palmerston, March 31, 1862, q. EDA, I, p. 277.
40. Bigelow to Seward, April 4, 1862, q. Case and Spencer, p. 267.
41. Slidell to Mason, April 12, 1862, q. Owsley, p. 279.

He sent Lindsay home to inform Russell and Palmerston unofficially of his views, and wanted him quietly to sound out Disraeli and Derby for an opposition response. Fiasco followed. The French minister in London, Flahault, threatened resignation because of the Emperor's apparent lack of confidence in his own ambassador; and Lindsay was icily snubbed by Russell who favored the usual channels for "the most confidential, as well as official communications." It was Cowley who had undermined Lindsay. Cowley passed on to Russell his suspicions that Lindsay wanted to make political capital with the opposition out of his visit, "and that you may hear of it in Parliament." A crestfallen Lindsay reported failure to Napoleon, repeating Disraeli's guess that Russell and Seward had a "secret understanding" not to challenge the blockade. The Emperor's Anglophobic nerve was momentarily touched, and he expressed what was to become a recurrent plaint about British ingratitude for his aid during the *Trent* affair.[42]

An unauthorized trip by Mercier to Richmond in mid-April touched off speculation that Napoleon was making a deal with the south—perhaps for trading privileges, perhaps to secure the flank for his impending expedition against the Juárez regime. Mercier accepted Seward's casual offer of a pass to the rebel capital because it offered him the chance to judge the real impact of the war on southern morale, and the opportunity to prepare the ground for an armistice and French mediation. Seward's motives in making the invitation are unknown. He may simply have hoped that Shiloh and other reverses would dispose the south to consider reconstruction—his old "conciliationist" plan—with himself a major negotiator. "You may . . . tell them that they have no spirit of vengeance to apprehend from me personally, and that they would be cordially welcomed back to their seats in the Senate, and to their due share of political influence." On this, he told Mercier, he was willing to risk his political career.[43] There might be advantage too in planting the suspicion in the south that Mercier was catspaw to the State Department, sent to represent the futility of expecting aid or recognition from the powers. Lyons was acutely aware of a further danger: Mercier's independent move would be interpreted as sign of a rift in the *entente cordiale*; it was certainly opposed to the spirit of the agreement to act in accord in America, and London was quick to suspect that sinister schemes

42. See Case and Spencer, pp. 269-275; EDA, I, pp. 289-296.

43. Mercier's report to Thouvenel, April 28, 1862, is fully printed in Case and Spencer, pp. 279-281.

were being hatched by Napoleon. Lyons failed to dissuade his colleague from the adventure, but advised him to emphasize that the Confederacy could expect no alliance from any European power.

Lyons was right, and the trip ended in diplomatic embarrassments. Nevertheless it resolved some important points. Mercier returned convinced of southern determination to achieve independence at all costs. Mercier met Judah P. Benjamin, bitterly censured in the south for his performance in the War Office and recently (March 19) promoted by Davis to the State Department. Benjamin admitted that "we have counted too much on Europe and the power of commercial interests," but utterly repudiated any reconstruction: " . . . it has come to the point where the North must exterminate us or agree to separation." Faced with northern naval onslaughts against their coastal cities, southerners would "retire into the back country" and continue a guerrilla war, a threat which impressed European opinion. Asked whether southern planters would resist the temptation of selling their cotton at ports opened for commerce by the Union, Benjamin replied:

> How can you suppose we won't burn cotton and tobacco? . . . Besides there's very little cotton in the cities. Only 600 bales in New Orleans. All this year's crop is still on the plantations where it is hard to get. Any planter who tried to sell would be exposed to the retaliation of his compatriots.

This was a blow to Seward's "open ports" policy. But hints of a "scorched earth" psychology, and of cotton scarcity, hardly brightened prospects for direct overseas intervention to obtain cotton.

In Paris, Thouvenel sent Mercier a tart reprimand for threatening the Anglo-French accord, and labored to smooth ruffled feelings in England. Napoleon also was upset—too many people had jumped to the conclusion that he was up to his old game of behind the scenes diplomacy—and this seems to have strengthened his resolve to march in step with England. News of Farragut's capture of New Orleans from the sea, and its occupation by Union troops under the soon-to-be-notorious General B. F. Butler, arrived in Europe on May 11, and plunged the Confederate camp into deep gloom. Seward could now begin haggling for an appropriate *quid pro quo* for relaxing the blockade, under a license system, at New Orleans, the only significant southern port under Federal control. Withdrawal of belligerent rights from the south was his first demand. Thouvenel would have no truck with what he regarded as a form of economic blackmail.

A legalist by temperament, he believed that France had acted scrupulously in granting belligerent rights. He could claim that the north had so far suffered no disadvantages from proclamations regularizing the status of a southern navy, for the south had no navy. In any case, as he told Dayton: "It would not be a handsome thing in a great government, at once upon the south being worsted, to withdraw a concession which had been made to them in their day of supposed strength."[44] The fall of New Orleans lessened the impact of Mercier's report from Richmond, but stalemate on the military front seemed likely. Hence Slidell began to advance the idea of a six month's armistice—it would be supervised by the powers, include the raising of the blockade and resumption of overseas trade, and permit plebiscites in the border states to determine their future.

Seward's diplomacy in this period displayed a fundamental cogency. It was designed to prolong and exploit the season of Atlantic harmony which followed the *Trent* settlement. Fitting the pattern were his plans to appease the Canadians, capitalize upon antislavery zealotry in Britain, and allay European anxiety about cotton. We shall examine each briefly.

The war scare in Canada over the *Trent* affair had had the effect of subduing provincial rivalries and welding the French and British populations into a semblance of national unity. Such results were later of immense use to the Canadian movement for confederation. But Canadian unity was built on the rock of anti-Americanism, and the affair sealed the estrangement between Canadian and northern peoples. In the aftermath, northern resentment against Britain was canalized against the Canadians, whose defense efforts were ridiculed and future security put in mortgage. Militant northerners threatened to avenge English insults at the first opportunity by making a *putsch* against the puppet state to the north, America's by right of manifest destiny. Owen Lovejoy, Illinois abolitionist, declared in the House of Representatives that the United States would aid Irish rebels after the war, inspire the French Canadians to revolt, and stir up Chartist insurrection throughout England.[45] Northerners felt that it was Canadians who had been provocative in recent events, arming to the teeth despite military passivity from the Union, and creating an unofficial theater of war along the border. Canadians had betrayed

44. Reported in Dayton to Seward, May 22 and 26, 1862, q. Case and Spencer, p. 296.

45. *Cong. Globe*, 37 Cong. 2 sess., 333, q. Winks, p. 99. For detailed treatment, Winks, Chapters 6 and 7. The Buffalo *Express* quote below appears in Winks, p. 100 (circa December 30, 1861).

democratic and antislavery principles, making their country a promising refuge for disaffection and a potential base for Confederate guerillas. In this atmosphere of distrust, rumors flew that the north would abrogate the reciprocity treaty, symbol of happier days and not due for reconsideration by the two countries until 1865. The New York *Herald* kept up a running fire against the treaty, while the Buffalo *Express* exhibited border irascibility in these words:

> The old, natural, instinctive, and wise distrust and dislike for England is revived again in the American heart, and will outlive all the soft words and sniveling cant about international brotherhood and reciprocity. These are 'our Canadian brethren', these suckling Britons to whom, like fools, we have opened our ports. . . . These reciprocal brethren of ours have been ready to fly at our throats from the moment when they felt it safe to be insolent.

Seward, however, had no intention of killing a measure which he had steered through the Senate in 1855 and in which his faith was still unbroken. Despite the war he believed that unimpeded trade between the United States and its neighbors would soften animosities, and was the best instrument for achieving a peaceful expansion of American power, of "informal empire," in the hemisphere. He intimated as much to Lyons when the latter transmitted British anxiety that the treaty be continued. For more than a year Canadian-Union relations had the chance to cool. They blew up once more when a series of festering disputes erupted from 1863 to 1865, but by then, as Robin Winks shows, war-weariness in both nations had taken its toll and the troubles were contained.

On April 24, 1862, the Senate unanimously approved a mutual-search treaty with Britain designed to suppress the oceanic slavetrade. Agreement was reached to search one another's ships for slaves and slaving equipment, with mixed courts to be set up at strategic points around the globe to adjudicate cases.[46] By providing for a peacetime right of search under strictly prescribed conditions, the treaty resolved a problem which had bedevilled Anglo-American relations for half a century: how to permit the Royal Navy to destroy the slavetrade on the high seas while preserving immunity for American neutral rights. Persistent disputes had been occasioned between the two nations by the United States' refusal to allow British warships to visit and search

46. See Conway W. Henderson, "The Anglo-American Treaty of 1862 in Civil War Diplomacy," *CWH*, XV, No. 4 (December, 1969), pp. 308–319; A. Taylor Milne, "The Lyons-Seward Treaty of 1862," *AHR*, XXXVIII (October 1932), pp. 511–525.

ships suspected of slave-trafficking under the American flag. Abuse of the American colors by slavers was prevalent, because the United States alone of the great maritime powers refused cooperation with the Royal Navy. Bitter memories of the impressment issue had prevented America signing mutual-search treaties sponsored by Britain after the Napoleonic wars. Also largely unsuccessful was the compromise attempted in the Webster-Ashburton treaty of 1842, whereby an American squadron (operating independently but cooperating with the British) was to police the West African coast to stamp out slave-trading under the American flag. Sectional animosities prevented effective collaboration, and clashes between the two countries over right of visit were still sharp in the last years of Buchanan's administration.[47] With the outbreak of war the Union cruisers stationed off West Africa withdrew to invest the south, and slave-trafficking threatened to assume scandalous proportions. Seward assured the British that the Republican administration would have "none of the squeamishness about allowing American vessels to be boarded and searched which had characterized their predecessors"—Lyons perceived "a desire to rally the Anti-Slavery feeling in England to the Northern Cause"—but the British Foreign Office preferred a more formal arrangement.

Lincoln had shown his determination to enforce the country's existing laws by hanging a slavetrader who breached an 1820 law providing the death penalty for transporting slaves to the United States. The departure of pro-slavery groups from national politics made possible the Anglo-American treaty, which was skillfully managed by Lincoln and Seward so as not to arouse public opposition and to avoid any impression of submissiveness to the British. The latter would have been fatal in the aftermath of the *Trent*. The Republican administration had sounded out the British on a convention as early as May 1861, but the draft proposal (already printed and complete with instructions for the mixed court commissioners) was sent out by Russell in February and March, 1862. Lincoln preferred that the treaty should appear to have been originated by the United States, and requested that the agreement be subject to renewal after ten years. Lyons, in charge of the negotiations in Washington, collaborated with Seward to give the impression to the world that America was the initiator of the treaty. (It was made to appear that Seward had invited Lyons in March to sign a

47. R. W. Van Alstyne, "The British Right of Search and the African Slave Trade," *JMH*, II (1930), pp. 37–47.

draft measure, which was actually the identical, printed British draft with the formal headings reversed in red ink.[48]) Lyons also pretended that he had had an unwelcome ten year limitation forced upon him, although he regarded the alteration as unimportant. The treaty was then rushed through the Senate with minimum publicity during an executive session.

Sumner and Seward were exultant, the latter claiming: "If I have done nothing else worthy of self-congratulation, I deem this treaty worthy to have lived for." Seward was skillfully bidding for British friendship by identifying the north more clearly with antislavery. Lincoln had been flooded with advice from patriots abroad to convert the Union's war aims to Negro emancipation. The cordial reception given the mutual-search treaty in London, Paris and elsewhere probably hastened the President's cautious progress toward that goal.

Whether the issue of Negro freedom was capable of affecting the diplomacy of the powers is a difficult question, like so many other issues of the Civil War. Fashion now denigrates the view that moral outrage against slavery significantly qualified the calculations of power politics. The fevers of our own age may have encouraged cynicism. John Bigelow, writing in a different climate, three decades after the war, believed that slavery "fatally handicapped" the rebels, was their "shirt of Nessus. . . . Their success in war meant the perpetuation of slavery—that and nothing else. This in due time became apparent to the people of Europe."[49] Even pro-southern tracts, such as James Spence's *American Union* (1861), perhaps the most effective to appear during the war, rejected slavery: "a gross anachronism, a thing of two thousand years ago; the brute force of dark ages obtruding into the midst of the nineteenth century."[50] Moral outrage against slavery strongly affected public sentiment in Britain, and cannot be lightly dismissed in an age when public sentiment exerted unprecedented sway over weak executives in foreign policy.

On the other hand, many believed that the war was about empire not slavery. The Negro debate was often tangential to the sectional controversy. Anti-Yankee and antislavery feelings were commonly combined. W. R. Greg, a freetrader on the conservative

48. Milne, p. 513. Seward's remark below is on p. 514.

49. John Bigelow, "The Confederate Diplomatists and their Shirt of Nessus," *Century*, XLII, ns. 20 (May, 1891), p. 113.

50. James Spence, *American Union* (London, 1861), p. 131. Spence, one of the south's best agents, lost his commission in 1864, for persisting in these views.

wing of the Liberal party, is a good example of British centerist opinion. Greg hated slavery, but saw the war as the price paid for America's unworkable populist institutions. Neither section, he felt, was morally superior to the other. There was widespread recognition in England of the deep-seated complexities of the Negro problem in America, and scepticism that force could resolve them. James Hunt's *On the Negro's Place in History* (1863) soon claimed that blacks were closer to the apes than whites, and were temperamentally fitted for slavery. Hunt's thesis was vociferously contended, but belief in black inferiority was prevalent and cut across the ranks of Yankee and rebel sympathizers. "They are not my men and brethren, these strange people with retreating foreheads, with great obtruding lips and jaws. . . . " Thus wrote the novelist Thackeray. Fresh from completing *The Virginians*, he extolled southern culture, but refused to countenance slavery. Edward Dicey, who supported the north in a popular travel account, shared white racialist views. But as Wilberforce's nephew, he approved the granting of full civil rights to the Negro, whose very weakness required it.[51]

One school of *laissez-faire* optimists rejected the theory of the African's hereditary inferiority; the liberated slave, participating in a free labor market, would attain higher civilization. The forecast blinked at the career of the free Negro in the north, where racial prejudice and economic discrimination had nullified black progress. Did not the north's "political" war aims bear out northern hypocrisy toward the Negro? The accomplished Liberian diplomat and black nationalist, Edward Wilmot Blyden, said so in a letter to Gladstone in 1862: "Both sections of the country are negro-hating and negro-crushing—intending and doing justice to 5 millions of oppressed people among them only as they are driven to it by European sentiment."[52]

Finally, British labor was deeply suspicious of the axis between antislavery, freetrade radicalism, and capitalism. Sermons against slavery seemed miserable affectation when made by those who had no compassion for the wages-slavery that enchained millions in

51. W. R. Greg, "The American Conflict," *North British Review*, XXXVII (November, 1862), pp. 491-492; G. N. Ray, *Thackeray: The Age of Wisdom* (London, 1958), pp. 216-217; E. Dicey, *Six Months in the Federal States* (London, 1863), I, pp. 69-70. For references on slavery, and a penetrating analysis, I am indebted to Neal Pender, "English Opinion on the American Civil War" (Unpub. B. A. thesis, Univ. of Queensland, 1967), Chapter 4.

52. E. W. Blyden to W. E. Gladstone, June 16, 1862, B. M. Add Mss., 44396, q. W. D. Jones, "Blyden, Gladstone, and the War," *J. Negro Hist.*, XLIX, No. 1, (January, 1964), pp. 57-58.

Britain. The Civil War seemed a struggle between two economic systems: the archaic ruralism of the south, and the new capitalism of the north. American and British capitalists condemned the southern system because it fettered the free movement of the individual as a unit within the economy. Their own industrial exploitation they justified, for it rested upon the free play of market forces. Reformist intervention was allowable in the case of slavery, but was indicted otherwise as contrary to the creed of economic individualism. Was not the war fought to tighten the grip of northern business over the south? Why should labor abet such an end? Was not the conflict an irrelevancy for international labor? Such questions were asked more commonly in the labor press in the early war years than the myth of solidarity with northern democracy would suggest.[53]

Seward knew that antislavery gestures would gain the north no immediate diplomatic windfall. He had higher hopes for his own brand of "cotton blackmail." His achievement in this respect has been commonly underestimated. He held out to the powers the vision of getting easy cotton with the compliments of the Union, and that lure exerted an insidious sway upon European imaginations. It weakened the case of the ardent blockade-busters for precipitate action; it heartened the timid, distracted the Machiavellian (like Napoleon), and pleased the peace-at-any-price school. Both Russell and Thouvenel welcomed Seward's plan of opening some ports to foreign ships, Russell because it diminished opposition to his blockade policy, Thouvenel because it gave him an alternative to propose to his emperor—Napoleon was becoming obsessed with the possibility of a popular revolt over cotton distress, and increasingly intent on a rash interventionist stroke. The trouble with intervention, as Mercier's trip indicated and as Lancashire knew well, was that it could easily prove abortive. As Henry Sanford, American minister to Brussels, said to Thouvenel in April: "The intervention of all Europe can not make cotton grow. On the contrary it might destroy it. It can not hasten

53. Files of *Reynolds' Newspaper*, *Bee-Hive*, etc. The range of labor attitudes is well brought out by Royden Harrison, *Before the Socialists* (London, 1965), Chapter 2. The older guard of anti-capitalists, regretting the benefits of the preindustrial corporate society, and some of the new style of socialists, abused the north more militantly. The newer labor aristocracy, and the younger generation of Trade Union leaders collaborating with middle class radicalism, are said to have been more pro-Federal. Karl Marx sided with the north, urging it to make a revolutionary onslaught upon the slave system. For Marx, the eventual emancipation of the American working-class depended upon the preliminary destruction of black slavery. See K. Marx and F. Engels, *The Civil War in the United States* (Citadel Press, N.Y., 3rd ed., 1961), a collection of articles and letters, 1861–1866.

its export."[54] But European, and particularly French insistence and alarm, could not be so easily quieted. In the same conversation with Sanford (duly reported to Seward, who was impressed) Thouvenel frankly admitted:

> . . . you know my wishes for the success of your cause, but above all for the early termination, one way or the other, of the war which is bearing heavily on us in France. We are nearly out of cotton, and cotton we *must have*. . . . Our people are getting to be irritated and some of the communications I have received from the Chamber of Commerce are even menacing in their language . . . we are going to have to have cotton even if we are compelled to do something ourselves to obtain it.

Baron Jacob Rothschild, also pro-northern, warned Sanford:

> I will admit to you that European intervention may not secure a bale of cotton, but here is a whole Continent in convulsion from this cause. When your patient is desperately sick, you try desperate remedies, even to blood-letting.[55]

Thurlow Weed added to the pressure on Seward; his conversations with Morny and Prince Napoleon convinced him that "this Government is in a tight place. Help as far and as fast as you can." Weed's urgent advice to Seward was: "If possible, open ports, and let the enemy refuse the cotton."[56]

During February to April, before battle victories enabled a gracious retreat, Seward tenaciously resisted trade concessions without matching compensation. He wanted withdrawal of belligerent rights from the south, on the grounds that they had been wrongly conceded, were prolonging the war and aggravating the cotton famine. According to this oddly superficial theory, the rebellion would collapse if the powers withdrew the moral support which the recognition of belligerency conferred. (Thouvenel was more impressed by southern contemptuousness of Europe, as indicated by harassment of foreigners through property confiscation.) Seward was right, however, in sensing that a European aboutface on the issue would be a propaganda coup of some magnitude for the north. The Union, he insisted, was not interested in depriving the Confederacy of any material advantages—lacking a navy or maritime commerce, it had

54. Interview Quai d'Orsay, April 9, Sanford to Seward, April 10, 1862, q. Case and Spencer, p. 290.

55. Conversation Quai d'Orsay, April 9, q. Case and Spencer, p. 290.

56. Weed to Seward, April 18, 1862; Weed to Seward, April 11, 1862; q. Case and Spencer, p. 291.

none to lose—but wanted only fair play, a speedy end to the war and the restoration of prosperity in France and England. Seward prudently retreated from this position when his agents represented the extreme unlikelihood of any reversal of policy by the powers, and reported the gathering clamor for direct action. He commented cynically to Chase on April 25:

> I incline to think that we may open three of four ports safely, this with restrictions, and thus pass through this last foreign peril without the South getting much aid or France (I fear) getting much cotton.[57]

After the fall of New Orleans, mail communications were restored between that city and the outside world (demanded by French merchants), and on May 12, Beaufort, Fort Royal, and New Orleans were opened by proclamation to all trade except contraband of war. Seward had thus sacrificed his bargaining power to obtain European concessions. The criticism applied by northerners to interventionist projects applied also, of course, to their own "open ports" policy—neither scheme guaranteed cotton on southern wharves. But a northern gesture indicated goodwill to Europe, and particularly to depressed workingmen (a democratic point worth accentuating), and would firmly place the blame on the rebels if cotton failed to materialize. As it turned out, the north managed to sell some cotton overseas, but cotton exports from opened ports proved disappointing. This was partly due to the embargo and cotton burning, and partly to United States customs regulations designed to prevent payment for staple in gold and silver. If allowed his way, Seward would have permitted foreigners to buy cotton from southerners and ship it out from New Orleans, even if they paid in specie.[58] Meanwhile he had obtained a short breathing space, and, by his bluster on belligerent rights, at least distracted the attention of European statesmen from the larger issue of southern sovereignty.

The cotton question had proved so far to be a much more complex and puzzling issue than uncritical southern theorists expected. Certain facts about Britain's cotton economy were commonly overlooked. It was a resilient industry, invariably one of

---

57. Seward to Chase, April 25, 1862, q. Case and Spencer, p. 292.

58. Van Deusen, *Seward*, p. 321. During the war, Lincoln permitted the licensed export of cotton from occupied territory, largely in order to reduce the foreign peril. See T. H. O'Connor, "Lincoln and the Cotton Trade," *CWH*, VII (1961), pp. 20-35.

the first to "bounce back" after cyclic depression. The big mill owners, with relatively low overhead costs and ample opportunities for stockpiling, readily "sat out" hard times by retrenching their armies of operatives. Crises, moreover, created sharp price fluctuations and thus speculative opportunities for those with wit and reserves. Nor was cotton still the lynchpin in the British economy. Heavy industries and transport had overtaken and supplanted cotton as the leading industrial sector as early as the 1840's. Comparatively self-contained, cotton had limited links with other producing sectors, so that the famine did not generalize itself to bring down the economy. On the contrary, the war brought a windfall to other industries, to noncotton textiles, armaments, shipbuilding and the merchant marine, while dislocations and readjustments were minimized and localized.

There was at the time, and has been since, much misunderstanding of the nature of the so-called "cotton famine." Lancashire knew to its embarrassment that cotton's dilemma was not shortage of fibre but glut, both in supply and markets. This was no new thing. The industry, compulsively addicted to self-improvement and the setting of astronomic output targets, habitually ploughing back profits, was paying the price of an overproduction crisis. This crisis cannot be dismissed as a superficial and short-term phenomenon, a problem soon to be driven from the scene by the American-inspired famine. A mass of evidence suggests that the overproduction crisis was deep-seated and prolonged. It is possible to go further. Economic historians are now testing the hypothesis that the fundamental cause of the cotton upheaval of 1861-1865 was this condition of overextension, with the war making an essentially contributory (even a distorting) psychological impact.[59]

Lancashire, in the boom years to 1860, was excited by the prospect of seemingly limitless expansion in world markets. Demand for calicoes soared in the "Far East" market, Britain's largest, with the ending of the Indian Mutiny in 1858 and the lapsing of the "Arrow" war in China in 1859. The Cobden-Chevalier treaty anticipated a lowering of French import duties on British textiles from October 1861. English mills overproduced on principle, greedily demanding raw cotton, helped by a series of bumper crops in Dixie. The timing of secession was palpably astray, for factories

59. See Eugene A. Brady, "A Reconsideration of the Lancashire 'Cotton Famine'," *Agric. H.*, XXVII, No. 4 (October, 1963), pp. 156-162; W. O. Henderson, *Lancashire Cotton Famine 1861-1865* (Manchester, 1934), Chapters 1-3, examines the overproduction crisis in a more traditional framework.

and warehouses were stockpiled high with cotton bales by the outbreak of war. The prudent and well-informed were already nervous about the imminence of a depression. "Everyone" observed a contemporary historian, "was looking out for buyers . . . they forced their wares upon apathetic speculators and unwilling manufacturers."[60] The crisis developed quite apart from the war, as a London journal pointed out in 1865:

> Two months after the fall of Fort Sumter, the markets of the world were gorged with cotton in all its forms. India and China had been overfed with manufactured goods; and the warehouses of Bombay groaned beneath the weight of 'shirtings' that found no wearers. Yet, notwithstanding a glutted market at home and abroad, production continued at about the same rate as in 1860 . . . at the end of 1861, although the rate of production had been checked during the last quarter of the year, there remained on hand not less than 300,000,000 pounds weight of manufactured goods; enough to supply every family in the U.K. for a year and eight months. Under these circumstances, and with cotton advanced 50 per cent, no marvel that mill owners began to run short time. . . .[61]

The American war at first hardly impinged upon the consciousness of Lancashire, in its way just as insular and wishful in its thinking as the south. Men predicted a quick finish and expected no serious run on stockpiled cotton. King Cotton theory was a washout in the first year of the war, a phony threat to those in the know. The close of 1861 saw the spectre of surpluses, not scarcity, still haunting the cotton interests. There was a sensitive indicator to this. Speculators were reluctant to gamble upon an American shortage pushing up prices for existing stocks of raw cotton and finished goods. It was not until the war had raged on well into 1862, not until the embargo and the blockade were having their effect, that the speculators came into their own. "Those were great times," Hemelryk wrote in his *Reminiscences of the Cotton Market*, "times of prosperity, when cotton brokers came down to business in their carriages or on horseback."[62]

There were many reasons for English stolidity about the American difficulty. One was a deep-seated confidence in the free trade dogma that supply always matched demand. Lyons had warned

---

60. R. Arthur Arnold, *History of the Cotton Famine* (London, 1864), p. 44. See also John Watts, *Facts of the Cotton Famine* (London, 1866), p. 112. Watts was on the Central Relief Committee and knew current attitudes.

61. *Quarterly Review*, (January, 1865), pp. 319-321, q. Brady, p. 158.

62. Quoted Henderson, p. 14.

Bunch at Charleston before the war about "the very exaggerated and very false ideas they have in the South about cotton:

> It is true that cotton is almost a necessity to us, but it is still more necessary for them to sell it than it is for us to buy it. Besides there are plenty of places where cotton can be grown. The only difficulty is to produce it as cheaply as in these States, the moment the price rises above a certain point it will be extensively cultivated in many parts of the world.[63]

There was indeed no long-term problem. Cotton would grow prolifically in warm temperate and tropical regions, and British newspapers were inundated with letters from zealous amateurs recommending the excellencies of numberless places. The *National Review*, endeavoring "to reduce the nebulous terror to definite outlines," put the issue plainly:

> If America were to be sunk in the sea, or if any circumstances made it clear or probable that we should never receive another bale from that quarter, English enterprise and English demand would in three or four years secure us an adequate supply from some part or other of the world. But this would be a work of time, of arrangement, of vast capital laid out with a view to future returns. We have to meet an immediate, not a prospective, deficiency. . . . What we have to do to meet the actual emergency is, not to set about growing cotton elsewhere, but to procure as large a supply as possible from quarters *where it is already grown.* We shall lack cotton in 1862, and most likely only then; and it is idle to tell us whence and how we may procure it by 1864 and 1865.[64]

The cotton experts calculated that, to meet the normal yearly requirement of around 2.3 million bales, Indian cotton—inconvenient but usable—could be made to supply about 1 million bales, and other sources (Egypt, Brazil, West Indies) perhaps half a million bales. As it was expected that higher prices for products would offset falling production, and given previously saturated markets, this would prove a reasonably satisfactory compromise. This was provided other conditions were met. One was that English prices for raw staple should rise sufficiently for Lancashire to corner available stocks. Trouble was anticipated from the United States and France. If the north raised a prohibitive tariff against British textiles, the result might be to create such an artificial boom in New England's industry as to enable it to win the scramble for raw materials in the

63. Lyons to Bunch, December 12, 1860, in *MHSP*, XLVIII, p. 214.

64. *National Review*, XIII (October, 1861), pp. 452, 456.

Liverpool market. Louis Napoleon too was capable of being commercially unscrupulous; dreading mass discontent, he might offer state subsidies to French cotton buyers, or even send government agents direct to Bombay to snap up available supplies of "Surat."

English prices in fact rose only sluggishly. "Middling Orleans" cotton, which stood at seven pennies per pound in November 1860, had struggled to only nine and a half pennies per pound by October 1861. Buyers were dubious that the 1861 American crop was really lost and, suspecting that it would be suddenly liberated and glut an already saturated market, refused to pay higher prices for fibres. More cotton was actually reexported from Britain in 1861 than in 1860. Advised to conserve cotton by working short-time and diverting production to finer quality fabrics, mill owners showed uncertainty and only grudgingly complied. Even so, nothing resembling a scarcity occurred in 1861. Over 2.2 million bales were landed at British ports—less certainly than the bumper 2.6 million bales of 1860 but close enough to the normal yearly average. Ominously however, 1.6 million bales came from the record American crop of 1860. More hopeful was the fact that India was able to supply almost a third of the 1861 cotton imports. Much was expected from cotton smuggling through the blockade and evasions of the embargo, piously deplored. For a generation renowned for moral earnestness, the Victorians had an overweening confidence in the ultimate triumph of men's material interests.

So much attention became rivetted upon India as a source of cotton that the French suspected a plot on the part of the British imperialists to create one more world monopoly. This might explain their acquiescence in the blockade and reluctance to end the war by intervention. Lancashire, indeed, made a great show of reviving the old pastime of promoting Indian cotton culture. The Manchester Cotton Company and other combines were formed to obtain Indian staples; the Cotton Supply Association sent its representatives to India and stepped up its propaganda activities; and pressure was mounted upon the government to secure an incentive system for cotton growing in areas such as the Gujarat and the Deccan, near Bombay. Manchester strove to encourage others to dynamic effort, although the cynics thought it coy in making heavy commitments itself in India. The colonial administration, responding to pressure, appropriated almost one hundred thousand rupees by late 1861 to improve roads from the cotton hinterland to the coastal ports. Gold medals and cash prizes were offered to successful growers. Beyond this the government would not budge. The Secretary of State for

India, Sir Charles Wood, a devoted freetrader, stubbornly resisted measures which would put the government in the role of private capitalist, cultivator, or promoter. He was also chary of disrupting settled Indian customs and institutions so soon after the Mutiny. And for what? Lancashire cupidity? It was well known that the cotton interests had serious reservations about India as a permanent source of supply, and would not hesitate to abandon its infant plantations once the war was settled. In the outcome it was high prices rather than any program which sent Indian production soaring. Bombay, the chief outlet, boomed tremendously, and was to remain the world's greatest cotton-export center until the 1870's. By 1862 India was supplying over one million bales; by the end of the war its annual average output was 900 million pounds, a rise of 50% on prewar levels. This constituted no small contribution towards foiling southern schemes.[65]

The year 1862 proved to be the year of crisis. By autumn short-time was being worked almost generally in the mills, many had closed down, the cotton prices had spiralled to twenty pennies per pound. Unemployment in November was over 330,000, leaving only 200,000 in full employment, and a massive relief campaign had begun. The distress was almost universally attributed to the disruption of supplies caused by the Civil War. Newspaper editors, cabinet ministers, backbenchers, radical orators, even economists took this view, although the latter pointed to contributory factors. From Lancashire's cotton interests and members of parliament came no rebuttal of such an obvious explanation, only a curious reticence. Richard Cobden, whose economic expertise cannot be lightly dismissed, wrote disconsolately to Sumner in July of the deteriorating situation:

> [In the spring] there was a large stock of cotton in the hands of rich spinners and merchants and they were interested in keeping out cotton. Moreover we had great merchants who had over-speculated in cotton goods which were shipped to India and China and they were glad of a rise in the raw material which enabled them to get out of their stocks. But all these motives for forbearance are now at an end. The merchants, manufacturers, spinners and operatives are all on the same footing, and they are all anxious to obtain raw cotton, and they will be all equally pressing on our

65. P. Harnetty, "The Imperialism of Free Trade: Lancashire, India and the Cotton Supply Question, 1861-1865," *J. Br. Stud.*, VI, No. 5 (November, 1966), pp. 70-96; Frenise A. Logan, "India: Britain's Substitute for American Cotton, 1861-1865," *JSH*, XXIV, No. 4 (November, 1958), pp. 472-480.

> government the necessity of 'doing something'. What that 'something' is to be is more than I can pretend to say. I am of course as strongly convinced as ever that nothing but harm can possibly be done by interference of any kind. But where the welfare and the lives of millions of persons are at stake you cannot present the alternative of a greater possible evil to deter a government from attempting to remedy so vast a present danger. I feel quite convinced that unless cotton comes in considerable quantity before the end of the year the governments of Europe will be knocking at your door.[66]

Cobden's fears were well-grounded. In the various attempts at British intervention explored later in this volume, a highly significant part was played by the belief, hardly questioned, that England badly needed American cotton. Recent research has now raised the fascinating possibility that this climate of crisis rested upon an economic misapprehension. Eugene A. Brady, after calculating the actual stocks of cotton held in mills and at ports in the United Kingdom throughout the "famine" years, claims that there never occurred a serious physical deprivation of raw cotton. It is true that the volume of raw cotton imported dropped markedly in 1862 (524 million pounds compared to 1257 million pounds in 1861). This impressed contemporaries more than the fact that ample stockpiling in earlier years was providing an effective cushion against real scarcity. In fact cotton stocks in 1862 were at virtually the same level as in 1858 (1862: 183.2 million pounds; 1858: 189.9 million pounds). The lowest ebb in reserves did not come until 1863 (137.7 million pounds), by which time unemployment was easing, alternative sources of supply were yielding more materials, and the value of exports was almost back to normal due to higher prices. As Brady says:

> The Civil War did have some impact upon the Lancashire textile industry, but it does not appear that its most significant role was one of cutting off supplies of raw cotton from British textile manufacturers. Its main effect was that of inducing *expectations* of a future input shortage. These expectations resulted in a greatly increased price for raw cotton as a result of a speculative bidding up of the price of fairly ample stocks of cotton housed in factories and in warehouses of the United Kingdom, which made cotton manufacturing operations relatively unprofitable.[67]

---

66. Cobden to Sumner, July 11, 1862, *AHR*, II, No. 2 (January, 1897), p. 307.

67. Brady, p. 157. Quote below is from *Quarterly Review*, October, 1864.

Strengthening this interpretation is the fact that every year between 1862 and 1866 Britain, far from striving to conserve its supply, increased its reexports of raw cotton to countries such as France. The evidence suggests that overproduction and overfed world markets were still the fundamental problems for the industry. High prices induced by the war merely offered a further incentive, perhaps a convenient excuse, to impose voluntary checks upon production until markets should improve. "To the operative" as the *Quarterly* noted, "this means 'short time'."

The ramshackle structure of goodwill for the north created by battle victories collapsed with the failure of the Peninsular campaign. Lee's transformation of the Army of North Virginia, and his brilliant counteroffensives after the relief of Richmond, seemed convincing evidence of the south's capacity to survive, while the awesome and bloody grappling of the two great armies in campaigns such as the "Seven Days" caused humanitarian outcry and a demand for peace. The Victorian mind experienced enormous difficulty in accepting that such a terrible war could be persisted in, or that modern states were capable of the unprecedented mobilization of resources that it needed. Predictions of the rise of a peace party in the north, and tales of northern disgust with the war, were eagerly repeated, but expanding recruitment programs sponsored by the Lincoln government were surer signs of future trends. Northern bankruptcy was commonly declared to be imminent, yet freetrade England turned sourly anti-Yankee at the upgrading of Union tariffs for revenue purposes. From the time of the siege of Yorktown to that of the battle of Antietam occurred perhaps the most intense public discussion of the question of foreign intervention by the powers. In France the Emperor's hot desire to act was faithfully reflected in the official and Bonapartist press, while the regime's growing opposition groups retaliated by playing the old tunes of Franco-American amity. In Britain a time of crisis for the north seemed fast approaching. Despite the public adamance of the Liberal government in a "hands off" policy, there appeared to be maximum receptivity at large to the need for intervention of some sort. General Butler's draconic regime in captured New Orleans alienated support; his instruction that women who insulted an officer or the flag should be treated like women of the streets outraged Victorian consciences. (Palmerston went into a remarkable passion, and was most undiplomatically rude to poor Adams over the affair, which roused much more indignation than the considerably more savage execution of a New Orleans citizen for tearing down the Stars and Stripes.) The Yankee camp in London relapsed into despondency as the tide ran against them in Virginia, and then in the European capitals.

Henry Adams railed against the unanimous hostility of Englishmen, and warned in May of the imminent peril of mediation projects: "the idea here is as strong as ever that we must ultimately fail." By July his father was coldly calculating that Confederate sympathizers "constitute much the greater part of the active classes." A month later the southern publicist Henry Hotze estimated them as comprising five-sixths of the Commons and all except two members of the Lords.[68]

The public debate over intervention raised certain major problems. The idea of a ceasefire arranged by the powers was appealing to all but a few. Disconcertingly, the exceptions included the most dedicated partisans of both sides; the one group implacably opposed to an armistice which should presage any diminution of the Union; the other preferring to win independence on the field and wary that attempts might be made to impose a reconstructionist settlement upon the south. What was the value of a ceasefire which neither side would accept? Seward's refusal to countenance mediation placed the issue four square before Europe's politicians: any offer to mediate would need to be backed by a covert threat of force. And without at least southern cooperation, the powers would intrude advice at the risk of rejection and diplomatic embarrassment all round. Richmond perhaps made a serious error in being cool towards mediation. Slidell at least—even though his pet project was recognition—kept open the question of accepting good offices. Let the north spurn an armistice initiative, he reasoned to Napoleon in July. This would throw the responsibility of the war's continuance on the Yankees, and open the road to recognition and armed intervention. The north must then back down, for northern policy was based on bluff and bluster. Slidell's case was for a piece of skillful gunboat diplomacy by the powers in combination. His plea was bolstered by the *Trent* experience, and would be vindicated if it achieved a bloodless capitulation by the north. But the prospect of a real war with the United States warmed few hearts in England, or even in imperial France (more dedicated in reality to peace than to the foreign adventurism which historians have so lovingly made

68. Henry Adams to C. F. Adams, Jr., May 8, 1862, in *Cycle of Adams' Letters*, I, pp. 138-143; C. F. Adams to Seward, July 11, 1862, Henry Hotze to Benjamin, August 4, 1862, q. Owsley, p. 300.

characteristic of the regime). Nobody in England countenanced the sacrifice of national interests in the abstract pursuit of peace in a distant continent, and not even for the more immediate gains (if they should accrue) to Lancashire. People wanted an American peace at no price. The question was whether such a bargain was in fact on offer.

Mediation, on closer look, bristled with difficulties. What should be the basis of any settlement? Separation and abolition (as proposed by the Bonapartists) or abolition and reunion (as favored by Paris Liberals)? Were the Negroes to be freed? As war needs and radical pressures in the Union inexorably brought closer the day of Negro emancipation, the slavery issue was debated lengthily in Europe. As in America, there appeared immediatists, gradualists, emigrationists; and the specter was raised of emancipation causing servile insurrection, wholesale massacre of whites, and permanent destruction of the cotton industry. But proslavery arguments *per se* were conspicuously absent in Europe, and most of the talk was distasteful to the south.

What, again, would be the boundaries separating Union and Confederacy? Napoleon hardly recognized the names of some of the border states whose fate hung in the balance, but his ministers confidently produced compromise plans. Presumably the military situation would dictate the lines of any peace settlement, although the use of plebiscites was canvassed. (Cavour had popularized them during the unification of Italy.) Throughout the debate ran consistent themes: belief in the impossibility of the north reducing the south, dismay at the human and economic ruin caused by the war, a growing sense of the need for European reappraisal of the situation, and a spreading conviction that steps were about to be made to put a stop to the carnage.

Such ideas were, of course, not necessarily antinorthern, although it was hard for New Englanders like the Adamses to appreciate the distinction. Walter Bagehot favored peace negotiations, he said, in the interests of the north, the negro, civilization, and humanity. The north should settle for the *uti posidetis* before "the Confederates should reconquer New Orleans, drive the Federals out of Tennessee and Missouri, obtain a secession vote in Kentucky, again defeat M'Clellan [sic] and again menace Washington." Peace could then be bought only at a disastrous cost. Bagehot thought the south had a right to independence "by every rule of justice and every principle of republicanism." But slavery was "so fatal to industry, to social progress, to sound views, to real elevation of principle or purpose" that he grieved to see it expand its empire where it was now disputed. Indeed he claimed that any boundary line giving Maryland, Kentucky and Virginia to the south ought not to be submitted to by the Union "except as a transition measure, or as the issue of a most exhausting defeat." Most important, a prompt peace might save the civil liberties of "the freest republic in the world," which the growing savagery of war was threatening to extinguish. Bagehot bitterly condemned the draft laws, Seward's use of arbitrary arrest, and the employment of military sanctions against those refusing enlistment in a war which divided men's loyalties and consciences.[69] Under Bagehot's control, the *Economist* joined the *Times* in urging mediation, preferably by the French: the Yankees hated England too well to accept her offers. All of the usual preconditions for mediation existed: the north's war aim (to restore the Union) was unattainable; the combatants were evenly matched and might fight on indefinitely; the war showed signs of degenerating into a barbaric war of extermination; neutrals were being injured, especially through the cotton famine, beyond the bounds of endurance; and the military situation provided the guidelines for a settlement.[70]

The Confederacy's new Secretary of State, Judah P. Benjamin, thus took office at a time when the south's overseas fortunes were at the flood. Yet lack of recent information on a quickly evolving European situation prevented him playing the effective role in foreign policy for which his undoubted intellectual ability and administrative skill fitted him. In this, as in his earlier career at the Confederate War Office, Benjamin was deserted by luck. He assumed office inauspiciously, kicked upstairs by his faithful superior, Jefferson Davis, just before a congressional investigating committee censured him as war minister for responsibility in bringing about the Roanoke Island fiasco. He became a convenient scapegoat for southern unpreparedness and lack of resources, and a target for those sniping at the president's handling of the war—a better target because of prejudice against his Jewish origins, his tactlessness in dealing with powerful and proud southerners, his lack of military training or expertise, and a certain sense of cynical realism which failed to win him popular support.

Yet it was precisely his realism which promised to make him, and did make him, the south's best foreign minister. He had other

69. Bagehot in *Economist*, XX (August 30, 1862), pp. 953-954.

70. *Economist* (June 14, 1862).

qualities for the job: legal training (he was immensely successful after the war as a practicing barrister in England), knowledge of Europe and European languages, a close liaison with Davis, and a necessary acquaintance with the arts of *realpolitik.* His biographer describes Benjamin as a man who saw the difficulties in winning the war and was willing to make the necessary sacrifices to do so, as "a revolutionist of the breed of Danton and Lenin, not Dumouriez or Kerensky."[71] He had doubted the wisdom of secession, prophesied a long and bloody war, and proposed that large shipments of cotton be sent to Europe as security for the purchase of arms. Less than a month after his appointment to the miniature State Department (housed in the Richmond Customs House along the corridor from Davis's staff) Benjamin showed that he was prepared to wield the cotton bludgeon more purposefully than his predecessors. What he proposed was a piece of blatant economic bribery, designed to appeal to Napoleon's cupidity. The Confederacy was prepared to make a treaty conceding to France the right to introduce its products free of duty into the south for a defined period in the expectation that Napoleon would abandon "the policy hitherto pursued."[72] In case this bait was not appetizing enough, Benjamin offered to make cotton available to French vessels "at certain designated points." 100,000 bales, he speculated, would cost the south $4.5 million, but would represent to France a grant of $12.5 million at the current price of twenty-five cents per pound in Europe. "Such a sum would maintain afloat a considerable fleet for a length of time quite sufficient to open the Atlantic and Gulf ports to the commerce of France." Here was proposed just the type of deal which northerners feared Napoleon, through Mercier, was angling for: free cotton and economic privileges in return for the smashing of the blockade (and inevitably, recognition). Mercier arrived in Richmond on April 16, four days after this dispatch was prepared, but he did not report any conversations with Benjamin on the "bribe"; Benjamin no doubt preferred to negotiate directly with Napoleon through Slidell. However Mercier's visit highlighted the issue, for on April 18 the Confederate Senate authorized the President to draw up a treaty with Britain, France and Spain offering special trade privileges and other inducements to break the blockade. But for the time-being Benjamin was making the offer exclusive to France, and Slidell adroitly exploited this fact to mature his plan of dividing the allies.

---

71. Robert Douthat Meade, *Judah P. Benjamin: Confederate Statesman* (N.Y. 1943), p. 239.

72. Benjamin to Slidell, April 12, 1862, q. Meade, p. 253.

The Atlantic Ocean and the blockading squadrons forced Mason and Slidell to act essentially on their own initiative. The blockade not only deprived the south of strategic materials, but disastrously interrupted the flow of intelligence, dispatches and instructions between Richmond and its agents—particularly in the vital period from late 1861 to mid-1863. The tiny staff of the Confederate State Department (a mere half-dozen) was obliged to obtain overseas news from northern newspapers and out-of-date European papers, journals, and parliamentary papers. Even basic reference books were lacking in the government library. Southern dispatches were often lost, or captured (to be published, to the chagrin of southerners, in Union newspapers). Before Benjamin began using fast steam blockade-runners based on Nassau or Bermuda from mid-1863, delays of six months were commonplace between mailing and receipt of documents.

Mason and Slidell had planned to present simultaneous demands to England and France on June 20, asking recognition, but the idea was dropped pending more decisive victories by the Army of North Virginia. Before these came Slidell almost despaired: "The position of our representatives in Europe is painful and almost humiliating . . . I am disposed to believe that we would have done better to withdraw after our first interview with Russell and Thouvenel."[73] He was revived, however, by McClellan's retreat across the Chickahominy; and, armed with Benjamin's "cotton bribe," he launched an intensified campaign for recognition. In interview with the Emperor at Vichy on July 15 Slidell clarified the advantages that would accrue to France if her powerful navy cleared the federal blockade, paving the way for recognition. He pictured prospects of an early peace—decisive foreign action would destroy the credit of the war party in the north—and added Benjamin's offer of cotton and economic privileges, an alluring invitation to France to forestall the British in creating an economic hegemony in the new nation. Napoleon was intrigued but cautious. Intelligence from Mercier had been less reassuring on the certainty of the north backing down in any confrontation with the powers. Mercier had sounded Seward on mediation early in July, and been met with threats:

> Be assured . . . that the Emperor can commit no graver error than to mix himself in our affairs. At the rumor alone of intervention all the factions will reunite themselves against you and even in the border states you will meet a resistance unanimous and desperate.[74]

---

73. Slidell to Mason, June 21, 1862, q. EDA, I, p. 307.
74. Mercier to Thouvenel, July 11, 1862, q. Owsley, p. 309.

On his own initiative Slidell raised the stakes by offering southern assistance in destroying the Juárez regime in Mexico. The Yankees, he claimed, were already in Mexico propping up the war effort against the French. According to the Corwin treaty they planned to subsidize Juárez to the tune of eleven million dollars. Delivering a homily on the expansionist tendencies of the section from which his people had just delivered themselves, Slidell declared that France and the Confederacy shared a common interest in setting up in Mexico "a respectable, responsible, and stable government." Slidell's criticisms of French acquiescence in the blockade were equally acute. What purpose did it serve other than prolonging the war by depriving the south of money and rifles? French action now would kill England's "torturous, selfish, and time-serving policy" of reviving "exploded" principles of blockade and securing a cotton monopoly for her Indian colonies. Napoleon's regret was obvious at his "great error" in not repudiating the blockade and recognizing the south a year earlier. But what could now be done?

> To open the ports forcibly would be an act of war; mediation would, if offered, be refused and probably in insulting terms by the North; and mere recognition, while of little advantage to you, would probably involve me in a war.[75]

Slidell, however, had clearly made an impression. The Emperor indicated that his government had no objection to receiving a formal demand for recognition. Intervention seemed to have moved closer, although Napoleon still regarded it as conditional on English cooperation. Soon after the interview at Vichy Napoleon sent a coded telegram to his Foreign Minister, who was in London for the International Exhibition, by coincidence at the time of a Commons' debate on mediation. It said: "Ask the English government if they don't think the time has come to recognise the South." The telegram could have had a decided impact on events, but it arrived after Thouvenel had departed for Paris:

> I should have hesitated a great deal to use [it] . . . [Thouvenel told Flahault] I think right now a foreign intervention would arouse the susceptibilities of the Northern masses to the point of committing some act of folly. Besides I could not conceive how we should be in more of a hurry than England or that we should risk to take on the sole burden of a job from which she would obtain the benefit and draw down upon us all the resentment which Americans now feel toward her.

---

75. Slidell to Benjamin, July 25, 1862. For interview, Case and Spencer, pp. 300-305.

For the moment he was able to stop the Emperor swerving from a policy of "abstention." Confederate demands for recognition were presented at Paris on July 20 and at London on July 24 but were fended off by the respective foreign offices. Thouvenel took a month before advising Slidell indirectly not to press for a reply as he did not want "to send an unmeaningful reply," but could at present do no other. In London Mason was brusquely refused an interview with Russell, and informed on August 2 that cabinet had decided against recognition because of the "fluctuating events of the war."[76] However there were straws in the wind that these were by no means irrevocable determinations.

Meanwhile counterpressures had been maintained upon the British from Washington. A strong note from Seward, presented on June 20, complained that rumors of intervention had "encouraged and sustained" the Confederacy from its birth, and were "highly injurious" to the north. Intervention, or mediation favouring the south, were entirely unacceptable to the United States, and if undertaken would force her to foment a retaliatory "servile war." Forster repeated this gloomy prognostication in the Commons' debate on mediation on July 18. Lindsay's plan of forcing a mediation resolution through parliament had had to be postponed when on June 20 the government denied in both houses that it had received mediation overtures from France or that it was contemplating action at present. The issue was a poor one for a direct parliamentary challenge to the administration: it had the numbers and the opposition was disunited on America. Lindsay made the mistake of baiting Russell, who had snubbed him as Napoleon's unofficial emissary. Lindsay bragged to Russell that a fortnight would see a majority of M.P.'s willing to defy the whip on a motion for southern recognition. He spoke of private members "undertaking a duty which belonged to the Executive," covertly threatened to precipitate a cabinet crisis, and declared that if the Civil War "is settled *without* our recognition of the South, he might rest certain that the Northern Armies *would* be marched into Canada."[77] The motion was belatedly brought before the house on July 18, after postponements and changes of form which served to irritate members. The opposition showed little interest in an issue which promised no

76. Thouvenel to Flahault, July 21, 26; Slidell to Benjamin, August 20, 1862; Russell to Mason, August 2, 1862, q. Case and Spencer, pp. 307-308, 312, 313.

77. Lindsay to Mason, June 18, 1862, paraphrasing Lindsay's letter to Russell, q. EDA, II, pp. 305-306, n6.

political advantages. Ralph Earle, Disraeli's trusted adviser on foreign policy, counseled him before the debate:

> I should be sorry if, in taking up a Southern line, we were to alienate the Manchester party. This House is much too timid to interfere with the Govt. in such a question & [sic] it seems to me to be one upon which Ministers are quite safe . . . In fact, it seems that there is nothing good to be got out of this American question, at present, & [sic] if we are forced to speak, it might be well . . . to say that you think it well to leave the Executive unfettered to act according to their own discretion.[78]

At a meeting of top strategists of the Conservative party it was decided to hew to a line of strict neutrality, and only a few minor members were permitted to express southern sympathies. Stanley, son of the opposition leader, advised against recognizing a country whose whole coast was in Federal hands. In a letter to Disraeli he thought it advisable to wait:

> If the autumn campaign ends without decisive results, the south will have held its own for two complete years: debt, taxes, failure of trade will have begun to tell in the north, which they have not as yet done. . . . If we want to protract the war—to stimulate the combatants to the utmost, let us talk of interfering to stop it. If we want it to die out, let us carefully stand aloof.[79]

The debate rehashed the polemics being heard generally. The pro-southerners, including Lindsay, Vane Tempest, Seymour Fitzgerald, Whiteside and Gregory, cited the unalterable determination and capacity of the south to win independence; declared separation justified on principles of self-determination, and mandatory to the powers on grounds of humanitarianism and self-interest. Mediation would save lives, preserve both sections from economic ruin, and advance the negro cause better than any northern victory. (Lincoln's failure to accept emancipation as a war aim here paid dividends to his enemies, who pictured slavery being maintained in any reconstruction of the Union, but gently passing away in an independent south.) The southern brief was helped by McClellan's retreat in the Peninsular (some newspapers printed reports that his army had capitulated), by intimations that Napoleon was eager to intervene, and by growing pressure for relief of the cotton distress. The recently published Farnall report, work of the special commissioner for the

---

78. Earle to Disraeli, July 14, 1862, q. W. D. Jones, "British Conservatives and the Civil War," *AHR*, LVIII, p. 532.

79. Stanley to Disraeli, July 15, 1862, q. Jones, pp. 532-533.

distressed areas, had revealed that 80,000 operatives were unemployed and 370,000 averaging half-time; and that cotton stocks had fallen to less than 200,000 bales. Such statistics undermined expectations of relief from the nominal reopening of New Orleans and other cotton ports. Lyons, who was in London on sick leave, thought that the government might be placed under irresistible pressures. Speakers in the house, with the interesting exception of the members for Lancashire, harped ominously on the famine. Lindsay produced a letter from Ashton-under-Lyne to show that workingmen favoured southern recognition; but Taylor, representing Leicester, rebutted the charge. The working classes, he said, saw that "intervention would involve a sin and produce a stain on the antislavery flag of England."[80]

Opposition to the motion came most vigorously from Forster of Bradford, and Taylor of Leicester. Forster's speech made a neat illustration of Manchester doctrine: intervention meant war, and the dubious benefits of war were outmatched by its economic and social costs. He spoke of the chance of a "corn famine," adding: "we could keep the working population of Lancashire in luxury for less than the price it would cost us to interfere." Both sides were sticking to their war aims, both powerful, furious, sure of success: "How was it possible to end the war short of the utter defeat of either party?" An offer of "friendly mediation" which favored the south, and was accompanied by a threat to the north, would only provoke the Union to more titanic fury. Would England submit to outside dictation of this sort if Ireland erupted? Forster's peroration took the theme that America was being wracked by a revolution, "an entire change in the social system" provoked over the place of slavery in society. Expedient intervention by the powers in such a struggle, without the acceptance of any responsibility for the social outcome of their acts, would be immoral, and would serve only to intensify the horrors of the revolution. As Taylor commented in an effective supporting speech: "Never was so tremendous an issue so easily, so lightly . . . raised." What was the point, he asked, of arranging an "armed truce" which would last only until the south felt strong enough to strike again, or the north strong enough to overwhelm the seceders?

Palmerston insisted that the house dispose of the issue; and successfully asked that a difficult and delicate matter be left in the hands of the executive. He regretted the debate, as things had been

---

80. *Hansard*, 3rd Ser., CLXVIII (July 18, 1862), pp. 522, 525-526.

said "which must tend to irritate and wound the feelings of both sides." He administered a setback to the advocates of recognition by flatly declaring that the south had not yet "firmly and permanently" established its independence. ("A fortnight ago it was doubtful whether the Confederates or the Federals would be in possession of Richmond.") He conceded "the vast importance to this country of a speedy termination of the war," but agreed with Forster that interference would only produce "greater evils, greater sufferings" for English workingmen. Palmerston was clearly impressed by the vast scale of the war:

> The Thirty Years' War in Germany was a joke to it in point of extent and magnitude. It was but the other day that I saw a map sent by the Quarter-master General of the Federal forces, on which were marked out the positions of 720,000 Federal troops—we now hear that 300,000 more men are to be called into the field—making 1,000,000 of men on one side; and probably there is something not much less on the other . . . is that the moment when it can be thought that a successful offer of mediation could be made to the two parties?[81]

Palmerston's restraint over America had been a significant factor so far in chastening the ardor of parliament. The seventy eight year old Prime Minister was at the height of his carefully nurtured popularity, still exhibiting consummate skill in the arts of parliamentary management and—despite rivals like Gladstone—maintaining his dominance over the ministry. He was close friends with Delane and the two usually worked closely together. The *Times* promptly endorsed Palmerston's stand:

> We are evidently approaching a crisis when a most solemn decision will be demanded of the British people, and every step should now be taken with the utmost thoughtfulness and caution.[82]

The government, it added, was more able to judge the fitting time for action than private individuals. Still, it believed:

> . . . we are but uttering the thoughts of nine Englishmen out of ten when we say that should it appear that the army of M'Clellan has been so totally defeated as to be incapable of resuming offensive operations, then the propriety of treating the Confederates as an independent people may be justly discussed by the British Cabinet.

---

81. Hansard, p. 572.
82. *Times*, July 19, 1862.

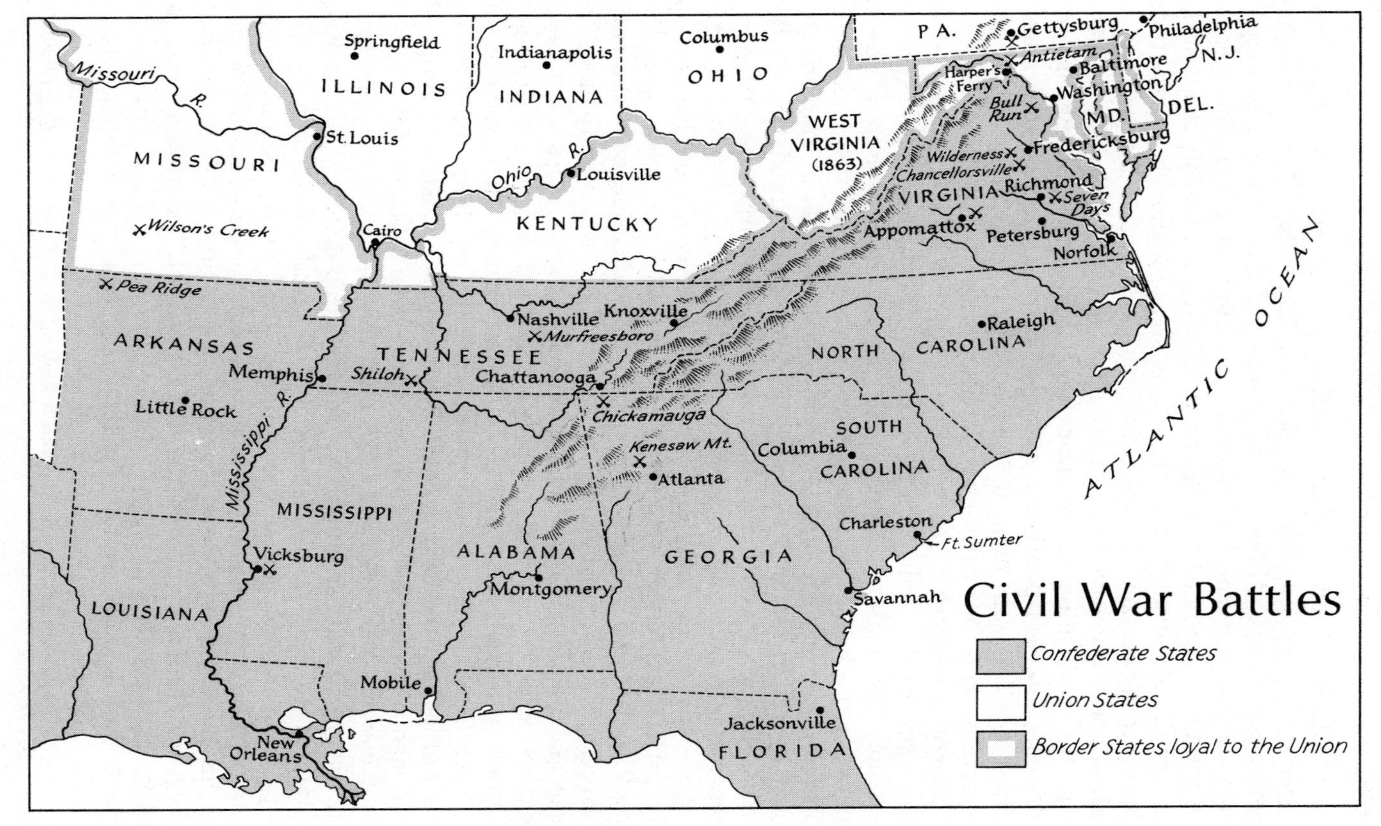
Civil War Battles
Confederate States
Union States
Border States loyal to the Union
Missouri R.
Springfield
ILLINOIS
St. Louis
MISSOURI
Wilson's Creek
Cairo
Indianapolis
INDIANA
Ohio R.
Louisville
KENTUCKY
Columbus
OHIO
WEST VIRGINIA (1863)
PA.
Gettysburg
Philadelphia
N.J.
Antietam
Harper's Ferry
Baltimore
Washington
MD.
DEL.
Bull Run
Fredericksburg
Wilderness
Chancellorsville
Richmond
Seven Days
VIRGINIA
Appomattox
Petersburg
Norfolk
ATLANTIC OCEAN
Pea Ridge
ARKANSAS
Memphis
Little Rock
Mississippi R.
Nashville
Knoxville
Murfreesboro
TENNESSEE
Shiloh
Chattanooga
Chickamauga
NORTH CAROLINA
Raleigh
SOUTH CAROLINA
Columbia
Kenesaw Mt.
Atlanta
MISSISSIPPI
Vicksburg
ALABAMA
Montgomery
GEORGIA
Charleston
Ft. Sumter
Savannah
LOUISIANA
Mobile
New Orleans
Jacksonville
FLORIDA

Palmerston's mind, as revealed in his private letters, was rapidly becoming more receptive to the idea of an armistice proposal. Always attuned to the political climate, Palmerston could not fail to notice the considerable sympathy for the southern cause in the house; and he had been much involved in mid-July in attempts to ameliorate distress in the cotton areas. Although intervention promised no certain cure for his difficulties, the Civil War had been a considerable domestic bugbear to him. The loss of American markets, and the dislocation of Atlantic trade, had made commercial and shipping interests politically irritable, and had cut into government revenues. The war created irreconcilable demands for ministerial economy and an expanded defense program, Gladstone at the Exchequer wielding a heavy Peelite axe against "Extravagance under the Impulse of Panic," Palmerston stoutly resisting retrenchments eroding the nation's defense capability. Irascible letters passed between the Prime Minister and the Chancellor of the Exchequer. With Disraeli and the radicals in unholy alliance, all of Palmerston's skill had been required to stem a parliamentary humiliation on the issue of expenditure (Stansfeld's resolution) in early June. Although scrupulously adhering to an official policy of rigid abstention from interference in the domestic affairs of other countries, Palmerston in private exhibited extreme irritation and impatience with the north during the post-Trent months.[83] Gratification over the anti-slavetrade treaty, for long a pet project of his, was overwhelmed by anger at the activities of the Union navy. British ships were being hauled into New York as prizes "without rhyme or reason"; Britain could not be subjected to "the scandal and inconvenience of having Federal and Confederate squadrons watching and fighting each other" off the English coast; convoys would need to be supplied for merchantmen passing through home waters, British ports closed to American warships, and offending Yankee captains "dealt with in a very summary manner." So ran his letters before July. He even confided to Russell his feeling that England would gain by the separation of south from north, one of the rare expressions of this class to be found in the private papers of government members. But as his biographer cautions concerning such letters, "at their worst they reveal the jingo, not the interventionist," and stand out in sharp contrast "to the very cool and correct official pronouncements which were issuing simultaneously from the Foreign Office

83. Bell, *Palmerston*, p. 314 and following for extracts from Palmerston's letters in early 1862.

and Admiralty."[84] Palmerston's July 18 speech accurately reflected his realistic prudence. But within a fortnight the mounting evidence of northern disarray established in him a deepening conviction that the south's independence was assured. On July 29 Gladstone revealed to his wife that "Lord Palmerston . . . has come exactly to my mind about some early representations of a friendly kind to America, if we can get France *and* Russia to join."[85] By early August discreet plans had been initiated for an armistice proposal. Palmerston wrote to the Queen on August 6, just prior to the Parliamentary adjournment, that October would apparently be the proper time.[86] Russell, about to accompany the bereaved Queen on a trip to the Continent, suggested a cabinet on the matter when he returned before October. He agreed that an armistice should be the first step, "but we must be prepared to answer the question on what basis are we to negotiate?"[87] An answer was never satisfactorily devised.

---

84. Bell, p. 315.

85. Quoted Morley, *Gladstone* (London, 1904), II, p. 75.

86. Palmerston to Queen Victoria, August 6, 1862, Windsor MSS, q. Bell, p. 327.

87. Russell to Palmerston, August 6, 1862, q. EDA, II, p. 32. The July 18 debate seems to have been a watershed to Russell. The day after it he wrote: "The great majority are in favour of the South and nearly our whole people are of opinion that separation wd. be benefit both to North and South." Russell to Lyons, July 19, 1862, *PRO* 30/22,96; q. W. D. Jones, p. 529.

Chapter VIII

The Current Turns Awry

Union humiliations mounted in the summer of 1862. Lincoln's abandonment of the Peninsular campaign, the Union defeat at Murfreesborough, McClellan's demotion and the elevation over his head of Pope and Halleck, the continuing insecurity of Washington seemed to provoke a crisis of confidence in the north, wracked also by deep differences over the issue of emancipation. As Lincoln's stocks, and those of his party, slumped, a Republican defeat loomed in the coming Congressional elections. Arbitrary arrests and the suspension of civil rights aroused dissent in the north, and the enlistment program slowed ominously. ("If this fails," forecast the London *Times*, "then all is over.") The battles of the Seven Days had impressed the world as among the foremost military events of the age, or any age, but they had decided nothing, it seemed:

> After pouring forth blood like water and fertilizing the fields of Virginia with thousands of corpses, the North finds itself obliged to begin all over again, with credit destroyed, a ruined revenue, a depreciated currency, and an enormous debt.[1]

In Paris, Slidell pondered England's puzzling failure to notice officially these massive signs of the south's sweeping success. He was in the dark on Russell's and Palmerston's secret moves (known only to Gladstone and a few others). "I think it may be assumed that

1. London *Times*, July 22, 1862. Preceding quote, *Times*, July 26, 1862.

England will not move," Slidell wrote shortly after Russell had made a cautious statement on the war to the Lords on August 4:

> I can only account for the inaction of the English ministry on the hypothesis that they desire to see the North entirely exhausted and broken down, that they are willing in order to attain this object to suffer their own people to starve, and play the poltroon in the face of Europe . . . France will for us be a safer ally than England.[2]

Characteristically, southern diplomacy played no part in the events of the next critical six weeks. Slidell thought that "the Emperor has been treated with a rudeness approaching to indignity" by the English, and rejoiced that this would push Napoleon into southern arms. Ironically Russell was at this time preparing to coopt the French for a joint intervention. But Slidell was not the only one to be caught napping by the British reversal. So were the French. As it turned out Napoleon failed to exploit the only occasion during the war when the British neared voluntary involvement. But the intrusion of Italian events into French politics, not Slidell's attempt to divide the powers, brought about this stroke of luck for the north.

During September, Russell, the recent convert to a policy of action, became an enthusiast in the cause. The disaster of Second Manassas (August 29-30) discredited Pope, effected the restoration of McClellan, and pushed southern morale to a wartime zenith. Lee's invasion of Maryland threatened to isolate Washington and inflict morale-crushing thrusts within Pennsylvania itself (Map 4). Stonewall Jackson's daring exploits in support of Lee excited admiration abroad.[3] To Russell, and many others, events seemed to presage the end of the war. Palmerston (who thought the Federals "got a very complete smashing . . . even Washington or Baltimore may fall into the hands of the Confederates") was willing, by September 14, to consider a Franco-British approach to the warring parties, recommending "an arrangement upon the basis of separation." Russell's response (sent from the Continent) offered mediation "with a view to the recognition of the independence of the Confederates. I agree further that, in case of failure, we ought ourselves to recognise the

---

2. Slidell to Mason, August 6, 1862, q. Charles Francis Adams Jr., "A Crisis in Downing Street," *MHSP* (May, 1914), p. 381. Private papers are used in Frank Merli and T. A. Wilson, "The British Cabinet and the Confederacy," *Maryland Hist. Rev.*, LXV, No. 3 (Fall, 1970), pp. 239-262.

3. M. Charles P. Cullop, "English Reaction to Stonewall Jackson's Death," *West Virginia Hist.*, XXIX (1967), pp. 1-5.

Southern States as an independent State."[4] Cabinet approval was deemed necessary for such a step, and a meeting was tentatively slated for October 23 or 30.

Unexpectedly, the first signs of hesitation came from France, which Russell had assumed to be eagerly awaiting the call. On September 16 Cowley, on Russell's orders, privately sounded out Thouvenel on the idea of "an armistice without mediation." To counter French doubts the English minister suggested a "safety in numbers" theory, also held by Palmerston: if a group of major powers made a joint proposal "and let it be seen that a refusal would be followed by the recognition of the Southern States, the certainty of such recognition by all Europe must carry weight with it."[5] The north would cave in without international war. But Thouvenel saw difficulties. He was increasingly at loggerheads with the Emperor over America, as well as over Italy and Austria. Expecting to be axed in a ministerial reconstruction, he was inclined to stick fatalistically to policies he thought best suited to French interests. The French had had their fill of war and diplomatic impetuosity. Thouvenel thought that the French were less enthusiastic than the English for recognition of the south; and he advised awaiting the results of the mid-term Congressional elections. Thouvenel's scepticism was aroused by the too-obvious ploy of involving Russia in the scheme as a sop to the north and a sign of the good intentions of the interveners. The French had in fact separately approached the Russians in late July with the Emperor's idea of a joint Anglo-French-Russian conciliation, and had been unceremoniously rebuffed. Gorchakov had indicated flatly that Russia favored reunion in America and supported the north; conciliation in company with England would appear as a threat to the north and was thus out of the question. Russell was obstinately to ignore this problem. He also discounted Thouvenel's misgivings: Thouvenel was under a cloud, his political credit nearing exhaustion, and Russell was no doubt confident of winning over the Emperor. In any case he went ahead in October without formal French assurances. Thouvenel for his part apparently retained little hope of averting precipitate action. But he wanted a postponement pending a thorough reappraisal with Napoleon of the French synoptic position

4. Russell to Palmerston, September 14, 1862; Palmerston to Russell, September 14, 1862; Russell to Palmerston, September 17; quoted EDA, II, p. 38.

5. Cowley to Russell, September 18, 1862; q. EDA, II, p. 39.

in Europe and America. Thouvenel had admitted in confidence to Dayton (September 12) that "the undertaking of conquering the South is almost superhuman"; nor was it the nature of a democratic republic like the United States to force millions of hostile people into subjection. He was toying with a compromise settlement which envisaged a weak confederation of south and north, united merely for defense and foreign relations—a reflection, as Case remarks, "of Thouvenel's—and France's—desire to see America strong in armed forces and in diplomacy to act as a counterweight to the power of the British Empire."[6]

On his return from Europe (September 22), Russell thrashed out possibilities with Palmerston, who by now wanted Russia added to England and France as the mediating powers. Gladstone, their obvious supporter in the cabinet, was kept informed, Russell describing the latest proposal to him on September 26 in the formula: "Mediation on the basis of separation and recognition accompanied by a declaration of neutrality." Palmerston's version of the plan included cessation of the blockade as a key ingredient. But Palmerston was never blind to crude realities. Throughout he accepted that the issue might well turn on the outcome of McClellan's attempts to stem Lee's offensive at South Mountain and Sharpsburg: "If the Federals sustain a great defeat, they may be at once ready for mediation, and the iron should be struck while it is hot. If, on the other hand, they should have the best of it, we may wait awhile and see what may follow. . . ."[7]

The battle of Antietam is often described as a critical turning-point in the diplomatic history of the war. But it is by no means certain that a southern victory at Antietam would irresistibly have produced British intervention, for events were to illustrate a surprisingly virulent opposition in cabinet to any departure from "strict neutrality." On the other hand, Palmerston, Russell, and Gladstone were—as Lord Granville observed—a formidable phalanx when united on foreign affairs. The significance of the setback to southern arms which took place at Antietam was twofold: it eroded the unity of the triumverate, by making Palmerston lukewarm; and it seriously weakened the legal (and hence moral) basis for recognition, a major component of Russell's original project. The plans thus actually considered were mild by comparison. Antietam also produced Lincoln's preliminary emancipation proclamation, which compli-

6. Case and Spencer, p. 336.

7. Palmerston to Russell, September 23, 1862.

cated, if it did not at first seriously divide, cabinet and public opinion.

Opposition to Russell's first plan had come from Granville even before Britain realized the full significance of Lee's enforced retreat across the Potomac after the gory battles of Antietam Creek. Granville had a freetrader's dislike of imperial dashes into distant lands, or gratuitous entanglements in dubious affairs. A senior Whig-Liberal statesman, an ex-foreign minister, his opinion carried weight. Nevertheless he wrote without much hope to Russell from Germany (where as Lord President of the Council he was in attendance on the Queen) giving a "long rigmarole" of reasons for opposing a "decidedly premature" move. European governments which did not really understand American politics were not fitted to arbitrate the questions of boundaries, slavery and other issues vital to any negotiations. If one, or both, belligerents accepted an offer of mediation, it would probably be for the purpose of gaining time, intriguing politically and renewing their military resources. If the north alone refused, Britain would face the dilemma whether to recognise the south. Granville was concerned to expose those who spoke glibly of recognition, but who really meant a forcible raising of the blockade. Recognition was meaningless as a practical measure, as a means of getting cotton, unless accompanied by force, and those who wanted peace must face the fact. Even a meaningless gesture of recognition would probably render inevitable a drift into war: "The North will become desperate, and even against their intentions will give us innumerable *casus belli.*" Granville reminded Russell that a war, "whether the French went with us or not," would remove English constraints from Napoleon III, who might gasconade more freely in Italy and elsewhere. Granville's point was unassailable; an Anglo-American war would not necessarily be a localized affair. It could throw the whole of Europe into the melting pot. Safer, he thought, to stick to the policy of neutrality which despite "the strong sympathy with the South, and the passionate wish to have cotton, has met with such general approval from Parliament, the press, and the public." Russell's scheme, he confided to Lord Stanley, "appears to me a great mistake."[8]

The uncertainty of the military situation, plus Granville's doubts, set Palmerston backpedalling. Southern success in the field

---

8. Granville to Russell (from Gotha), September 27, 1862; Granville to Stanley, October 1, 1862; q. Lord Edmond Fitzmaurice, *Life of Granville, George Leveson Gower, 2nd Earl Granville* (London, 1905), I, pp. 442-444.

he recognized to be a precondition for a successful offer of mediation. He believed that the south would accept mediation, based on separation, its war aim; but the north "would be unwilling to give up the principle for which they have been fighting so long as they had a reasonable expectation that by going on fighting they could carry their point." Lee's retreat seemed merely to have postponed the north's moment of truth—for how long no one knew, although the papers viewed Antietam as only a temporary rebuff for the south. ". . . we do not yet know the real course of recent events," Palmerston told Russell, "and still less can we foresee what is about to follow." The whole matter, he said querulously, "is full of difficulty, and can only be cleared up by some more detailed events between the contending armies."

One of the difficulties was Canada. Neither Palmerston, nor as it turned out, Newcastle at the Colonial Office, wanted a repetition of the winter mobilization and trauma of the previous November. If England was going to risk a Yankee war, it would be more expediently done in the spring of 1863 "when communication with Canada was open, and when our naval force could more easily operate upon the American coast. . . ." Palmerston saw two ways of salvaging Russell's scheme: Britain could act in tight conjunction with a group of powers (the Yankees could with difficulty single out England for a quarrel, and would balk at tackling a "European Confederation"); and might water down "an absolute offer of mediation" into "a friendly suggestion" that the time for an inevitable separation had arrived. He was even prepared to consider what he thought a very pro-northern arrangement, an armistice "not accompanied by a cessation of blockades."[9]

Russell meanwhile kept tinkering with mediation plans. Their rationale was at times baffling and not calculated to cut the ground from under potential criticism. Russell never came to grips with the question of Russian participation in any intervention. By October 1, through Baron de Brunow, the Russian ambassador in London, Russell had invited the Tsar to join with England and France in offering "good services" for peace. His invitation was sincere, and he even confessed to Palmerston that Russia's "separation from our move would ensure the rejection of our proposals." Yet no one with diplomatic knowledge seriously believed that Russia would join in a patently antinorthern move. Her power interests demanded a strong United States as a counterweight to Britain navally, she was

9. Palmerston to Russell, October 2, 1862, q. EDA, II, pp. 43-44.

self-sufficient in cotton, and had succeeded in cultivating a good image in the Union. Russell's note would need to contain arguments highly compelling to the Russian foreign office. Instead it begged the outstanding questions. Despite his plan's "excellent chance of success," Russell granted the possibility of a northern rejection. In this case Britain would recognize the Confederacy "as it seemed likely that this could be done without giving the United States a just ground of quarrel."[10] This blandly ignored Seward's long-standing public threats that recognition would be regarded by the north as a *casus belli.* Moreover, it is virtually certain that Russell knew unofficially the terms of a dispatch received by Adams on August 16 from Washington declaring American hostility to any form of mediation. If Britain (alone or jointly with other powers) approached Adams with any proposal "to dictate, or to mediate, or to advise, or even to solicit or persuade, you will answer that you are forbidden to debate, to hear, or in any way receive, entertain or transmit, any communication of the kind. . . ." If southern independence were acknowledged, Adams was immediately to suspend his functions. Russell was probably relying upon the rise of northern defeatism and peace movements to neutralize Seward's threats, or even to overthrow the Lincoln government. Such possibilities seemed not at all far-fetched in October 1862, despite Antietam, and were widely canvassed in the press. Again, should mediation be aggressively refused by Washington, it was open to Britain to defer the question of recognition. On October 4, Russell told Palmerston of two essentials: "that we propose separation" and "that we shall take no part in the war unless attacked ourselves." To the realists Russell was the victim of wishful thinking.

Gladstone meantime was engaged in a triumphal procession through Tyneside, and was unaware of Palmerston's revived hesitations after Antietam. Had he known, he may not have made what was close to being one of the more inspired "leaks" of the age, when on October 7 he publicly proclaimed at Newcastle his faith in the imminence of southern independence. It seemed a preliminary announcement of cabinet determination to recognize the south. In fact the Chancellor of the Exchequer acted without authority: and his celebrated phrase that "Jefferson Davis and other leaders

10. Brunow's summary of Russell's note, Brunow to F.O., October 1, 1862, q. EDA, II, p. 45. For Seward to Adams, August 2, 1862 (received August 16), EDA, II, p. 35; and Russell to Palmerston, October 4, 1862, EDA, II, p. 46.

of the South have made an army; they are making, it appears, a navy; and they have made what is more than either, they have made a nation [loud cheers]" may have been a piece of spontaneous oratorical virtuosity. But there is no doubting that Gladstone was deadly serious in his convictions, which represented for him long-maturing sentiments and reflected the conventional wisdom of the day.

Gladstone's ideas poignantly reflected the ambiguities of the liberal mind concerning the Civil War. He sympathized with the American experiment in popular government; and he was impatient with those who made blatant political capital out of the north's civil war difficulties. Such sympathies overshadowed his irritation with northern conduct of the war and distaste for protectionism and Sewardesque diplomacy. Nor, at least before Lancashire distress began to prey upon his conscience (a very well developed organ), did Gladstone believe that British national interests would be served by disruption of the Union. As he said at Leith just after the *Trent* crisis, England had nothing to fear from the growth of the U.S.A.[11] Rather, the division of the continent posed dangers to strict British interest. The creation of a cluster of northern states would threaten Canadian security, while a cluster of slave states would no doubt covet a Latin American empire—a situation less favorable to England than "the balanced state of the old American Union."[12] During the *Trent* crisis (which he described as "a new and fearful anxiety—may God guide us all His erring children") Gladstone had written "I am deeply convinced it was for *our* interest that the old Union should continue. . . ."[13]

What provoked Gladstone's anguish, and his sponsorship of a negotiated peace based on southern independence, was his ineradicable commitment to the principle of local self-determination, and his classical liberal preoccupation with the need to preserve free institutions and liberties menaced by the monolithic and centralizing tendencies of a wartime democracy.

Gladstone was unsympathetic to the slave philosophy of the south, and the cynical program and methods of secession. But he was in good company with liberals like Bagehot and Lord Acton in opposing any attempt to maintain the Union by war. As a colonial

11. *Times*, January 13, 1862.

12. Speech in Commons, *Hansard*, XLXXI (June 30, 1863), p. 1802.

13. Gladstone to Archdeacon Sinclair, December 19, 1861, *B.M. Add Mss* (Gladstone Letter Book), 44532/128.

reformer he had borrowed American principles of local freedom to apply to British imperial problems, and he was later—and quite consistently—to apply similar principles to the Irish situation. Tocqueville was the schoolmaster of the liberals in this regard; from the splendid example of New England's municipal self-government the Frenchman had derived the view that democracy in the locality was the school and safety-valve of democracy at large. Tocqueville's *Democracy in America* provided canonical text against the menace of democratic absolutism. In 1861 and 1862 it seemed to Gladstone, and many others, that the choice in America, consequent on the breakdown of federalism, was between the acceptance of slaveholding independence, or the suppression of rebellion by denial of the Republic's foundation ideals and destruction of individual liberties in the north. Gladstone's respect for movements of national independence was already becoming legendary, but it was more of a piece with Woodrow Wilson's Fourteen Points than Lincoln's neomystical vision of Union nationalism. Nationality was a matter, if not of linguistic unities, of cultural, intellectual and economic affinities, and its acid test was regional or local loyalty to a particular form of government. In this view the Union readily appeared in the same dress as, say, the Habsburg Empire, asserting nominal allegiance over subject peoples. Southerners were only inferior to rebellious Hungarians or Italians in the lack-lustre moral quality of some of their aspirations. As long as the Union did not officially fight an antislavery crusade even that reservation was weakened.

Those, like Bright, who saw the war in clear moral terms, as democracy versus slavery, progress versus the forces of darkness, resented Gladstone's "enigmatic" stand on the Civil War. But he was, in point of fact, putting the common view, if with exquisite unctiousness. Slavery had already, through political association, tainted northern ideals. Why clasp the viper to the bosom? "If (and what an if!) they could conquer the South they would only find themselves confronted by political and civil problems which are . . . wholly insoluble."[14] In the long run, the law of political dynamics would ensure separation between communities based on irreconcilable differences of civilization. He sympathized with the European view that the Union was too big to last, even within the

14. Gladstone to Sinclair. For an admirable account using valuable manuscript sources, see C. Collyer, "Gladstone and the American Civil War," *Proc. Leed's Philosophical Soc.*, VI, part 8 (May, 1951), pp. 583-594.

bounds of a sophisticated federal state. At Newcastle he admitted: "I can understand those who say that it is for the general interests of Nations that no State should swell to the dimensions of a continent."

All the ingredients of the Newcastle speech can be found earlier in Gladstone's thought, but as the carnage mounted in Virginia, as arbitrary arrests and "Mr. Lincoln's lawless proclamations" proliferated, his tone became more intense. Only weeks before Newcastle the war was "an immense mischief, not merely to democratic but to all liberal and popular principles whatever."[15] By September Gladstone unequivocally favored recognizing southern independence. Even pro-northerners like John Elliot Cairnes and John Stuart Mill seemed to concede the end of the Union. Gladstone later claimed that Professor Cairnes' advocacy of a peace settlement weighed heavily with him. Cairnes' *Slave Power* despite its special pleading for the north, abandoned the idea of reconstruction of the Union "in its original proportions," and called for a "Mississippi Compromise." Independence should be granted to that tract of land east of the Mississippi and south of the border states, with Louisiana "reserved for the North and for freedom."[16] Mill also was pessimistic about reducing the south to unconditional submission; he now focused publicly on the urgent need to preserve as free soil in any peace settlement the regions west of the Mississippi.

Gladstone's visit to Newcastle was a landmark in his rapid progression from Peelite conservatism to a markedly liberal, even radical, standpoint. He had taken the plunge of joining the Whig-Liberals in 1859 partly on behalf of the Italian cause, which was popular and invoked the rights of nationalities. Now another political leap was to be associated with similar international issues. Banqueted, and applauded by the vast crowds who assembled to witness his aquatic processions through Tyneside—a Tyneside immensely impressive as a seat of new industrial power, wealth and potential political weight—Gladstone made speeches which glowed with pleasure. He appears to have discerned within himself a latent power to move popular audiences, and he may have been carried away on America, the greatest topic of the day. Victorian public

---

15. Gladstone to the Speaker, August 16, 1862, and to Argyll, September 19, 1862, q. Collyer, pp. 588–589.

16. See J. F. Cairnes, *Slave Power* (London, 1862), p. 285 and following; Mill in *Westminster Review*, LXXVIII (October, 1862), p. 510.

meetings demanded magisterial pronouncements. He praised the resignation and self-command of Lancashire's operatives, and foreshadowed a future reward in franchise extension (a theme he was often to develop in the next years.) Privately he feared riot in the cotton centers. Gladstone wanted mediation before Lancashire erupted, for in that case the world would delight in accusing Britain of intervening out of stark self-interest. Now soberly, almost sorrowfully, he advised the north to drink the bitter cup of misfortune, disappointment, and mortification. Peace were best made before the slaveholders carved out an inconveniently large empire by the inspired success of their arms. A hint of Europe's duty to mediate alarmed Adams: "If Gladstone be any exponent at all of the views of the cabinet, then is my term likely to be very short. . . . We are now passing through the very crisis of our fate."[17]

Whether Gladstone in fact spoke as cabinet's mouthpiece was not clear to the public. The *Times* and *Morning Post* were reticent, suggesting ministerial embarrassment. It existed, but it was not acute. Palmerston complained mildly to Clarendon about the political inconvenience of Gladstone's utterance, but he thought the prediction of southern independence "not far wrong." Russell reproved the Chancellor: "Recognition would seem to follow, and for that step I think the cabinet is not prepared."[18] Convention held that ministers should not poach on the preserve of their colleagues, and foreign policy was the province of the Foreign Secretary or Prime Minister; nor should ministers independently foreshadow likely cabinet decisions. But the fact was that the doctrine of cabinet collectivity had been erratically enforced during the generation following Repeal of the Corn Laws, the golden age of the parliamentary member and a time of indifferent party discipline. Palmerston himself had overridden colleagues in the cabinet during the Italian-Austrian war of 1859. He had committed himself in speeches to policies not acceptable to cabinet, and even by sending dispatches without cabinet sanction. So had Russell. Now the Premier was wont to complain wryly of the inconvenience of being surrounded by able and articulate ministers—and Gladstone was the most fractious of them all. Palmerston's liberalism was of the old fashioned

17. Adams, *Diary*, October 8, 9, 1862, q. Morley, *Gladstone*, II, p. 80.

18. Palmerston to Russell, October 12, 1862, q. Adams, "Crisis in Downing Street," p. 402; Russell to Gladstone, October 20, 1862, q. Morley, *Gladstone*, II, p. 80. The radical sheets were preoccupied with the Garibaldi riots (October 12) but *Reynolds'* remarked that Gladstone's policy was merely that which it had advocated for over a year.

Canningite variety, and his politics posed no challenge to the political supremacy of "the Lords and Great Proprietors of the Soil." Gladstone was tapping new sources of political support for a more widely appealing liberalism, and Palmerston squarely thwarted his ambitions. Inevitably there was conflict. Palmerston had been unable to curb his Chancellor's criticisms of financial policy in the house and in public. Gladstone only too often felt a compelling moral obligation to tell the world the truth, or to state his personal convictions, on particular matters, with or without embarrassment to his cabinet colleagues. His Newcastle statement threatened, in this respect, to compromise British impartiality. As Palmerston had warned in the July 18 debate the English could make friendly offices towards peace in America "only by presenting ourselves in the shape of impartial persons, not tied by opinions either one way or the other."

In 1872 at Geneva, before the arbitration tribunal adjudging American wartime claims against Britain, the Americans cited the Newcastle speech as evidence of "conscious unfriendly purpose" towards the Union on the part of British cabinet members during the war. Gladstone replied to the charges in a letter to President Grant's ambassador at St. James, written after the case had closed.[19] Penned during Gladstone's historic first ministry, and at the height of his powers, the letter spoke of the "unexampled circumstances which misled me, and, in a great degree misled the world;" it justified his desire to terminate the war by reference to "motives of sheer humanity, and hatred of the effusion of blood," and to his belief that severance was in the best interests of the American people. In old age he repented this misjudgment in what Guedalla describes as "almost an excess of sackcloth." The charge of his animus against the north, which persists in the literature, can stand no longer. But it is also true that people of the best intentions have been prolific breeders of impetuous programs, and the secret record of Gladstone's cabinet role in the last months of 1862 makes a fascinating commentary when placed alongside the apologia of 1872.

The rumors of an armistice caused cotton prices to plummet, momentarily revealing the element of speculation present in the

19. Gladstone to Robert C. Schenk, November 28, 1872. The Grant administration, loath to revive controversy, shelved the letter. It was recently discovered and printed by Robert L. Reid, ed., "William E. Gladstone's 'Insincere Neutrality' during the American Civil War," CWH, XV, No. 4 (December, 1969), pp. 293-307.

famine and the desire of large interests to see the war continued. The *Times* city editor (October 11) reported that the commercial classes of London were strongly opposed to formal recognition. Gladstone's speech also dragged from their shooting, and other pleasures of a parliamentary adjournment, the pronortherners and "do-nothing" advocates amongst ministers. They were soon pitched into controversy against the interventionists.

The Secretary for War, Cornewall Lewis—one of the "do-nothing" school rather than a partisan—gave a public rebuff to Gladstone in a speech at Hereford on October 14. Lewis apparently acted on his own initiative to check speculation caused by Gladstone's speech and to show that the cabinet was yet uncommitted (although rumor had it, then and later, that the Prime Minister "had put him up to it"). The war, Lewis asserted, was yet undecided: "Its battle-fields were still reeking with the blood of thousands of soldiers killed on both sides." Until the north was incapable of continuing the contest, southern independence could be granted only in defiance of the historic criteria of international law. "Sir G. C. Lewis," derided the Liverpool *Courier*, "is great upon the astronomy of the ancients, and still greater upon the mythical history of Rome"; but it had no time for a doctrine which said "if the North be only dogged enough, the South can never be independent. . . . Here is a doctrine preached by a member of that Cabinet which bored the house and the country with its merits for recognizing Italy!" Palmerston was evading the issue: ". . . to set one Cabinet Minister to contradict another, while the Premier is silent, is neither the best nor the wisest way to secure respect or peace" (October 18). Lewis's speech proved to be the first shot in a high level controversy which effectively killed the chance of an interventionist decision being made at the cabinet projected for October 23.

In preparation for this cabinet, Russell sent a circular to ministers on October 13. Lewis sent around a countermemorandum on October 17, and more memos followed.[20] Russell's case postulated the existence of military stalemate, a seepage of support away from the Union in the border states Kentucky, Missouri, Tennessee, Arkansas, and the growth of war-weariness in the western states. (His intelligence came from the British *charge d'affairs* acting for Lyons in Washington—Lyons in London urged caution and his

20. These documents are largely unpublished. For extracts and analysis see E. W. Ellsworth, "Anglo-American Affairs in October of 1862," *Lincoln Herald*, LXVI, No. 2 (1964), pp. 89-96.

absence from his post was bad luck for the Union at this stage.) Unionism in the south was dead, and impossible of resurrection because of northern vindictiveness. Even if defeated, the south could be held only by military subjugation and civil despotism. This last was an obvious bow in Gladstone's direction. Russell proposed that it was the duty of the powers

> to ask both parties, in the most friendly and conciliatory of terms, to agree to a suspension of arms for the purpose of weighing calmly the advantages of peace against the contingent gain of further bloodshed and the protraction of so calamitous a war.

Britain, he later added, would act only in conjunction with France, Russia, Prussia and Austria. For the time he prudently dropped his previously emphatic threat to recognize the south if mediation was spurned by the north. Russell's language was humanitarian, but as Nevins says, "in effect he was proposing Northern acknowledgement of defeat under foreign pressure."[21]

Russell's difficulty was one of method: how to gain the prizes of peace—a reopened cotton trade and lucrative southern markets—without losing northern goodwill and trade, or being sucked into a war which would threaten Britain's vulnerable shipping trade, and the loss of Canada. There was less support in the nation for such a war now than in the heated atmosphere of the *Trent* days. War would put at stake that financial stability for which Gladstone had labored so brilliantly. The prospect of high war taxes probably curbed proletarian demands for action on cotton as effectively as any sympathy for Unionist democracy.

Lewis's countermemorandum was based, characteristically, on a sober and plain analysis of national self-interest and legal obligations. Lewis was something of a phenomenon in English politics—a scholar politician with a flair for business and a rooted aversion to intellectual frills or rhetorical vagueness. His mind, Bagehot once said, was "complication-proof."[22] In the practical assembly of Parliament, Lewis was highly respected, and his influence extended to both sides of the house. He had been a success at the Exchequer in the difficult circumstances of the Crimean War, and at the Home Office; and, while less at home in the War Office, had acquitted himself well during the *Trent* affair. Lewis and Gladstone were rival heirs for the Liberal leadership after Palmerston, but political motives do not

---

21. *War for the Union*, II, 269.
22. *National Review*, XVII (October, 1863), pp. 493–494.

explain their disagreement on mediation; both were high-minded, serious men and neither attempted to make political capital out of the issue. Lewis wanted British aims clearly spelt out, believing it a mistake to deliberate on expedients when there was a fundamental discrepancy respecting ends. His writings on the war in the *Edinburgh Review* (of which he was the former editor) had proferred little solace to the north. He shared the current view of the war's insanity and the desirability of relieving Lancashire distress. He wrote to Bagehot in March 1861:

> I have never been able, either in conversation or by reading, to obtain an answer to the question, What will the North do if they beat the South? To restore the old Union would be an absurdity. What other state of things does that village lawyer Lincoln contemplate as the fruit of victory? It seems to me that the men now in power at Washington are much such persons as in this country get possession of a disreputable joint stock company. There is almost the same amount of ability and honesty.[23]

But he cut sharply through Russell's optimism to ask what Pandora's box the powers might throw open by interference. "We may doubt" he suggested dolefully, "whether the chances of evil do not preponderate over the chances of good." In his memo of October 17 he asked what Britain intended on slavery, the border states, and the territories. Was she in a position to be honest broker in such perplexing matters? Would the embattled sections listen to offers of mediation? The north seemed unyielding in prosecution of the war, and would surely resent as one-sided an armistice which proposed to lift its stranglehold at sea. Had Russell faced up squarely to the chance of an open break with Washington, to Canadian vulnerability, to the likelihood of an expanded defense budget?

Lewis elaborated the legal doubts he had raised at Hereford from an analysis of historic British recognition policy, which forbade acknowledgement of sovereignty while a *bona fide* struggle for supremacy was still taking place between an imperial power and insurrectionary subjects. Antietam showed that the Union had not abandoned its drive to subjugate rebellion. In those circumstances, as William Vernon Harcourt later expressed it "a recognition of the inchoate independence of the insurgents by a foreign state is a hostile act towards the sovereign state which the latter is entitled to resent as a breach of neutrality and friendship."[24] Lewis was

---

23. Cited *Economist*, XXII, (September 10, 1864), pp. 1136-1137.
24. "Historicus" in *Times*, November 7, 1862.

strongly influenced by the antirecognition arguments of Harcourt, his brilliant young relative (he was married to Lewis's stepdaughter), and the two men worked closely in harness during the crisis months of October and November. Writing in the *Times* under the pseudonym of "Historicus," Harcourt had once given valuable support to Russell on his blockade policy. But now Russell encountered his opposition, backed by industrious researches and voiced in incisive barrister's style. An aspirant for political honors, for which his marriage gave him powerful connections, Harcourt was to establish in a range of civil war controversies a reputation as an international lawyer which later won him election to the first Whewell Chair of International Law at Cambridge.[25] His perennial theme was the peril of intervention, and the necessity of deference to solemn precedents and usages in relations between nations. The justice and equity of British practice, he pleaded, were immeasurably more important than considerations of expediency or partisanship. Britain's duty was to offer not only political but "moral" neutrality: "the solicitations of interested partisans and the clamour of ignorant passion" must be resisted. For his part, "the principles of one party and the aims of the other seem to me alike so indefensible as to leave to the impartial spectator little room for sympathy with either." The models he held up for British emulation were Washington and the great American statesmen of the era of the French revolutionary wars. They had stood out nobly against the excited passions of their people to resist intervention against the mother country. In their state papers he found an "inflexible attitude of strict neutrality" which repudiated rash short-term policies. (Their papers, he added caustically, bore the same relationship to the papers of modern transatlantic politicians as "that of the literature of Rome under Augustus to that of the Lower Empire.")[26]

Emancipation of the slaves bulked large in the battle of the memoranda. On September 22, Lincoln had issued a preliminary edict, declaring free, as from January 1, 1863, all slaves in areas still in rebellion. The traditional historical view has held that Lincoln's Emancipation Proclamation marked a watershed in the international history of the Civil War by mobilizing new support for

---

25. A. G. Gardner, *Life of Sir William Harcourt* (London, 1923), Chapter 7.

26. *Letters by 'Historicus' on Some Questions of International Law, reprinted from the Times* (London, 1863), pp. ix–xiii. Written a little later this preface represents his views at the time of the events narrated.

the north from the autumn of 1862. Thomas A. Bailey stated that the proclamation "elevated the conflict into a holy crusade against human bondage," adding that it "helped nerve the workingman to withstand the famine" and "demonstrated that the masses in England would be loath to stand behind the government in intervention."[27] Research has diminished the popularity of such interpretations. Although mid-Victorians condemned slavery on moral, religious, liberal, and economic grounds, the new biology strengthened dominant ideas of negro racial inferiority, while Britain's experience in her West Indian colonies seemed to show the ruinous social and economic effects of immediate and unplanned emancipation. Britain's Irish experience also indicated the difficulties of imposing social change upon a recalcitrant people by imperial force. Immediate emancipation could also be condemned on moral, religious, liberal and economic grounds. Ellison's study has revealed apathy and opposition to emancipation from working-class groups in Lancashire, and the persistence there of pro-southern sympathy. Again, Joseph Hernon has argued with persuasion that hindsight into the final triumph of the Unionist and antislavery causes in 1865 caused historians to oversimplify wartime British opinion, caused them to exaggerate the strength of support for Unionism and its antislavery program. The extreme revisionist position is represented in Hernon's statement: "The belief that the Emancipation Proclamation effected a great change in British public opinion appears to be totally fallacious."[28] He cites the example of abolitionists such as Lord Brougham who supported the Confederacy because it fought for self-determination; and others who were sceptical of northern sincerity, or were willing to accept the inevitability of secession, hoping that slavery would be doomed in the outcome.

The mixed reception accorded the preliminary proclamation in Britain bears out some of these criticisms, but an overall assessment must await more intensive study of proletarian and nonconformist opinion. Much evidence still stands to the effect that the northern image abroad improved, in the long run, after Lincoln adopted a war aim which was more intelligible to European opinion. While revisionist views offer valuable perspective on the complexity of British attitudes, they run the danger of analyzing out of existence the repercussions of the proclamation. It did not

27. For a brief survey of the literature on this, see Joseph M. Hernon Jr., "British Sympathies in the American Civil War: a Reconsideration," *JSH*, XXXIII (1967), p. 357.

28. Hernon, p. 359.

cause an immediate and wholesale conversion to the northern cause, or against intervention; but its very existence added a new dimension to the dialectics on mediation which cannot be ignored.

In this respect it seems significant that Russell felt it necessary in his cabinet circular to expatiate on the fallibility of the proclamation as a legal and moral *fiat.* For the activists, it was necessary to repudiate the idea that Lincoln had changed anything, that he had converted the war into a moral crusade. Russell piled up evidence from Lincoln's speeches to show that the north fought for preservation of constitutional government, not for negro freedom; he cited Lincoln's agonizing over the decision to emancipate, and highlighted his admission that he viewed emancipation as a practical war measure, "to be decided upon according to the advantages or disadvantages it may offer to the suppression of the rebellion." Russell was caustic about the cynicism of an edict which freed no slaves in states which remained in the Union: "The right of slavery is made the reward of loyalty; the emancipation is not granted to claims of humanity but inflicted as punishment on their owners." Plunder and incendiarism would follow in the wake of the "liberating" Union troops, while racial prejudice and indifference to the social plight of the Negro on the part of northerners would prevent any real amelioration of his lot. It was an impressive indictment, sharpened by the claim that the proclamation was legally dubious and an abrogation of the constitution (ignoring Lincoln's conviction that he was justified in acting under the war powers available to him as Commander-in-Chief). America was ripe for an armistice:

> . . . military forces equally balanced, and battles equally sanguinary and indecisive, political animosities aggravated instead of being softened, social organisation not improved by a large and benevolent scheme of freedom for the human race, but embittered by exciting the passions of the slave to aid the destructive progress of the armies.[29]

Gladstone, predictably, was in agreement. He shared the widespread impression that the north fought for political dominion, and not for the objectives of the abolitionist minority; and he refused to take seriously his friend Argyll's theory that a protracted

29. Quoted, Ellsworth, p. 90. The Emancipation Proclamation seems to have caused an abrupt change in Roman opinion, producing sympathy for the south, thought to be at the mercy of slave uprisings. See A. B. Lalli and T. H. O'Connor "Roman Views on the American Civil War," *Catholic H. R.*, LVII (1971), p. 31 and following.

struggle for the Union would lead to a general offensive against the institution which was the proximate cause of its disruption. But even more fundamental to Gladstone's position on emancipation was his abiding liberal distaste for the imposition of freedom by forcible methods. In Manchester in April, 1862, he had asserted that he had "no faith in the propagation of free institutions at the point of the sword." (Argyll held that free institutions had always been propagated by the sword.) At Newcastle and elsewhere Gladstone pointed out that slavery had been sheltered beneath the power of the whole Union, and would be more exposed to the force of world opinion if the south were left to bear the responsibility alone.[30] The Liverpool *Courier* put the case bluntly in these words:

> . . . it was the North that shielded the domestic institution of slavery from the detestation and hostility of the world. It was the Northern navy which menaced the English cruiser that dared to board an American slave ship. The North admitted slavery as part of its own institutions, and to this moment acknowledges the right of loyal masters to work, breed, buy and sell human 'chattels'. The fidelity of an owner to the Washington Government washes away the guilt of slavery . . .[31]

Gladstone, in one of his own cabinet circulars, spoke of the southern cause "being seriously tainted by its connection with slavery." But he maintained that successful mediation by the European states would enable them to put pressure upon the Confederacy to remove or mitigate the evils of slavery. The idea that an independent south would be reliant upon European goodwill for national survival, and would thus be forced to confine if not extinguish its appetite for a slave empire, may have shown deformed insight into the mind of the south, but it was surprisingly prevalent. Even Cairnes, in his *Slave Power*, opposed immediate emancipation at the "bayonet point," accepting separation as the only successful method of transforming the slave regime.[32] Cairnes wanted a *cordon sanitaire* of slavefree states drawn around the south, so that slavery should be penned into the smallest possible area. Gradual emancipation should be begun in the border states, where he believed the greater productivity of free negro workers would

30. See Collyer, pp. 584–585 for Gladstone's views on slavery; Argyll, *Autobiography* (London, 1906), p. 190. Gladstone claimed in his support the three antislavery champions, Brougham, Buxton, and the Bishop of Oxford.

31. Liverpool *Courier*, October 11, 1862.

32. Cairnes, *Slave Power*, pp. 285, 303.

compel the slaveholders through self-interest to change their system. With the Mississippi the limit of its westward reach, Mexico to the south, and an entirely freesoil Union to the north, the Confederacy would be a miniature empire, impotent to expand. Slavery would die a natural death. A great deal of English writing elaborated such points to demonstrate—what the twentieth century can hardly moralize about too glibly—that harmonious race relations depended upon fundamental changes in white racial attitudes and the existence of favorable economic opportunities. These were not automatically provided by proclamations and guns.

It was not necessary, however, to disagree with the above arguments to discount them as a signal for British intervention. Lewis and Harcourt recognized the element of expediency in Lincoln's edict but interpreted it as a sign of renewed martial determination. Russell might deplore the proclamation as a military rather than a moral act (so did Palmerston), and one which threatened servile war before negro freedom, but these things augured ill for the prospects of an armistice. The north seemed bitter and in deadly earnest, and the war likely to be prolonged. There was another scruple to be considered too. Was the distant hope of slavery's natural death in a separate south worth the immediate establishment of a stark slave state through blatant British act and sponsorship? As Harcourt was soon to write: "If we refuse to become the dupes of Northern insincerity, we are equally determined not to make ourselves the abettors of Southern iniquity." Could England become slavery's virtual guarantor?

> To my mind, in the one word 'slavery' is comprehended a perpetual bar to the notion of English mediation as between the North and the South; a bar to amicable mediation, because it would be futile; to forcible intervention, because it would be immoral. . . . A joint mediation, involving the settlement of this question, would practically place our honour in the hands of our copartners in the intervention. We might find ourselves placed in a position in which it would be equally difficult to advance with credit or retire with safety.[33]

Palmerston, ever the pragmatist, reverted to his earlier stance after the news of Antietam. The retreat of Lee's mauled army to Virginia, commercial uncertainty, Tory opposition and cabinet rifts

---

33. "Neutrality or Intervention?" *Times*, November 17, 1862, printed in *Letters by Historicus on some Questions of International Law* (London, 1863), p. 49.

put uncomplicated action momentarily out of the question. The "Yankees" in the cabinet—Argyll, Milner-Gibson, Grey, Villiers—rallied to the peace cause, but their advocacy suffered the defect of predictability. It was the Lewis-Harcourt approach which turned the scales. It was reminiscent of an earlier style of politics from which Palmerston had often encountered trouble, a style supported by the weight of middle-of-the-way Whiggery. Legally scrupulous, traditionally open to merchant opinion, it was in tune with the sober pacifist desires of the "intelligent middling classes." Instructively, such misgivings crossed party lines. Palmerston took care to sound out Lord Derby, through Clarendon, a week before the projected cabinet. The Opposition leader's reluctance probably sealed the fate of Russell's design. Derby's outlook had been moulded by the conciliatory diplomacy which Lord Aberdeen had pursued toward America during Peel's great administration of the early 1840's. He was against war and against making gestures which would only goad the north without procuring cotton. Moreover, "as each party insisted upon having that which the other declared was vitally essential to its existence, it was clear that the war had not yet marked out the stipulations of a treaty of peace."[34] This was the "hands off" policy which was to be adhered to by Derby, Disraeli, and the ranking Conservative officers during the war. They tried to rein in the impulsive southern sympathizers on the backbench, and resisted the clamors of the warhawk Tory press. Derby's solution to the Lancashire problem was private charity; as the greatest landowner in Lancashire he gave generously. Intervention, however, was both dangerous to world peace and inconvenient politically. The "Tory Democracy" program—looking to the inevitable widening of franchises—aimed not to alienate unnecessarily the Manchester School. So guarded were Derby's speeches on the war that party members were confused. One complained to Disraeli, after studying a Derby address at Buckinghamshire:

> All that I can make out from that, is compressed in the following summary: (1) Gloomy prophecies. (2) Impossibility of foreseeing any termination to the war & [sic] ergo to the Distress. (3) An oracular silence as to the merits of the two sides.[35]

---

34. Clarendon to Palmerston, October 16, 1862, q. EDA, II, pp. 51-52; W. D. Jones, *Lord Aberdeen and the Americas* (U. of Georgia P., 1958).

35. Henry Lennox to Disraeli, September 23, 1862, q. W. D. Jones, "British Conservatives and the Civil War," AHR, LVIII, p. 533; also pp. 532, 539.

Another motive may, perhaps unworthily, be attributed to Palmerston. The prospect of allowing the troublesome Gladstone to be torpedoed from within the cabinet may have had allure to one of Palmerston's mentality. (He had terrorized his office clerks when foreign secretary, was rude to his social inferiors, and had contrived the ruin of numerous rivals. Lord William Russell, who served under Palmerston in the 1830's, complained: "When I was at Lisbon, my views did not agree with his, so he attacked my wife's reputation . . . no gentleman can in the end consent to do business with him."[36]) Perhaps if circumstances forebade bullying Brother Jonathon, some rough handling for Gladstone might make a diverting and salutary alternative. An opposition paper accused him of enjoying the hubbub around him: "It is hard to unearth an old fox . . . The whelps, indeed, may break cover, and 'track', 'double', and 'loop' [Lewis and Gladstone?] . . . but the old stager knows better."[37]

On October 22 Palmerston told Russell he was "much inclined to agree with Lewis." Asking for an armistice in America would court "injury to our position." Requesting that the parties arrange peace themselves would be futile—each would stick to its war aims, and become pledged more strongly to them. "I am very much come back to our original view of the matter, that we must continue merely to be lookers-on till the war shall have taken a more decided turn." Russell, displeased, and recognizing that "no good could come of a Cabinet," postponed the October 23 meeting. On that day, Palmerston remained at Broadlands, but an informal meeting of ministers listened to Russell defend his armistice proposal as consistent with neutrality. However he and Gladstone found themselves outnumbered by followers of the Lewis position. That afternoon Adams was assured by Russell that the government was not inclined at present to change its neutrality policy, but that no promises could be made for the future. The Confederate *Index* was acidulous:

> . . . while our people are starving, our commerce interrupted, our industry paralysed, our Ministry have no plan, no idea, no intention to do anything but fold their hands, talk of strict neutrality, spare

---

36. Jasper Ridley, *Palmerston,* p. 113 and *passim.*

37. Liverpool *Courier*, October 18, 1862.

> the excited feelings of the North, and wait, like Mr. Micawber, for something to turn up.[38]

Lyons had been kept in London pending a cabinet decision, and was now much pleased to be allowed to return to his post without instructions on mediation. Clarendon was soon congratulating Lewis on his "smashing the Foreign Secretary's proposed intervention." ("He had thought to make a great deal of his colt by Meddler out of Vanity, and you have shown his backers that the animal was not fit to start and would not run a yard if it did."[39]) But any anticipation that the north's perils had ended was premature. Should the Confederates again begin sweeping all before them, mediation was sure to be revived. Palmerston and most of the ministry regarded the matter as closed, if only temporarily, but Gladstone and Russell were embarrassingly reluctant to accept any deferment. Russell was piqued by Lewis's sarcasms, and replied to them in a postcabinet memo which defended mediation by no less than five great powers. Gladstone, in yet another memo (October 24), continued to urge action, this time by England, France, and Russia. The concept of using international sanctions, and applying international moral force, to preserve world peace was to become Gladstone's controlling ideal, later developed in his Concert of Europe philosophy.[40] In this he was at one with the arbitrationist theory of the Manchester School. But they had incurred the charge of inconsistency by spurning an American mediation which should seal the fate of their favorite democratic republic. Cobden's scathing denunciations of war, made during the Crimean conflict, were now heaped back upon him.[41] Cobden seemed willing to accept peace dictated by Union bayonets, Gladstone wanted peace by moral

38. *Index*, October 23, 1862. The *Index*, a weekly newspaper, published in London by Hotze, in charge of the Confederacy's system of propaganda in Britain, first appeared on May 1, 1862. It became remarkably successful with "polite society," attracting the support of James Spence and employing at least seven writers from London newspapers. Hotze wrote leaders also for the *Morning Post*, *London Standard*, and Derby's *London Herald*. See Smith, *Confed. Index*.

39. Clarendon to Lewis, October 26, 1862; q. Maxwell, *Clarendon*, II, p. 266.

40. Ellsworth, p. 93.

41. See letter to editor from "A Man of Peace," *Times*, July 19, 1862, p. 7.

force. The defect in Gladstone's view, from Cobden's standpoint, was that he failed to discriminate between the Concert ideal and what would be the reality—gunboat diplomacy by the powers, spawned out of interest and threatening general conflagration.

The persistence of the activists fed off public opinion. Newspaper reports spoke of the bloody "draw" at Antietam having strained the north's resources and brought the country to the verge of utter disintegration. High prices for gold and railroad stocks on the New York market were interpreted as symptoms of failing government credit, the result of a crisis of confidence following a deluge of paper money poured forth from the Treasury. Habeus corpus had been suspended and martial law proclaimed in states under the sway of Federal troops. The drafts, it seemed, were being filled only with great difficulty, and rumor had it that another half million were about to be called up. All this smacked of desperation, not determination. The *Times* had forecast draft riots when the north's German and Irish mercenaries had been used up: "Foreigners and rowdies are now all but exhausted. Whether the respectability of the country will take their place remains to be seen."[42]

Many believed that Lincoln's administration was tottering, with the radicals usurping his authority, and the likelihood of a takeover by the man on horseback, the now indispensable McClellan. Whatever the outcome, liberty would be the victim: "There will be a spy in every household, a police agent in every company, a gaoler in every street." The Liverpool *Courier* demanded recognition for a people who, with scanty resources and no outside help, had repelled three invading armies and three times placed their enemy's capital in peril: "A vast, productive, and commercial multitude must not be shut out from intercourse with the rest of the world because a tyrannical clique of impotent officials claim ineffectual authority over it."[43]

The counterargument against recognition was that it might aggravate the horrors of the war by uniting conflicting parties in the north. The *Manchester Guardian* took this view, and warned against "a new outburst of that unreasoning anger against this country, which is so utterly unintelligible to Englishmen."[44] The *Times* threw up its hands in helplessness and thought it best that

---

42. *Times*, July 26, 1862.
43. Liverpool *Courier*, October 11, 1862.
44. *Manchester Guardian*, October 10, 1862.

the war should be allowed to wear itself out:

> Already the Northern States are gradually awakening to the fact that two nations are not like two pike, and that it does not follow because one is somewhat larger than the other, that the larger can swallow and digest the smaller. After a further quantity of useless butchery and carnage, and after the inumerable hospitals have been some more times filled and emptied, this truth will grow into a familiar fact.

While the British debated mediation, Paris was strangely quiescent. France, and Europe, were distracted by upheaval in Italy. The Italian question was both central to Napoleon's European diplomacy and entwined with hemispheric affairs. The Emperor's obsessive desire was to obtain Venetia for the Italians by cession from Austria. He would thus fulfill his pledge to free Italy from the Alps to the Adriatic, destroy one of the remaining territorial arrangements of 1815, and restore the credit he had lost in Italy during the 1859 war. Austria had defied French arms and retained Venetia, so would have to be persuaded by diplomacy. Napoleon planned to compensate Austria for her sacrifice in a number of ways: France would underwrite the fragmentation of the recently established Kingdom of Italy (into the Papal States, Sicily and Piedmont); enter an alliance with Austria; and—as this was not enough—would offer to place the Habsburg prince Ferdinand Maximilian on the throne of Mexico. (Napoleon also considered the Greek and recreated Polish thrones.) The Austrian court, determined to keep Venetia, refused to rise to the bait, and carefully dissociated itself from the Mexican venture, advising Maximilian to do likewise.[45] Any tentative interest Austria displayed in the Mexican proposal faltered with the withdrawal of England and Spain from the military expedition, and evaporated as the invading French armies encountered pugnacious Mexican opposition. By the summer of 1862, after the French defeat at Puebla (which necessitated massive reinforcements from France), Napoleon's policy was in serious difficulties. Maximilian, under pressure from Richard Metternich, the Austrian ambassador in Paris, seemed likely to withdraw from the entire affair. Moreover Napoleon's pro-Italian strategy threatened to alienate his Catholic and conservative supporters, who feared the evacuation of French troops from Rome where they protected the Papal States against

45. Nancy Nichols Barker, "France, Austria and the Mexican Venture, 1861-1864," *Fr. Hist. Stud.* (1963-1964), pp. 224-225.

the nationalists. Napoleon was forced to appease this opposition when Garibaldi precipitated a crisis by marching to "liberate" Rome in August 1862. The Turin government, playing a highly equivocal role under Ratazzi, gave covert encouragement to Garibaldi—hoping that the threat of a radical coup would force Napoleon to hand Rome over to the less dangerous national government—but later repudiated Garibaldi, and Italian troops dispersed his volunteers at Aspromonte (August 27). Italy was plunged into political confusion, verging on civil war in the south. In France the clerical and pro-Austrian groups at court were strengthened. This was reflected in the dismissal from the Quai d'Orsay of Thouvenel, liberal and pro-Italian. He was replaced by the experienced conservative diplomat, the pro-Austrian Edouard Drouyn de Lhuys.

Thouvenel's disposition to obstruct imperial recklessness on the American question was doubtless a contributing factor in his fall. Ironically, Drouyn de Lhuys turned out also to be an advocate of strict neutrality, almost an isolationist, on America.[46] As Blumenthal points out, Thouvenel and Drouyn differed only in degree respecting France's civil war policy. Algeria had convinced Drouyn that France dissipated her energies in colonialist adventures, when her destiny would be fulfilled or lost in Europe. The true focus of her attention should be upon the vital power changes promised by the unification movements taking place in Italy and Germany. The abiding peril for France was that of diplomatic isolation in Europe, hence Drouyn's advocacy of British and Austrian alliances. Hence also his fear of estranging France's friends by acting alone, or overambitiously, in the new world. Suspicion of Napoleon's world-ranging designs was already high enough over the acquisition of Nice and Savoy, French penetration of Syria, the occupation of Rome, and Mexico. Although politically aligned with Empress Eugénie and the clerical party, Drouyn was unsympathetic to the program of French involvement in Mexico which they sponsored.

Paradoxically, Drouyn came to preside over a series of interventionist moves on America. Good intentions, of course, do not necessarily pave the way to heaven in foreign affairs, and Drouyn was to preside reluctantly over a series of bewildering disasters for France during his four years of office. Nor was it a case of a weak minister caving in to the Emperor's demands, for Drouyn was patently no cypher and had broken with Napoleon in the past as

---

46. See Spencer's Chapter 10 in Case and Spencer; and Blumenthal, *Reappraisal of Fr. Am. Rels.*, p. 139.

foreign minister. The fact was that Drouyn tolerated arrangements which took no serious risk of war with the United States. Like most European statesmen he wanted an end to the uncertainty of the war. Moreover he and Napoleon were driven by domestic factors to make gestures for peace in America—especially by the need to appease dangerous emotions of outrage over unemployment caused by the cotton famine. In the outcome France risked little by suggesting mediation in conjunction with a safe number of other big powers, or by offering harmless suggestions for direct negotiations between north and south.

A fortnight before he departed the Quai d'Orsay, Thouvenel leaked to the Americans the informed suggestion that Britain might be about to recognize the south. The news gave Dayton a nasty shock. He also learnt Thouvenel's opinion that there was "not a reasonable statesman in Europe" who expected reunion to come about. The Russians, who were not really opposed to a north-south agreement, sent similar warnings: the United States had little time before Europe intervened. Northern resentment waxed strong at the prospect of the envious nations of the old world blighting Seward's "ripening civilization of the West." Ironically, resentment's focus became trained upon France, which (for motives as expedient as those behind British secrecy) proclaimed in open diplomacy its designs to end the war.

Luck, and European events, had caused Britain and France to move out of step, a disastrous stroke of fortune for the Confederacy. Napoleon's response to the British initiatives of September—it was also a response to the Federal defeat at Chattanooga, and to Mercier's promptings for a truce—came belatedly at the close of October, *after* the lines of battle had been drawn in the British cabinet. The emperor suggested a joint proposal by the three maritime powers for a six-months truce in America on land and sea. His armistice proposal was made in notes sent to London and St. Petersburg on October 30, a week after the collapse of Russell's cabinet proposal. Drouyn was sceptical—he shared his predecessor's doubts on Russian cooperation and thought "the fruit hardly seems ripe"—while Slidell had been curiously equivocal in interview with the Emperor. Slidell was still preoccupied with the idea of British poltroonery and the necessity of getting unilateral action by the French. At St. Cloud he poured cold water on a project of joint mediation. The south preferred "umpirage" by France alone, and would not welcome a scheme which permitted France to be outvoted by a pro-northern Russia and an ultracircumspect England.

Slidell feared that England would not go so far as to recognize the south if mediation was refused by the north. Napoleon, on French behalf, suggested that a northern refusal "will afford good reason for recognition and perhaps for more active intervention." His sympathies were entirely with the south. But Slidell was banging his head against a stone wall in trying to weaken the English alliance, for Napoleon was tied to it by European imperatives. Drouyn shared the Emperor's "grave objections to acting without England." Palmerston could be more thoroughly trusted if pinned in the friendly bearhug of his ally. Otherwise, as Napoleon confided to Slidell, "if he [Napoleon] acted alone, England, instead of following his example, would endeavour to embroil him with the United States and . . . French commerce would be destroyed."[47]

The French note of October 30 justified an armistice in lofty language about the conciliationist mission of neutrals, who desired to end the "prodigious shedding of blood" before servile war was touched off by the emancipation edict. Less unselfishly, it pointed to the advantages of ending the cotton crisis, which was "preventing the growth of one of the most fertile sources of public wealth" and causing a "most painful situation" for the great centers of labor. Reports from the procureurs-general were indicating a more insistent demand for mediation or relief. Napoleon was simply reacting in accordance with his dictum that "it is public opinion which wins the last victory." Drouyn's dispatch was characteristically prolix, but there were some interesting omissions. Nothing was said of recognition, or of that "more active intervention" which Napoleon had forecast to Slidell. The note was studiously vague on the role to be taken by the powers: they would be nonpartisan, they would smooth the way for negotiations "which might hopefully follow" between the belligerents, they would intervene "only to the extent allowed by both parties." Finally the plan seemed superoptimistic in hoping that the north would accept the opening of southern ports.

It is possible to explain British rejection of the French overture—often interpreted as the death stroke to southern hopes of foreign intervention—as the culmination of the situation which arose in October. Certainly Drouyn's note precipitated much the same division of forces in cabinet, and resulted in the same negative outcome (this time formalized in a vote). But the context had been

---

47. For detailed account of joint mediation, Case and Spencer, Chapter 10; also Owsley, pp. 328-336, 353-359.

changed to some degree by Napoleon's assumption of initiative and by American events. For Napoleon to thrust himself into the forefront was to risk British suspicions of his deeper designs; certainly it evoked a chauvinistic reluctance to be led from Paris. The *Manchester Guardian* thought there would occur "a considerable divergence in the spirit with which intervention would be undertaken by the two powers concerned."[48] At Bradford, W. E. Forster warned a sympathetic audience that "it was undesirable that our foreign policy should be inextricably involved in the wishes and plans of Louis Napoleon."[49] There was widespread criticism in England of an armistice which favored the south, by lifting the blockade. The alarm was raised that Napoleon sought a northern rebuff as a pretext for recognition and forcible intervention. England should steer clear of such intrigues. This trend was exquisitely embarrassing to those Englishmen who were unantagonistic to such a train of events.

Meanwhile the news from America was of McClellan's pending dismissal, and of mounting Democratic successes in the mid-term Congressional elections. (News of the Republicans' loss of New York, and the full extent of the electoral swing was not, however, known until almost a week after cabinet had made its decision.) Various interpretations could be placed upon these events and few were rash enough to forecast an immediate end to the war. It was appreciated that the Democrats, and other opponents of the regime, had fallen short of a complete triumph; residual Republican strength in Congress, together with Lincoln's monopoly of the Presidency for another two years, ensured no revolutionary changes. The *Times* (which compared the President, during his four years, with an emperor elected for life) declared that the election had "only created a protesting minority," and, moreover, one which could not yet afford to espouse a policy of "surrender." But, it added, "it is a threat of what may happen hereafter."[50] The English papers absorbed the rhetoric of opposition politics in the United States and it became fashionable to picture the Democrats as the party of conservative constitutionalists opposed to a faction of nationalist-centralists. The Republicans were "for absolute power, to be obtained

48. *Manchester Guardian*, November 18, 1862. "The impression thus produced is certainly not weakened by the position now occupied by the French in Mexico and the favour shown to the Southern Envoy at Paris. In short, it may be doubted whether the imperial policy is inspired solely by an impartial desire to bring the war to a close."

49. *Guardian*, November 22, 1862.

50. *Times*, November 17, 1862.

by the sword, and to be exercised under the dictation of mobs led by a few frantic parsons and fanatical laymen."[51] Democrats were not traitors, but realists who admitted that the Union could not now be restored by arms. Their numbers and boldness would grow with "every fresh evidence of the monstrous expenditure of national energy which is being wasted on a hopeless and unjustifiable enterprise."[52]

Who could disagree? The evidence seemed clear of a swelling tide of disgust with Republican mismanagement of the war, with their abridgement of civil liberties, emancipation policy and conscription intentions. Centrifugal forces were at work tearing apart the north. But whereas the French government contended that foreign interposition would accelerate them, and force a north-south accommodation, the British feared it would have the opposite effect. Interference would slow down the disintegrative process by creating temporary national unity against an outside threat.

The *Times* approved cabinet's caution; it came out against "the very dangerous and far-drifting policy of American mediation," and gave as the most cogent reason against interfering the danger of weakening opponents of the war:

> It would be, indeed, a fearful reflection for us at a future day that we had by an untimely meddling defeated the efforts of the American Constitutionalists, and forced the nation once more under the power of a faction which must have fallen without our aid.

Even the Democrats must exclaim against an armistice "so manifestly an act of favouritism to the South." England would lose the merit of its long self-denial without obtaining cotton that winter. The *Times* agreed with Cobden that it would be cheaper to keep all Lancashire on turtle and venison than to plunge into a desperate war with the north, even with all Europe at Britain's back: ". . . in defence of our honour, or of our rightful interests, we are as ready to fight as we ever were; but we do not see our duty or our interest in going blindfold into an adventure such as this."[53]

The French proposal offered embarrassment for Palmerston, renewed challenge for the noninterventionists, and hope resurrected

---

51. *Times*, November 13, 1862.

52. *Manchester Guardian*, November 3, 1862.

53. *Times*, November 13, 14, 1862. "We very much doubt" it added "whether, if Virginia belonged to France as Canada belongs to England, the Emperor of the French would be so active in beating up recruits in this American mediation league."

for Russell and Gladstone. Russell however, fumbled his opportunity. The surviving records bespeak a sense of bafflement in those exposed to the Foreign Secretary's arguments, and deservedly so. He wanted an intervention which would (he thought) strengthen the hands of the Peace Democrats; at the same time he expected both north and south to rebuff any approach from the powers. On neither the use nor consequences of an abortive overture was he enlightening, but spoke vaguely of making good offices "such as would be creditable to us in Europe."[54] This may have reflected, as Lewis guessed, a fear of displeasing France.[55] Perhaps he merely yearned, like Napoleon, to deflate anger over the cotton catastrophe. But his vagueness raised suspicions that he wished to speed up British recognition of the south (which he had been predicting would take place next spring), or that he was sponsoring a program of forcible intervention. For the puzzle of slavery, which perplexed Palmerston ("we could hardly frame a proposal which the Southerns [sic] would agree to, and people of England would approve of."[56]), Russell had his solution. Negotiations would result either in restoration of the Union, when all slaves should be emancipated with compensation to owners, or in separation, when "we must be silent on the trend of slavery, as we are with regard to Spain and Brazil."

On November 7 Cornewall Lewis circulated to cabinet a twenty-five page memorandum which bore unmistakeable marks of Harcourt's forensic eloquence. In it were re-presented the objections to an intervention which would "abet southern iniquity," would prove utterly unable to discover an acceptable moral foundation for solving the problems of slavery and boundaries, and which only puerile optimism expected to be short, simple or peaceable. Harcourt put much the same case in influential letters to the *Times* on November 7 and 17, later printed as tracts.[57]

The stumbling block in the French plan, as far as Palmerston, most ministers, and diplomats like Cowley were concerned, was the suggestion of raising the blockade. As the *Times* asked (and Dasent was presumed to be peddling Palmerston's opinion):

---

54. Russell to Palmerston, November 3, 1862, q. EDA, II, p. 61.

55. Lewis to Clarendon, November 13, 1862, in Maxwell, *Clarendon*, II, p. 268.

56. Palmerston to Russell, November 2, 1862, q. EDA, II, p. 61.

57. See "Historicus," "The International Doctrine of Recognition," *Times*, November 7, 1862; "Neutrality or Intervention?", *Times*, November 17, 1862. Printed in *Letters by Historicus on some Questions of International Law* (London, 1863).

> What hope can we have that the Federal Government would submit to a suspension of arms by sea and land for six months? Such an armistice would undoubtedly be very convenient to the South, very convenient to England, and very convenient to France. The South, relieved from the blockade of their coast, would be able to exchange their now valueless millions of cotton bales for sugar, salt, tea, coffee, calico, broadcloth, leather, and every other article not contraband of war, under the want of which they now so desperately suffer. England would be able to set her mills to work. France would recover her lost customers for her silks and wines and her Paris articles, and would also obtain the cotton which she now buys through us at fabulous prices . . . But what would the North get by it? To her it would be a request to allow us to tie up her right arm. (November 12)

There seemed only remote chance of the powers "going into this matter as a European league" on such a dubious mandate. Even if they did, there seemed remoter chance of preserving unity in a retaliatory stroke against the north involving recognition. As Lewis quipped: "A single intervening Power may possibly contrive to satisfy both the adverse parties; but five intervening Powers have first to satisfy one another."[58] The powers had, after all, fallen out among themselves in almost every instance of intervention since Navarino. Asked "Historicus":

> Has England no interests in Canada, France no views in Mexico which might lead to a divergence on various points in the negotiation? What security is there that, as in the case of Belgium and Greece, dissentient sections of the mediating Powers should not end by ranging themselves in hostile camps side by side with the original belligerents: and that thus, in an ill-judged attempt to quench the American strife, we should in the result endanger the peace of Europe?

Intervention, he contended, was like revolution: ". . . its essence is illegality, and its justification is its success. Of all things, at once the most unjustifiable and the most impolitic is an unsuccessful Intervention."[59]

During the deliberations it became known that Russia had refused to act jointly with Britain and France. The Russians would accept a north-south rapprochement; and had in fact secretly instructed their minister at Washington, Stoeckl, that he might act in concert with the other powers if Washington were to become

58. November 7, memo, q. EDA, II, p. 62.
59. "Neutrality or Intervention?", *Times*, November 17, 1862.

genuinely conciliationist. But they opposed a premature move which would discredit them with their northern friends and prejudice future peace overtures. Russell was prepared to risk acting without Russia, but he had few followers among his colleagues.

At cabinet meetings on November 11 and 12 prudence prevailed, and the French were politely informed that overtures would be best postponed until better prospects existed of their being accepted by the contending parties. Palmerston (according to Gladstone) "gave to Russell's proposal a feeble and half-hearted support," while Russell "rather turned tail" after ministers had picked his plan to pieces.[60] According to Lewis: "Everybody present threw a stone at it of greater or less size, except Gladstone, who supported it, and the Chancellor [Westbury] and Cardwell, who expressed no opinion."[61] Russell admitted, under questioning from Lewis, that there was no chance of Washington accepting the proposal, and this clinched the matter for the majority. Confederate independence was inevitable. Why risk war to speed the process? The *Moniteur* considered the British response not a refusal but an adjournment, and Gladstone shared the sentiment. (The other Paris papers were unindulgent towards Albion, the Orleanist *Débats* declaring it impossible "to descend lower in the depths of what may be called deliberate Machiavelism. . . .") Like Slidell, Gladstone hoped the French would act alone: "It will be clear that we concur with them, that the war should cease."[62]

Across the channel, Drouyn and Napoleon splashed their peace plan in the press. They gave the impression of acting with indecent haste to make maximum political capital out of the affair. But there was an unwanted effect which they did not foresee. Northern animus was transferred from the British—whose mediation deliberations had been decently shrouded in secrecy—to the French. Drouyn published his October 30 note on November 13 (before he had even received an official reply from London) and followed with the British and Russian rejections on November 16. The Emperor's wooing of opinion was largely successful. He was given credit for attempting to procure cotton, while being able to shift the blame

60. Gladstone to his wife, November 12, 13, 1862; q. Morley, *Gladstone* (London, 1904), II, p. 85.

61. Lewis to Clarendon, November 13 (?), 1862; q. Maxwell, *Clarendon*, II, p. 268. Westbury belatedly came out in favor of Russell's plan.

62. Morley, *Gladstone*, II, p. 85. I have taken the *Moniteur* and *Débats* quotes from NYH, December 5, 1862.

for continuing unemployment on Britain and Russia.[63] (Britain, forced into publication, blamed Russia, northern obstinacy, and the danger of Atlantic war.) But Dayton was indignant, and Franco-American relations began a downward slide. Dayton learnt of the French armistice plan, humiliatingly and after equivocation from Drouyn, only one day before it appeared in the *Moniteur*. He suspected a cynical plot to feather the French nest in Mexico or to silence enemies of the regime at home, and reacted with a display of patriotic temper which impressed Drouyn.[64] The American minister aptly blended a sense of aggrieved national innocence with a salutary reminder of his country's historical mission and power. It was unfeasible to ask the north to forsake its war aims, to disband armies and navies raised at immense national cost, just when victory was about to materialize. Europe should put up with cotton shortages. Such hardships were the common result of every war. Spreading a large map on Drouyn's desk, he indicated the huge slave populations still held in bondage in the south. Was it worthy of the world's great nations to prevent their emancipation, now at last made possible by exercize of the presidential war power? Jabbing at Louisiana, Florida, and Texas, Dayton exclaimed that the people of the *whole* United States had either paid large sums or fought wars for those territories. The north would never "yield them up without a death struggle; France, I am sure would not!"

Slidell and his colleagues had ridden the crest of hope in early November but they were not too downcast by the British and Russian rejections. Susceptible to conspiracist theories, Slidell speculated that the British had deliberately enticed the emperor into a commitment, then snubbed him with premeditated malice. (Russell's clumsy handling of events had at least permitted such an hypothesis.) If it was true, Napoleon would go on out of pique. "If on the contrary he did not expect the acceptance of his proposition, judging from his character and antecedents, he will not be disposed to leave

63. This motive was appreciated in England. Cf. *Manchester Guardian:* "A season of distress is only too likely to awaken the slumbering fires of revolution, and the Emperor hastens to show that the continuance of the cotton famine cannot be justly laid at his door." (November 18, 1862).

64. Dayton to Seward, November 12, 1862, q. Case and Spencer, pp. 368-369. American suspicions had been raised when, on October 28, Admiral Reynaud commanding the Antilles and America station arrived at New Orleans on the frigate *La Guerriere.* The French-speaking and secessionist residents hailed the visit with delight. It coincided with the mediation note and was held in England to show French determination to intervene.

his work unfinished and will act alone."[65] But Louis Napoleon was not Napoleon I, and he was not willing to persist in a strong interventionist move without the security of allies. France was still willing to make available its good offices, would indeed soon offer them unilaterally, but Seward could safely ignore such anodyne interference. For his part Drouyn showed no disappointment that Britain and Russia were determined to "maintain a role of absolute abstention," and he informed Mercier that France was resuming its previously passive attitude.[66]

---

65. Slidell to Benjamin, November 29, 1862, q. Owsley, p. 358.

66. Drouyn de Lhuys to Mercier, November 13, 1862, q. Case and Spencer, p. 369.

Chapter IX

"A Dead Cock in the Pit"

The damage inflicted upon northern morale by the great European debate on Intervention has never been adequately assessed. That debate accompanied a string of military reversals after the Seven Days Battle which threatened to turn the whole Unionist world dry and crackly. From foreign nations an avalanche of words preached the war's futility and the impregnability of the south. From the English, worse than their official acts, came "the studied, systematic, persistent reviling of our cause, which is to us as grand as liberty, as sacred as the memory of our fathers, as priceless as the national life itself. . . ."[1] By late 1862 a fund of bitterness had been built up in the loyal states against the powers, and its legacy was to be potent. Increasingly difficult to discover were those evidences, present even during the *Trent* affair, of sentimental regard for the mother country or historic friendship with France. Russia was virtually the sole beneficiary of events.

As this chapter will illustrate, the strains of war were warping the integrative bonds within the Atlantic world which had previously offset power rivalries. That world would now remain at peace, Americans believed, only if peace was dictated by the stark considerations of power politics, economic and political interest. Reliance could no longer be placed upon tradition, sentiment, cultural affinities, or "the crimson thread of kinship." More

1. *NYT*, December 9, 1862.

accurately, such reliance was misplaced as far as Europe's governing elites were concerned. Interestingly, this realization stirred a reawakening of America's missionary revolutionary ideology as northerners perceived, perhaps wrongly, that their true friends were the masses and submerged subclasses of Europe.

The building of Confederate vessels of war in Britain precipitated enormous resentment in the north over England's "pseudo-neutrality." The escape of the raider *Alabama* from British jurisdiction in July 1862 started a ruckus which was not to end until the Geneva arbitration of 1872. The facts of the *Alabama* case are now well-known.[2] Working against considerable odds—poor communications with Richmond, money shortages, no official representation in London—the south's chief naval agent in Europe, James D. Bulloch, skillfully brought to fruition the first stage of Mallory's ambitious naval program for the Confederacy. Deprived of dockyard facilities at home, the south would commission the building abroad of a small but superior fleet of swift propeller-driven cruisers. Heavily armed for their size, fast enough to elude capture by more ponderous Union warships, the raiders would frighten Yankee shipping from the high seas, weakening enemy morale. The cost of imports to the north would soar, as American trade was driven to neutral flags. Backed by the south's fiscal agents, the Liverpool firm Fraser-Trenholm, Bulloch in mid-1861 arranged the construction in Merseyside docks of two gunboats, to become the *Florida* and *Alabama*. The *Florida*, 191 feet, screw-propelled, three-masted, sailed out of Liverpool without armaments on March 22, 1862. The British government refused to act, holding that the building of an unarmed ship did not violate existing neutrality laws. Nor had Adams' agents and spies, under the energetic control of Consul Dudley in Liverpool, been able to unearth usable evidence of Confederate ownership of the ship. The *Florida* steamed to Nassau in the Bahamas where her armament was completed. British inaction was a triumph, at this stage, for a more traditional legal interpretation of the Foreign Enlistment Act of 1819 (soon to be associated with the "strict

2. The following account is indebted to Frank J. Merli, *Great Britain and the Confederate Navy* (Indiana University Press, 1970); Douglas H. Maynard, "Plotting the Escape of the *Alabama*," JSH, XX, No. 2 (May, 1954), pp. 197-209, and "Union Efforts to Prevent the Escape of the *Alabama*," MVHR, XLI (June, 1954), pp. 41-60; Rupert C. Jarvis, "The *Alabama* and the Law," *Historic Soc. Lancs. and Cheshire Trans.*, III (1959), pp. 181-198.

construction" of the statute).[3] The act forebade the "equipping, furnishing, fitting out, or arming" in British territory of any vessel with the intent that such vessel should be used to commit hostilities against any state with which Britain was at peace. Lawyers who harked back to the original intention of the act claimed that it had not meant to prohibit the right of neutrals supplying contraband in the form of ships to belligerents. The veto on arming, equipping etc., was designed to prevent armed vessels waging war immediately they had cleared port, thus transforming neutral territory into a base of military operations.[4] On this view it was unexceptionable to build unarmed ships (akin to ordinary contraband), and it was open to a belligerent buying such a ship to fit it for war outside British jurisdiction. Bulloch acted on such legal advice. No comparable case had, however, been brought under the act, and more stringent views of neutral obligations existed—not least among Foreign Office advisers apprehensive about Britain's naval interests in a future war. When Adams redoubled his efforts to prevent the escape of Bulloch's second, more powerful, cruiser—Number 290 in Laird's yards, 220 feet, capable of over twelve knots from twin engines—Russell found himself in a perplexing situation.

After construction delays, the 290 was launched on May 15, 1862, given engine trials on June 12, and seemed likely to clear Liverpool in mid-July. Adams on June 23 asked Russell to stop the projected expedition; he offered circumstantial evidence, obtained by Dudley's spies, indicating that the 290 was constructed as a vessel of war and was being built for the south. The Crown Law Officers advised an investigation to test the truth of the allegations, and favored the vessel's detention if the charges were corroborated. At the same time the Board of Customs advised against unwarranted detention, claiming that customs surveillance of the 290 had failed to uncover evidence to justify a prosecution. There is little doubt, given the weakness of the American evidence and the verdict in the *Alexandra* case a year later, that a test case against Lairds would have failed. Russell accepted the customs view: the onus of proving violation of the act was put upon American agents. On July 21 Dudley submitted sworn depositions to the collector of customs at Liverpool and demanded the 290's arrest. (One affidavit alleged that an attempt had been made to enlist a seaman in the Confederate

3. The legal tangle is discussed more fully below, Chapter 10, "Neutrality on Trial."

4. Jarvis, p. 182 and following.

service aboard the 290. Had this charge been sustained, the ship could have been detained only so long as the fine of £50 per recruitment remained unpaid!) The collector requested an urgent ruling from the Board of Customs "as the ship appears to be ready for sea." Two days later the northerners learned that the Board had rejected their seizure request. Pressure upon the Foreign Office seemed more likely to succeed. From Robert P. Collier, Q.C. and Judge Advocate of the Admiralty, Adams obtained an acrid opinion against the immobility of the customs, and sent it to Russell's department with the most recent documentation of "contraventions" of the act. Collier warned that the *Alabama*'s escape would give the Federal government serious grounds for remonstrance. Treasury, in charge of customs, had already suggested the wisdom of a legal opinion from the Crown Law Officers. On July 23 Russell ordered an urgent decision by the officers. So far, as Douglas Maynard comments, the speed at which the American documents had been processed set an enviable record for any bureaucracy. A Union success was blocked by two things: the Board of Customs stubbornly adhered to its original stand; while the Queen's Advocate, Sir John Harding, was incapacitated by mental illness from dealing with the documents which had been delivered to his care. The papers were not retrieved from Harding's desk until July 28. Meeting hurriedly that evening, the Solicitor-General and Attorney-General recommended immediate seizure of the ship. They advised against a "narrow construction" of the act which would "give impunity to open and flagrant violations of its provisions." The *Alabama*, however, fled to sea the next morning, ostensibly on trials, leaving without armaments, "not as much as a signal gun or musket." Official procrastination, later criticized at the Geneva arbitration, prevented the Treasury telegram ordering seizure from reaching the Liverpool collector until July 31, or other officials who might yet have detained the *Alabama* on the British or Irish coast until it was too late. Eluding Union naval pursuit, the *Alabama* made its way to the Azores, where it was armed according to Bulloch's carefully matured plans. Under Captain Raphael Semmes, it began a two year career of havoc to Union commerce.

The escape, and news of the building of sister raiders to the *Alabama* in shipyards at Liverpool and Birkenhead, stirred a hornet's nest in America. Seaboard interests grew progressively alarmed at the damage inflicted upon northern shipping by the "privateers." Such perils attracted high insurance rates to American vessels and goods, and caused a flight of trade to neutral flags. To the northern mind, the activities of Lairds, Thompsons and other British shipbuilders exceeded the legitimate commercial proceedings of neutrals. Although Americans had been notoriously ardent in the cause of neutral profiteering in other people's wars, they viewed in a new dimension the stakes at issue in the present controversy. Britain (and later France) seemed verging dangerously near to war by remote control, intervention without the drawbacks of actual war. This view, despite its exaggerations, embraced a more modern concept of neutrality which made allowance for developing war technology, impossible under the antiquated terms of England's Foreign Enlistment Act. The sinister implications of events were obvious to the *Herald*:

> The fact must stand apparent to the world, that a great combination of British capital has been made, embracing, without doubt, the shipping, the manufacturing and the *political* interests of the Kingdom, for the purpose of giving success to the American rebellion. And to make sure of their work so gigantic a scheme as the creation of an iron-plated navy, equal to the task of effectually raising the blockade, is boldly entered upon. The reward for this enterprise will pay well for its hazard. No doubt the last and the present year's cotton crop . . . is offered freely as the fund from which all expenses and risks are to be paid. Four hundred millions of dollars would not be too high an estimate probably, in a commercial view, of the value of the stake played for—a sum that overshadows quite the seductive millions that the speculators of the French Ministry are supposed to be seeking in Mexico, at the cost to the Empire of a foreign war.[5]

From all sides remedies were urged upon the government: intensify the Union navy's striking power, equip special raider-hunters, tighten the blockade (one effect would be to stop the exodus of cotton bales used by Bulloch to pay for his cruisers), use strong diplomacy in London. Seward, who had threatened to issue letters of marque to American privateers in mid-1862, sympathized with moves to have an enabling bill on the matter introduced in Congress. British shipping would be the obvious target. To this threat of reprisal, which made due impact in England (even in Liverpool, where maritime interests were starting to chafe at the damage caused by raiders to neutral property on belligerent ships), was added a clamor for reparations against the British for war losses caused by the *Alabama* and her cohorts. The clamor intensified with each sinking, and hardly ceased for a decade. Reparations might

5. *NYH*, October 10, 1862.

not be a practical proposition in 1862; but as Bennett said darkly they could be filed away, "to be brought to light and urged with the whole power of the nation as soon as we have put down the rebels and restored the republic to all its former greatness." Who should be surprised then if, in retaliation for England's villainous treachery "in our time of tribulation," Canada was seized and held "until full and satisfactory retribution be made . . . ?"[6]

Meantime, events to the south were already showing, as General Phil Sheridan later claimed, that "the French invasion of Mexico was so closely related to the Rebellion as to be essentially part of it."[7] The United States had exerted diplomatic pressure to forestall intervention in Mexico, and failed. Now caution forebade it unnecessarily adding France to its enemies. France's right to exact its claims by force from Mexico was reluctantly recognized. Accepting the patent fictions that France renounced territorial conquests for itself, and that its troops were engaged in mere police action, the State Department assumed a stance of neutrality in the Franco-Mexican war. An implied threat of retribution was held over for the future. Seward deliberately refrained from invoking the Monroe Doctrine. But he made clear United States opposition to intervention, which was "injurious and practically hostile to the most general system of government on the continent of America." Northern opinion did not dispute Seward's case that the nation was in no position to challenge France. But there was much stifled frustration as Mexico's fate hung in the balance. The idea of an American mission to civilize, even conquer and colonize, Central America, and to expel all foreign influence, had exercised powerful sway in the antebellum north. This was true despite qualifications induced by the sectional dispute and fears that any new empire would be dominated by the southern slave power. Mexico had delivered up prized possessions to the United States at bayonet point, was regarded by expansionists as an American appendage, and more generally as within an American sphere of influence. Now it was in mortal danger of becoming a French colony, and the unappetizing prospect existed of a return of the powers to an unstable hemisphere. (The rebels accepted this as the price to be paid for independence, and as an opportunity for ultimate Confederate expansion.) Northern

---

6. *NYH*, October 19, 1862.

7. General Phillip Sheridan, *Memoirs*, q. Barry M. Cohen, "The Texas-Mexico Border, 1858-1867," *Texana*, VI, No. 2 (Summer, 1966), p. 153.

anger at France had all the quality of imperial resentment of a rival who was taking retribution for the haughty insolence of Monroe's exclusivist dogma. The *New York Times*' influential Paris correspondent, "Malakoff," plied his countrymen with warnings of Napoleon's, and Empress Eugénie's, intentions: the French were resolved to stay in Mexico, set up a government, "lines of travel between the two oceans, and other sources of military and political strength, which will not only neutralize the power of the American race on the Western Continent, but offer a permanent barrier to their future extension to the southward."[8]

French arguments that South America was better suited to the spread of Latin, Catholic and monarchical institutions would not wash, predictably, among a people convinced of their own biological and political superiority. Horace Greeley (himself under fire from Bennett for making the "beastly, filthy proposition" to amalgamate white and black races "and produce a deteriorated hybrid race, like the races of South America, Central America and Mexico") ridiculed the arguments of racial destiny used to clothe Napoleonic ambitions "The Latinity of the Indians, blacks, and mezzotints of Mexico!"[9] Greeley saw Mexico's conquest being projected by a dictator plotting against the liberties of the world. Aspromonte had released a torrent of liberal criticism against the ruler who, despite his constitutionalist posturings, had suppressed Roman freedom, permitted Garibaldi's humiliation, and turned upon the path of ultramontanism. Now Napoleon was maturing a plot for which he had long bided his time, waiting an opportune moment of American weakness. The reinforcements sent out to retrieve France's unexpected disaster at Puebla on May 5 were, according to Greeley, directed "at the power, the liberalism, the Democracy of the North; and for the aid of the Southern slavedrivers . . . there are the war materials in Mexico, the mines; and there are mines in California, and there is much booty."[10]

French credibility dwindled to disappearance point as details leaked of French intrigues. In October the Juárez government expelled from Mexico the French banker Javier Jecker, whose intrigues with the interventionist party in France and the invading

---

8. *NYT*, October 3, 1862. Later it declared the French conquest of Mexico "so against the regular order of human affairs as marked out by the God of Nature, that . . . the ultimate results must be disaster and defeat, involving directly the overthrow of the author." November 2, 1862.

9. *NYH*, October 19, 1862.

10. *NYDT*, October 2, 1862.

expedition had been exposed from intercepted correspondence. Jecker was the nephew of Jean-Baptiste Jecker, head of the Swiss banking house whose dubious claims against Mexico for default on loans made by the company to the Miramón regime were being protected by French arms. (The house of Jecker, Torre and Co. had a long history of Mexican involvements; it had underwritten the *La Restauradora* venture, aiming to exploit the mines of Sonora, which ended in open rebellion against Mexican rule in 1852.) The captured correspondence was published in the north, and indicated the extent of Napoleon's ambitions. The Mexican project, according to one letter from Paris, was "capable of inspiring serious alarm in England."[11] The plotters referred to assurances of "colonization, a throne, protectorate, etc., etc. . . ." Mexico would become another Algeria. Maximilian would prove no obstacle to French control; he was a "pilot-balloon without any importance." One captured letter forecast that General Forey "with his 40,000 men will go even to the Rio del Norte, to subdue Alvarez, the King of the South. I believe also that these forces have in view to restrain the United States, drunk with pride and vain boasting." Further proof of the duplicity of French diplomacy became available when the Spaniards disclosed that France had entered the joint expedition with the predetermined purpose of installing a puppet monarch. In the Cortes, General Prim declared that Almonte had received orders from Paris to urge Maximilian's candidature for the Mexican throne, a plan to which Napoleon stood guarantor. At the same time French diplomats had been loudly proclaiming French innocence of political designs in Mexico. Disturbingly, the Rue de Mexique and Rue de Puebla were named in Paris before the year ended. (The irony of perpetuating a defeat was lost on the Parisian bureaucracy.)

With impressive cogency Americans put Mexico and the Civil War squarely in the context of French *Weltpolitik.* The balkanization of North America as the result of southern success would certainly, as Van Alstyne suggests, have exerted a profound influence on the state system of Western Europe; and may well have "strained the resources of British foreign policy to the breaking point" in dealing with mutually hostile American nations while supporting Canada.[12] At the same time, success for the south would severely have curtailed the United States' capacity to build the big navy which

---

11. Elsesser to Jecker, August 24, 1862. (Letters published in *NYEP*, November 25, 1862.)

12. Van Alstyne, *Rising American Empire*, p. 196.

became an instrument of American expansionism in the latter nineteenth century. An astute French diplomacy might have made rewarding pickings from these fundamental changes. (A weak one, of course, might merely have accelerated Prussian hegemony in Europe, for there is weight in the traditional case that French interest demanded a strong British ally.)

As 1862 closed, reports circulated that France would recognize or enter an alliance with the Confederacy. "Malakoff" habitually scorned easy talk of French intervention in America's Civil War, but he conceded that Mexico introduced an incalculable factor into the equation. Napoleon was unlikely to move if the Union disintegrated without his aid, ensuring painless success for his enterprise. But otherwise? In a classic misprediction, but a cogent one, "Malakoff" warned that any real prospect of northern victory might force France into the arms of the Confederacy, all for the sake of Mexico. It would be, he speculated, a ticklish situation: "for, since the Southern Confederacy also has its eyes fixed on Mexico, and the gradual extension of Slavery, it becomes a delicate point for the rebels to know how far they can go with France in such a coalition."[13] The *Herald* defiantly welcomed foreign intervention as "the speediest solution of the national difficulty." A reunited American people would combine their armies to wrest Canada from England, Mexico from France and Cuba from Spain: "We have been cutting each other's throats for the profit and amusement of the monarchs and aristocracy of Europe . . . to settle an abstraction of no practical importance to any section of the country—a conflict which might have been prevented at first by statesmanship, conciliation and compromise."[14] For the moment, however, United States power was paralyzed, and Mexico and other Latin American republics called in vain for protection against the pending rape of their countries.

The problems of the maritime war and Mexico were disturbing ones, but it was American policy to make them containable ones, and there was underlying confidence in the north that they would not be allowed to explode into war. The constant stimulation of interventionist rumors had dulled the nation's nerve, and it was not appreciated until much later that the Union had survived an international crisis in October and November 1862. Antietam merely

13. *NYT*, October 3, 1862; also November 27, 1862.

14. *NYH*, October 5, 1862.

bred mild optimism on grounds that failure in the field was the clearest invitation to meddlers. Gladstone's Newcastle speech stirred few ripples; if anything the eastern papers were heartened by the cry against intervention which the address evoked, and simplistically interpreted signs of cabinet division in London as signifying mediation's death knell. Lyons' return to Washington was accompanied by "leakages" of information that Britain would hew to a strict "hands off" line. By November 3, the *Herald* could describe intervention as a "dead cock in the pit." America's safeguard resided in "our immense military levies, our rapidly increasing navy of impregnable ironclads, and the desperate valor exhibited by our soldiers." Even the south appeared defeatist. The *Richmond Examiner* was severely disenchanted by Cornewall Lewis's speech at Hereford: "it extinguishes the light and closes the last prospect of European intervention in the active stages of the war: for it is England that controls the action of Europe on this question."[15] The Confederacy would be well advised to rely for salvation upon its own resources and fighting will, and foresake prideless and useless fawning upon the powers.

The south suspected, and the north hoped, that rivalries between the major powers, exacerbated by an unstable balance of power in Europe itself, would dictate an uneasy reconciliation between the United States and its envious onlookers. Near-civil war in Italy, a looming Austro-Prussian war, imminent insurrection in Poland, French and Russian anger at the prospect of a British candidate on the Greek throne and eclipsing of their influence in the eastern Mediterranean—such complications could lead to a major European war, in fact presaged the struggle for mastery which was to change the face of Europe in the next half-century. The fact was highly relevant to America, for as Greeley put it: "The greater the danger of collision among themselves, the less European Governments will feel an inclination to meddle in transatlantic strife." Ironically America might be saved by "the unprincipled egotism that is the soul of European diplomacy."[16]

While the strains imposed upon the Anglo-French alliance in the early sixties were real enough, and inhibited joint agression in the hemisphere, northerners tended to exaggerate the fraility of the accord. Editors such as Bryant hammered the view that "neither

---

15. *Richmond Examiner*, November 8, 1862. This editorial was widely publicized in the north.

16. *NYDT*, December 12, 1862.

power will move without the other in an effort to end this quarrel of ours, and neither can afford to interfere. With France, as with England, it is a question of pounds, shillings and pence; and the game of forcible intervention is too costly to play at."[17] Too vulnerable to interfere singly, the powers were too distrustful of each other to combine. Distrust sprang from history: England could not forget that the grudge of Waterloo was yet to be avenged. Bennett indulged in freer speculation, prophesying an Anglo-French war before any American one: Napoleon, presenting the strange anomaly of a revolutionary emperor, had by sponsorship of oppressed nationalities opened a Pandora's box of troubles in Europe. From it he was now recoiling. Always despotic at home ("in his judgment the French are unworthy of free institutions"), he now embraced the cause of the "ultramontane, bigoted clerical party," and was reviled by the revolutionary party. He had betrayed Italy, and smothered his liberal tendencies abroad—this was the wider significance of the Mexican aberration—making mockery of his slogan "empire should be peace." The suffering masses of Europe—including the minorities of the Habsburg empire, Poland, Italy, Prussia—no longer honored his name. Radical and socialist leaders were rousing his own subjects against him and ridiculing his expeditions into far off countries. His only salvation would be a distracting war against the traditional foe. Whether Napoleon sought to humiliate England as a symbol of aristocratic reaction, thus retrieving his liberal reputation, or as a rival for revolutionary leadership ("Mark how England sustains Garibaldi, how she speaks out for the Poles, and how she sympathises with the Hungarians") Bennett did not discriminate. War would be the signal for a general rising of Europe's oppressed peoples seeking independence and democracy, and to that cause the United States would lend all aid as soon as it had disposed of treason at home. Should England fall "none will heave a sigh over her ruin."[18]

Power jealousies might even retrieve Mexico for the Mexicans. The suspicion was abroad that Britain had urged France into Mexico so that a major rival might be brought into collision with the United States. The plot had gone awry, for neither north nor south now seemed likely to emerge from armageddon powerful enough to contest French occupation of Mexico. The dangers of French

17. *NYEP*, November 7, 1862.

18. *NYH*, November 12, 16, 1862.

domination of Central America would surely stir Britain, with its entrenched strategic and commercial interests in the area.

Another belief also obtained widespread expression in the north. It was that profound economic considerations would bring to heel nations such as Britain, which might otherwise be tempted into atavistic expansion at American expense. Such factors were "bonds to keep the peace." It was with some irony that eastern financial and commercial interests ignored the standing reproof of their own national crisis—where war had broken out despite all their pleadings that it would undo the work of generations of economic consolidation—to claim the superior power of economics over emotion in the international arena.

The United States continued to be, regardless of war, one of Britain's most valued customers, a significant market for a range of manufactured goods including fine fabrics, steel and metal goods, liquor, and pottery, and an important outlet for investment. An Atlantic war would place this trade in jeopardy, by direct disruption in the short run, by economic retaliation and alienation in the long run. As it was becoming obvious that war against the north would not necessarily guarantee Britain cotton, its likely immediate consequence would be merely to plunge into distress millions more English workingmen. In any case the gains of neutral profiteering, and the weakening of American commercial rivalry, would accrue to England merely by permitting the war to take its natural course. The *Richmond Examiner* saw that the exhaustion of north and south would remove from England's side "the painful thorn of American rivalry in commercial enterprise and empire."[19]

Furthermore, there existed in the north tenacious confidence—genuine, if wrongheaded, and not merely Federal propaganda—that British dependence on American wheat and foodstuffs was a powerful factor guaranteeing British neutrality. The trade facts lent plausibility to this "King Corn" theory. By the eve of the war the Mississippi valley had begun to live up to its reputation as the potential "Granary of the World." From the century's beginning, America had supplied respectable supplies of "corn" (mainly wheat and flour) to Britain; but with the dismantling of English protection in 1846, and revolutionary improvements in American agricultural outputs from the 1840's, began the change in trade patterns which was to result in Britain's almost total dependence on American

---

19. *Richmond Examiner*, November 8, 1862.

grain by the end of the century. Needing to feed an expanding population, Britain had become by the later 1850's the center of a large-scale international wheat market, within which the major competitors for dominance were the United States and Russia, with Prussia and France of only slightly lesser significance. Although the prairie wheat economy had not yet established decisive superiority in the British market, it had entered a period of strong commitment to production for that market. British imports of grain from the U.S. expanded massively in the 1850's, amounting in some years to one-quarter of the computed real value of all imports from America.[20] In twenty years of widely fluctuating trade patterns (1850-1870), the U.S. was able to capture peak shares of the British market (exceeding one-third) during the Crimean War years, which eliminated Russian competition, and during the first three years of the Civil War. (Between 1846 and 1861 the U.S. was the main supplier of grains and flour in total in no fewer than ten years.) Official U.K. statistics (which slightly exaggerate American over European performance) reveal that the U.S. furnished an average 23.5% of the U.K.'s wheat, flour and maize imports across the 1850's; that the average rose to 33.3% for the war period (1860-1865) and then declined to 23.2%, 1866-1870. Corn shipments from America were abnormally heavy in the years 1861-1863: 22 million hundredweight or 44.7% of total imports in 1861; 27 million hundredweight, 45.3% in 1862; 15.8 million hundredweight, 37.3% in 1863. (Real values for corn imports in these years were £15.5 million, £18.3 million, and £9.6 million.[21]) Potter's adjusted figures still show marked American dominance in the British market in 1861: out of a total 16.1 million quarters of grain and flour imported, the U.S. furnished 5.4 million, Russia 1.9 million, Prussia 1.5 million, France 0.4 million.

A variety of factors explain the remarkable northern export performance of 1861-1863: poor harvests in the U.K., causing reliance on foreign corn imports to rise from an average of 25-30% from 1855-1860, to almost 50% from 1860-1863; similar crop failures in France, 1860-1862, eliminating one important supplier; the superior competitiveness of northern wheat. The latter was a product of expanding acreage, increased mechanization, and the release of

---

20. J. Potter, "Atlantic Economy, 1815-1860: the U.S.A. and the Industrial Revolution in Britain," in A. W. Coats and R. M. Robertson, *Essays in American Economic History* (London, 1969), p. 21 and following.

21. Robert H. Jones, "Long Live the King?," *Agric. H.*, XXXVII, No. 4 (Oct., 1963), pp. 167-168. The volume figures refer to wheat, wheat meal and flour, and maize imports; the value figures include other grains.

surpluses for export caused by the disappearance of the southern market after Sumter. The American commissioner of agriculture considered, in his annual report for 1862, that Europe's dependence on the U.S. was "permanent:" breadstuffs and meat now had "a controlling influence at home and abroad. Unitedly, too, they stand arrayed against the kingly prerogatives of cotton. . . ." Cobden, in speeches widely publicized in the north, reinforced such confidence. Before the Manchester chamber of commerce on October 25, 1862, Cobden cited estimates that food imports from America between September 1861 and June 1862 "was equal to the sustenance of between 3,000,000 and 4,000,000 of people for a whole twelvemonth." He had been assured by an eminent corn-dealer, and M.P., "that if that food had not been brought from America, all the money in Lombard Street could not have purchased it elsewhere."[22]

The King Corn theory was rescued from the oblivion into which it had fallen in the postbellum generations by Louis Schmidt, writing in 1918 with revisionist conviction that economic forces were the key to international power politics. Careering to extremes, Schmidt claimed that northern wheat "may well be regarded as the decisive factor, counterbalancing the influence of cotton, in keeping the British government from recognizing the Confederacy." His assessment of the strategic impact of the wheat-peace argument upon English public opinion was later questioned by critics, and its impact at the decision-making level openly denied by diplomatic historians such as E. D. Adams who had examined the documents. Exaggerations in his economic analysis invited buffeting from business historians such as Eli Ginzberg. The consequent undermining of Schmidt's thesis became almost complete. His view that continental wheat-exporting nations such as Russia and Prussia were inelastic in export capacity ignored the respectable improvement in their performance in the latter 1850's and war years, despite American competition. (Prussia is the clearer example, raising exports of corn to Britain from 3.3 million hundredweight in 1859 to 6.2 million hundredweight in 1862; Russian figures fluctuated between 3.8 million hundredweight in 1859 and 5.7 million hundredweight in 1860 and 1862, and it is at least contendable that the Polish troubles from 1862 would have inhibited any spectacular expansion beyond this level.)[23] The contention of Schmidt's critics is that higher wheat prices would, in the event of northern wheat being withheld, have

22. Cobden, *Speeches on Q's of Public Policy* (London, 1880), pp. 457-458.

23. *BSP*, 1865, LV, Paper No. (3513), "Statistical Abstracts U.K., 1850-1864," p. 42.

attracted sufficient supplies from alternative sources to offset American losses. Owsley's conclusion, that American predominance was a matter of price not necessity, has received general acceptance.[24]

Reaction to Schmidt has, one suspects, gone too far. That continental suppliers could respond rapidly to price temptations is, so far, as much a statement of faith as Schmidt's assertion to the contrary, and until pragmatic study is made of the dynamics controlling individual industries in Europe, must remain an open question. What cannot be gainsaid is that an Atlantic war would have left a gaping hole in corn imports (shipments from the North American continent amounted to more than half of 1862's intake); to retrieve this loss entirely would have required Russia and Prussia, as main suppliers, to multiply exports by a factor between two and three.[25] Reduced imports, or the situation of nonreplacement of American supply, would have entailed higher prices and raised the complex question, evaded by Ginzberg, of the political tolerability of inflated bread prices. The curves of bread prices and popular disturbances ran in remarkable parallel in eighteenth- and nineteenth-century Britain; the threat of dear bread had been an explosive political factor during the Corn Law agitations; and dear wheat had contributed to the unpopularity of the Crimean war. At the least, there is force in the view that sudden interruption to the American corn trade would have caused considerable short-term dislocation while market adjustments took place. Nor were northern arguments

24. Ginzberg, noting the rise of per capita consumption of wheat between 1858-1862, argued:

> If Great Britain had not imported a single quarter of wheat from the United States during the critical years, the supply would have permitted the per capita consumption to remain at the same level as in 1858-1860. That the price would have risen is beyond dispute, but it probably would not have approached the high level of 1854 when wheat sold for more than 10s. per bushel.

25. Comparative figures are shown in the series below taken from official statistics of the U.K., *BSP* (1865), LV, (3513): Total wheat, wheat meal and flour, and other grains imported into U.K. (millions of cwt)

	1858	1859	1860	1861	1862	1863	1864
U.S.A.	4.7	0.4	9.3	15.6	21.7	11.8	10.0
Russia	2.6	3.8	5.7	4.5	5.7	4.5	5.1
Prussia	2.7	3.3	4.9	4.4	6.2	4.4	4.9
France	5.5	8.1	4.5	1.3	1.9	1.8	2.8
Br. Nth America	0.7	0.2	1.3	3.3	5.1	3.1	1.8
Totals (All Countries)	23.2	21.4	31.8	37.6	50.0	30.8	28.8

on the point unsophisticated: anxiety over corn would be only one of a mosaic of economic and social factors inhibiting war, because war would become politically insupportable. Commentators cited the impossibility of areas such as Russia, Poland and Germany growing grain at prices competitive with the midwest. England itself was regarded as unlikely to expand significantly its own grain production because of commitment to technological development and the ingrained opposition of aristocrat landowners to agricultural innovation.[26]

If power rivalries and economic interest should prove powerless to restrain European atavism, northerners hoped that ideological attachment to the United States on the part of Europe's common people and bourgeois liberals would generate popular resistance to any idea of war. The prospect of social crisis and class war would quench the blood-thirst of elitest governing classes against the model republic of their subject masses. (They did not know that Gladstone, the model of a modern liberal, had used the spectre of class war to urge intervention: Gladstone's was the heresy that the proletariat were impelled by hunger not by ideology.) Such reasoning was maintained in the north despite disenchantment over the war's actual legacy to date. After more than a half-century of missionary activity, of giving generous moral (if only limited material) sustenance to world democratic movements, Americans might be pardoned for muttering of ingratitude. Repudiation of debts was offered when realization of credits was most needed. The Civil War, like wars since, discouraged outsiders from relentlessly probing the causes and consequences of conflict. The participants interpreted with little sympathy the attempts of overseas observers to come to terms with a confusing totality of factors. Lack of commitment seemed fatally close to hostility. Thus was explained much of the "temporising" of England's journals, Whig politicians, monied and business classes. They were being led by either oligarchic political theory or sinister venal interests into secret anti-Yankeeism. The thought, however,

---

26. *NYT*, November 9, 1862; November 16, 1862. For the debate see L. B. Schmidt, "The Influence of Wheat and Cotton on Anglo-American Relations during the Civil War," *Iowa J. Hist. and Politics*, XVI (July, 1918), pp. 400-439; and criticisms by E. Ginzberg, "The Economics of British Neutrality during the American Civil War," *Agric. H.*, X (Oct. 1936), pp. 147-156; and Jones; Owsley, p. 547 and following; Claussen. Contrary to assertion, at least one cabinet minister, Milner-Gibson, president of the board of trade, argued nonintervention on grounds of American wheat and foodstuffs. See speech at Ashton, dated January 1863, *NYT*, February 9, 1863.

that overseas populaces and genuine progressives had deserted the chosen people, or were apathetic, would be unbearable. It could only be that the people of Europe were still in chains, their opinions manipulated or suppressed by the governing classes. Hence the eagerness, not without pathos, with which the northern press seized upon the slightest evidence of Federal sympathies among groups and individuals outside the established centers of power and prestige. Vigorous mythologizing turned such phenomena into significant peace and northernist movements well before the latter had in fact eventuated.

Cobden and Bright assumed the stature of true hero figures in this process. Cobden's speeches paraded forceful arguments against recognition of the south—which would elicit no cotton, only protract the war and risk a wider conflagration which the British people could not afford. His fundamental pacifism (he understood the north's insistence on war but opposed all but defensive wars) Northerners deemed less relevant; so too his "amicable theorizing" on the need to abolish blockades and privateering, or the need to accept American doctrine on the inviolability of private property in war. What was crucial was Cobden's loyalty to the cause he had long espoused "under the torrent of bitter abuse that has been poured upon him by the tory and secession Press of England."[27] John Bright's letters of encouragement to American well-wishers also received much publicity.

Pamphlets by the pro-northern Count de Gasparin and Edouard Laboulaye, Cairnes' *Slave Power*, and John Stuart Mill's appraisal of it in the *Westminster Review*, were prominently and favorably reviewed in the big northern papers, and contributed to the mood of complacency existing in late 1862. Laboulaye reminded his readers that not all Frenchmen had been carried away by the new authoritarianism of the second empire. Some remembered that until recently "it was a maxim received on both sides of the Atlantic, and almost an article of faith, that America and France were two sisters, united by a community of interests and by glorious memories. The North remains faithful to this friendship, and can it be that for the love of slavery we shall, after eighty years of mutual regard, break the only alliance which has never imposed upon us a sacrifice, or caused us a regret?" France's commercial interests, he

27. *NYT*, November 18, 1862. On Bright, see Roman J. Zorn, "John Bright and the British Attitude to the American Civil War," *Mid-America*, XXXVIII (new ser. v. 27), No. 3, pp. 131-145.

went on to demonstrate, committed her to neutrality, and so too French need to preserve the unity of the only maritime power which could serve as a balance to England. Cairnes' work, pruned of some heterodox tendencies, could also be recommended. He exposed the barbarities and despotism of the slave system, and showed the political ruthlessness with which slaveholders had wrenched down the national structure for their own narrow class interests. True, Cairnes had raised the prospect of a balkanized America, but he also, like Mill and Harcourt, proclaimed intervention "forbidden by the dictates of selfish policy and by the maxims of morality and law." He understood the northern cause, said the *New York Times*, "not simply because his hand has been diligent and his head clear, but because his heart has been in the right place."[28]

Even more symptomatic of the north's emotional need for democratic support from abroad was the manner in which was created the legend of Staleybridge, an acorn from which was to grow a considerable oak. Lancashire, as recent research has shown, was slow to exhibit any marked feeling for the north. If public meetings are an index, the climate of opinion in the cotton districts was veering in favor of mediation or intervention by late 1862, was if anything inclined towards the south. However on October 1 the north won a minor triumph at Staleybridge, a depressed cotton town. A meeting organized by southern supporters to press for recognition was taken over by workingmen, who overwhelmingly voted that "the distress prevailing in the manufacturing districts is mainly owing to the rebellion of the Southern States against the American Constitution." The incident, quietly reported in England, was given tremendous coverage in the U.S. "The capitalists" according to the *New York Times*, "desired to inveigle workingmen into sympathy with the oppressors of labor, and were defeated."[29]

> . . . the British laboring classes are not blind to the fact that the interest of labor and of democratic institutions is identified with the success of the North, and that the South is a simple embodiment of that veteran domination and tyranny which the capitalist has always struggled to maintain over the workman. No suffering, not even famine itself, will ever alter this conviction or make the English masses unfaithful to it.

Echoing Cairnes, this analysis served to counteract southern claims that slavery, through its paternalism, was more humanitarian than

---

28. *NYT*, November 6, 1862.
29. *NYT*, October 16, 1862.

the industrial slavery of the north's *laissez faire* factory system. (Anticapitalist resentment in Britain had, in fact, already formed itself into antinorthern or antiwar attitudes among certain labor groups.) The *Herald*, claiming that it had heard "the ring of the genuine metal," exulted that "we will, we must, we shall conquer a peace, a glorious peace, a reconstruction of the Union as our fathers left it to us; and when our great efforts are ended we shall look for the beginning of that uprising, that great popular demonstration, which European governments now dread. This must be the inevitable result of the American rebellion. . . ."[30] Staleybridge elicited from the *Herald* a classic statement of American mission, threatened but not destroyed by the despots of the old world:

> The yearnings of the nations of Europe after our free, our enlightened, our civilized form of government were [previously] but illy repressed by their frightened despots, who, with dismay, saw their downtrodden, unhappy subjects flocking to our hospitable shores by thousands, by millions. The governments of Europe stood aghast with wonder and fear at our gigantic strides towards power and influence, and, as . . . the force of our example was to be the signal for the downfall of their despotisms . . . schemes and base intrigues were brought to bear against that mighty tree of liberty which we were so proudly rearing heavenwards. In our fond imaginings its branches were to spread far and wide, casting over all the oppressed and tyranny ridden of the earth a genial shade, that of an untrammeled, manly independence.

America's enemies had openly encouraged the diabolical scheme of secession:

> Bitter comments, vile misrepresentations, scandalous lies, have been circulated throughout the whole of the European continent, with the purpose of impressing upon the people, the masses, the governed, that republics were unfeasible; that the people could not govern themselves; that the many were to be guided by the few; that freedom was but a name . . . [but] the people . . . are not convinced . . . the masses judge our present struggle correctly. . . .

Ideology and war strategy may be discerned as more potent motives than humanitarianism or economics in the setting-up of a Lancashire relief fund in America. That is demonstrated by the deliberate exclusion of French workers from the scheme: they were not a sufficiently strong political force, nor so unambiguously pro-northern as the English masses. Begun in early November, apparently as the brainchild of the *New York Times*, the idea of

30. *NYH*, November 6, October 20, 1862.

sending large consignments of grain and foodstuffs direct to England's starving operatives gathered strength with the renewal of French overtures for mediation. The campaign acquired massive press support (the papers printing harrowing stories of distress taken from the English press) and the adherence of clergy, chambers of commerce, public bodies and societies. In Congress, Senator Fields of New Jersey brought a motion "to manifest the sympathy of Congress toward the suffering operatives in Great Britain"; but public opinion preferred a homely and unofficial gesture of brotherhood from the American to the British people. The American International Relief Committee, including prominent members of the New York Chamber of Commerce, launched an appeal on December 4. At the Committee's meeting, merchant and grain companies vied with each other to fill the subscription list—one anonymous donor giving a thousand barrels of flour worth $7,000, while the owners of the 1800 ton vessel *George Griswold* offered free carriage for a cargo of food to go to Liverpool.[31] Objections that relief might be misinterpreted as a reproof to England were brushed aside; America had a duty to provide from her overflowing silos of grain for those who innocently suffered from her internal difficulties.

For those who, like the wealthy New York merchant Royal Phelps, were "not sure that this movement originated in pure disinterested philanthropy and charity," the decision to send food rather than money to Lancashire might have overtones of economic interest: not only was it costlier to send cash, since the rate of exchange was unfavorable, but the whole operation would ensure immediate benefits to midwestern farmers. Buying operations on the eastern seaboard would bail the wheat states out of the difficulty of low prices caused by surpluses by giving farmers some hard currency.[32] The nation might ultimately benefit, too, from emigration of sturdy operatives and artisans touched by American generosity. The real strength of the movement, however, was centered in New York and Philadelphia, where commercial houses had close links with England. The campaign effectively integrated the work of

---

31. See *NYT*, December 5, 1862. The owners of the ship acted on behalf of "our suffering friends abroad" and out of respect for the Queen, whose "regard for the opinions . . . of her excellent husband, Prince Albert, alone prevented a rupture between Great Britain and this country." Details of the movement in D. Maynard, "Civil War 'Care': Mission of the George Griswold," *N. Eng. Q.*, XXXIV (September 1961) pp. 291-309.

32. *NYEP*, December 4, 8, 1862.

separate committees, including the New York exchange, and funds exceeding $190,000 were raised. The response was weak in Boston, and inland states preoccupied with local war distress. (The bloody battles of Fredericksburg and Murfreesboro also interrupted the drive for funds in some states.) The *George Griswold*, stuffed full of flour, pork, bread, bacon, and grain, loaded without charge by New York stevedores and skippered without pay, finally sailed on January 9, 1863. Decorated with gay bunting and flying British and American flags, it was cheered by British sailors off Governor's Island. It was to be greeted by some in England as America's answer to the *Alabama*.

The international consequences of emancipation of the Negro had figured intimately in the raging debate which preceded Lincoln's edict in September. Inevitably the political nation was divided on this, as on the ethics and domestic expediency of emancipation. Lincoln's overseas agents and friends counseled overwhelmingly on two themes: don't provoke Europe into hostile acts; and try to impress "the great party of Human Progress, which is substantially one throughout the world" with the antislavery character of the war.[33] But Europe proved lukewarm when Lincoln frankly accepted Negro emancipation as a war measure. The beneficiaries of European criticism were the anti-emancipationists in America and, less expectedly, the militant abolitionists. Overseas objections to the "conditional and prospective" character of the proclamation embarrassed the out-and-out opponents of Negro freedom, and strengthened the hand of those (like Charles Sumner) who wanted the issue presented as a frank redress of a great national wrong. Greeley represented the radicals when he predicted that European support for the north would swell "in proportion as the proclamation becomes more than mere waste paper and a living reality."[34]

New York politics were inextricably involved in the controversy. In the bitter contest for the governorship of New York, the Democrat victor, Horatio Seymour, obtained his party nomination with the support of old-line Whigs opposed to emancipation. His platform—"the Union as it was, the Constitution as it is"—duly assailed emancipation as "a proposal for the butchery of women and children, for scenes of lust and rapine, and of arson and murder, which would invoke the interference of civilized Europe." Seymour

33. The words are Horace Greeley's; *NYDT*, October 3, 1862.
34. *NYDT*, November 19, 1862.

became the darling of the London *Times* as he heaped invective on the government for its arbitrary stand on civil rights, press control, the draft, the confiscation laws, and its "revolutionary" war program which was designed to overthrow the southern social system. (This was an age of "new loves and unwonted affections," Greeley observed with sarcasm. When the Democrat party was

> young and wickedly vigorous, the queer old women who create public opinion in England always denounced it as dangerous and disreputable; and it is only now when its vices have brought it to a premature dotage, with no virility to improve its fortuitous conquests, that they have suddenly grown in love with its stammering speech and shattered corporation.[35])

Bennett and the *Herald* originally favored the moderate John A. Dix as governor, but swung behind Seymour when the radical Republicans associated with Greeley, Bryant, and Chase secured as the Republican candidate the uncompromising emancipationist, General James S. Wadsworth. The *Herald* gloated when Sumner's predictions came unstuck, and even "thick and thin" partisans of the Union such as the *Opinion Nationale* disfavored the emancipation edict. On the other hand, the *Herald* held that the proclamation was an irrelevancy, an empty gesture to appease clamoring radicalism, and nothing for the north's negro-hating masses to become furious over. Foreigners should cease their flow of crocodile tears over an edict which was, in the President's phrase, like "the Pope's bull against the comet." But radicals were somewhat consoled when London's *Morning Star* and *Daily News* welcomed the edict, the free trade *Star* proclaiming it as "indisputably the great fact of the war—the turning point in the history of the American Commonwealth—an act only second in courage and probable results to the Declaration of Independence. . . ."[36]

In Washington, Seward's backstairs intrigues against emancipation almost achieved his political ruin. In December, he narrowly survived a cabinet crisis precipitated by a Radical Republican caucus, including followers of Treasurer Salmon Chase. Dissatisfied with the prosecution of the war, they attacked Seward's ascendancy over Lincoln. Charles Sumner was one of the caucus. Although chairman of the Senate Foreign Relations Committee, Sumner was now an open detractor of Seward's diplomacy. Seward's policies seemed

35. *NYDT*, November 19, 1862.

36. *Morning Star*, October 6, 1862.

to Sumner to be unprincipled, and they neglected to appeal to universal antislavery opinion. During the crisis Sumner did little to dispel rumors that he would be Seward's successor in the near future.

In the new year, 1863, the French attempted unilateral mediation. On close inspection it turned out to be a mild proposal, part window-dressing to placate social unrest in France, part endeavor to exploit the growth of the Copperhead peace movement in the north.[37] A French note, originating in cabinet, was sent on January 9. It proposed north-south negotiations to end the war. To evade the flaws in his earlier armistice scheme, Napoleon suggested that such negotiations might be held during hostilities (as were peace talks during the American War of Independence). The south would then be denied the chance of reorganizing its forces during a truce, a main objection of northern sympathizers to the earlier plan.

Napoleon was in fact keeping open his lines of retreat on America at a delicate time in Europe. The January uprising in Warsaw menaced accord between Paris and St. Petersburg, but the resultant European confusion offered Napoleon a possible revision of the settlements of 1815. Something, if only little, needed to be done—with maximum publicity—on America to quell local criticism. Unemployment caused by the Civil War was not in fact massive—at the height of the crisis, late 1862 and early 1863, it was probably little more than 220,000 and was largely confined to the cotton districts of Lille, Roubaix, and Tourcoing in the north, and Rouen in Normandy, and to specialized industries affected by loss of American trade (e.g., Bordeaux shipping, Aix hats and perfumes, Besancon gem-cutting). However, distress had been magnified by the press and was becoming politically significant, opponents of Bonapartism using slogans such as "Bread or Death. Vive la République!"[38] Revealingly, Drouyn published his new mediation dispatch in Paris before it reached America, leaking the plan to the press initially, then splashing the actual details to dispel "false rumours." The news made a pretty background for the Emperor's annual report to the legislature. Whether the government expected

37. See Case and Spencer, Chapter 9.

38. Case and Spencer, pp. 377-379. Cf. *NYDT*, December 1, 1862, Paris correspondent: "While, on the industrial side, France does not want as much cotton as England does, she does on the political side want her comparatively little cotton a great deal more."

any real effect from its move is a moot point. King Leopold of Belgium and influential southern sympathizers urged action; McClellan's sacking and the Union disaster at Fredericksburg seemed favorable omens; while interest demanded that any truce should be patched up before spring planting, if cotton was to be picked in Dixie in 1863. Slidell objected that the whole idea was impractical, but he was brushed aside: the government had received intelligence of an acquiescent attitude from Richmond.

The Quai d'Orsay had been encouraged by Mercier to believe that France might catalyze a northern reaction against the war. Mercier's influence gives perhaps the key to distinguishing the French from the British approach to mediation. Mercier consistently underestimated the fact that conflict in the north over the war took place within a closed system, that the fiercest of disagreements were nevertheless over ways and means of achieving essentially American ecopolitical objectives, or "destiny." Outside intrusion risked almost unanimous rejection because it flowed from alien, and probably competitive values. Significantly London appreciated the political necessity which forced even the Democrat press to oppose foreign meddling, whereas Paris was to court unpopularity. Mercier interpreted the political swing to the Democrats (they had won New York and Pennsylvania in the midterm elections, and come within challenging distance of the Republicans in Congress) as a "definitive" change in public opinion. Copperheadism had become overt. The people were becoming "altogether in opposition to the policy of war to the end," a policy which must lead to "complete servile insurrection, to the complete devastation of the South and to the ruin of its public liberties." The Emperor might opportunely prepare "some conciliatory act" before the sitting of a new and less militant Congress.

Congress however showed no inclination to censure Seward when he gave a polite but unyielding negative to Drouyn's proposal. To Washington's relief, the French demarche was revealed to be a case of the mountain laboring: direct "conversations" between commissioners of north and south could obviously precede a truce at any ripe time—indeed Congress could provide a natural forum for the reconvening of the whole country's representatives and discussions on a national peace. French interposition was superfluous, and only likely to aggravate the forebodings of Americans concerning French designs in Mexico: "They do not like to see His Majesty's hand always in their business" Dayton observed, accurately enough. Napoleon's European embarrassments, and intimations of widening rifts in the Anglo-French accord, gave Seward the chance to play from strength. Mercier did his cause no help by indiscreet attempts to drum up political and press support for mediation; his intrigues with Horace Greeley and the adventurer William Cornell Jewett had nettled Seward before the note's arrival.[39] The Secretary reiterated northern determination not to treat with armed insurrection in order to diminish constituted national authority. His reply offered no hope to Paris: the war was winnable, and was being won; contention was a sign, not of defeatism, but of democratic health, leading to renewed national vigor; nobody was in favor of "foreign intervention, of mediation, of arbitration, or of compromise with the relinquishment of one acre of national domain, or the surrender of even one constitutional franchise."[40]

Throughout the northern debate on intervention there occurred a highly interesting persistence of the idea of imperial mission. The habits of thought of the era of manifest destiny were not extinguished by the Civil War, nor would a new foundation need to be laid for the creation of a postwar empire. The quality and intensity of the idea were of course affected by the war. It was inclined to be muted among those preoccupied with the primacy of the antislavery moral issue: the prerequisite for healthy national expansion, based on the truly unfettered operation of the commercial and ideological energies of the American people, was national "radical reform"—extinction of the moral incubus of the slave system, and all it stood for, by the sword. It would be rash to regard this attitude as characteristic of the majority. Many of the opponents of abolitionism at heart condemned internal factionalism as an unintelligent and basically unnecessary interruption to America's destined fate. Seward had been sympathetic to this view; and it was the significance of the "foreign war panacea," whether in his hands or others, that it predicated a return to a style of national politics based on a unanimity of purpose and direction. But once the war was irreversibly under way, nostalgia for lost vigor emerged

---

39. Mercier became associated with an unofficial mediation scheme independently sponsored by Greeley, and Jewett, who became almost a professional "peace monger" in the latter war years. The intricacies of the episode, which bore no direct relation to the official French move of January 9, are unravelled in Warren F. Spencer, "The Jewett-Greeley Affair: a Private Scheme for French Mediation in the American Civil War," *New York History*, V, No. 51 (1970), pp. 238-267.

40. Mercier to Drouyn de Lhuys, November 10, 1862; Dayton to Seward, January 15, 1863; Seward to Dayton, February 6, 1863; q. Case and Spencer, pp. 384, 390, 396. See also Van Deusen, *Seward*, p. 362.

in impatience to win the war. The effect of events was, in the words of the *New York Times*:

> . . . to make us long for the time when, with treason crushed at home, we may be free from this half-patronizing, half impudent tone of European Powers toward us, and may again, as of old, go on in our own course of development without troubling ourselves about any 'joint action' of the three Powers, or of all the Powers together. We beg Heaven only that when that time shall come, our disgust at the irksomeness of this meddling may not make the recoil too violent.

It was the *Herald* which was most articulate in warning the powers to "beware of ruffling the pinions of the American eagle," and in predicting, with a disconcerting ring of authenticity, American hegemony in the hemisphere after the war: "We cannot brook the interference of any European Power on this continent, and those who take advantage of our present troubles to intrude will some day reap the whirlwind they are surely sowing."[41] The *Herald*, so often dismissed in the commentaries as an unrepresentative and irresponsible troublemaker in the international arena, in fact offered some of the more perceptive analyses of power realities in the new world, and of ideological possibilities in the old. Its attitudes were probably more deeply symptomatic of embedded American values than civilized Americans would like to admit. But it moved in a world of harsh reality. Spirited, aggressive, bigoted, cynical of motives, often wild and careless of consistency, the *Herald* stirred the pot. With a generation of European statesmen inclined only towards bloodless victories, it was a sensible thing to do.

---

41. *NYH*, November 30; December 3, 1862; December 26, 1862.

Chapter X

Neutrality on Trial

The classic works on civil war diplomacy by Ephraim D. Adams and Frank Owsley were rather too dogmatic in presenting as foreordained the failure of southern foreign policy after November 1862. The British decided in late 1862 to wait and see, not to do nothing everlastingly. A real and present foreign danger still threatened the Union should circumstances arise favorable to the Confederate States. Recent research has redressed the balance severely; emphasizing the peril of an Anglo-American war over southern shipbuilding operations in Britain, and highlighting the tension caused by the Union navy's brusque regard for neutral rights in its vigorous repression of blockade-running.

It is nevertheless difficult to escape the conclusion that Confederate diplomatic success depended upon two factors. The first was transformation of the war itself, either by decisive southern field victories or by growth of a massive peace movement in the north. The second requirement was maintenance of a stable power equilibrium in Europe, necessary to provide a secure base of operations for any interventionist project. 1863 fulfilled neither condition. Lee's magnificent triumph at Chancellorsville in May was more than counterbalanced two months later by the strategically decisive Union victories at Vicksburg in the west and Gettysburg in the east. Nor did the Copperhead movement assume the gargantuan proportions necessary to convince Europe of the imminent collapse of the war effort. Indeed the massive growth of the northern army, even under blundering generals, the gallantry of southern arms and skill of southern commanders threatened only to prolong an awesome conflict. In practice, that militated against foreign recognition of the south and against intervention.

In the second regard, trouble in Europe erupted spectacularly with the crises over Poland and Schleswig-Holstein. The outcome proved depressing for Jefferson Davis and his followers. Popular sympathy for small nations like the Poles and Danes (and Confederates) had barren international results, unless underpinned by overwhelming considerations of national interest leading the powers to interfere. Palmerston's government emerged irresolute, clinging to the policy of nonintervention at all costs. Events starkly outlined the difficulties of concerting the policies of the western powers in the face of mutual suspicions and diverging interests.

To view the Polish crisis of 1863 as a spectacular sideshow driving American affairs out of view in Europe, and relieving international pressure upon the Union, is to underestimate its significance. It did of course have a diverting effect—the evidence from Confederate and Union sources is overwhelming on the point. Take as example the rancorous complaints of the south's special commissioner to Russia, Lucius Quentin Cincinnatus Lamar, who never got to Russia because of Polish complications. Palmerston (Lamar complained to Benjamin in March) was "far more engrossed with the conferences, jealousies and rivalries between the leading Powers of Europe than with the fate of constitutional government in America."[1] On the other hand, Richmond might expect to benefit from popular sympathy for an insurrectionary movement which had parallels with the south's national struggle. It is instructive to note that, at a crucial stage of their campaign for British parliamentary support, the Confederate lobby in June considered pressing for an international congress which would settle both the Polish and American questions. More instructive still, the idea was shelved.

The global dimensions of the upheavals of 1863 need to be remembered. The European ramifications of the Polish crisis were serious enough, threatening general war and destruction of the existing power balance. A policy of nonentanglement in America was the elementary course for Britain and France to pursue if they were to have free hands for European action. And so they determined. But there was more to the matter than that. Russell, in a

---

1. Lamar to Benjamin, March 20, 1863, q. J. Kutolowski, "The effect of the Polish Insurrection of 1863 on American Civil War Diplomacy," *Historian*, XXVII, No. 4 (1965), p. 566.

flash of rare insight, forecast to Lyons in March that the Polish conflagration could lead to "great consequences," such as a Russo-American agreement or a new balance of power in the world.[2] Bungling European diplomacy might cause the beleagured colossi of east and west to join together to achieve the primacy on the world stage to which their resources entitled them. This might take place during the war, or in its aftermath. Ultimately they would divide the world into two great spheres of influence, an Asian centered on St. Petersburg and a Western centered on the Mississippi Valley. These are not words written with cold war hindsight. Prophecies of this kind had been made in the antebellum period by Tocqueville, and by Americans such as Perry McDonough Collins.[3] Collins' *Voyage Down the Amoor* (New York, 1860) recounted his travels in Siberia in 1856 and compared the Russian drive to the Pacific with American continental expansion. The conquering of the American West would achieve the fabled North West passage linking Europe to Asia, and cause a revolutionary realignment of world trade flows. The geopolitical theories of men like the southern oceanographer Matthew F. Maury, and Seward himself, postulated ultimate mastery of global commerce passing to the United States, because of its strategic geographical position, sea power, and control of international communications. Seward often spoke of America's historic mission to carry the torch of European expansion to "the seat of all civilization," Asia. When rallying the sections early in 1861, Seward assigned a world role to his country which seemed to allow a passive role to other countries. With the decay of a divided Europe, the United States had the obligation to extend by means of its institutions the "civilization of the world westward . . . across the continent of America," across the Pacific to Asia, on through Europe until it reached "the other side, the shores of the Atlantic Ocean."[4] In such theorizing, however, competition was peaceful, and there was much room for complementary relationships. Seward said in 1853: "The nation that draws most materials and provisions from the earth, and fabricates the most, and sells the most of productions and fabrics to foreign nations, must be, and will be, the great power of the earth." If he was right, the geopolitical revolution taking place would make America top dog but Russia would not be far behind.

2. Russell to Lyons, March 7, 1863, *PRO* 30/22/97, folios 9-10, q. Kutolowski, p. 565.

3. Charles Vevier, "American Continentalism: An Idea of Expansion, 1845-1910," *AHR*, LXV, No. 2 (January, 1960), pp. 328-329.

4. Congressional speech, January 5, 1861, q. Vevier, p. 331.

Russian friendship to the north kept such ideas in vibrant existence even in the midst of civil war. St. Petersburg's rejection of Louis Napoleon's armistice overture earned praise in the north, some of it extravagant. The *Washington Daily Morning Chronicle* declared:

> True in peril and faithful in adversity, Russia has obtained the deep gratitude of this country, and should the occasion ever arise for practically showing how much we feel the obligation, we shall not wait to be reminded of it.[5]

Much of the discussion of Russo-American relations was however harshly realistic. Imperial Russia supported republican north for balance of power reasons and because, as the London correspondent of the *New York Times* put it, "it was almost certain that in the future she would have some uprisings of her own to suppress."[6] The starkest appeal to naked interest came from the *Herald*, which now rejoiced at being able clearly to distinguish America's friends from its enemies. Russian interests, it stated, did not conflict but harmonized with those of the United States:

> In the Eastern hemisphere the destiny of Russia is to absorb all the minor states around her, and she is every day making rapid progress in that policy. She will soon be, if she is not already, the great Power of Europe and Asia. In the Western World the United States is destined to play the same part. One of these governments is an absolute despotism; the other is a representative democracy. But both are suited for the regions and the races where they prevail. Both are philosophical, and will fulfil their destiny without coming into collision or competition with the other. Not so the milk and water governments that stand between them. . . .[7]

As John Kutolowski points out: "Throughout much of 1863 critical moments and events in the Polish issue coincided remarkably with significant developments in American diplomacy."[8] In February occurred the first of such conjunctions fateful to the south. The long-awaited insurrection of Poles was finally proclaimed in Warsaw, after Russian attempts to conscript troublesome radicals. Warsaw erupted just as Napoleon awaited Washington's reaction to his offer of unilateral mediation, and cooled any ardor he had for

5. *WDMC*, November 28, 1862.
6. *NYT*, December 1, 1862.
7. *NYH*, November 27, 1862.
8. Kutolowski, p. 575.

developing an initiative which proved repugnant to the Lincoln government. Historians have not spared Napoleon for his meddling in Poland. It threatened death to the Franco-Russian rapprochement, difficulty with allies, self-defeating instability in Europe, and crippling limitations to his autonomy of action in North America and Mexico. Napoleon at first drew back. But liberal and catholic support for the Poles (one of the few uniting causes around), and the temptation to redraw the map of Europe according to the Bonapartist program, undid his caution. His Rhineland ambitions were reawakened when Bismarck made an overture of aid to Russia—in the Alvensleben convention by which Prussia helped quell disorder on Poland's German frontier. On February 21 the Emperor proposed an Anglo-French remonstrance against Prussia. Britain was suspicious of his restless strivings, and refused. Other Napoleonic attempts to promote an international settlement in Poland foundered on the reluctance of Britain and Austria to act effectively with France. Harcourt's strictures on the futility of joint interventions by Europe's squabbling factions were abundantly fulfilled. Napoleon harvested from events the alienation of his Russian ally, the estrangement of London, and the disenchantment of French opinion. While the Poles won only fair words from the west, and were duly crushed, the real beneficiaries were the Prussians and the Yankees.

Charles Francis Adams recognized this. As he reasoned to Seward in February, English apprehensions were rife that Napoleon planned a Machiavellian stroke to revise France's Rhenish boundary. The Polish complication thus provided a "favourable interlude" for that growth of northern military power "needed to protect us from the possibility of European intervention."[9] Poland had nicely achieved Seward's aim of rifting apart London and Paris, the north's insurance policy. The British were passive on the American question. Until north and south were heartily sick of tearing each other apart, Russell declared, "I see no use in talking of good offices."[10] Britain would await a decisive shift of events in North America. Rising support in England for the Emancipation Proclamation, and grinding pressure from the Union for preventive measures against shipbuilding for the south, precluded the politicians from any sense of reckless adventure, despite their perfunctory gestures against demagoguery and Yankee bluster. Here, according to Hotze's

9. Adams to Seward, February 26, 1863, q. Kutolowski, p. 563.

10. Russell to Lyons, February 14, 1863, q. EDA, II, p. 155.

Index, was a government that would let Lancashire starve, allow Welles' navy to plunder and burn British merchantmen off Nassau and Cuba, do anything but quarrel with Seward and Bright. It did not mean to intervene "unless there should occur some of those 'circumstances over which they have no control', which leave weak men and weak ministers no choice."[11] Confederate hopes abroad became pinned upon the pressure of the famine, Lee and his army, and the prospect of a Tory ministry at Westminster. Meantime Mason and his colleagues were overwhelmed with advice to await a better season for their annual attack on the blockade and demand for recognition.

In the south itself irrepressible resentment was mounting against powers which offered the south no skerrick of official recognition, whose neutrality in practice favored the north, and which recognized the obnoxious blockade. Mason had protested against Foreign Office doctrine on the blockade in July 1862, but received from Russell only a cold acknowledgement and a refusal to interview the Virginian. Benjamin regarded the British posture as a contravention of the spirit of the 1856 Paris agreement, to which the south was now a signator. But his request for explanation of the "evident danger" thesis—which he regarded as addendum to the Paris text—was ignored by Whitehall, whose behavior was "discourteous and even unfriendly" in Benjamin's eyes. Only one thing, he told Mason on October 31, 1862, prevented Richmond withdrawing the London mission—southern confidence that a distinction must be drawn between the ministry and the British people. Oddly, both parties in the Civil War were drawing that distinction. Much earlier in American history Benjamin Franklin was forced by the events of the revolutionary war to broaden his indictment of Lord North's administration into one against the whole nation. Jefferson Davis and his followers were to suffer much the same experience during the War Between the States. (The north, for its part, felt able to rest assured that the English masses at least cared for the cause of "an innocent and virtuous people, fighting only in defence of their just rights.") Another year elapsed, however, before the futility of treating with England was officially declaimed by the south.

Davis' new year message to Congress berated Europe for accepting a paper blockade, which he compared unfavorably with the Berlin and Milan decrees and orders-in-council of the Napoleonic

11. *Index*, January 29, 1863.

wars. Davis had a legalistic cast of mind, and his indignation at Britain's defiance of the Paris treaty's strict construction was genuine. Characteristically, in his two-volume *Rise and Fall of the Confederate Government* (New York, 1881), Davis focussed myopically upon this grievance in a brief treatment of diplomacy which showed minimal understanding of the complex international forces at work. Russell however may have felt stirrings of conscience at Davis's public rebuke, for in February he took the trouble to write Mason a courteous note on the matter. Mason had hinted at a stormy withdrawal in a starchy note of January 3, and this was to be avoided if Britain was to have an open door into a finally-independent Confederacy. But Mason won little except civility, for Russell stubbornly refused to waver from the stand taken by the ministry since February 1862. British passivity on the blockade, which was steadily improving in efficiency, ensured French passivity. Napoleon would not aid the Poles or the Confederates without the British. Together they might impose peaceful change; alone Napoleon dared take no risks.

Mason's hopes for a Tory takeover in Parliament underestimated the strength of Palmerston's political resources. The ministry maintained itself in office in 1863, even though Poland and Schleswig-Holstein made it a difficult year. In any case the Conservative program did not include the adoption of a "southern" position; the instincts of the leadership were, if anything, for a bipartisan agreement on the continuation of neutrality. At the opening of Parliament, February 5, Disraeli did not forebear from scoring political points off the government: it was, he indicated, split wide on the war, Milner Gibson at the Board of Trade berating the south's "hateful, infidel and pestilent" institution, Russell speaking of the north's war for empire, while the chief secretary for Ireland (Sir Robert Peel) thought "the Lord of Hosts was on the side of the South." But Disraeli advocated no change in policy. Indeed he excoriated Gladstone for suggesting one in the Newcastle speech. Research into the private papers of prominent Conservatives has shown little interest in the war as a foreign policy issue, and no proof of desire for America's permanent division. Considerations of party tradition and political expediency counseled a policy of neutrality and official restraint.[12] Derby prescribed the party line in February: ". . . regretting as I do to differ from any of my friends, I confess I cannot bring myself to the conclusion that the time

12. W. D. Jones, "British Conservatives and the Civil War," *AHR.*, LVIII, pp. 527-543. Quotes in this paragraph, pp. 534-535.

has arrived at which it is either wise, politic, or even legitimate, to recognize the South."

An attempt by Lord Campbell on March 23 to have the Lords reverse this verdict met with negative results. In a speech bristling with facts and skillfully marshalled arguments, Campbell urged the aptness of the season for recognition. A loan floated by the south through the French banking house of Erlanger had been offered on the London and continental markets only four days earlier. In two days it was oversubscribed three times in London, and by the time of the debate the bonds had rocketed from Erlanger's guaranteed price of 77 to over 90. The capitalists of London, Frankfurt, Paris, and Amsterdam were in no doubt of the war's issue. Such was Campbell's claim, but it was eroded within weeks as the speculative bubble burst. Cotton bonds fell below par and Confederate "bulling" became necessary to sustain the market and southern political credit.[13] Campbell's other premise—the rebels were unbeatable—was confidently held by military experts of the day. Hooker inspired little respect, and the rout of his army by Lee at Chancellorsville in May fulfilled the expectations of the Jeremiahs. If Europe blazoned forth the fact of southern nationhood, Campbell advised, the scales would fall from northern eyes: continued only because it was directed against "rebellion," the war could be honorably settled as a "foreign war" (i.e., war between sovereign states). Recognition thus promised "freedom to the Government of Washington from the necessity of hopeless war which weighs on it at present." Unhappily for the southern lobby this analysis was being directly negatived by the government's advisers abroad. Russell's reply to Campbell echoed their view that England could do nothing useful to end the hostilities.

Campbell made one comment unsettlingly to the point. If England refused to secure southern friendship while it was still available, it could end the war friendless in the North American continent. Whatever the outcome of the war, British power interests would be seriously jeopardized. Should the north win, the present policy of not giving umbrage to the United States would provide poor security for Canada: "As if aggressive Powers had ever been restrained, by wanting pretexts, from the wars they were inclined

13. Although the Erlanger loan did not go as planned, and has had a bad press from historians, it produced vitally needed funds for use in Europe in 1863 and 1864 in the face of great difficulties. See Judith F. Gentry, "A Confederate Success in Europe: the Erlanger Loan," *JSH*, XXXVI, No. 2 (May, 1970), pp. 157-188.

to." The north might attack Canada in the drunkenness of pride, if victorious, and in the bitterness of failure, if defeated. Campbell's preference was clearly for an alliance with the south in anticipation of the latter eventuality: ". . . the aggressive State will then have to contemplate the chance of an attack upon his rear as well as the bombardment of his cities and destruction of his commerce." The real peril of a policy of drift was the creation of separated powers in North America, both irrevocably hostile to England. "We may be forced, now to guard Canada from one, now the West Indies from the other." At the least Britain would be foolish to relinquish her chance of setting up a paramount influence in the new Confederacy. Was not that a rosier prospect than the resurrection of United States imperialism? Once the south was enthralled by northern arms "a power more rapacious, more unprincipled, more arrogant, more selfish and encroaching, would arise than has ever yet . . . multiplied the fears, and compromised the general tranquility of Europe."[14]

Poland continued to preoccupy the British. On March 18 the Foreign Office agreed to concert with Austria and France in remonstrating with Russia, and the next month was devoted to devising blueprints for a settlement. The trick was to convert Alexander II back to a program of constitutional reform in Poland by covert threat of western intervention. At the same time Napoleon must be restrained from an impulsive move leading to a European war. That provided sufficient grist for Whitehall's mill. As March closed, however, news came of the defeat of the rebels under the Polish general Langiewicz, showing that Russia was well-launched on a simpler solution to the Polish tangle. It was in this setting that Anglo-American relations became seriously strained over shipbuilding and maritime disputes. Poland might not prove a watertight guarantee of peace in the Atlantic theater, for as Russell was to write to Lyons: "we are not going to war abt [sic] Poland, & I shall be ready to meet the Yankees if they take to bullying."[15]

In the winter and spring of 1863 a remarkable spate of public meetings was sponsored throughout Britain by the Union and Emancipation Societies and radical sympathizers of the north. Significantly, the most striking of these mass meetings, held at St. James' Hall, London, on March 26, publicly proclaimed the

---

14. *Hansard*, 3rd ser. v. 169, Lords (March 23, 1863), pp. 1714-1734.

15. Russell to Lyons, June 20, 1863, *PRO* 30/22/97, folio 29, q. Kutolowski, p. 569.

reconciliation of Cobdenite radicalism with London Trade Unionism. Bright orated magnificently; but it was E. S. Beesly, the Positivist intellectual, who emphasized labor's class solidarity with American workmen. The causes of Northern Democracy, Emancipation, and Franchise Reform in England, were one, and reformers of all ilk must sink their differences to achieve that greater good.[16] The cry was widely taken up by the politically conscious wing of British labor.

This clamor provided symphonic background when on March 27 Parliament debated the escape of the *Alabama*. The pressure may have been counterproductive. The Prime Minister and the Solicitor-General defended the government against the charge that it had acted unneutrally by negligently failing to seize the *Alabama.* They did so by embracing a "strict construction" of the Foreign Enlistment Act, although their legal advisers had in fact been advocating a flexible interpretation more suited to Britain's future naval interests. The government was now declaring municipal law inadequate to justify seizure of the *Alabama.* Their arguments dovetailed with the legal advice upon which Bulloch had been consistently acting. (He had no other choice because Richmond rejected his advice to play safe and build ships at home with imported armor.) On that view there were gaping loopholes in the act: it was legal to arm and equip a ship within British ports, provided it was not intended for use against a state at peace with Britain; it was legal to build a ship ("unequipped" for war) within Her Majesty's dominions, the intent of building being irrelevant; it was legal to arm and equip such a ship outside British jurisdiction.[17] Palmerston informed Parliament that the *Alabama* could not be seized because it sailed from England unarmed and received arms, equipment and crew in a foreign port. Moreover any charge of intent to cruise in belligerent service must be established by evidence on oath and not mere suspicion. As the Solicitor-General, Roundell Palmer, put it in debate: ". . . laws are usually enforced against English subjects . . . on facts, and not on presumption: on satisfactory testimony, and

16. See Royden Harrison, *Before the Socialists* (London, 1965), pp. 64-77. Charles Francis Adams felt there was a distinct swing of working and middle class opinion toward the Union from late 1862, with rising support for Lincoln and Emancipation. He documented this, in dispatches to Seward, from letters and petitions with which he was inundated, and from resolutions of the numerous pro-Federal meetings being held. Federal funds undoubtedly greased some of these operations, but rebel efforts to compete fell very flat. See *Foreign Relations,* 1863, Vol. I.

17. See beginning Chapter 9 above.

not on the mere accusations of a foreign minister or his agents." These words were soon to be thrown back in his face; and they plagued the life of Charles Francis Adams who spent much of 1863 collecting less than satisfactory testimony on Confederate attempts to build a navy abroad.

The shadow of future "violations" of British neutrality on a mammoth scale lay across the whole dialogue. Although rumor inflated southern naval activities into a vast conspiracy, there were building in British yards a number of vessels destined for the south. They included two warships with iron piercers designed for blockade-breaking—the famous "Laird rams" begun in Lairds yard at Birkenhead in July 1862, scheduled for delivery in March and April 1863, and costing the Confederacy almost £94,000 each. There was also a 3000 ton armored frigate (larger than the rams) building at the Clyde yards of James and George Thompson, contracted for in May 1862 but not launched until February 1864. (This was the "Number 61" built for Lieutenant James H. North, costing £180,000 and later sold to the Danes as the *Danmark.*) Thompsons were also building, for Lieutenant George T. Sinclair of the Confederate navy, a raider modeled on the *Alabama*, but more powerful; part wood, part iron, combination sail and steam, eight-inch guns. Contracted for in October 1862 at a price of over £46,000, this vessel (secretly the *Texas*, christened the *Canton*, later *Pampero*) was behind schedule in April 1863, and fears of seizure led Sinclair to investigate the possibility of transferring to technical French ownership.[18] Customs officials, on orders from Whitehall, watched and reported upon all suspicious naval construction; but even more assiduous were the efforts of northern agents and hired detectives employed by Union consular officials, by far the most skillful and indefatigable being the Liverpool consul Thomas H. Dudley.[19] Dudley disagreed violently with British insistence that

18. Douglas H. Maynard, "The Confederacy's Super '*Alabama*'," CWH, V (1959), p. 82. For details of the financing, construction, legal and diplomatic repercussions of shipbuilding see: Frank J. Merli, *Great Britain and the Confederate Navy* (Indiana U.P., 1970), up to date and authoritative; and Wilbur Devereaux Jones, *The Confederate Rams at Birkenhead* (Tuscaloosa, 1961, limited ed.). In view of the wealth of the literature on this subject, detail will be reduced in this volume.

19. Brainerd Dyer, "Thomas H. Dudley," CWH, I, No. 4 (December 1955), pp. 401-413. (The article uses valuable unpublished papers but is unfortunately undocumented.) Dyer's *Public Career of William M. Evarts* (Berkeley, Calif., 1933) is also relevant. See also Thomas H. Dudley, "Three Critical Periods in our Relations with England during the Late War: Personal Recollections. . . ," *Penn. Mag. Hist. & Biog.*, XVII (1893), pp. 34-54.

the burden of proof lay upon the prosecution in the matter of unneutral shipbuilding. In a pamphlet issued in mid-1863 he urged that charges made by responsible American officials should elicit an investigation by the British authorities, who had access to shipyards, contracts and other papers, denied to the United States. Meanwhile in a hostile community, Dudley contrived from 1862 to amass a staggering amount of evidence of southern activity; affidavits were taken from shipyard workers, sailors, engineers, turncoat southerners, spies, boarding house owners, anybody who could testify to the warlike equipment of vessels or their Confederate connections, and furnished to Adams, who then bombarded Russell with them. The Bostonian businessman, John Murray Forbes, on a secret mission to England in early 1863, considered Dudley's work vital: it would, he thought, be worth £50,000 to stop the Laird rams, for if they sailed, war might result, and this would "cost 2000 millions."[20] On his return Forbes successfully recommended to Lincoln and Seward that Dudley's grant of £2000 per year for espionage service be greatly increased.

The move feared by the south came on April 5 at Toxteth dock, Liverpool. British customs seized, and marked with the broad arrow, the newly built wooden screw steamer, the 120 ton *Alexandra*. A celebrated trial followed, the first time a ship had been brought to trial in the history of the Foreign Enlistment Act. Detention of the vessel was ordered by the Foreign Office—on the advice of its law officers but against that of the solicitor of the Treasury—following a request to customs by Dudley, and diplomatic pressure on Whitehall by Adams. Russell had been under relentless pressure from a righteous Adams on the subject since the escape of the *Alabama*, which Adams hoped had pierced the Victorian conscience. The *Alexandra* was indeed destined for Confederate service, but the evidence which the government possessed from customs and Federal sources was far from conclusive in this respect.

As the seizure was the first of a series it can be readily viewed as a turning-point in British policy. Scholarly opinion, however,

20. Dyer, "Dudley," p. 407. The Forbes-Aspinwall mission was sent to Britain to purchase ships to prevent them from coming into the possession of Confederate agents. An open move along such lines would have placed north and south on the same footing. Seward heard rumors that the British government would have rejoiced to see the north enter the market for ironclads, thus getting London "off the hook" on the question of damages over the *Alabama*'s depredations. See: D. H. Maynard, "The Forbes-Aspinwall Mission," MVHR, XLV, No. 1 (June, 1958), pp. 67-89. Unable to purchase raiders in the British market, Forbes and Aspinwall poured money into the northern espionage system in England, and strove for the cause of Atlantic peace by making valuable contacts with parliamentary leaders and influential business interests.

has displayed minor disagreement on the matter. Frank Merli sees the arrest as an attempt to gain legal approval for a new approach, "a definite reversal of official British thinking"—an attempt to forestall an embarrassing diplomatic and legal confrontation with the United States.[21] This interpretation considers as representative of earlier policy the government's defensive parliamentary stand over the *Alabama*; any contrary view faces the inconvenience of assuming government insincerity on that responsible occasion. In the pre-*Alexandra* period, Merli makes allowances for hesitations and ministerial confusion in the face of an ambiguous law. Nevertheless he is inclined to see the seizure as sign of British conversion to a "flexible" from a "strict" construction of the statute. Despite its parliamentary protestations, the government was now acting on what looked suspiciously like "suspicion of intent" instead of proof, and had a case not markedly stronger than that which had existed against the *Alabama*. Merli concludes that the affair was an attempt to sanction a harsher stand against Confederate shipbuilding by court decision, in preference to a politically risky appeal for parliamentary changes in the act.[22] There were three objections to the latter course: it might be unpopular, an improved statute was difficult to devise, and the United States had already refused to concert with Britain in creating more acceptable laws all round—an appalling error of judgment often forgotten in discussions of the *Alabama* claims.

Earlier, Wilbur Jones had been impressed by the fundamental continuity of Foreign Office attitudes. He interpreted the *Alexandra* case as a victory for what had long been the dominant legal viewpoint in the department.[23] As early as November 1861 the law officers had favored stoppage of suspect shipbuilding, merely requiring "reasonable evidence" of contravention of the Foreign Enlistment Act. They later urged detention of the *Alabama*, over the objections of customs solicitors, on the grounds that the ship was constructed as a vessel of war. Although the *Alabama* carried no arms or ammunition in British waters, they believed that evidence

---

21. F. Merli, "Crown versus Cruiser: the Curious Case of the Alexandra," CWH, IX, No. 2 (June, 1963), p. 176. See also his *Great Britain and Confederate Navy*, Chapter 8.

22. E. D. Adams also suggests a "volte face" theory. Unfortunately he makes a serious documentary error in misdating a key letter from Russell to Palmerston, which justifies detention on policy grounds. The letter in fact was dated September 3, not April 3, and referred to the Laird ironclads. E. D. Adams, II, 135 and below, 323. (The error is an inexplicable slip by a usually reliable historian, for the September 3 document was well-known.)

23. Jones, *Confederate Rams*, pp. 26-58.

on its structure could be used to establish that the ship had been "equipped, furnished, fitted out, or armed" within the meaning of the act. Again, although they had no real proof of Confederate ownership, they intended to call witnesses who would make it "reasonably clear" that the 290 was intended to cruise for the south. Presumably the government accepted this advice when it tried to detain the *Alabama*—although the issue was complicated by allegations of enlistment of British citizens; and it is possible that Russell was still uncommitted, primarily wanting a test case to clarify Britain's neutral obligations. In the associated case of the *Florida* the law officers' zeal to bring a prosecution had outstripped discretion. When the raider was impounded by colonial officials in the Bahamas, Whitehall possessed frail evidence concerning her equippage in Liverpool and only hearsay evidence concerning her then southern ownership. Even that was irrelevant. As the judge of the local court of Vice-Admiralty ruled in August 1862, violations of the act must be shown to have occurred within the jurisdiction of his court. No satisfactory testimony could be produced on the matter, and the ship was restored to its owners. Undeterred by such setbacks, the law officers finally obtained in the *Alexandra* a case in which to test their "broad" theory of the act.

There is less disagreement concerning the mounting anxiety of Russell and other ministers to resolve the shipbuilding issue. American pressure was important—but not decisive—in precipitating this resolve. Yankee threats, even wielded gingerly by Adams, created backlash. Palmerston had a passion, almost a phobia, against appearing to be browbeaten by foreigners. The ministry's task was unenviable: it had to discharge its international obligations while preserving the sanctity of private enterprise; and Merli for one suggests that strategic considerations tipped the balance:

> The Queen's ministers had begun to realize that the North might win the Civil War, in which case the Confederate shipbuilding program in England might well cause troubled relations with a re-established United States for years to come. They therefore felt inclined to try to satisfy the American demands as a gesture of conciliation.[24]

The argument seems more appropriate to the post-Gettysburg period. Prior to Meade's triumph in July, Lincoln's advisers were themselves uneasy about Washington's security. The seizure of the

24. Merli, "Crown v. Cruiser," p. 169.

Alexandra occurred during a time of military confusion in America. It was soon followed by news of Hooker's battering at Chancellorsville (May 1-3) and Lee's invasion of Maryland and Pennsylvania. The British press treated Lee's offensive (even without Stonewall Jackson, killed at Chancellorsville) as a mortal threat to the north; and many expected Lee to succeed in forcing the north to a negotiated peace settlement.[25] Gladstone believed that, precisely because their cause was lost, "the Americans of the North seem to have a strong claim of honour upon us for the vigilant execution of the law. With my feelings of the certain & indeed practically the achieved issue of this contest, I am the more desirous that there may not even be a colour of a case against us with reference to minor matters of controversy."[26]

E. D. Adams' revisionist insistence that increased British vigilance was occasioned by Seward's privateering threat has itself become superceded.[27] British guilt feelings over the depredations of the *Alabama*, nervousness at the scale of the damages bill being steadily calculated across the Atlantic, dismay at marine insurance losses, and preoccupation with the Polish crisis might as plausibly be offered in explanation.

There was at least one other factor. By 1863 it had become clear that long-term British interests might be ill served by the *Alabama* precedent. According to popular dogma free trade was permitted in warships just as in ordinary armaments. But, with swift improvements in naval technology, that trade might enable nations without Britain's maritime resources to buy their way across the "battleship gap" of the 1860's. In fact, the class of ironclads building for the south at Lairds soon became obsolescent. But there was at the time considerable awe at their destructive power, while the speed of naval change promised bigger and better battleships. The experts forecast that England's predominance in seapower could be upset in future wars unless neutral nations, especially the United States, were restrained by international practice from supplying scores of lethal raiders to Britain's foes. (They did not

25. Charles P. Cullop, "English Reaction to Stonewall Jackson's Death," *West Virginia History*, Vol. 29 (1967), pp. 1-5.

26. Gladstone to Russell, April 27, 1863, *PRO* 30/22-33; q. Jones, p. 56. The presence of the northern abolitionist, Moncure Conway, in Britain in June did not inspire confidence in northern prospects, for he was reported to be offering a deal by which abolitionists would oppose prosecution of the war if the Confederacy emancipated its slaves under the supervision of a European commission. (*Manchester Guardian*, June 19, 1863).

27. EDA, II, Chapter 13; Jones, p. 52 and following.

envisage the contrary situation: with the destroyer deal of 1940 Britain itself was to obtain succor out of slanted neutrality.) Northern complaints were entirely relevant: traditional concepts of neutrality were being rendered archaic by advances in warfare. Prompted by its sister body in New York, the Liverpool Chamber of Commerce favored changing an act whose inefficiency "tends to expose our professions of neutrality to the charge of inconsistency, and to establish a precedent which may at some future time be turned with harassing effect against ourselves."[28] This logic led Britain a long way. After a Royal Commission, Parliament in 1870 framed more stringent legislation designed to prohibit even the building of ships for belligerent purposes.[29] The limits of neutrality were narrowed even further during the Washington Treaty negotiations in 1871. As a concession to the Americans, but also as a matter of self-interest, Britain agreed to arbitrate the *Alabama* claims upon the basis of a new code of rules—containing severe sanctions against commerce-raiding—instead of by reference to the 1819 law which applied during the alleged violations. This was giving the game away with a vengeance. As an "acknowledgement of certain great rules as rules of International Law for the future" it cost the United Kingdom over $15 million in damages, awarded in the famous Geneva Arbitration of 1872.

It is doubtful whether Russell's motives were particularly far-ranging in mid-1863; he wanted the nuisance of raider-building abated, but without appearing to stretch neutrality for the Yankees. Both sides distrusted him, but in practice the south suffered most in the tense interval before the trial took place on June 22. Proceedings were transferred from Liverpool—in Russell's words "a port specially addicted to Southern proclivities, foreign slave trade, and domestic bribery"—to the court of exchequer in London, where the government was protected against large damage suits. Adams and the prosecution collaborated closely, and a northern observer, William M. Evarts, was permitted to scrutinize the preparation of the case. Russell was thus being friendly to the northerners, and also offering them first-hand experience of the vexations of administering the

28. Quoted *NYT*, April 22, 1863. The *Manchester Guardian* agreed: "But on the other hand, she (Great Britain) cannot waive her own rules of judicial procedure to serve the purposes of a foreign power." *Manchester Guardian*, April 7, 1863.

29. Jarvis, pp. 194-198. The new act prohibited building, equipping, or dispatching any ship—armed or not—with intent, or knowledge, or even "having reasonable cause to believe" that it would be used in the services of foreign states warring with nations at peace with Britain.

law.[30] Moreover he kept his hands untied. Should the court rule against the crown, the government had a good excuse for doing nothing. If action became necessary the law would have to be evaded or changed. Meanwhile the litigation halted the south's entire naval program.

The trial indicated that the ministry was dangerously in advance of public opinion. A range of motives underlay the widespread opposition to the seizure: from the conviction that the south was getting a raw deal, to *laissez faire* zealotry, greed for neutral profits and resentment at executive autocracy. The sanctimoniousness of the Yankees on the issue was, to say the least, indecorous when northern agents were recruiting for the Union army in Ireland, and when the north was the main beneficiary of the massive export of arms and strategic stores from Britain. ("The trade with New York" said the *Times* six months earlier "is actually resuming its old proportions under the extraordinary and continued demand for munitions. . . . The soldiers of the South have been shot down by weapons 'fitted out in England'. . . . Their provinces have been invaded and their cities taken with armaments 'fitted out in England'. . . ."[31]). Why, men asked, were ships exempted from the grisly trade of war? Britain's neutrality regulations concerning prizes and access to neutral ports already in practice favored the north. Now that the south was trying to redress the naval imbalance which lay at the root of such a situation, Britain threatened to slam the door on neutral trade in ships. The United States, moreover, was inconsistent. American law had, in the past, permitted the sale of ships, which might arm in the manner of the *Alabama*, regardless of destination. Americans had built and sold the *Grand Admiral* to Russia during the Crimean War; while the north itself in July 1861 had applied to Lairds to build a completely armed ship for the Union.[32] Nor would the Lincoln government change its laws on the subject in tandem with Britain.

The trial proved a vindication for free trade orthodoxy. Sir Hugh Cairns, appearing for the claimants, contended that a verdict for the crown would paralyze British ports and drive naval construction to other countries. Roundell Palmer had himself asserted in the *Alabama* debate: "It would be a great mistake to suppose that the Foreign Enlistment Act was meant to prohibit

---

30. Jones, p. 45.
31. *Times*, October 30, 1862.
32. Owsley, p. 403 and following; Jarvis, 183.

all commercial dealing in ships-of-war with belligerent countries."[33] Now, in an unfamiliar trial role as counsel for the crown, Roundell Palmer was suggesting that a vessel's warlike structure was sufficient proof of its hostile character and intent. He was caught in his own trap and Cairns subjected him to a merciless courtroom savaging.

The *Alexandra* had three-inch teak bulwarks, a reinforced rudder, facilities for a crew of two hundred, hatchways and hammock racks suitable to a small class man-of-war; it was clearly convertible to a raider. The defense alleged it was built as a yacht, but also held that it was "perfectly competent for any person to build a ship easily convertible into a ship-of-war, and sell that ship to any belligerent power." The object of the act of 1819, according to Cairns, was very circumscribed; arming and equipping within port was proscribed simply "to prevent the ports of this country from becoming arsenals, out of which expeditions might issue. . . ."[34] The judge agreed. Even had the crown been able to establish that the ship was armed according to the act, it had no clear proof that the ship was being built for the CSA. In a dramatic move, the crown produced the ex-paymaster of the *Alabama*, Clarence R. Yonge, once Bulloch's private secretary, who had pawned information to Adams and Dudley. But Yonge was unable to show much beyond the existence of a connection between Bulloch, and the firm of Frazer, Trenholm and Co., well-known financiers to the south and allegedly "mixed up with" the building of the *Alexandra.* (One room in their offices was used, Yonge said, almost exclusively by Confederate army and navy personnel; but as Lord Chief Baron Pollock pointed out, what they did there was legally irrelevant.) There was a strong presumption that Confederates implicated in the escape of the *Alabama* were supervising operations in Toxteth dock. But as the *Alabama* affair had never been adjudicated, and as legal ownership of the *Alexandra* was indisputably vested in a British firm, the prosecution's case lapsed badly. Revelations of the activities of

33. The *Manchester Guardian* remarked of this speech that it left "some difficulty of understanding what is the nature of the obligation which rests upon this country to put the Foreign Enlistment Act into force. But although the Solicitor-General seemed to be in some doubt as to the character of the law, he was very clear as to the duty of obeying it, just as some philosophers who question the divine origin of Christianity, think . . . it is a useful instrument for regulating the passions of mankind." (May 1, 1863).

34. Trial proceedings, Court of Exchequer, Westminster, June 22, 1863, "Seizure of the Ship Alexandra"; printed *United States House Executive Documents,* 38 Congress, 1st session, CDS, 1180 (1863), p. 341. There is an evocative account of the trial in Merli, "Crown v. Cruiser," p. 172 and following, *Great Britain and the Confederate Navy,* p. 167 and following.

spies and detectives in British shipyards rebounded against the crown, which Cairns accused of warping the law "to suit the temper of a foreign minister."[35]

Cairns' reasonings were fully endorsed by the presiding judge, the octogenarian Tory Sir Frederick Pollock. Ships, he said, were legitimately part of that trade in munitions expressly permitted neutrals by American jurists such as Story. The object of the act was not to protect belligerents, but to maintain peace within Her Majesty's dominions. (Thus his lordship, in the first judicial pronouncement to be made on the *Alabama*, stated his opinion that, if the *Alabama* had cleared from Liverpool without arms "as a mere ship in ballast," and was armed outside British jurisdiction, then the act was not violated.) Provided builders avoided immediate equippage in British waters, they might legally fulfill a contract to build a ship, "leaving those who bought it to make what use they thought fit of it." The ship's structure, it followed, was irrelevant. In 1911 Brooks Adams, son of Charles Francis, portrayed Pollock as a sinister figure, and interpreted his charge to the jury as part and parcel of the British aristocracy's conspiracy against northern democracy.[36] The prosaic reality was that Pollock's ruling merely declared the legal orthodoxy of the time. The jury promptly returned a verdict for the defendants. It was received in the courtroom with wild applause.

The court's decision was unsettling to British merchant interests, while Minister Adams forecast the decimation of northern commerce by hosts of British-built raiders. However the case became snarled in legal complications as the crown attempted to appeal to the Exchequer Chamber over the objections of the Lord Chief Baron. Upset at the prospect of extended litigation, the builders offered to sell the *Alexandra* to the Admiralty. The Foreign Office urged the purchase as "highly expedient," but the Admiralty was lukewarm and Treasury objections killed the project. The case continued unresolved until early 1864. Leave to appeal was finally denied the crown after procedural rulings by the Exchequer Chamber and House of Lords; and the *Alexandra* was released.

---

35. Glasgow *Sentinel:* "It is assimilating our practice to the Continental spy system, and paying rather too high a price for the *entente cordiale* between the Cabinet of Abraham Lincoln and that of Lord Palmerston" (May 9, 1863).

36. Brooks Adams, "The seizure of the Laird Rams," MHSP, XLV (December 1911), pp. 270-287.

In the spring of 1863 another Atlantic fracas built up over the *Peterhoff* prize case. On February 25 the screw-propelled British-owned *Peterhoff* was captured by a Union cruiser five miles off St. Thomas in the Caribbean on suspicion of carrying contraband, despite being headed towards the neutral port of Matamoros in Mexico. The war scare which ensued, according to a recent authority, "reached a height second only to that which resulted from the *Trent* affair."[37] It was characterized by stock market disruption and spiralling marine insurance rates; and sparked demands for convoy escort for merchantmen trading with the West Indies. (The suggestion horrified the Admiralty as repugnant to Royal Navy interests.) Public hysteria in Britain was premature (it declined when unpalatable facts about the *Peterhoff*'s voyage and blockade-running emerged) and insecurely based on maritime law, which provided British precedents for the capture. The anger was visceral, beamed at Yankee arrogance. A generation bred on the dogmas of Bright and Cobden found itself out of accord with the "belligerent pretensions" practiced by England itself against the seagoing commerce of other nations in an earlier era. With exquisite irony, Washington was now employing those claims against British neutral trade with the Confederacy. Opinion at large was less ready than Whitehall to grasp the consolation that the Americans were surrendering historic doctrine on neutral rights, and that Britain was well placed to take shrewd advantage of the fact.

The naval war had produced an accumulating series of incidents involving Union interference with the British flag at sea. Particularly galling to Milne's squadron—whose secessionist sympathies and desire for retaliation the vice-admiral kept severely curbed—was the presence of the "demonic" Charles Wilkes in charge of the American West Indian station since the summer of 1862. From the northern point of view Wilkes' responsibility for sealing off the sealanes to the south was of vital importance, his respect for neutral sensibilities of secondary concern. The *Peterhoff* voyage (although it raised some novel points of law) typified the wartime profiteering pilloried by northerners. London and Liverpool had become bases from which British shippers, in close collaboration with southern purchasing agents and merchants, traded contraband for cotton. Supplies useful to the Confederacy were off-loaded from merchantmen

37. Bernath, *Squall Across the Atlantic*, p. 67, and generally Chapter 8. Also F. L. Owsley, "America and the Freedom of the Seas, 1861-1865," in A. Craven ed., *Essays in Honour of Wm. E. Dodd . . .* (Chicago, 1935), p. 203 and following.

at neutral ports—chiefly British Nassau in the Bahamas and St. George's in Bermuda, Danish St. Thomas, and Spanish Havana—whence blockade-runners attempted the perilous last leg of the voyage. Neutral Matamoras, near the mouth of the Rio Grande, became a thriving center of munitions trade with Brownsville, just across the river in Texas. Vessels sailed from Europe to Matamoros, confident that they were legally immune from Union harassment. The passage of goods to Confederate territory was then completed by a safe land transit from Mexico (see Map 5).

The Union navy struck at the indirect trade with the south by harassing the big merchant ships on their primary cruise to neutral ports. In justification the navy flexed British maritime doctrines. Wilkes, now rear-admiral, had his warships hover off—virtually blockading—Nassau and St. George's and intercepting suspicious vessels. During the Napoleonic wars the British fleet had lain off New York and Boston, and seized vessels entering and leaving, but without claiming the practice as a right. (This iniquity was remembered in July 4th folklore.) Welles emulated the example, apologizing for blatant departures from modern usage but winking at the overall practice. British shippers yelped that arbitrary seizure was being made of vessels whose names appeared on Union blacklists, lists drawn up by Adams and his consuls naming ships suspected of trading with the south. The close surveillance of British colonial harbors, and their use by Union ships as bases of operations and coaling stations, created numerous incidents and encroachments upon neutral rights, and turned the colonists into philo-Confederates. Welles had ordered his squadron not to "chase, fire upon, board or seize" vessels within the three-mile limit marking off neutral territorial waters; but reckless officers sometimes observed the command in the breach. A heated quarrel arose between Spain and the United States when the U.S.S. *Montgomery* pursued the *Blanche* (which had been running the blockade from Texas to Havana under British ensign) into Cuban waters and took possession of her.[38] Although the steamer was beached by her captain on the Spanish shore, she was boarded by an armed crew of Americans who allegedly insulted a protesting Spanish official and destroyed the ship by fire. An American disavowal of the act averted a serious breach between Madrid and Washington. The *Montgomery*'s captain was

38. Bernath, p. 100 and following. The incident occurred on October 7, 1862. The *Blanche* was actually an American warship taken by the rebels and illegally transferred to British ownership, a fact which weakened seriously the British claim for damages.

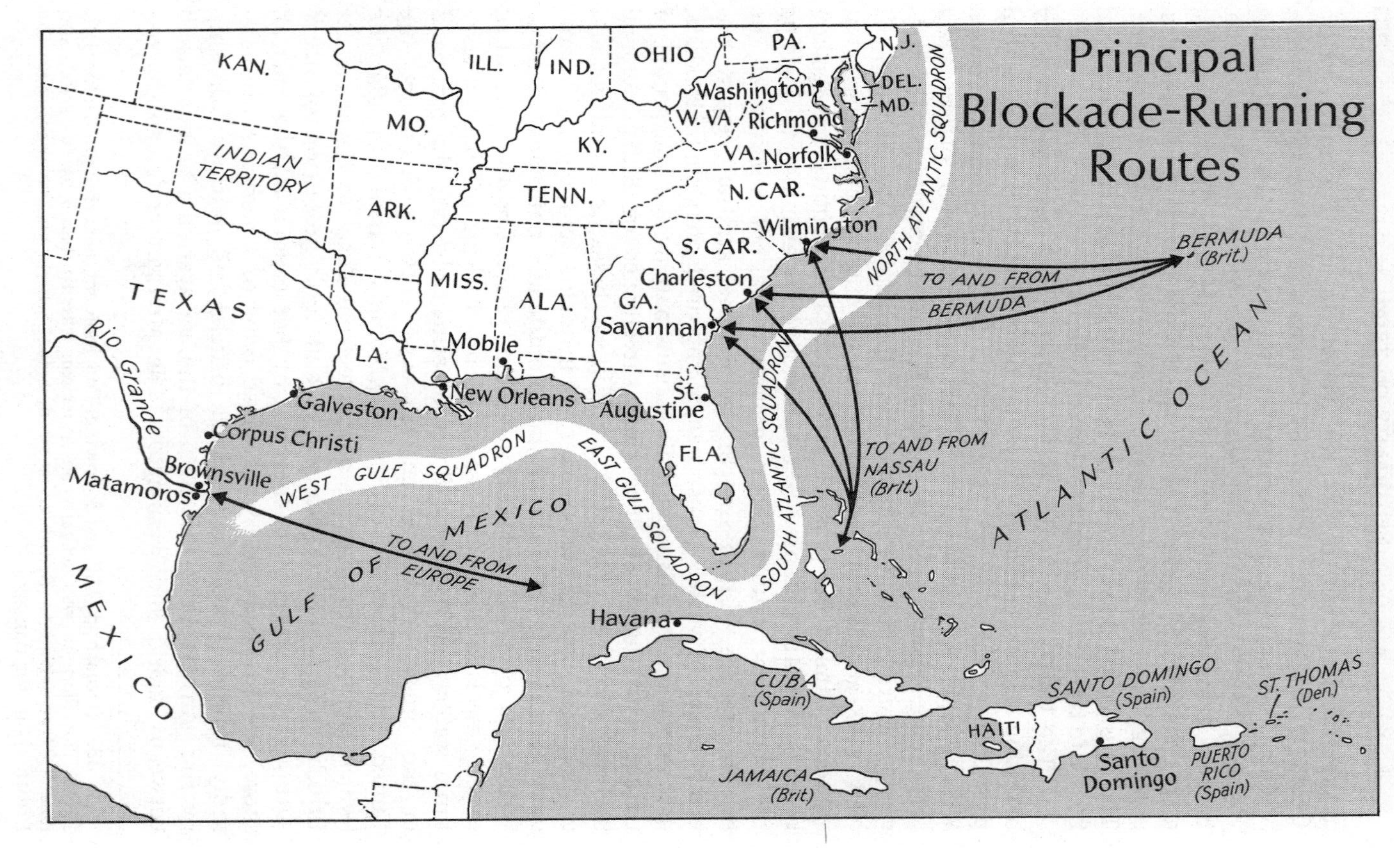

Principal Blockade-Running Routes
KAN.
ILL.
IND.
OHIO
PA.
N.J.
DEL.
MD.
Washington
W. VA.
Richmond
VA.
Norfolk
MO.
INDIAN TERRITORY
KY.
TENN.
N. CAR.
ARK.
Wilmington
S. CAR.
Charleston
GA.
Savannah
MISS.
ALA.
TEXAS
Rio Grande
LA.
Mobile
New Orleans
Galveston
Corpus Christi
Brownsville
Matamoros
St. Augustine
FLA.
NORTH ATLANTIC SQUADRON
SOUTH ATLANTIC SQUADRON
EAST GULF SQUADRON
WEST GULF SQUADRON
TO AND FROM BERMUDA
BERMUDA (Brit.)
TO AND FROM NASSAU (Brit.)
TO AND FROM EUROPE
ATLANTIC OCEAN
GULF OF MEXICO
MEXICO
Havana
CUBA (Spain)
JAMAICA (Brit.)
HAITI
SANTO DOMINGO (Spain)
Santo Domingo
PUERTO RICO (Spain)
ST. THOMAS (Den.)

dismissed from the navy on Lincoln's insistence, and Consul Shufeldt was replaced at Havana, but neither Britain nor Spain received compensation for damages. On another occasion (May 30, 1863) a Union cruiser landed shells upon Eleuthera Island in the Bahamas in an attempt to disable a Confederate steamer it had forced ashore there. A Union navy court ruled that the guns had been fired from international waters, but this hardly satisfied the English press: "If at Eleuthera, why not at the Isle of Wight, in Southampton Water?" enquired one editor.[39]

Patience was stretched thin in the Atlantic world as a result of such frictions, but governmental restraint on both sides was ordained by considerations of enlightened self-interest. The *Peterhoff* case is a particularly instructive instance of the medley of forces at work. In order to stop a trade threatening the Union's entire war effort—the neutral trade to the West Indies and Mexico—Lincoln's navy was forced to capture merchantmen according to the doctrine of continuous voyage (or ultimate destination). It was a doctrine entrenched in decisions of British prize courts; it had been directed classically against American neutral trade in past wars; and had been fiercely disputed by American jurists and opinion. It had matured as a device to counter the ingenuity of American traders during Britain's war with Napoleon. British orders-in-council of the 1790's restricted a booming American trade between the French West Indies and metropolitan France. Merchants tried circumvention by landing cargoes from the French colonies in the United States, paying duty upon them, and re-exporting them as American goods.[40] British courts ruled (as in the 1805 *Essex* case) that such voyages were not "broken" (i.e., constituting a bona fide importation into America) but were "continuous": the intent of the transaction being to complete an illicit trade to an ultimate destination in a belligerent port. The essential principle developed that voyages between neutral ports must be *bona fide*: expedients designed to conceal a cargo's ultimately hostile destination were illegal. Thus for a ship to touch at a neutral port (usually its ostensible destination) before running into a blockaded port (its real destination) did not exempt the ship from seizure and condemnation by a prize court. Nor did the device of transmitting cargo to hostile places via a succession of voyages in separate vessels. During the Civil War British ships such as the

---

39. *Army and Navy Gazette*, July 4, 1863; q. Bernath, p. 114.

40. Patrick White, *A Nation on Trial: America and the War of 1812* (Wiley, N.Y., 1965), p. 7 and following.

Bermuda, Stephen Hart, and *Springbok* were seized under this rule, which clearly forbade the trans-shipment of goods from big ships to blockade-runners at Nassau and nearby ports. That such ports were adjacent to the southern coast, and could themselves hardly pose as genuine markets for munitions, was strong incentive for closely scrutinizing neutral trading in the area. Inevitably, neutral sensibilities were offended by strict application of the doctrine. Naval captains, and later prize courts, had to decide upon difficult questions: of intent to run a blockade, true destination, ownership of cargo, and whether cargo could be classed under a variety of types of contraband. As ships' papers were commonly destroyed on capture, or were falsified, and because ingenious methods were used to conceal irregularities, American courts admitted circumstantial evidence to sustain captures. English merchants claimed that the north was deliberately driving British trade away from the Caribbean—probably with a motive of supplanting Britain's position in the islands' economy—and was exploiting the delays of prize litigation as a war measure. The situation created by the dictates of war, interest, and chauvinism was worthy of Gilbert and Sullivan: American courts condoned belligerent practices in the words of their eighteenth century enemies, while Englishmen protested the sanctity of trade between neutral ports in language reminiscent of Madison.

The *Peterhoff* capture introduced an extension of the theory of continuous voyage. That vessel carried a cargo of artillery harnesses, army boots and blankets, quinine and chloroform—subsequently classed by an American court as contraband when intended for Confederate use. The ship was to anchor in neutral waters off the mouth of the Rio Grande, and lighter its cargo up river to Matamoros. The United States government contended that an ultimate destination for the cargo could be established in Brownsville, in belligerent Texas. The New York district court accepted, in July 1863, that a voyage became illicit if completed by *overland* route to a hostile destination. The cargo and ship were thus forfeit. (This precedent was cited by Britain in World War I to justify closing off wartime trade with Germany through ports in Holland and Scandinavia.) The court was outdoing even British doctrine. An 1801 ruling of the British court of Admiralty recognized the legality of neutral trade to or from a blockaded country by inland transportation. After the Civil War, the American Supreme Court, presided over by Salmon Chase, held that carriage of the *Peterhoff*'s cargo inland from Matamoros to Brownsville did not render the ship itself liable for violation of blockade.[41] Treaty arrangements between Mexico and the United States guaranteed free navigation on the Rio Grande. Although Union cruisers had tried a *de facto* blockade of the mouth of the river, and harassed trade with Matamoros in a variety of ways, Matamoros was legally unblockaded. Chase held that overland transit to Texas did not breach any blockade, and he released the ship. The cargo, however, he condemned according to continuous voyage, as destined for rebel use.

As in the shipbuilding controversy, considerations of future naval interests strongly influenced the Admiralty and Foreign Office. The British government made representations on behalf of the *Peterhoff*'s owners—as it consistently supported merchant interests believed to be *bona fide* victims of Union aggression—but accepted the district court decision with equanimity. Milne's squadron continued to respect orders not to interfere with Union seizures of British ships, except in territorial waters. For his part Welles renewed his general order that officers conform to international usages in search and seizure. Despite British pressure, Seward generally followed the policy of referring cases such as the *Peterhoff* to the prize courts, foreswearing government interference in questions of claims and compensation. The restoration of British mail captured on the *Peterhoff* constituted a significant exception to this practice. Welles and Seward quarrelled over the matter. Welles (and also Sumner) wanted sealed packages of letters which had been taken from the ship's mailbag opened, as they might contain evidence against the *Peterhoff*, and opposed any knuckling-under to London. Seward ordered the mail kept inviolate in line with an agreement he had made with Britain in 1862, a pact to which Welles was not a party.[42] Seward urged release of the mails to reduce the war risk with England, and to safeguard America's future requirements as a neutral. In a celebrated arbitration between his ministers, Lincoln ordered the mails forwarded and forebade future belligerent interference with neutral mails.

A parliamentary debate on the prize cases took place at Westminister as Lincoln settled this affair. Adams, for once imprudent, had pulled a hornet's nest upon his head by granting a note of immunity to northern merchants wanting to ship arms to Matamoros to aid the Juáristas. He fulminated therein upon "the multitude of fraudulent and dishonest enterprises" being financed by Englishmen

41. A number of complex issues were involved in the decision, handed down in 1867. For details, Bernath, Chapters 4 and 5.

42. Van Deusen, *Seward*, p. 351.

to Mexico. This leaked to the press. "That foolish letter" commented Moran, "has caused an immense amount of gossip among all classes . . . and has supplied the clubs with a new sensation."[43] Adams was excoriated in Parliament for setting up to license foreign trade. The Quai d'Orsay protested at Adams' concurrence in an intervention project in Mexico, a violation of American neutrality. Whitehall added its support. Seward offered regrets to the French, and disclaimed to Lyons any wish to interfere with lawful British trade. His apology, the release of the *Peterhoff* mails, and the transfer of the abrasive Wilkes from the West Indies station, did much to abate exasperation abroad.

Despite talk of war, the Jingos in Britain by no means held the field. There were abundant commonsense appeals for peace, stirrings of conscience on the arms trade, and maledictions made against troublemakers like the London *Times* and *New York Herald.* From Sydney, nervous of a maritime war which should have dismal consequences for the Australian colonies, came reproaches concerning Americophobia in England. A *Sydney Morning Herald* editorial typified the sense of fatalistic gloom widespread at the time:

> That there will be war between England and America at no remote period is to us as certain as any undeveloped event. . . . Any Englishman may well look with concern on this unfortunate state of two great and kindred nations. The supercilious contempt of American power is, we suppose, by this time over. We have now a spectacle of what such a nation can do when roused by strong passions. To us it seems absurd to attribute either to North or South any monopoly of the good or evil in the national character; but this we clearly see, that they can sacrifice on each side both money and men to an extent unprecedented. . . . A war with England would be prosecuted with a vigour and fierceness of which no nation has hitherto afforded an example, and it is not at all improbable that the Continental nations would avail themselves of such a conflict to . . . circumscribe the influence, if not the dominion, of Great Britain.[44]

Similar themes were adopted by the *Glasgow Sentinel* and *Reynolds' Newspaper*, who called for an end to the fitting out of more

43. Moran, *Diary*, II, p. 1150 (April 22, 1863); Bernath, p. 73 and following; Dayton thought "the chances of peace with England seem to me growing less and less daily; that the exasperation upon that side of the channel growing out of the seizures, searches, etc. of British vessels fully keeps pace with that in the U.S. growing out of the depredations of the rebel privateers." Dayton to Seward, April 27, 1863, q. Owsley, "Freedom of Seas," p. 240.

44. Cited fully in *Glasgow Sentinel*, April 25, 1863. See also May 9.

Alabamas. Writing for *Reynolds'*, "Gracchus" (who was no great friend of the north) declared: "Earl Russell must turn a deaf ear to those selfish and headstrong men who would urge him to precipitate this country into a fearful, a terrible, and a deadly strife." War would drive British commerce from the seven seas ("We know, by the doings of the Alabama and Florida, what a vast deal of damage can be inflicted on a commercial marine by only one or two fast-sailing, well-equipped steamers, commanded by dashing, devil-me-care-officers."). Canada's defense would be problematical, and enormously expensive given the apathyof Canadians in defending themselves. England would be saddled with an unbearable national debt and intolerably heavy taxation; widespread starvation and irremediable social divisions would ensue . . . England was neither so rich, so prosperous, or so powerful as to court such calamities.[45]

The Confederacy's last formal attempt to win the British Commons to official recognition of its legal rights and its revolutionary success—the Roebuck intervention—has been described as a fiasco and an anticlimax. And so it proved. But at the outset it seemed to promise much, and with reason. J. A. Roebuck's intrigues with Napoleon III were founded upon the Emperor's very real readiness to join England in a peace move which would elicit cotton, and secure his flank in Mexico. If that could be achieved before north and south splintered themselves entirely into fragments, thus depriving him of possible future counterweights against England, so much the better. The United States regarded the whole affair—drenched in publicity—as perhaps the most menacing of the war, and threatened a break with France over it. Nor could the British government regard lightly the political perils of seeming once again to demonstrate spinelessness towards the Yankees. Public anger over the *Alexandra* and *Peterhoff* cases placed the ministry on the defensive. When Roebuck gave notice of a motion on recognition in May, Palmerston's minions sought to kill the idea and put out rumors that Louis Napoleon no longer favored joint intervention. Such at least was the story going the London rounds. In order to scotch it Roebuck and Lindsay journeyed to obtain reassurance from Napoleon himself at Fontainebleau on June 22. They left the interview convinced they had obtained what they wanted, i.e., an affirmation of French willingness to move in conjunction with England on recognition, and authorization from Napoleon to deny any contrary rumor in parliament. They understood that the French

45. *Reynolds' Newspaper*, May 10, 1863.

ambassador in London, Baron Gros, was instructed to straighten the record and to sound out the Palmerston government on a joint move. Duplication of official and amateur diplomacy led to endless complications. Napoleon's first inclination (expressed to Slidell) was to make a direct and formal proposition of joint intervention to the British. This would have been the simplest and most effective strategy. His cabinet, however, feared another rebuff from London, an unendurable wound to French pride. The legacy of Anglo-French distrust engendered by Mexico and Poland was now having its effect. Russell was thought capable of betraying the French by passing on a direct proposition to Washington. The United States might retaliate with a punitive stroke in Mexico (Spencer aptly interprets this anxiety as implying "a clear lack of confidence in the Confederate ability to aid the Mexican designs of France"), and Napoleon would be dragged unwillingly into a war of England's deliberate making.

Napoleon indiscreetly conveyed these fears to Roebuck and Lindsay, charging that England had previously leaked an intervention proposal of his to Seward.[46] With incredible artlessness Roebuck repeated the charge in the Commons. Napoleon was chagrined at betrayal of a confidence, and the Commons erupted in chauvinistic dudgeon against the French. Members of the house thought it odious enough that Roebuck should present himself as Napoleon's "courier" to parliament. But his credit collapsed entirely when, contrary to his confident assertion, it appeared that no French communication on joint intervention had been sent to London. Russell, then Layard and Grey, denied having received any written or verbal indication from Napoleon showing a wish to join England in intervention. Moreover, they added, Baron Gros had made a point of calling on Russell, stating that he had no orders on the subject. There seemed two possibilities to the thunderstruck southern lobby: they had been double-crossed by Napoleon (on intelligence from Paris they soon rejected this) or by the British government. Roebuck, it turns out, was the victim of his own impetuousity, contingency, and a touch of Foreign Office casuistry.[47] Napoleon had in fact

46. This at least was the Lindsay-Roebuck version of the interview. If Napoleon referred to the only formal proposal acknowledged by the British, the armistice plan of October 30, 1862, his complaint has no force; the plan was openly printed in the *Moniteur* before the British had even formally replied, and it was conveyed to Seward by Mercier, not Lyons.

47. Much ink has been spilled on the mystery of the Roebuck affair, and it is still not completely solved. For a detailed study, Owsley, Chapter 13. Case and Spencer add valuable material from the French archives.

acted. He told Drouyn that he wanted Palmerston unofficially informed "that I am resolved on recognizing the independence of the Southern Provinces." This was strong, if unofficial, and exceeded the French cabinet's position: ministers were against making an initiative, insisting that France should only follow a British lead. However Drouyn, approving the cabinet's caution, watered down Gros' orders to: "See Lord Palmerston and in the course of conversation give him to understand that the Emperor has no objection to recognize the independence of the South." Gros, understandably, read no sense of urgency into this injunction. Unable to see Palmerston, who was ill, Gros did not interview Russell until June 30—the day of the debate on Roebuck's motion—and then on the subject of Poland. As Gros explained to his superior: ". . . it is very likely that I incidentally said to him that having no official communication to make to him on this subject of the recognition of the Southern States, I was personally persuaded that the Emperor was disposed to recognize them." Gros was angry at the gloss placed on this exchange by Russell in parliament. If it was exceedingly informal, Gros' approach was "very likely" not quite nonexistent, and certainly not a direct rebuttal of Roebuck's claim. Moreover Russell already had intelligence from Cowley indicating that Gros had received orders remarkably similar to those described by Roebuck. As Owsley observed, the French should have known "the old British custom of denying the existence of all unofficial, informal communications to or from the British Foreign Office. A thing did not exist unless it went on record. . . ."[48]

Inevitably, Roebuck's motion flopped. He did his cause no help by a rasping attack on the ministry, or by his light disposition to wage war upon a shabby and "mongrelised" northern democracy. Roebuck's is an illuminating minor saga in the annals of Atlantic radicalism. In the mid-1830's he had edited *Pamphlets for the People*, which disseminated a highly idealized, and doctrinaire Benthamite vision of America in the interest of parliamentary reform. Roebuck was, in this respect, one of the more dogged defenders of his old patron, Jeremy Bentham, against the eroding influence of younger liberals such as John Stuart Mill and Alexis de Tocqueville. He would permit no warts to be seen upon the visage of Jacksonian America, and campaigned in the Commons for the ballot and a scheme of national education on the lines of the Massachusetts schools system. But, as with many a Victorian radical,

48. Owsley, p. 462.

the less torrid years of mid-century drew Roebuck towards a more patriotic position, and by the 1860's he was finishing a gradual transition to Toryism. American expansionism, "insolent and overbearing", shook his faith in popular government. In the June 30 debate he made a renowned attack on the Western Colossus, "the great bully of the world: I am determined to do all I can to prevent the reconstruction of the Union, and I hope that the balance of Power on the American continent will, in future, prevent any one State from tyrannizing over the world as the Republic did." England should stop crawling on its belly to the United States, take time by the forelock, and intervene: "we shall be a much greater people, and London will be the Imperial city of the world." Roebuck was an Anglo-Saxon racist, explaining the failure of the American experiment in self-government as due to a mistaken policy of immigration. This had permitted the entry into the north of the "scum and refuse of Europe," and would ensure the victory of the south. Rich and educated northerners had withdrawn from politics, to be replaced by "mere political adventurers." After the war, in one of his last addresses to his Sheffield constituents, his disillusion was apparent: "Beware of trade unions" he wailed, "beware of Ireland; beware of America."[49]

The strong meat dished out by Roebuck was too much even for Gladstone and pro-southerners such as Lord Montagu. Montagu doffed his cap to "Historicus," and reluctantly compiled an impressive list of objections to acknowledging the south: recognition and neutrality were incompatible while a contest still raged for supremacy—other nations could either remain neutral (granting belligerent rights but none else) or espouse the cause of one party. In practice there was no middle ground, as history had always shown. Why should England respond to what was essentially a cry for alliance against the north? War against kinsmen would be unpopular; war meant heavy taxes and loss of English lives; and war would be difficult to wage at a distance of three thousand miles with English shipping vulnerable to American privateers, and Canada an easy prey. Conflict would also cut off a major

---

49. See my *American Democracy in English Politics*, pp. 42-43, 55-60; R. E. Leader, ed., *Life and Letters of J. A. Roebuck* (London, 1897), pp. 299-300, 321-324, 330; *Hansard*, 3rd ser., v. 171, (June 30, 1863), pp. 1771-1842, for full debate on motion.

supplier of grain.[50] Nor would recognition, without a war, produce a bale of cotton, or much beside except undying northern resentment. Was intervention an apt policy, when England itself had resisted, and would resist, outside interference in India and Ireland? Was intervention, even mediation, realistic unless Englishmen were agreed upon a proper and lasting peace settlement? What territorial limits should be assigned to the two sections, what was to be done about slavery? Lastly, why defraud the south of the glory of a self-won victory? After Chancellorsville, the rebels appeared on the point of irresistable triumph, and arms would decide irrevocably—as foreign interposition never could—the points at issue between north and south.

Gladstone, in a temperate speech, accepted the absurdity of venturing upon recognition when monumental and momentous battles were pending in the eastern and western theatres. Perhaps the overriding theme of the debate was a fatalistic acceptance of the fact that the war had acquired such a destructive momentum that outsiders—whether motivated by humanitarian outrage at its hopelessness and waste of life, or by realpolitik—were powerless to end it. Although Gladstone reiterated his belief that high British interest disfavored the Union's rending to pieces, his pain was obvious over the war's exactions and futility:

> Look at the embittering and exasperations of the relations between the black man and the white man in the South. Look again at the suspension of constitutional liberty in the North—the utter confusion of all the landmarks that separate between right and power—the danger into which the very principle of freedom has been brought in that which used to boast itself the freest, and which we, perhaps most of us, admit to have been at any rate one of the freest nations of the earth. Look at the discredit of liberty abroad—the discredit, not only to democratic, not only to popular, but I venture to say to all liberal and constitutional principles . . . [Look at] the desperate political extremities to which the free popular institutions of North America have been reduced. Why, Sir, we must desire the cessation of this war.

But by now Gladstone had come to reject England's being capable

50. Montagu's use of the corn scarcity argument has been much criticized, but his points were made with restraint and accuracy: more than one-third of imports were coming, he said, from the American northwest, England's chief supplier; Poland was unlikely to step to the rescue during the rising; elimination of American wheat would "aggravate" existing distress. *Hansard*, 1795. Obviously he did not see the corn situation as a single-cause factor preventing intervention.

of impartial intervention: "The very fact of our enormous interests in the American Continent, make us, as it were, a party in the struggle. . . ." So was France disqualified, even more decidedly because of its engagement in Mexico. England and France "would not be able to stand up in the face of the world and say, we claim to represent the impartial opinion of Europe." Peace-mongering would be resented by the north and would only retard the growth of the American peace movement. Such reasonings were becoming the conventional wisdom of the day. The south should be allowed to prevail by way of manly self-reliance and historical inevitability. Hopefully, all rancorous hatreds would be dissipated through the exhaustion of war. If England was the key, and England would not move, this spelt the end of Confederate diplomacy. There was little solace in Montagu's confidence that the south was better off without diplomacy—"diplomatic ability was the ruin of states."

Slidell was not surprised by the outcome of Roebuck's move. Slidell had long prophesied England's unreliability, and his policies had the virtue of being consistent with that prediction. Whether he helped it to self-fulfillment is another matter. His favorite project now was to free France from the English embrace, and push it into a continental league pursuing concerted policies on America. Considering that Napoleon could not create a similar league to act against Russia on the nearer problem of Poland, the plan had obvious difficulties. A Franco-Spanish axis seemed a promising possibility. Spain had been building up its navy, and the Serrano government saw advantages in confirming southern independence. An entente between Spain and the infant C.S.A. would provide protection for Spain's slave colonies in the Caribbean. But Madrid had no intention of acting without powerful friends, risking the loss of Cuba, "the pearl of the Antilles," to a resurrected United States. Slidell attempted to cajole Isturitz (Spain's minister to France) into acting with Napoleon, but without England. His efforts were interrupted by the fall of Serrano's regime. Napoleon by no means scorned Spanish aid, but he must have doubted whether the combined naval resources of Spain and France would be enough to deter the north from war. There was no certainty even that the ultimate deterrent of the British navy was sufficient protection for an allied intervention—on February 28, Congress had resolved that any proposal of outside interference in the rebellion would be regarded as an unfriendly act—but the risk of acting with less than that was high. Napoleon, moreover, had no intention of allowing England to sit on the sidelines while he got tangled in an American war likely to extinguish his scheme for empire in Mexico. That would play into Palmerston's hands. Better to allow events their head in America, keep at least nominal friendship with both sides, while hoping for southern success. With the United States playing a reduced postwar role in hemispheric affairs, Maximilian's kingdom might yet be kept intact.

The Roebuck fiasco brought about precisely what Napoleon and his cabinet had been at pains to avoid, wide publicity to his interventionist desires and a first class row with the United States. (This was besides the critical failure to gain a commitment from England, plus an interchange of recriminations between Confederates, French and British officials.) On July 7 the New York press printed accounts of the French cabinet meeting of June 18 and the Roebuck-Lindsay interview with Napoleon. France it appeared, was making fresh propositions to England. Rumors also flourished of French overtures to Spain on joint recognition, given color by the presence in Paris of Pierre Rost (Confederate delegate to Madrid). Seward, treating the reports with utmost seriousness, demanded explanations of the French, and threatened a rupture of diplomatic relations "if the emperor shall by any official act violate the sovereignty" which Dayton represented. Any new demonstration of activity "prejudicial to the unity of the American people, will be necessarily regarded as unfriendly. . . ." Urgently dispatched only days after the battles at Vicksburg and Gettysburg, Seward's protests reflected a nervousness that Napoleon might act impulsively before receiving news of the north's great victories. His alarm was needless for Drouyn was at work mending bridges. Napoleon made that task more difficult by publishing his version of the Roebuck interview in the *Moniteur* (July 5). There he disclosed that, should the English cabinet favor southern recognition in order to end the war, "the Emperor would be disposed to follow it. . . ." This dared the Yankees with a vengeance. Dayton had already warned that recognition "might extend and enlarge the war by drawing other nations into it." Drouyn took refuge in the evasion that no official communications had passed between London and Paris on the matter (all transactions had been kept carefully unofficial for just this contingency). An atmosphere of cordiality was restored between Dayton and Drouyn when the latter made appropriate assurances of France's benevolent intentions and renunciation of unilateral intervention. Dayton was abundantly aware, nevertheless, that it was the transformation of the military situation which acted as a bromide to cool the emperor's passions.

Meanwhile the powers had their hands full with Poland. In April, Britain, France, and Austria sent notes of protest to the Tsar, who returned unsatisfactory replies. The old Crimean coalition came closest to a new war with Russia in June and July despite mutual suspicions among the allies. Britain cooperated with Napoleon so as to prevent him marching into the Prussian Rhineland on the pretext of the Alvensleben convention, and in order to end his friendship with Russia. The Austrian-French alliance depended on a fragile truce over Napoleonic ambitions in Italy. Napoleon was urged on by his ambitions, and the need to appease public opinion, sympathetic to the Poles and already alienated over the Mexican affair. On June 17 the powers remonstrated once again with the Tsar, demanding a truce and a European congress to settle the Polish crisis on the basis of amnesty, reforms, and Polish independence. This was almost exactly the type of international precedent the Confederacy would have liked set, and the Union abhorred. But in practice the expectation of a Polish war unwhetted European appetites for more distant complications. Bright remarked in the Commons debate of June 30 that if Napoleon "is to engage at the same moment in dismembering the great Eastern Empire and the great Western Republic, he has more ambition than Louis XIV. . . ." Russian intransigence, however, soon revealed the gap between promise and performance on the Emperor's part. His suggestion of a punitive stroke against Russia in the Baltic elicited from the British only an offer of neutrality. The project of western intervention on behalf of the oppressed Poles foundered on the shoals of divergent national interests, despite almost undiluted public support for their cause. Polish exiles launched an effective propaganda campaign in Britain; but, as Kutolowski explains: "When the realities of possible war and moral protest converged, virtually every group, class, and interest (except the Radicals and some Catholics) reappraised the Polish issue on a self-interested, nationalistic, and materialistic basis."[51] In that reappraisal the fear was pre-eminent that France "would reap the spoils and tear asunder the European order." The moral in all this for America, a more divisive issue in Western Europe, was obvious.

In April, Napoleon had, against all logic and perhaps merely to flatter Washington, invited the north to join in the note of protest to St. Petersburg then being prepared. Washington had only one

---

51. J. F. Kutolowski, "Mid-Victorian Public Opinion, Polish Propaganda, and the Uprising of 1863," *Journal of British Studies*, VIII, No. 2 (May, 1969), p.110.

possible reason for accepting: to negotiate a deal by which American support for Poland would be traded for French guarantees not to recognize the south. What a volatile press, daily subjecting Napoleon to metaphoric disembowelling, would have said about such guarantees was entirely predictable. The case was overwhelming against rebuffing Russia, America's major friend in Europe; and against endangering traditional American attachment to the principle of nonintervention, when its erosion might prove fatal.[52] In brushing aside the offer, Seward cited the exhortation of the Father of the Country against "foreign alliances, intervention, and interference." The American people must be content to recommend the cause of progress by peaceful example. (This was not a convenient time to parade Editor Bennett's offer of patronage to revolutionary movements in other countries.) The problems of the gallant Poles, Seward professed to believe, would be solved through the enlightenment and humanity of the Tsar. A copy of the reply was sent to Cassius Clay to show to Prince Gortchakov, and the latter's request to publish it was graciously assented to. Alexander II conveyed his gratitude to Seward:

> His Majesty has greatly appreciated the firmness with which the government of the United States maintains the principle of non-intervention, the meaning of which in these days is too often perverted; as well as the loyalty with which they refuse to impose upon other states a rule, the violation of which, in respect to themselves, they would not allow.

In September 1863 a sensation was created in New York when a "fleet" of six Russian warships straggled into harbor, a move widely interpreted on the seaboard as an overt show of Russian friendship to the Union in its time of crisis. "We were seized with a Russian mania," the *Herald* reflected afterwards, "We indulged in banquets, speeches, we even went so far as to compare Alexander with Lincoln."[53] There was loose talk of an impending defensive alliance between free America and Tsarist Russia: Lincoln had freed the slave in America, Alexander had freed the serf in Russia; both shared common enemies, the treacherous powers of Western Europe; both would become superpowers who were capable of dividing the world between them. In the welter of rhetoric, traditional American sympathy for the Polish cause was repressed,

---

52. Harold E. Blinn, "Seward and the Polish Rebellion of 1863," AHR, XLV (July, 1940), pp. 828-833.

53. *NYH*, November 12, 1863.

although Charles Sumner and others of the Polish "lobby" reminded their countrymen of "Tartar tyranny" in Poland.[54] Sumner delivered a long analysis on American foreign policy at Cooper Institute on September 10 (just before the Russians arrived). In it he noted that western intervention in Poland was as yet unarmed, and at least on the side of liberal institutions: ". . . we have but one friend—Switzerland—in Europe." Sumner, and a number of prominent eastern newspapers, suspected the real purpose of the Russian naval maneuver. It was, as Sumner guessed in a letter to Bright, to keep the ships from being "sealed up at Cronstadt," should the Polish crisis erupt into a European war.[55] Rear-Admiral Lisovskii, commanding the Russian Baltic fleet (a not very seaworthy three frigates, three clippers and two corvettes), had been instructed in July to proceed to New York. In case of war between Russia, England and France, Lisovskii was to destroy allied commerce and attack weakly defended enemy possessions.[56] In obedience to similar strategic needs, Rear-Admiral Popov brought his small Pacific squadron into San Francisco harbor in October. There it was in a handy position to harass the Pacific trade routes. To its admirals St. Petersburg was silent on aiding the north, on an alliance or naval cooperation with the United States. The ships stayed in American waters for seven months, during which time a portion of the press began to regret the popular hysteria whipped up on behalf of the Russians. But the affair, with its hints of a secret Russo-American alliance, aided Seward's diplomacy, and passed into American folklore.

---

54. See Joseph W. Wieczerzak, *A Polish Chapter in Civil War America* (New York, 1967), especially Chapter 7. For writings on the "fleet" myth, see pp. 177-178. See also Albert A. Woldman, *Lincoln and the Russians* (New York, 1952). "Copperhead" and anti-war papers tended to be more pro-Polish, as did American ethnic papers for their own politico-religious reasons: e.g. *Chicago Times, Columbus Crisis, Boston Courier, New York Express, Irish American, New York Staats-Zeitung,* and *Echo z Polski.*

55. Sumner to Bright, October 6, 1863, q. Wieczerzak, p. 155.

56. F. A. Golder, "The Russian Fleet and the Civil War," *AHR*, XX, No. 4 (July, 1915), pp. 803-804.

Chapter XI

After Gettysburg

Fatalist acceptance of a protracted American war was deep set in Europe by mid-1863. It was not dispelled even by the striking victories of Meade and Grant in July. Gettysburg spelt the end of Lee's desperate last throw to achieve a peace settlement by an offensive feat of arms. But by good generalship and enemy indecision he had managed to keep intact the remnants of the Army of Virginia in its retreat across the Potomac. Meade's inability to interfere with Lee's escape was clear proof of the terrible price which the Federals paid at Gettysburg,

> . . . it should rather be said, perhaps, of the handbreath by which they escaped defeat . . . the moral to be drawn from it is the same which has been taught by many previous passages of the war. Neither of the two main armies can manage to make way in the country of its antagonist. . . .[1]

The huge strategic significance of the joint victories in the east and west eventually sunk in (Map 4). But the prospect of a quick peace was dashed by the failure of reunionist projects. Political squabbling and resistance to the draft in the north handicapped any rapid storming of the south. Seward's private opposition to the emancipation proclamation was well known; and he was reputed in July to be sponsoring negotiations with Confederate Vice-President, Alexander H. Stephens, and offering repeal of the proclamation as a preliminary step to reunification of the sections. Rumor had the cabinet

1. *Manchester Guardian*, July 20, 1863.

divided, Chase and Seward at loggerheads, and the Republican party split between its moderate and abolitionist wings. Seward's plan evoked no noticeable enthusiasm in Britain where there was growing acceptance of emancipation of the slaves. Even the *Glasgow Sentinel*, regarded as secessionist in sympathy, predicted that the emancipation edict,

> should it ever be fully acted upon, will be the glory of Lincoln's Presidentship, and to repeal it now would be an act of cowardice and imbecility . . . To have the Union recovered with a single slave state within its boundary is to run the risk of having the whole system reproduced . . . the confinement of slavery within a recognised Confederacy [east of the Mississippi] is the only solution of the American conflict our national sympathies can wish for.[2]

The New York draft riots occurred in July. Police in pitched battles reportedly shot tens of hundreds of rioters, the majority Irish-Americans, and public shock outside America sickened even ardent Unionists against the war. The riots had complex motivation: they were class insurrection against conscription laws which favored the rich ($300 was the price of exemption), an outgrowth of anti-Republican politics in New York, a sign of warweariness, and uncontrollable ghetto pogroms by the Irish against the Negro. The detested targets of the mob were the abolitionists. They were seen as bible-thumping ideologues for northern capitalism, which wanted to create cheap pools of labor from freed blacks. Caches of captured arms, and the presence of Copperheads among the gang leaders, caused accusations that the riots were a Confederate conspiracy, planned to coincide with Lee's attack on Washington. (Historians now dismiss this theory.) However, the atrocities perpetrated by the rioters—widespread Negro lynchings and murders, destruction of a hospital for black children—weakened sympathy for the uprising abroad, as did the anarchistic attack on property. In England moreover deeprooted national prejudice against the Irish, and the Irish disposition to rebellion (tabood in the context of British imperial control over Ireland), tempered horror at the Union's draconian war methods. (English methods had not been noticeably milder than the north's in past wars, although conscription was eschewed as a violation of the Englishman's historic liberties.) But in Ireland itself the riots catalyzed and confirmed opposition to the war and to forcible reconstruction of the Union.

---

2. *Glasgow Sentinel*, July 25, 1863.

They proved a propaganda bonanza to the south.[3] For Ireland they were probably the single most important happening of the war, the culmination of a progressive disillusionment with the north. Irish pride had been high, entering into legend and song, over the heroism of Irish-born troops fighting for the Union army. Meagher's Irish Brigade won immortal fame at home after being cut to pieces in direct assault upon Confederate entrenchments at Fredericksburg. But pride was overwhelmed by horror at the slaughter and feckless waste of life inflicted by northern generals. Earlier nationalist euphoria for the north—the democratic utopia, the emigrants' refuge from English tyranny—evaporated as the Irish-Americans emerged as victims of northern discrimination. "Our countrymen" according to the *Cork Examiner*,

> have played the part of dwarf in this war, to the giant—the Native Americans—the Know-Nothings—the abolitionists. They have fought the battles, got the blows, and bear the wounds, while their companions receive the glory and the plunder. For the latter are the colonelcies and the generalships, the army contracts, and all the other sources of honor and profit which a great war opens to the unscrupulous.

Now, through Congress's draft law of April 1863, the future of the Irish was proclaimed: they were to be cannon-fodder in an unwinnable war. The savage suppression of the uprising in July provoked wrath from all classes of Irish opinion, Catholic and Protestant, nationalist and conservative. Some saved the Irish name by denying Irish participation in the worst outrages, others defended men goaded beyond endurance. A leading Anglo-Irish paper, the conservative *Irish Times*, asked:

> . . . will the Irish soldiers continue to fight for a government which insists that the Irish should struggle for the aggrandizement of the North, perforce, or else be bayoneted, shot down, and blown to pieces by cannon in the streets of New York?

Despite the upswing in northern military fortunes from Gettysburg, Ireland was to remain a Confederate stronghold to the end of the war. After peace, a convenient lapse of Irish memories occurred. The Irish brigades who fought for the north were remembered,

---

3. Joseph Hernon, *Celts, Catholics and Copperheads* (Ohio State U.P., 1968), especially pp. 19-23 and *passim*. Following quotes from *Cork Examiner*, October 20, 1862, *Irish Times*, July 29, 1863, q. Hernon, p. 21. The reader is referred to Hernon's definitive work for analysis of the complexities of Irish opinion.

pacifism and rebel sympathies in Ireland itself were forgotten. Thus was historical legend adjusted fuzzily to accord better with the political alliance which grew up between the Irish independence movement and its American supporters.

In London news of Gettysburg and Vicksburg caused southern bonds to drop thirty-two points, and aided the Emancipation Societies in their propaganda war with the Dixie lobby, Henry Hotze conducting. As the cotton industry was showing signs of a leisurely, but encouraging, return to health, Richmond's pessimism about British intervention deepened. It became total when the ministry detained the Laird rams in early September. Historians once regarded the rams affair as the major crisis of the war.[4] It can no longer be seen in that light, but neither is it justly treated as a mere postscript to the momentous diplomacy of 1862, or a near-automatic working-out of British postures taken before Gettysburg. Genuine uncertainty lurked in the minds of English policymakers until the last moment concerning the proper course of action to be taken over the Birkenhead ships. Had the decision gone the other way—no doubt the odds in the historical calculus were longer against that chance—the course of Anglo-American relations over the next generation would have been even stormier. As it was, Americans threatened to visit their vengeance upon Canada in return for the devastation wreaked by the *Alabama* and its consorts. After the war, so astronomical was the damages bill served upon Britain for alleged violations of neutrality that men on both sides of the Atlantic considered swopping Canada for settlement of the account. The experts are now inclined to doubt that the Laird ironclads could have upset seriously the naval balance of the war.[5] But their release could well have smashed the uneasy diplomatic balance of the postwar years. Inescapably, the actors in the events had a more opaque perception of consequences than historians blessed with hindsight.

---

4. James Ford Rhodes, *History of the U.S. etc.* (N.Y. 1893-1906, 7 vols.), Vol. 4; Brooks Adams, "Seizure of the Laird Rams," *MHSP*, XLV (1911).

5. A rare admission of this from southern sources comes from the *Richmond Dispatch*, October 28, 1863, "Our Naval Heroes," which frankly admitted Confederate ownership of the rams. The *Dispatch* favored the building of more ships like the *Alabama*: ". . . we are inclined to think that such ships may be of more value to our cause than the rams, which are, after all, a problem so far as sea-going qualities are concerned, and which may never have come up to the expectations of the people in breaking the blockade . . . If we had only twenty Alabamas and Floridas upon the seas we could make the Northern cities howl, and cause the Stars and Stripes to trail ignominiously the waves of every sea."

The battles at Cemetery Ridge, where Lee lost vital casualties in frontal assault upon Meade's entrenched soldiers, and the siege of Vicksburg, which gave control of the Mississippi to Grant's army of the west, were barely over when Dudley and Adams moved to have the Laird rams seized. The launching for trials of one ram, the "294," forced Dudley to apply for detention from Liverpool customs on July 7. Adams took the case to Russell, although it was by no means watertight. The design of the ships was obviously warlike, and would have given the crown law officers their strongest case yet for testing the theory of "intent inferred through structure." On orders from Mallory the vessels had been planned specifically as blockade-breakers. According to Bulloch's expert specifications, Lairds were plating 350 horsepower, 10 knot cruisers with armor, and fitting turret batteries. (These recent innovations gave heavy firepower while permitting maneuverability and shallow draft for operations in American coastal waters and rivers.) Added to the prows were seven-foot iron piercers designed to sink wooden blockaders.[6] However, the *Alexandra* decision had rejected the theory by structure. As the rams lacked arms, ammunition, or legal signs of Confederate ownership, the law office was understandably dubious about its prospects of success in any prosecution. A lost case could mean heavy damages, although it might prove cheaper than Yankee revenge for what Moran dubbed England's "bastard neutrality."

Bulloch had been placed by Mallory in charge of the Confederate ironclad program abroad, a program at last efficiently backed by cotton bonds. He went to extreme lengths to disguise the rams' connections—nevertheless a matter of notoriety in Liverpool—and to keep the transaction with Lairds legal within the scope of the *Alexandra* ruling. In this he was eminently successful. Ownership was originally vested in Bulloch himself, but was transferred to a compliant French firm, owned by Francois Bravay who claimed to be acquiring the vessels for the Pasha of Egypt. Bravay's middle eastern connections gave color to the assertion. Such were the intricacies of the affair that a full scale mobilization of Foreign Office resources in Britain, France and Egypt, undertaken to justify the seizure, never entirely unearthed the facts.[7] Bulloch was

6. Merli, *Great Britain and the Confederate Navy*, pp. 179-180. In the following section I have relied heavily on the researches of Merli and Jones.

7. The British investigation is skillfully described by Jones, *Confederate Rams* Chapter 4. For the *Alexandra* Trial, above, Chapter 10, p. 292, and following.

nevertheless apprehensive. Rumors flew of imminent intervention by Her Majesty's government, whose advisers conducted an investigation of the ships in late July. Customs officials and northern spies haunted Lairds' yards, where workmen worked overtime under gaslight to speed the project. (Technical problems caused by Bulloch's design innovations had delayed the original deadline.) Bulloch had no alternative but to wait and hope, meanwhile trying to organize another warship program across the channel, Richmond's illusory second line of offense.

The north, as well as its enemy, had been left in unbearable suspense by the outcome of the *Alexandra* trial. Seward had been distinctly mollified by the original British seizure of the *Alexandra*. He ceased threatening to issue letters of marque if Britain failed to stop shipbuilding; and in August took Lyons with him on a symbolic joint tour of New York State (rather to the embarrassment of the shy Englishman). But if Seward believed that the crisis was over, that the British were now "pledged" to suppression of "unneutral" construction, the reception from mid-August of anxious dispatches from Adams threw the whole matter back into the melting pot.[8] Adams' diary entries, and the tone of his protests to the Foreign Office, attest to his belief in the menacing seriousness of the situation. It was now only too likely that Russell would profess his government hamstrung by Lord Chief Baron Pollock's ruling in the *Alexandra* trial. The British government was in a fork stick: the prospect of the rams' escape was becoming increasingly unpleasant, yet their stoppage could be effected only by an act outside the law. Legendary British respect for the rule of law, and the certainty of political embarrassment for the ministry, combined to make an arbitrary action distasteful. On the other hand, if Britain dodged its international obligations (as usual in a state of obscurity) by taking refuge behind inadequate domestic legislation, the United States might legitimately sue for reparations.

A strong note from Adams on July 11 (which spoke of "active malevolence" by Britain) had no apparent effect. Reports in late August suggested that the "294" was about to be towed to sea to

8. Cf. EDA, II, Chapter 13, especially 141 and following. Adams' cursory account of the rams crisis was a reaction to older versions: he justified brevity on the grounds that the British had made a firm commitment with the April seizure of the *Alexandra*, that an understanding existed between the British and the north (perhaps only tacit) on the point, that Russell's delays in acting against the rams caused a belated (but unfounded) American doubt of British sincerity. According to his reading, Russell's purpose throughout was to stop the rams; the whole crisis was phoney.

have its turret fitted, perhaps, like the *Alabama*, never to return. Foreign Office enquiries had begun to unearth mildly suspicious, but legally useless, information on the Bravay connection. Russell wavered until September 3. He was, according to Merli, "not fully satisfied with the advice of his legal advisers . . . [but was] reluctant to override it, especially if by so doing he appeared to be responsive to foreign pressure."[9] On September 1, Russell's attitude (as conveyed by Layard, his undersecretary, to the Home Office) was that the ironclads ought to be detained pending further investigation, but only "if sufficient evidence can be obtained to lead to the belief that they are intended for the Confederate States of America." The same day Russell, holidaying in Scotland, wrote to Adams declaring the government's inability to interfere with the ships on existing legal grounds: Dudley's depositions depended on hearsay evidence; the ships belonged to Bravay; and nobody had been able to disprove their Egyptian destination. However by the time Adams received this note, on September 4, and sent off an angry and famous reply, Russell had changed his mind. Arrangements were made to prevent the rams putting to sea until thorough investigations had been completed. This was acting on suspicion, but Roundell Palmer concurred in the measure "as one of policy though not of strict law."[10] The fact that the government had determined merely upon detention, and not yet upon seizure, rendered the act less challenging to the law. Roundell Palmer, Harcourt, and the *Times*, opposed repetition of government laxity as in the *Alabama* affair, and this may have carried weight with Russell. "We shall thus test the law," Russell told Palmerston, "and if we have to pay damages, we have satisfied the opinion which prevails here as well as in America, that that kind of neutral hostility should not be allowed to go on without some attempt to stop it."

Palmerston agreed, and the matter would no doubt have been quietly resolved and stirred little historical dust had not Adams—unaware of the turn in events—made a desperate last minute play to stop ironclads on "hostile errand" against his country. Historians

---

9. Merli, p. 199.

10. Russell to Palmerston, September 3, 1863, q. Jones, p. 72. Quote below from same letter. Russell requested a cabinet on the matter if Palmerston did not agree. Jones describes the events leading to seizure as "the climax, the crisis which caused the British Government to attach itself irrevocably to the policy of legal obstructionism." (p. 194). Moran thought it a "wonderful revolution of Ministerial policy." *Journal* (September 8, 1863) II, p. 1208. The move was generally supported by government officials and ministers although there were misgivings about its legality. See also p. 293 above, footnote 22.

have superabundantly demonstrated that Adams' September 5 note was penned two days *after* the critical British decision had been taken. Britain did not bow before this particular Yankee menace. Adams' tone was harsh: he regarded Russell's do-nothing approach as "opening to the insurgents full liberty in this kingdom," and in celebrated phrase stated: "It would be superfluous in me to point out to your Lordship that this is war." The language, however, was only a more provocative version of that used by Adams in his earlier July 11 protest. Then he had described the application of British industrial skill to this particular art of naval destruction as the "gravest act of international hostility yet committed." The rebels were waging war from Liverpool to break a fully recognized blockade. Americans had no choice but to regard British policy as "tantamount to a participation in the war by the people of Great Britain to a degree which . . . cannot fail to endanger the peace and welfare of both countries."

Having already retreated, the ministry had no relish for salt rubbed in the wounds. Moreover there was political peril in appearing to submit to bluster (as opposition sniping showed in the Parliamentary debates of early 1864 on the affair). "It seems to me" Palmerston coached Russell, "that we cannot allow to remain unnoticed his [Adams'] repeated and I must say somewhat insolent threats of war. We ought I think to say to him in civil Terms 'you be dammed'. . . ."[11] Honor was satisfied on both sides only after a choleric interchange of notes between Adams and Russell. Threats, said the Englishman, would not induce the government "either to overstep the limits of the Law or to propose to Parliament any new Law which they may not, for Reasons of their own think proper to be adopted." Adams denied being minatory, but submitted that "the interests of two nations are of too much magnitude to be measured by the infinitesimal scale of the testimony permissible before a jury in a Common Law Court."

The heated language should not be allowed to obscure the ultimately satisfactory outcome to all parties but that of the unlucky Bulloch. Adams suffered a snubbing from Russell, who made a point of going over his head to Washington on the topic, "These matters" he rebuked Adams, "will no doubt be duly and dispassionately considered . . . at Washington however they may

11. Palmerston to Russell, September 24, 1863, PRO 30/22/22 q. Jones, p. 77. For the battle of notes between Russell and Adams, Merli, p. 204 and following.

have been understood in London." But Adams won the larger battle of getting the rams stopped, a victory his son Henry regarded as a "second Vicksburg . . . the crowning stroke of our diplomacy":

> We come with victories on our standards and the most powerful military and naval engines that ever the earth saw. If our armies march on . . . [Henry forecast cynically]; above all if emancipation is made effective; Europe will blow gentle gales upon us and will again bow to our dollars.[12]

The ministry's position was still tricky legally, but became politically stronger as the facts of Bulloch's activities slowly turned up, and as public opinion solidified against a permissive stand dangerous to British naval and marine insurance interests. Palmerston's strong tactics in September were to pay off in the new year when the ministry parried a Conservative attempt to embarrass Russell for his handling of the affair. The government did better in Parliament than it might have expected or deserved, for it was susceptible to charges of illegal fiat by executive usurpation of Parliamentary right. Again, ministers who believed the enlistment act to be inadequate, yet who permitted politics to deter them from remedying its defects (or invoking other legislation, such as the customs act, to impose a license system upon trade in ships), were unimpressive claimants for statesmanship. But the debate is instructive, for it was entirely symptomatic of the death of America as an international issue for the British. The Opposition confined itself to scoring minor political points off a government which it had not the resources to replace. The critics did not declare for a reversal of policy on the rams, and showed no enthusiasm for resurrecting quarrels with the north when the world's attention was focused on the impending crisis of Schleswig-Holstein.

The south, as so often, turned out loser. Detention of the rams became seizure on October 8, 1863. The government disregarded a warning made earlier by its legal officers that seizure was probably unjustified by the evidence. Since then Bulloch's original ownership of the ships had been discovered; the Pasha of Egypt had disavowed interest in Bravay's ironclads; while scare rumors spread of a conspiracy to free the vessels from navy surveillance at Birkenhead. (The scare may have been deliberately manufactured by northern agents.) Against palpable Treasury trepidation the Foreign Office obtained a gunboat guard on the rams; and after hostile demonstrations

12. Henry Adams to Charles Francis Adams, Jr., September 16, 1863, q. Merli, pp. 209, 212. For the 1864 debate on the rams, Jones, pp. 105-108.

by Lairds' dockyard workers, had the rams moored under the guns of a British warship in the Mersey. No case can be made for British half-measures in what followed. With classical skill the ministry employed legal procrastination to prevent the release of the rams. They gave brusque regard to Lairds' or Bravay's property rights, thereby putting paid neatly to the south's naval program. The crown went to extraordinary lengths to build a cast iron prosecution case. Court proceedings were finally scheduled for May 1864 and then only after crown efforts had come to nothing to appeal against the inconvenient *Alexandra* ruling. For the hearing the Foreign Office tried to obtain an affidavit, sworn on the Koran, from the Viceroy of Egypt, and proposed to subject him to cross-questioning from crown and defense lawyers. A special delegation was sent to Cairo. The Pasha's refusal to compromise his dignity and political interests by appearing as a chief witness in these proceedings hampered the prosecution. As war seemed about to break out between Denmark and the German powers, the case was quietly dropped and the rams were brought from Bravay for the Royal Navy. The southern agents were let down by Napoleon III, who refused to press his British ally for the release of ostensibly French ships. It seemed necessary to Bulloch in May 1864 to cut his losses, retrieve £188,000 from the sale, and to contrive other means of continuing the naval war.

In the north, Anglophobia had been whipped up to the point of war hysteria on the rams affair. Charles Sumner denounced English neutrality in a celebrated oration at Coopers Institute, delivered (unluckily for Sumner) two days *after* Russell had ordered the rams detained. In the event Seward, not Sumner, got the credit for preserving peace, while England's retreat stopped Sumner from leading a noisy campaign for a war of revenge.[13] During the crisis even the sober *New York Times* was combative. It appealed to the precedent of the *Caroline* affair, set by the British during the Canadian rebellion (1837), to justify a punitive raid by the Union navy to destroy the rams in British port. The *Herald* demanded an embargo on English shipping, and the sequestration of property belonging to English firms, as soon as the "Anglo-rebel iron-clads" attacked northern forts: "Better war a thousand times with the

13. David Donald, *Charles Sumner and the Rights of Man* (New York, 1970), pp. 125-137. Donald argues that Sumner was trying to oust Seward from control of foreign policy. The oration was wrathfully received in Britain, alienating even Sumner's friends Richard Cobden and the Duchess of Argyll.

governments which are guilty of these mean and treacherous acts than to allow them to furnish our enemies with the means of destroying us." Although not the administration's attitude, this was not an unpopular response to what the *New York Times* described as "the most immediately threatening question in our foreign relations." Surprise and initial doubt of British sincerity greeted Russell's detention decision. "We . . . shall expect to hear" said Bennett, "that, by some quibble, the rams have evaded the restriction and sailed." British good faith seemed established with the October seizure, but cynical explanations of the change-of-face abounded. Greeley commented: ". . . only in proportion as the Confederacy began to show the clearest indications of a speedy collapse, the [British] Government awoke to a consciousness of its duties as a neutral power." W. C. Bryant's *Evening Post* was more charitable:

> . . . we have no doubt that England has been influenced by a growing enlightenment as to the merits of the case . . . we have had powerful advocates, not only in her eminent statesmen and writers, such as Bright, Cobden, Forster, Cairns, John Stuart Mill and others, but in her traditional anti-slavery policy and a genuine love of freedom and right which lies at the heart of her people. These have already overcome to a considerable extent the malice of her aristocracy and the cupidity of a part of her merchants. . . .[14]

The rebel press was despairing. "Water, salt or fresh, seems to be an element decidedly hostile to the Confederacy" reproved John Moncure Daniel's *Richmond Examiner.* Britain seemed in unholy, if uneasy, alliance with the north. Its policies helped to implement Union ocean strategy in order to maintain its own naval predominance.[15] Unparalleled invective was heaped upon Britain after the seizure of the rams, which gave impetus to the advocates of salvation through self-help. The *Richmond Dispatch* raged: "As for England, her course has been so decidedly hostile it is hard to say which are our bitterest enemies, she or the Yankees." Seizure, the editor thought, "would furnish ample ground for an instantaneous declaration of war." At the least economic retaliation must be tried: he urged the southern Senate to exclude England

14. See *NYT*, October 3, 1863; *NYH*, September 7; *NYT*, September 22; *NYH*, September 24; *NYDT*, September 24; *NYEP*, October 21; also *WDMC*, October 10.

15. See Davis' Message to Confederate Senate and H. of R., December 7, 1863, in *Richmond Dispatch,* December 9, 1863. The quotes in this paragraph come from: *Richmond Examiner,* October 7, 1863; *Richmond Dispatch,* September 29, October 24, October 10, 1863.

from the free trade Arcadia to be established after independence, and to offer a privileged position to her rival France. The *Dispatch* attributed British treachery to "the radical and fanatical influences of Exeter Hall," which had grasped the power reins from "the English aristocracy and the conservative middle classes, who embrace all the worth and intelligence of that country:"

> The swinish elements of her society, marshaled by a handful of aristocratic demagogues, have undermined the foundations of all that is venerable in the British Government. . . . The Confederacy is fighting [Britain's] own battles . . . of her commerce, trade, manufactures, and of those conservative political principles which are the only bulwark of England against the tide of republican democracy and anarchy which, unless checked here, will one day topple down her crown, her church, and her nobility, and finally their rulers in England, as they are aiming to do in America by the establishment of a vast military despotism.

In an analysis curiously reminiscent of antiradical northern writing, the editor proclaimed the "un-Americanism" of the Atlantic abolitionist movement, which had wrenched down the Union—and in doing so forever alienated both sections from the mother country. The true and latent forces of friendship between kindred peoples had been destroyed by the plots and subterfuges of malignant minorities in both countries. If the north won, let England look to her possessions in the hemisphere; if the south succeeded, it would remember the humiliations of 1863: ". . . the last strand of confidence and good feeling between Great Britain and the American States has parted forever, and can never again be restored."

The final estrangement soon took place between London and Richmond. In August Benjamin ordered Mason to withdraw from London at his discretion. He did not linger long. With a curt note to Russell on September 21, Mason ended his mission and joined Slidell in Paris. Napoleon was now the rebels' last foreign hope. "I am at a loss to understand why this step has been taken. . . ." Henry Adams wrote home:

> Mr. Mason's mere presence at this place has been a source of annoyance both to us and to the British Government. His departure will tend greatly to allay the dangers of our foreign affairs. Either England or France must take the brunt of our ill will. Why should Mr. Davis aid our diplomacy by himself directing all our causes of alarm towards France, a nation whose power we have no real cause to fear, and away from England, with whom we have been on the very verge of war?[16]

16. H. Adams to C. F. Adams, Jr., September 25, 1863; q. Ford, *Cycle*, II, p. 87.

In October, Benjamin, in the absence of the President, called together the Confederate cabinet and expelled all British consular agents from the Confederacy. This was an extraordinary step to be taken by a Secretary of State, but nobody objected. The act followed months of rancorous quarrels involving the consuls, state governors and Confederate officials. Attrition of the south's battered legions led the states to call up domiciled British subjects, and consular resistance to the moves stretched southern patience to the limit. There was precious little public sympathy for foreign draft-dodgers, many making a tidy profit from the war, or for Earl Russell's contortions in declaring that military service was not required of domiciled aliens in a civil war. (In normal war this was a belligerent right sanctioned by international law.) The Foreign Office advised that conscripted British citizens should throw down their arms in battle. Southerners read this as arrogant contempt for Confederate sovereighty. Sections of the press, most vociferously the anti-Davis papers, had long condemned the presence of consuls officially accredited to an enemy power. They were an offensive reminder of the world's humiliating refusal to acknowledge the south's nationality. But Davis and Benjamin had defended the practice by reference to states rights theory and expediency. With secession, they claimed, individual southern states had withdrawn the foreign relations power granted under the original compact to the Union, and conferred it upon the Confederacy. Exequaturs granted by the Union under that power retained validity, as the south honored constitutional obligations predating the rebellion. Further, the Confederacy had no desire to extort "inferential recognition" from outside nations by insisting upon new exequaturs.[17]

Official impatience with the consuls rose in June when the English agent George Moore was expelled from his Richmond post. Moore had protested against a new militia law in Mississippi—outside his jurisdiction—which permitted conscription of aliens. He topped this by accusing the War Department of despotic and brutal behavior in cases involving Irish-born conscripts, and blatantly disregarded the authority of Benjamin and the State Department. A British attempt to revoke Moore's exequatur, and appoint Cridland of Mobile in his stead, was rejected by Benjamin, who now forebade direct communication between consuls and the United States. The newspapers demanded the ejection of agents who took orders from

---

17. For details: M. L. Bonham, *British Consuls in the Confederacy* (N.Y., London, 1911), Vol. 43, *Columbia University Studies in History, Economics and Public Law*, 18, pp. 88-89; Owsley, Chapter 14.

Lyons, ambassador in an enemy capital, or who advised Englishmen not to serve in the army of an unrecognized "rebel" state. (Fullerton of Georgia and Walker of Charleston offended in the latter respect.) But the final break with England was really the culmination of a year of bitter affliction and frustration for Confederate diplomacy. Richmond's patience, so long primed by recurring reports of a British breakthrough, had finally run out. That was entirely understandable, given British nonrecognition, Russell's hauteur and cynicism on the blockade, and the seizure of southern ironclads. Some still made muted appeals for maintaining links with Britain on grounds of self-interest: renewed military success by the rebel armies might yet create conditions favorable to British mediation. But for the moment despairing pride and latent Anglophobia triumphed.

As opposing armies swept to and fro across huge areas of the southern homeland, devastating its resources, symptoms appeared of approaching collapse. Eroding morale bred more desperate schemes of salvation. After Gettysburg, R. G. H. Kean, head of the Bureau of War, memorialized Benjamin on the great need for a foreign alliance "even at the expense of some pride and independence:"

> It might be expedient to sound the Emperor of the French on the basis of large commercial privileges, a sort of protectorate guarantee of our territory, say 11 states, and entire freedom of domestic administration as to all laws and institutions, etc. This accepted would involve him at once in war with the United States but would give him control of cotton, abundance of ship timber and naval stores, and make France a first class naval power. War with Great Britain we would have to apprehend, but *per contra*, Great Britain would be benefitted by a hook being put in the nose of the United States. . . . I have conversed with several thoughtful persons who agree with my ideas on the subject.[18]

A similar blend of hopeful fantasy and despondent cynicism was to mark the south's last years of diplomacy. Benjamin may have been responding to Kean's plan when on August 4 he questioned Slidell on the feasibility of another cotton bribe. The Confederate government might offer to sell to Napoleon eight million dollars worth of cotton at the bargain price of 8 to 10 cents a pound. The move was made over the head of Treasurer Memminger, who did not relish such direct government intervention in economic

18. Edward Younger, ed., *Inside the Confederate Government: The Diary of Robert Garlick Hill Kean* (N.Y., 1957), p. 82. See also p. 42.

matters, but it aroused no interest in Paris.[19] However, there had been from the formation of the Confederacy a strong theme in press comment favoring the French as more reliable friends to the southern people than the British.[20] Faith in the French died hard, particularly when it became obvious that there was noone else to turn to.

Mexico seemed the obvious theater to apply leverage on the French. Accustomed to regard Central America as their natural sphere of influence, southern officials expected to manipulate, not to be manipulated, with respect to Mexico. They adjusted slowly to the realization that Paris and Richmond were at dangerous cross-purposes on the matter. The infant Confederacy's first bearings toward its neighbor had been predatory: agents such as John T. Pickett hardly concealed their belief that northern Mexico's "boundless agricultural and mineral resources" were staked out for the south, or that access to the Pacific across the Isthmus was vital to their nation's future. Projects of expansion were discussed with quasi-independent chieftains of the area such as Santiago Vidaurri, who was anxious to head a league of states allied with the south. Vidaurri was reported willing even to annex his "Republic of Sierra Madre" (centered on the states of Coahuila and Nuevo León) to the Confederacy (see Map 6). As long as the war made overriding demands on rebel energies, and as long as it was expedient not to upset the French, Richmond's ambitions were kept subdued. But southerners shared with northerners the confidence that imperial success went to peoples who could colonize from short range, using emigration and commercial control to fasten an unchallengable grip on new lands. The end of the war would see the fulfilment of southern territorial destiny. The French, for all their high phrases on the superiority of the Latin races, feared such an outcome: there is an underlying thread of worry in their Mexican correspondence to that effect. Hence the attractiveness of the idea of containing the south by bartering for Union acquiescence in the Maximilian experiment. Ultimately the two sections might be

19. Meade, *Benjamin*, pp. 292-293; Blumenthal, *Fr. Am. Rels.*, pp. 160-161. On the illicit trade in cotton between southerners and the Federal invaders during the latter phase of the war, see T. H. O'Connor, "Lincoln & the Cotton Trade," *CWH*, VII (1961), pp. 20-35.

20. There is an analysis of southern newspapers in Caroline Ayling, *The Confederates' Relations with France and Britain during the Civil War* (Unpublished thesis, B.A. Hons., 1969, University of Queensland).

CALIF.
N. MEX. TER.
TEXAS
El Paso
SONORA
Rio Grande
CHIHUAHUA
Chihuahua
COAHUILA
NUEVO LEÓN
Monterrey
Matamoros
TAMAULIPAS
Gulf of California
Gulf of Mexico
DURANGO
Mazatlán
Tampico
San Luis Potosí
PACIFIC OCEAN
Mexico City
Vera Cruz
Puebla
Isthmus of Tehuantepec
Mexico

played against each other. Napoleon would have found acceptable a package deal by which the United States gave a genuine undertaking not to intervene in Mexico (irrespective of the Civil War's outcome) and recognized Maximilian's government, in return for the withdrawal of French troops and French refusal to recognize or aid the Confederacy. He didn't get it, but he thought he had got something near it from Seward which would do as well (especially if the south won). The alternative of a Franco-Confederate alliance not only raised a host of unsurmountable domestic and international problems, it posed two other nasty possibilities: lasting enmity from the United States in the hemisphere; and a potential takeover bid for parts of Mexico by dynamic allies quite capable of penetrating local centers of power.

On June 10, 1863, Mexico City was once more in its history occupied by foreign troops. Against spirited resistance by Juârez's guerrillas, exciting respect in the United States, General Forey's reinforced army captured Puebla in May, and then marched successfully on the capital. Forey formed a provisional government, his nominees making up an assembly of 215, with an executive junta of thirty-five electing a ruling committee of three. Supposedly exercising the people's right of self-government, the handpicked new regime voted on July 11 for a monarchy. It offered the imperial crown to Maximilian (or to any other Catholic prince acceptable to Napoleon III). The United States State Department formally treaded with restraint, but never considered these proceedings as anything other than an exercise in political rigging, Bonapartist-style. In fact the settlement was a *fait accompli* by the French military, who acted without waiting advice from Paris. Napoleon's strategy, at least until Gettysburg, had been flexible. Had Maximilian withdrawn his candidature, as seemed likely on a number of occasions, Napoleon was willing to consider other than monarchical institutions for Mexico. During the January project for mediation, when French optimism flared over peace prospects in America, Napoleon and his foreign minister had meditated an ingenious hemispheric solution to the American problem.[21] Both northern and southern expansionist tendencies might be curbed, and a satisfactory balance of power created, by setting up a "hyphenated confederation." Modeled on Germany, and administered by a diet

21. "Note on Affairs of Mexico and the U.S., January 21, 1863," *Corresp. Politique, Mexique*, LX, q. Kathryn A. Hanna "The Roles of the South in the French Intervention in Mexico," *JSH*, XX, No. 1 (February 1954), pp. 9-10.

similar to that of Frankfurt, the confederation would consist of roughly equal states: the North, the South, the West, and Mexico. The plan was kept top secret, as it would have pleased nobody but the French. While the United States would be completely dismembered, there were intimations that a French-controlled Mexico would be expanded to include Texas, and possibly the old colony of Louisiana.

Richmond was already worried that the French coveted Texas. Saligny, once *charge d'affairs* in the Texan Republic and now the French representative in Mexico City, favored the detachment of Texas. Theron, the French vice-consul at Galveston, was suspected by the Texan governor, Francis R. Lubbock, of conspiring to the same end. Lubbock's complaints to Davis resulted in Theron's expulsion in the fall of 1862. Tabouelle, chancellor of the French consulate at Richmond, had his functions temporarily suspended at the same time for pumping Senator Oldham of Texas on his state's resources.[22] Benjamin reported on these intrigues to his agents abroad, but his dispatches were captured and published in the north. In them was blazoned forth Benjamin's distrust of Napoleon III, suspected of resurrecting France's old Texan policy of creating a client buffer state to obstruct southern imperialism. The Emperor was further accused of wanting to secure an independent source of cotton supply to offset that possessed by Britain in India. Edward Everett, now special adviser to the State Department, added his authority to the view that France was reviving visions of a project which it had attempted in 1844—namely, to join together in a dynamic and independent league Texas, the Mexican territories west of Texas to the Pacific, including California, the northern states of Mexico, and possibly Louisiana.[23] The south predictably would be resentful of latter day efforts to create a "larger Texas" affiliated to Paris.

Seward, as with the Polish issue, hewed scrupulously to a policy of nonintervention and neutrality, the attitudes he expected of overseas governments to American issues. Outright support for Juárez would have appealed to the Hispanic Americans and to northern emotion. But it might also precipitate French intervention and create a Franco-Confederate alliance. (Richmond was puzzled that so obvious a means of protecting the French expeditionary force from Union interference had not been embraced by Paris.) On the other hand, too soft a policy on Seward's part might have

22. Hanna, p. 10.
23. *NYT*, February 20, 1863.

unduly encouraged the French campaign against Juárez' irregulars—it had seemed to be bogging down in the first part of 1863—and undermined Seward's domestic political position. He has been rightly praised for skill in following a difficult middle path which preserved the forms of Franco-American amity, avoided diversions the Union could not afford ("why should we gasconade about Mexico when we are in a struggle for our own life?" he asked Bigelow), while "compromising nothing, surrendering nothing."

The French and Yankees avoided acute antagonism by choosing their own interpretations of French intentions. Seward professed to rely upon assurances that France abstained from "political change which should be in opposition to the will of the Mexican people." He ignored the subtle but menacing qualifications which the French added to this formula as their military campaign prospered. They would not interfere in the Mexican form of government, but they would have no objection if anarchy was ended, or if the Mexicans chose a monarchy (April, 1862). A year later, they had no intention of "controlling" the government of Mexico. At the outset of French action, Seward had offered the unsolicited advice: a monarchical government established by foreign force "has no promise of security or permanence." A new government headed by a "person alien to Mexico" would fall unless sustained by European alliances, while the return of the powers to the American continent was opposed to the historical trend of the century. The United States was neutral, but its sympathies were openly on the side of hemispheric republicanism.[24] This was worrisome to Napoleon. Seward had referred to peaceful forces which ensured ultimate American hegemony in the area—expanding population, limitless resources, the attraction of American democracy. But it was not clear if the Union would go to war or not over French armed intervention "for political ends" in a neighboring republic. This uncertainty was Seward's trump card. The defeat of the French at Puebla in May 1862, the famed Cinco de Mayo, struck a severe psychological blow at their military morale, more severe than Seward realized. He was able to capitalize richly on the subsequent reluctance of the Emperor to risk his mercenaries against highly trained Union forces. Confederate hopes of recognition broke on this rock, for Napoleon preferred to finesse a friendly Union into grudging acceptance of the Maximilian

24. Seward to U.S. legations, March 3, 1862, q. J. F. Rippy, *The United States and Mexico* (N.Y., 1926), pp. 258-259. For the role of the Juáristas, Walter V. Scholes, *Mexican Politics During the Juárez Regime, 1855-1872* (Columbia, Missouri, 1957).

regime than to provoke more overt northern financial and military aid for Juárez.

While Forey's occupation of Mexico City might have been expected to strengthen French commitment in Central America, appearances were deceptive. Gettysburg and Vicksburg underlined Union power, and enabled Seward to tighten the screw. The United States refused to recognize the anti-Juárez provisional government, and in August withdrew Corwin to Washington. In the American view the existence of the Juárez government at the town of San Luis Potosí indicated the continuance of a state of civil war. Through Dayton, Seward expressed continuing concern that the French might betray their pledge against annexation. Napoleon was advised "that a solution of the present complications of Mexico be made, as early as may be convenient, upon the basis of the unity and independence of Mexico." Hints were made that the Lincoln government with difficulty resisted popular clamor for a more martial policy against Napoleon's puppet state. But there were other pressing factors urging Napoleon to extricate himself from the Mexican morass.

One was the war's general unpopularity in France, clearly demonstrated in the June elections of 1863. Considerable gains were made by republicans and anticlericals, a sign that political fortune was beginning to run once again in favor of the anti-Austrian, pro-Italian faction at court and against the conservative and clerical advocates of monarchy in Mexico.[25] Most significant of all, Napoleon's *raison de'être* for all-out support of Maximilian—the hope of making a package deal with Austria which should net Venetia for the Italians—had disappeared as Austro-French relations deteriorated. New world complications now emerged as contributing factors in weakening both France and Austria, thus paving the way for the hegemony of Prussianized Germany in Europe in the latter nineteenth century. Napoleon hoped to obtain the critical support of Austria for his Polish policy by dangling certain prizes before the Habsburgs: French friendship (insurance against Prussia), the division of Italy, vaguely specified gains in Silesia and the Danubian provinces, plus the gift of the Mexican throne to a Habsburg prince. The price Austria would be required to pay was high—loss of Venetia to Italy and Galicia to a reconstructed Poland—and on March 27, 1863, after serious consideration, Austria made its

25. Nancy N. Barker, "France, Austria, and the Mexican Venture, 1861-1864," *French Hist. Stud.* (1963-1964), p. 229 and following. Barker's interpretation is followed below.

fateful rejection of the terms. Playing its part in the decision was Austrian reluctance to be associated with the Napoleonic theory of nationalities (an acute embarrassment for the multinational Habsburg empire), or with Napoleonic designs to redraw the map of Europe. Relations between Paris and Vienna worsened as the Emperor accused the Habsburgs of dragging their feet over Poland out of fear of offending Russia. (The Austrians were in fact secretly assuring the Russians that the western protests were mere talk.) Understandably, Napoleon no longer felt much incentive to continue an expensive and difficult campaign in Mexico which would gain no rewards in Europe. Late in 1863 he admitted to Sir Charles Wyke, former British *charge d'affaires* in Mexico: "I realize that I have gotten myself into a tight corner, but the affair has to be liquidated." When he publicly accepted the principle of Italian unity, he also pronounced the closure of his grand project.

The Emperor's unscrupulously pursued objective hereafter was to install Maximilian in Mexico with minimum French commitments, and to leave the archduke to his own resources as soon as possible. Maximilian could not resist the temptation of the throne. Too ready to take at face value Napoleon's indefinite talk of French protection for the new empire, he allowed himself to be maneuvered into a dangerous position. Austria was in no position to extract guarantees of support from the Tuileries for Maximilian. It had formally dissociated itself from the Mexican affair, and feared a storm of anger from Napoleon who was already deeply offended at Austrian "ingratitude." Once again the course of events in America was to be shaped by European power politics. In November, 1863, Austria effectively refused to participate in Napoleon's grand plan for a congress of nations which should settle Poland and other European questions. Napoleon was furious. Austria formed an alliance with Prussia involving joint invasion of the Danish provinces of Schleswig-Holstein, claimed by Prussia. In February 1864 the allies entered Denmark, alarming Napoleon and the rest of Europe. Vienna strove desperately to head off possible French retaliation against Venetia and other vulnerable provinces of the sprawling Habsburg empire. Maximilian's negotiations with Napoleon took place at this unlucky time, and a promise of French neutrality over Denmark enabled the Emperor to take a hard line on Mexico.

In the convention of Miramar, Maximilian had finally to be content with a guarantee that French troops would gradually withdraw from Mexico over a three-year period, leaving a rearguard of 20,000 men in 1867. This fell far short of his earlier requirement of a joint Franco-British guarantee of the empire, a loan and a military occupation of up to 15 years. Maximilian obtained his agreement at fearful cost. France promised not to fail the empire "however events in Europe turn out," but the convention was silent on new world developments: "Napoleon did not pledge himself to defend the new empire from its enemies. In view of the hostile attitude of the United States, this was a major omission."[26] Mexico promised to bear the expense of the occupying troops, and to indemnify France for the cost of intervention (presumably from the fabled wealth of the Sonora mines). This satisfied the demands of the French chambers, but it augured ill for the prospects of Maximilian's empire, soon wracked by factional rivalries, burdened by debt, and menaced by the local nationalists.

Neither Richmond nor Washington appreciated the real significance of these secret negotiations. The Confederate government had anticipated no hitch in exchanging ambassadors with the provisional government newly set up in Mexico City. That achieved, recognition would then be exacted from Napoleon: "France needs an ally as a shield to interpose between her new province of Mexico and the gigantic power of the United States."[27] In October 1863, the rumor spread that the Marquis de Montholon, who represented the second empire at Mexico City, had personally pressed Napoleon to recognize the south. Otherwise, the Marquis reputedly said, Napoleon might as well renounce the idea of founding a throne in Mexico. Napoleon did not respond, and by the year's end it was clear that the south needed to do more than talk.[28]

On January 7, 1864, William Preston, a former United States minister to Spain who commanded a unit at Chickamauga, was appointed Confederate envoy to Mexico. To those who thought the

---

26. Barker, p. 238.

27. *Richmond Examiner,* July 21, 1863.

28. The *Richmond Sentinel* (re-established in March as a pro-government organ) preached realism:

> ". . . we must place no reliance upon Napoleon or Maximilian for direct and material aid in our war . . . Napoleon, what with European complications and the Mexican war has his hands full . . . and Maximilian . . . will have an arduous task to keep peace at home without engaging in war abroad. Yet the time must come and cannot long delay when a common interest will bring about intimate and friendly relations between Mexico and the Confederacy . . . neither Mexico nor Central America can ever be safe from the ambitious and rapacious designs of the United States and *England* except by entering into close alliance with the Confederacy."

Richmond Sentinel, November 18, 1863.

Monroe Doctrine banned new European imperialisms from the hemisphere, Jefferson Davis had a simple answer: "If the Mexican people prefer a monarchy to a republic, it is our plain duty cheerfully to acquiesce in their decision. . . ." (Message to Congress, December 8, 1863). Before making the appointment, Benjamin had received overtures from Juan Almonte, regent in Mexico pending Maximilian's arrival. The overture came in December through the south's man in Monterey, Juan Quintero, who conveyed Almonte's anxiety to receive a commissioner from Richmond. Almonte revealed that he had advised Napoleon to recognize the Confederacy. At this time Maximilian himself simplistically identified the fortunes of his empire and that of the south. In December 1863 the archduke went out of his way to inform Davis, through Slidell, that he regarded Anglo-French recognition of the Confederacy as a precondition for his acceptance of the crown. His insistence was short-lived; this became another of the "essential guarantees" he was forced to sign away in the convention of Miramar.

Preston and his friends were to find official doors shut to them in Mexico and Europe. Preston's persistence and peregrinations deserved better reward. After a fruitless stay in Havana waiting to be welcomed to Mexico, Preston journeyed to London and Paris, where he and Slidell worked unavailingly to negotiate with Maximilian. Napoleon, it proved, had no intention of having his hands tied over Mexico through Maximilian's impulsiveness. Maximilian was informed that it would be inconvenient for France if he opened official relations with the Confederacy. (The evidence, at least, points strongly to this conclusion.) At the time of the Miramar signing (March 1864) Slidell was cold-shouldered by Maximilian. Slidell and Preston became impatient and angry, and tried veiled threats with Maximilian's Mexican advisers Estrada, Hidalgo, and Arrangoiz. Such threats were to become a feature of the south's desperate final diplomacy. France should beware lest a reconciled north and south enforced the Monroe Doctrine, and extinguished the new monarchy. Drouyn was also served this notice. Already alarmed by moves in the United States Congress demanding withdrawal of French troops in Mexico, Drouyn must have felt caught in a tightening trap.

Had the French or Maximilian known the secret terms of Preston's commission, they may have congratulated themselves on keeping a dangerous ally at arms length. If the chance offered itself, the southern price for a treaty of alliance with Mexico was to be raised to include "the right of free passage across Chihuahua and Sonora to Guaymas which would be of great value to Texas and Arizona."[29] The Sonora mines would be exposed to southern avarice. Portent of a possible future westward thrust of Confederate power was given in the plans of Matthew F. Maury—the same oceanographer and geopolitician of antebellum fame—for the annexation of California to Mexico. In letters to Maximilian in late 1863, Maury offered himself as a commander of imperial ironclads to do the job.[30]

Meanwhile, undercurrents accompanying the Miramar negotiations suggested that Seward had cleverly outflanked the rebels. Rumor had it that a bargain had been struck between Lincoln and Napoleon: Washington would recognize Maximilian if France abandoned plans of acknowledging the south. The southern lobby wrathfully accused Seward of inspiring the leak to sabotage the Preston mission. Seward certainly reaped the harvest, but the deception (according to one historian) was Napoleon's.[31] He was floating a trial balloon. Even temporary northern tolerance of the Maximilian regime would ease his problems: his objective was swift extrication from Mexico without losing face by appearing to act under northern pressure. For that he was willing to talk of troop withdrawals and an ultimate end to intervention. But without some sign of American restraint French troops must stay to bolster Maximilian. This would be criticized in France, and was a needless contradiction of the thesis that the monarchy was popularly based in Mexico.

Seward was in no position to offer as much as Napoleon wanted, or the south feared. But he took care to hold out some carrots for the Emperor, while making sure that his declared policy had the stamp of appropriate firmness. The French hoped to give an aspect of legitimacy to the new empire by means of carefully managed plebiscites, but the official Union reaction verged upon an accusation of fraud. The installation of Maximilian seemed to depart "very materially" from imperial assurances of free choice of institutions for the Mexican people and speedy withdrawal after liquidation of French claims.[32] But subsequent silence from

---

29. P. W. Kennedy, "Union and Confederate Relations with Mexico," *Duquesne Rev.*, XI, p. 60.

30. Hanna, pp. 13-14.

31. Owsley, p. 526 and following. Benjamin feared that Seward would go to extreme lengths to frustrate Preston's overtures; he warned that Seward would offer an alliance between the north and Maximilian to keep the south isolated.

32. See Seward to Dayton, February 13, 1864, q. Owsley, p. 517.

Washington indicated that no further action was contemplated until conditions were ripe to enforce reparation. Indeed Mercier had been primed by Seward to hope for ultimate acceptance of Maximilian's *fait accompli.* After all, as Mercier reported home, from 1863 the U.S. had refrained from open protest at the establishment of a monarchy; Seward had damped down inflammatory tendencies in Congress (with the aid of Sumner, devoted to "one war at a time"); while Juárez found himself kept prudently at arms length by the State Department. Incensed that the French had been allowed to collect a large army and navy in the Gulf without complaint by the Union, Romero (Juárez's representative in Washington) protested early in 1864 that strict neutrality had not been observed in the Mexican civil war.[33] Mercier, in behind-the-scenes interview with New York financial interests, acquired an impression that business was not averse to a *modus vivendi* with the French which should permit opportunities for American economic penetration of the area. The motives of American business have not been recorded, but they may not have been unlike those of the anticolonialists of the McKinley era who deemed formal American control of potential markets unnecessary to economic expansion. Peace and reconstruction of a normal economy probably assumed a higher priority in their minds, and would more rapidly create economic dependencies abroad, than filibustering in the name of Monroe. Nor should Seward's caution be attributed entirely to a temporary failure of American military strength. His too was a faith in the inevitability of the historical forces dictating peaceful conquest of the continent by the North Americans. As he told Bigelow:

> . . . those who are most impatient for the defeat of European and monarchical designs in Mexico might well be content to abide the effects which must result from the ever-increasing expansion of the American people westward and southward. Five years, ten years, twenty years hence, Mexico will be opening herself as cheerfully to American immigration as Montana and Idaho are now. What European power can then maintain an army in Mexico capable of resisting the martial and moral influences of emigration?[34]

---

33. On Romero's able diplomacy, Robert R. Miller, "Matias Romero: Mexican Minister to the United States during the Juárez-Maximilian Era," *Hispanic Am. Hist. Rev.*, XLV (1965), pp. 228-245.

34. Quoted James M. Callahan, *American Foreign Policy in its Mexican Relations* (New York, 1932), p. 297.

Chapter XII

The South in Extremity

As the tide of war slowly turned against the south, the diplomatic focus of the powers changed from projects of interference and positive action to defensive strategies devised to protect national interests against a revanchist United States. The success of northern foreign policy in the war's closing phase was essentially the product of this situation, whose potentialities Seward exploited with high competence. Unavoidably, Canada and Mexico became major theaters in which were played out the underlying international tensions of the time. Behind the shadow-boxing there lay the real menace of blows, for the world's greatest military machines now rolled in North America.

In Canada, Confederate activity caused a series of crises which plagued Anglo-American relations between Gettysburg and Appomattox, turning the border with America into an armed frontier.[1] Like neutral countries in the world wars of the twentieth century, Canada was a hotbed of wartime intrigue and a center of rival intelligence networks. British neutrality had been carefully observed in the provinces; but that task became more arduous as Confederate bands—at first without official backing—plotted hit-and-run attacks into the north from neutral territory. Paradoxically the raids produced closer cooperation between the colonial and American authorities at the same time that they heightened acrimony between

1. See Winks, Chapters 8-17. Winks' definitive research provides the foundation for the following account.

the neighboring peoples. When this was required to protect Canadian neutrality, Monck and his officials passed on to Washington news they obtained of rebel plots, and enforced sanctions against unneutral activities. Naturally, this did not sit well with Richmond or with the numerous and vocal southern sympathizers in the provinces.

In November 1863 Monck informed Seward of a "serious and mischievous plot" by rebels in the Canadas to release Confederate prisoners of war held on Johnson's Island. Just off Sandusky, Ohio, on Lake Erie, the camp held more than two thousand Confederate officers, including Morgan's raiders, and was guarded by the U.S.S. *Michigan*, part of the American naval contingent permitted on the lakes under the Rush-Bagot agreement. Schemes to rescue the prisoners became a feature of the war. In this instance, the plotters were financed by Confederate Secretary of Treasury Memminger and supported by Benjamin. Quick action by Union Secretary of War Stanton, who moved to place the border area on alert, caused the abandonment of the plot. The affair quickened border nervousness, but Monck's warning won praise from the northern press, even from the *Herald* (whose personal column had been exploited to organize the raid). The British were blamed in the Confederacy for aborting the raid.

In December, however, the south came close to getting its war between the hated Yankees and British when the *Chesapeake* capture "created a situation potentially as explosive as the 'Trent' affair."[2] Masterminded by the London-born adventurer John C. Braine, the conspiracy was hatched in New Brunswick in the autumn. Together with Vernon Locke, a Canadian citizen long resident in South Carolina, and a group of others (the majority British subjects), Braine planned to seize the American-owned coasting steamer *Chesapeake*, which worked the New York-Portland run. Under the dubious authority of a Confederate letter of marque held by Locke, under another name and applying to a vessel which had been captured in the Bahamas, the *Chesapeake* would be converted into a rebel privateer. Posing as passengers, sixteen men captured the steamer on the high seas on December 7, killing the second engineer. Short of coal, the *Chesapeake* was cornered in Sambro harbor, Nova Scotia, by the U.S.S. *Ella and Annie*. Abandoned by almost all of the conspirators, the *Chesapeake* was seized in British waters by the Union warship, which also boarded and searched a Nova Scotian vessel carrying coal to the "prize." A

2. Winks, p. 244.

Nova Scotian raider, John Wade, was captured. On the order of Navy Secretary Welles, the *Chesapeake* was handed over to the colonial authorities at Halifax. Under Halifax batteries, and with an angry pro-southern crowd on Queen's Wharf, Nova Scotian officials demanded the release of the captured Nova Scotian Wade. Five Federal gunboats in the harbor were poised for action. "A shot from the shore, accidental or planned, might have drawn return fire that would have wrought havoc in Halifax, a flimsy city of wood."[3] Eventually Wade was taken ashore, in chains, but intervention by onlookers prevented his arrest by county marshal, and Wade escaped.

Seward (remembering the *Trent* fiasco) promptly denied that the United States had authorized or countenanced any violation of Nova Scotian authority. But he hammered at the British for ineffective enforcement of their neutrality laws. Withdrawal of the south's belligerent rights, he claimed, was justified by the incident. Withdrawal would be a friendly gesture which would assist him in keeping the question of terminating the reciprocity treaty from the floor of the House of Representatives, as wanted by the House Ways and Means Committee. Adams was asked to revive in London the whole question of the Queen's proclamation, whose injustice was by now Seward's *idee fixe.* But Winks considers that Seward and Lyons handled the affair well and quietly (explaining its scant attention in the history books). Moreover the colonial and northern press, war-weary, behaved with restraint. The complicated issues at stake emerged in three court trials which grew out of the affair from December to March in Nova Scotia and New Brunswick. Benjamin assigned J. P. Holcombe, professor of law at the University of Virginia, to assess whether the case might be turned to the south's advantage. Holcombe advised inertia: neither Braine nor Locke had lawful claim to Confederate citizenship, while Locke had violated both Confederate and British law in using a letter of marque issued to another person. The magistrate presiding over the first trial (New Brunswick, February 24) decided that the raid was piracy and not an act of war. This was upset when a higher court ruled that if piracy was the offense, proceedings should have begun in a United States court. Imprisoned conspirators, arrested through the zeal of provincial officials, were discharged on the ground of incorrect processing of their arrest warrant. Seward did not press for extradition: to execute British subjects for piracy

3. Winks, p. 251.

would needlessly have invited discord. The *Chesapeake* was returned to its owners as the victim of piracy, a decision made by the Halifax Vice-Admiralty Court in February. But the border remained tense. Scares multiplied of daring Confederate exploits being planned against Yankee ships at sea, and on the lakes and canals, or of harassment of Union military and civil targets from provincial bases. Maine, Vermont, and Upper New York clamored for protection, and General John A. Dix, commanding the eastern military district, was sent to control the American side of the frontier.

Confederate hopes were pinned less on the direct military, than on the diplomatic, repercussions of their guerrilla activities in the provinces. Richmond, after its break with England, became more willing to risk irritating London by taking a highly flexible view of its belligerent rights in the Canadian theater. Previously, no sideshows had been allowed which might interfere with the European intrigues of Mason and Slidell. By 1864, Europe was embroiled in the Schleswig-Holstein emergency, and passive to the American question.

The fact was neatly illustrated in the final demise of the south's shipbuilding program. As insurance against the collapse of the Laird rams project Bulloch had turned to France. By July 1863 he had contracted for the construction of six warships—including two ironclad rams—in Bordeaux and Nantes, under the auspices of the leading firm of Arman.[4] Napoleon (who had not hesitated to egg on such a scheme as early as October 1862) allowed Slidell to believe that he would turn a blind eye to the armoring of the vessels and their secret delivery into Confederate hands. But when the nature of Arman's activities was revealed to the United States embassy by a French informant (an employee in the Nantes shipping yard who conveniently supplied original documents showing that Arman intended fraudulently to arm the ships and send them to the rebels), Napoleon was embarrassed. After prolonged diplomatic pressure by the United States, the Emperor was forced to crack down upon the conspiracy. Playing a key role in his calculations was fear of angering Washington at a delicate stage in his effort to obtain northern acceptance of Maximilian as emperor of Mexico. In May 1864, Drouyn directed Arman and his agents, on pain of government seizure of the vessels, to make a *bona fide* sale of the ships to a neutral government. Arman managed, in violation of this order

4. The intricate details of Confederate naval construction in France are recounted in Case and Spencer, Chapter 13. Artillery for the rams was being built by the British firm of Armstrong.

and to Drouyn's anger, to spirit one ironclad, the *Stonewall*, to southern hands, after an attempted sale to Denmark had fallen through. Unseaworthy and poorly designed, it arrived in the American theater too late to participate in the war. In June 1864, the *Alabama*'s career finally ended when it was sunk off Cherbourg by the U.S.S. *Kearsarge*. Other southern raiders were bottled up in neutral ports, including the *Rappahannock*, detained at Calais. There were few consolations left for Bulloch and his team. One of them arose out of a brilliant coup by which the Confederacy purchased the graceful but deadly Clyde-built *Sea King*, which became the renowned *Shenandoah*.[5]

It was becoming clear to Richmond that Britain and France could be stirred to blows against the north only through hemispheric agitations, if at all. Jefferson Davis, in April 1864, appointed a three man commission in British North America. Their verbal instructions said little concerning British neutrality, and left much to the agents' discretion. Their job was to "crystallize anti-Northern feeling in Canada and mould it into some form of hostile expression." Where possible they were to lend aid to the antiwar movement in the north, and promote opposition to Lincoln in the November presidential election. Conditions seemed auspicious for the mission. Joshua Giddings, the ageing and inefficient consul-general at Montreal, had launched a campaign at Washington against the reciprocity treaty—in pique, it seems, at personal insults he had earned in Canada. (His death in May was an inconvenience for the south.) The election of the Liberal-Conservative coalition under John A. Macdonald and Etienne Tache brought to power in the united Canadas a party dedicated to Canadian union. The stock-in-trade of the "confederationists" was fear of American expansionism, and the necessity of political centralization to provide effective defense against the future menace of Grant's army. In the event, the new government's policy turned out to be cautious toward a prickly neighbor, awaiting the movement to mature for closer union. But the materials lay at hand for anti-Yankee propaganda. As commissioners, Davis appointed Jacob Thompson (Buchanan's Secretary of the Interior, an able politico), Clement C. Clay (former Alabaman senator, ill and ineffectual), and the inexperienced Holcombe. Closely associated with the mission was the Kentuckian Thomas Hines, sent by Secretary of War Seddon to Toronto to dispatch a marauding band of rebel soldiers into the north. Placed under

---

5. See Merli, Chapter 11.

Thompson's wing, Hines was instructed to observe British neutrality. The originator of the St. Albans' raid, George Sanders, a fiery "Young Americanist" of Pierce's era, joined the group, which was reportedly financed to the tune of a million dollars.

Thompson's aspiration of remaining within the letter of the law was tested in the ambitious Lake Erie raid of September, 1864. It was planned by the Virginian, John Yates Beall, and endorsed by Thompson. On September 19, Beall and a group of Confederates took control of the lake steamer *Philo Parsons* on the American side of Lake Erie. Another steamer was scuttled to prevent its crew raising an alarm. Beall planned to board the U.S.S. *Michigan*—its captain and crew previously drugged by an accomplice—which would then train its guns on Johnson's Island while Confederate prisoners were freed. The accomplice was discovered and Beall, realizing the scheme had miscarried, scuttled the *Philo Parsons* off Windsor. He was arrested in December after failing to derail an express near Buffalo, in order to free Confederate officers; and was executed for sabotage and treason. The plot had been prepared in Windsor, underlining northern complaints that Canada was becoming a rendezvous and base for Confederate subversives. In self-protection the Americans unofficially—they hoped temporarily—suspended the Rush-Bagot arms limitation on the lakes. Without publicity, armed tugboats were readied to patrol harbor entrances. Another regiment was sent to Detroit and Buffalo. Monck also ordered tighter vigilance and pressed a parsimonious home government to strengthen British forces on the lakes. The sensational St. Albans raid in October gave totally unwanted force to the Governor-General's warnings on the combustibility of the situation.

The raid was matured in Canada East and was the brainchild of George Sanders. Clay verbally authorized the raid. Clay and Thompson were on poor terms, and the latter disapproved of the raid when he learned of it. Thompson later asked the C.S. State Department for post-dated authorization to legitimize the affair as an act of war. On October 19 a group of some twenty Kentuckians led by a commissioned officer, Lt. Bennett H. Young, attempted to take possession of St. Albans, Vermont, in the name of the Confederacy. They robbed three banks and a citizen and tried unsuccessfully to fire the town; in the ensuing melee one townsman was killed and several injured. A Vermont posse pursued the raiders into what the latter had fondly hoped was Canadian sanctuary, captured Young and some others, but delivered them over to the Canadian authorities. On Monck's orders, fourteen of the raiders were arrested by October 23. The full scale border panic which ensued was to condition Canadian-American relations to the war's end, and after, providing heat to the quarrels over wartime compensations, Fenian retaliation, and Yankee annexationism.[6]

With difficulty Seward and Monck tried to contain a situation which the indiscretions of individuals threatened to throw out of control. Shortly after the raid, General Dix, without consulting Washington, ordered Union troops in Vermont to pursue the offenders into Canada if needed and destroy them. When Judge Coursol of Montreal discharged the prisoners (December 13) on what even Canadian papers described as a blatantly partisan technicality, Dix issued a second order: his troops were to chase future raiders into Canada, and either destroy them or bring them back to be tried by martial law. Although Stanton and northern sentiment supported Dix, his directive was perilously close to being (as the London *Times* said) "a declaration of war against Canada." For a time Washington permitted Dix's threats to stand. Seward could not safely lift military pressure from the backs of the Canadians until he obtained a *quid pro quo*: watertight neutrality enforcement. Until then he took the risk of another St. Albans, Union retaliation, border violations and war, thus springing an obvious Confederate trap. To be soft on the Canadians—as he was accused of being soft over Mexico—would have eroded dangerously his political credibility: the country's mood was triumphant as Sherman speared north toward Richmond, and the generals were having their day. From Cincinnati General Hooker chafed at "the conscious weakness of our Govt. in its foreign policy . . . in case a raid should be attempted from Canada I intend that somebody shall be hurt if I have to go into Canada to do it."[7]

Seward asked the British for extradition of the raiders and, although in principle favoring a demilitarized border, gave notice of American desire to end the Rush-Bagot agreement within the required six months. Unofficially, he proposed a review of the situation at the end of that time. If Canada failed to protect the lakes, the United States would feel free to increase its naval arms there, and Britain would bear responsibility for any future naval arms race. The release of the St. Albans raiders converted a critical number of Congressmen against the reciprocity agreement with

6. See Brian Jenkins, *Fenians and Anglo-American Relations During Reconstruction* (Cornell Univ. Press, 1969) and Leon O'Broin, *Fenian Fever, An Anglo-American Dilemma* (London, 1971).

7. Hooker to Chandler, December 19, 1864, q. Winks, pp. 319-320.

Canada. Whereas Elijah Ward had, in April 1864, failed in a House bid for abrogation and renegotiation of the treaty, Justin S. Morrill in December carried a House resolution calling for unconditional abrogation. On January 12, 1865, the Senate called for abrogation, 38 votes to 8, with Zachariah Chandler and Charles Sumner strongly in support.

The significance of such stormclouds was not lost upon the provinces. At the right moment Seward made a peace gesture: on December 17 he obtained the revocation of Dix's order from Lincoln. Coordination between Quebec and Washington had occurred from the outset of the trouble, helped along by the presence of Preston King in Quebec as Seward's peacemaker and horsetrader. Canadian opinion, moreover, showed signs of contrition (mixed with awe) toward the north, and mounting irritation at the south's abuse of provincial neutrality. Cartier (Quebec's strong-man in the cabinet) had suspended Judge Coursol and disavowed his act. Young and other raiders were rearrested. Monck responded to Lincoln's revoking act by pressing the united provinces government for a more stringent neutrality law. He was helped by pressure from Seward who instituted a burdensome passport system to apply on the border as long as subversion was a serious problem. In London Earl Russell's anger at St. Albans rebounded against the south when he rebuffed the Kenner mission (below), and the British government quietly recommended stronger Canadian laws. Seward eventually got most of what he wanted: Macdonald's Frontier Outrages Bill proposed to expel foreign nationals suspected of engaging in hostile acts against a friendly nation. Militia were mobilized for border duty, a secret detective force appointed to operate among Confederates on the Niagara and Detroit boundaries, and the Thompson mission was in effect almost totally neutralized. Seward also paid his debts. The last pieces of a complex diplomatic jigsaw were put into place in March, 1865, when the State Department ended the passport system for the Canadas, and announced that the Rush-Bagot convention would remain in force.

In the meantime Sherman's famous march through Georgia had capped Napoleon's monumental troubles in Mexico. Since the Mirimar convention, which fatally limited French options, the Emperor's concern had been to appease domestic criticism of the Mexican adventure: it was rife even in the cabinet. He tried to do so by squeezing the Mexicans dry for the profit of French creditors and sundry swindlers. Maximilian was to be maintained on a shoestring, and French sons brought home as fast as decency permitted. The policy was self-defeating and might alone have caused the death of the Maximilian regime. While the luckless Maximilian was stripped of the financial and military resources required for the pacification of the country, his helpless dependence upon French support eroded his authority and popularity. The French goals of troop withdrawals and "Mexicanization" of the war (uncannily reminiscent of Indo-China in the 1970's) rested on assumptions of expanding imperial control of the countryside, growing stability and prosperity. The patent reality was widespread Juárista control, perennial guerilla warfare, insurrection, an empty treasury, no organized national army, bickering between court factions, and an unavailing struggle by Maximilian to assert his authority over French generals (such as Marshal Bazaine) whose first loyalty was to the Tuileries (or themselves). There was another unspoken assumption underlying Napoleon's hopes—success for the south in the Civil War. When that failed to eventuate, the awesome probability had to be faced that Maximilian could be shored up only by an open-ended French commitment of massive proportions. That had never been contemplated and—in a context of utter French weariness with Mexico, resurrected American power, and prospective European war—was destined never to be contemplated.

Napoleon trusted to luck to salvage something. Right up until Appomatox, he hoped for the prolongation of the war. Perhaps the north would be too exhausted to worry about Mexico; perhaps the Anglo-French alliance (admittedly in shreds since Schleswig-Holstein) might be patched up to secure the *status quo* for colonial powers in America. Meanwhile Marshal Bazaine was plagued by orders plainly irreconcilable: he was to crush the enemies of the state and build a foundation of national unity and peace on which Maximilian was to build a lasting empire; at the same time he was to concentrate his forces, cut expenses, and prepare for ultimate evacuation. As large areas reverted to Juárista control, and loyalists were abandoned to the vengeance of the republicans, defeatist sentiments spread infectiously through the populace and government. Under the French spur, Maximilian began a draconian policy of reprisals which rendered very bitter the last phase of hostilities and ensured the Emperor's own tragic execution. Probably because he needed some camouflage to cover the inevitable withdrawal, Napoleon professed to believe Bazaine's rosy reports on Mexican conditions (deliberately rosy so that blame for any later collapse should fall on his military successors).

Pride forebade Maximilian conceding (even to himself) the full desperation of his position. Had he done so openly, he may conceivably have embarrassed Napoleon into concessions, for French pride resisted the appearance of bowing before the Americans. But Maximilian clung despairingly to his illusions. He deluded himself that Napoleon would never desert him; that the people were loyal to him; that his liberal reforms would not alienate his conservative and clerical supporters; that he could raise the lowly Indians without resentment from the Spanish-descended; that he could treat with Juárez; that, in the last resort, his good intentions were enough to win him the day. Even after the surrender of the Confederacy, he persuaded himself that Washington could be cajoled from intervention, even into recognition, and was touchingly secure in believing that the powers would guarantee his empire.

The Quai d'Orsay had no such illusions. On the occasion of Maximilian's elevation to the throne, Seward had made his warning for the future with the opinion "that the destinies of the American continent are not to be permanently controlled by political arrangements that can be made in the political capitals of Europe." That the United States desisted from stronger threats for the next year and more is explained by the exigencies of war. 1864 nevertheless brought angrier demonstrations in America in favor of the Monroe Doctrine. "Defenders" of the doctrine met in clubs, and shipped arms illegally to Juárez through New Orleans (proceedings winked at by the Union government). The Republican nominee for vice-president, Andrew Johnson, favored a punitive expedition into Mexico as "a sort of recreation" for northern soldiers after the rebellion had been crushed (June 10, 1864). Criticisms of Seward's caution on Mexico damaged his political stocks at home—they were not in any case particularly high in 1864 and he did not seriously consider himself a Presidential candidate that year—but strengthened his hand abroad. There the impetuous fire-eater now appeared the responsible statesman, with difficulty curbing the chauvinist emotions of his countrymen in the interest of international conciliation. The difference between the Secretary of State and his critics within the ruling party was narrowed in June, when a majority of Republicans at the Baltimore national convention passed a resolution acceptable to the administration. The Radical wing had favored a sweeping condemnation of antirepublican governments anywhere on the continent. Avoiding this trap, the convention viewed as menacing to American independence any European efforts "to obtain new footholds for monarchical governments, sustained by foreign military force in near proximity to the United States." As Grant made his final onslaughts on Richmond in the new year, it seemed that the politicians might be placed under insuperable popular pressure to mobilize a grand army which would drive the French invaders into the Gulf of Mexico.

Geopolitical considerations added cutting edge to northern ire. Reports, some of them originating in Mazatlán, circulated that Maximilian had ceded to France the north Mexican states of Sonora, Sinaloa, Chihuahua, Durango, and Lower California in payment for French subjugation of the old Mexican republic. William L. Gwin, ex-senator from California and a man long interested in developing the Sonora mines, was said to have been created a Duke of Mexico and Napoleon's Viceroy over the new colony. Paris had in fact abandoned plans to exploit the Sonora mines in November 1864, but the Washington State Department, unaware of this, demanded explanations.[8] They received an official denial of cession in February.

The northern press seethed. Advocates and opponents of American control of north Mexico could agree on the need to kick out the French. It all smacked of a last-ditch try by the French to complete a vital link in their supposed schemes for world commercial ascendancy. Napoleon was known to have placed high priority on construction of a transit railroad across the Isthmus of Tehuantepec. By forestalling the Anglo-Americans with their plans for a canal across Panama, France would have a stranglehold on interoceanic trade in the western hemisphere. With the completion of the Suez canal under French auspices, control of the world's major trade routes would pass to France. Less grandiosely, Napoleon's assertiveness in northwest Mexico could be construed as a flank movement upon California and preparation for the establishment of a large French naval and commercial base on the Pacific coast.

North Mexico was indeed a turbulent area, inviting to the rapacious: at varying times late in the war it promised to be a new base of Confederate resistance, the possible nucleus of a larger Texas, and the subject of a Yankee takeover masterminded by business and army interests. In July 1865, Seward received intelligence from the War Department of attempts by the Mexican imperial authorities to whip up support for the regime in west Mexico by creating the impression that Texas would be annexed. No doubt the brainchild of the local commander Meijia, such a plan would have been fatal

8. Hanna, p. 15; *NYH*, January 26, 1865.

to Maximilian's diplomacy, and no more was heard of it after American representations in Paris. Not enough is known, again, of projects floated in the north by private enterprise, in shadowy association with Juárista officials and Union generals like Lew Wallace, by which bond issues to the republicans would be secured by mineral land rights and colonization privileges in Tamaulipas and San Luis Potosí, and by prerogatives to build railroads and telegraphs.[9]

On April 22, 1864, the *Herald* had declared:

> . . . let the French and Austrians build railroads, open the mines, and develop the resources of Mexico. We shall reap the benefits thereof when we are prepared to enforce the Monroe Doctrine, which is now tied up in red tape and laid on one of the shelves of the State Department. . . .

That pledge seemed about to be fulfilled in 1865.

Meanwhile the Confederacy, in its moment of extremity, had to consider coming to terms with the north at the peace table. Duncan Kenner's doomed mission to Europe was a last-minute bid to avoid any such humiliation. The south had suffered from two disabilities in Europe: the prejudice against slavery, and belief in the inevitability of the rebellion's success without outside aid. Kenner's task was to sweep away both obstacles. The south would abolish slavery, would pay "even this fearful price" (Hotze), if that was the barrier to British or French recognition. Kenner was to make it abundantly clear, moreover, that his country stood on its last legs. If the powers expected to reap rich benefits from America's division, they must act. Otherwise a reconstructed United States would bestride the hemisphere, evicting the British from Canada and the French from Mexico. Kenner, Confederate Congressman for Louisiana and friend of Benjamin, was a leading turfman and gambler, a symbolic appointment. Long convinced that a diplomatically isolated south could not wage a winnable war, Kenner urged emancipation of the slaves as a precondition for foreign recognition or aid. Davis and Benjamin were plied with similar views from their agents and friends abroad. The Southern Independence Association of London had "steadily but kindly" advised the south "to combine the gradual extinction of slavery with the

---

9. Callahan, pp. 306-307; *NYH*, April 22, 1864, May 6, 1864. In 1866 Thaddeus Stevens proposed to the Committee on Foreign Affairs a loan of $20 million to Juárez secured on Lower California, Sonora, Sinaloa or Chihuahua.

preservation of property." In Paris, De Leon had been told repeatedly by warm friends of the south—including Persigny, de Lesseps, and court officials—that "France cannot take the lead in acknowledging the Southern Confederacy without some promise for prospective emancipation." Benjamin admitted to Hotze in 1864 that abolitionist sentiments were axioms in France; even the powerful Napoleon was "too sagacious to act in direct contravention of the settled public opinion of his people, while hampered by the opposition of the English Government."[10] (Napoleon in interview with Slidell showed fewer scruples on the score of slavery.)

By the tailend of the war the Confederate government was willing to put survival ahead of embedded racial dogma. Negroes were finally to be armed and enlisted in the army, despite fears of black uprisings and more economic chaos. There seemed little point in refusing complete emancipation. The alternative was emancipation by the conquering Yankees, plus subjugation of the south. Papers like the *Richmond Enquirer* preferred that the south become a European colony to reincorporation in the Union.[11]

By the time Kenner reached Europe, the Hampton Roads conference had taken place. Driven to seek a respite from hostilities, Confederate representatives met with Lincoln and Seward in February 1865 on board the U.S.S. *River Queen*. The Kenner mission's original goal of forestalling peace talks was thus already lost, and changed tactics were needed if anything was to be salvaged. Leverage might yet be applied on the powers, for the peace discussions on the *River Queen* were known to have raised the issue of a divertive war against either Britain or France. Rumor flew of north and south forming an offensive and defensive alliance. The Richmond press had been speculating freely on the imminence of a war between the Union and France over Mexico, or between the Union and England over the *Alabama* claims and St. Albans affair. If the powers allowed the Confederacy to sink, why should it not join the Union in vengeful retaliation against them? The *Enquirer* warned England that Canada would not survive for six months against a joint attack. "America for the Americans" was now its

10. Mann to Benjamin, January 29, 1864; De Leon to Benjamin, June 19, 1863; Benjamin to Hotze, January 9, 1864; q. Bigelow, "Shirt of Nessus," pp. 119, 122, 124. The mission is treated in Owsley, Chapter 17; William W. Henry, "Kenner's Mission to Europe," *Wm. and Mary Q.*, XXV, ser. 1. (July, 1916), pp. 9-12.

11. *Richmond Enquirer*, December 30, 1864, *Richmond Examiner*, January 2, 1865, *Richmond Whig*, January 4, 1865, *Index*, January 19, 1865.

theme. The southern people hated Lincoln and his faction, "but he is a rare bird in these States that loves England or France."[12]

All this brow-beating was to no avail. An emancipation gesture made when the Confederacy's fortunes were at the flood may conceivably have worked: that is hypothetical, and it is historically unlikely, given the nature of southern society, that such a concession would have come at such a juncture. In 1865 it was irrelevant. The south was beyond salvation. For other nations, recognition would have been a legal absurdity and a political blunder of gigantic proportion: at the simplest, it would have brought the wrath of what was now the world's most formidable army upon the offender, with no corresponding recompense to be had from the south. When Slidell broached Kenner's offer to Napoleon on March 4, 1865, he was gently rebuffed: France could not move without England; England had so decisively rejected previous imperial overtures on recognition that Napoleon was disinclined to risk a further snub. Napoleon had in fact been genuinely alarmed by the Hampton Roads talks. Geofroy, the French *chargé* in Washington (Mercier had returned to France in December 1863), warned of a possible rapprochement between the contestants. If so, "alliance against a foreign power will be the pivot of reconciliation; and we would, within the next six months, see the war transplanted to the borders of Mexico and Canada."[13] Seward had hastened to reassure Paris that nothing had changed: the United States would maintain neutrality on Mexico—Napoleon's chief worry—and entertained no aggressive designs after the war's end. However Geofroy's reports of a rift between Lincoln and Seward kept up the uncertainty: Lincoln, according to Geofroy, "would be perfectly capable of making some great decision without consulting his advisors."[14] Napoleon requested a military appreciation from his experts. It was gloomy. The French navy was not competent to convey 100,000 troops to Mexico, and carry on naval warfare single-handed against the north. A successful result was predicted for an Anglo-French combination. As that was hardly on the cards, French policy toward the Union thawed perceptibly as the war ended. In London, Mason fared no better with Kenner's deal. Palmerston (after fathoming what Mason meant with his circumlocutions on the tabooed topic of emancipation) discounted slavery as the cause of British inertia:

---

12. *Richmond Enquirer*, January 19, 1865, March 22, 1865.
13. Geofroy to Drouyn, January 24, 1865, q. Case and Spencer, p. 561.
14. Geofroy to Drouyn, February 7, 1865, q. Case and Spencer, p. 565.

> On the question of recognition, the Government had not been satisfied at any period of the war that [southern] independence was achieved beyond peradventure, and did not feel authorized so to declare when the events of a few weeks might prove it a failure.[15]

The Hampton Roads conference had of course raised the possibility of a north-south "war of liberation" in Mexico—but only for Lincoln to dismiss it. The war was almost won, and Lincoln had no intention of presiding over a peace which did not achieve full restoration of the Union and abolition of slavery. In any case, recent demonstrations of the Confederate Congress and press in favor of the Monroe Doctrine—despised for four years in the south—were transparent attempts to induce aid from Napoleon. (The *Richmond Examiner* spoke in classic terms of applying the doctrine from Bering Strait to the Isthmus of Darien.) Perhaps, the Yankee papers speculated, Jefferson Davis feared desertion of his disheartened followers to William L. Gwin's confederacy of north Mexico. The emigration of Confederate soldiery to Mexico which occurred in the war's dying phase was welcomed by many northerners: an exodus of troublesome spirits from the devasted south simplified the problem of reconstruction; it also promised, by repetition of the pattern of the 1830's and 1840's in Texas, to add a new domain to the American empire. The emigrants proved a source of embarrassment to Maximilian, threatening to embroil him with the United States over breaches of neutrality. The State Department kept eager watch for southerners carrying arms across the border, mass enlistments in the imperial army, and continuing Confederate operations against the north from Mexican bases. Nor was Maximilian enchanted by the prospect of men like Kirby Smith's battle-hardened veterans carving out a New Texas for themselves in north Mexico. Ex-Confederate volunteers for the French Foreign Legion in Mexico were carefully scattered through various corps.[16]

The involved history of Confederate colonization schemes, undertaken under Maximilian's patronage after the war, illustrated the propensity of southerners to assume leadership, and the depth of Mexican suspicion towards the newcomers. In a round-table conference at Puebla in June 1865, Maximilian made clear to his advisers, including the new French Minister, Alphonse Dano, that

15. Quoted by Mason to Benjamin, March 31, 1865, q. Owsley, p. 540.

16. See Hanna for Confederate immigration into Mexico, p. 16 and following. Also R. L. Kerby, *Kirby Smith's Confederacy: the Trans-Mississippi South 1863-5* (Columbia Univer. Press, 1972).

he hoped to reach agreement with the United States on the delicate issues of emigration and resumption of commercial relations. He rejected plans proposed by the southern agents Gwin, Pierre Soule, and the ubiquitous Matthew Maury, for Confederate soldier settlements in the northern provinces: "They would be loyal for a while, but I must think of the future. What will happen when a compact Anglo-Saxon group is established on the frontier? They will become rich and will they follow our rule or want to be independent?" He would give asylum to an unlimited influx of southerners, but only into central Mexico where they must blend with the indigenes. They were to be kept away from the Isthmus of Tehuantepec and border areas where many had had investments before the war.[17] Maury, appointed imperial commissioner of colonization in September 1865, had grandiose ideas of settling 200,000 southern families on plantations in Mexico. Although only a few thousand arrived, a land office was set up under General John B. Magruder, land surveys initiated, and a Confederate newspaper started. Maximilian's colonization decrees, however, blundered in permitting southerners to bring with them former slaves on an apprenticeship basis. Romero brought the matter to Seward's attention, Bigelow applied pressure on Drouyn, and Maximilian was persuaded by Dano to drop a scheme his country could not afford. So petered out the Confederacy's variant version of American mission.

---

17. Dano to Drouyn, June 11, 1865, q. Hanna, p. 18.

Chapter XIII

After Appomattox

> *The danger is, that public sentiment will gradually rise until it becomes uncontrollable. As in the recent civil war, the people will suddenly place in office politicians who sympathise with and will carry out their ideas. Then, without warning, the Senate will declare war; the President will call for a million of men; our veterans will take down their muskets; the Secretary of the Navy will provide transports and a convoy, and before the news of the declaration of war reaches France the first shot will be fired and the first battle won. After Mexico will come Canada, and after Canada will come Cuba. The crash will be heard, like Horace's thunder, from a clear sky.*
>
> (*New York Herald*, August 1, 1865)

One of the puzzles of civil war history is to explain why the immense anger generated against foreign foes during the war was not translated into expansionist revenge after Appomattox. Why did an imperialist outburst await postponement until 1898, when unexampled scope existed in 1865 for making a *fait accompli* which would achieve at a stroke the master design of the geopoliticians? Grant's Juggernaut awed the world; Welles' navy was (at a conservative estimate) among the top three; and Europe's distractions on the eve of the Austro-Prussian war matched those of the United States in 1861. Yet the Canadians were allowed to create their non-republican Dominion, in Van Alstyne's phrase "the great surprise of North America," which "while still in swaddling clothes . . . placed a permanent barrier against the American northward advance."[1] And the French were driven out of Mexico by "the un-American plan of matching diplomacy with diplomacy."[2] Seward's superbly pacific and self-denying strategy restored the Mexican republic, even kept intact formal friendship with the French, and gained America not an inch of territory. This extraordinary restraint determined the essential contours of the modern United States.

It did not take long even for the *New York Herald*—rarely at a loss in such matters—to see that there was dwindling political capital to be made from a campaign of zenophobia. It was still boastful: the United States had generals like Grant, Sherman, Sheridan, and Thomas, unequalled in the world; Union finances were in quite as good condition as England's, and better than those of France and Spain: "Besides this, a foreign war is the very thing we require, in order to quickly weld together in the heat of battle the divided sections of the country." But Bennett, it turned out, preferred to drive the powers away by the show, rather than the exercise, of strength. It was a remarkable climb-down from his wartime posture. As did Henry Raymond of the *Times*, Bennett now supported Seward's strategies:

> Our wisest statesmen prefer a slower, but a more peaceful process of reunion. If France will retire from Mexico, England from Canada, and Spain from Cuba, the situation will be greatly simplified and our government can afford to make some concessions in return. Let the Mexicans themselves take care of Maximilian, and he of them, the troops of France being withdrawn, and we shall not interfere. We do not want Mexico. We conquered it once and relinquished it, as we expect France to do now. England could make no more satisfactory settlement of our claim for damages inflicted by the Alabama and other rebel privateers than to quietly slip out of Canada and allow the Canadians to manage their own affairs. We do not want Canada, any more than we want Mexico; but the point is to have European Powers withdraw. . . . As for Spain, we would pay her a round sum for Cuba, as we bought Louisiana from France. Thus the whole matter would be peaceably and satisfactorily arranged and the Monroe Doctrine vindicated without a war.[3]

It was within the choice of the powers whether to accept this adjustment by treaty or by war.

Antiannexationist feeling may perhaps be sufficiently explained by reference to war-weariness and a natural desire for a return to

1. Van Alstyne, *Rising American Empire*, p. 176.
2. *NYH*, August 1, 1865.
3. *NYH*, August 1, 1865.

normalcy and time for economic and social recuperation. The expansionist vision persisted, but the American nation seemed psychologically unprepared yet to accept the full implications and responsibilities of imperialism. The ravages of war may, in this respect, have caused a deepening of certain embedded reservations about empire. It was enough for the moment within the hemisphere to expel the invaders, preferably by persuasion, and to reestablish there the regenerative principle of republicanism, while giving first priority at home to development of the existing domain. White supremacist ideas discouraged the incorporation of lesser breeds within the American sphere. The racialist theme was severely underplayed during the war when necessity dictated support for sister American republics fighting foreign aggressors. But it re-emerged when reconstruction promised a surfeit of racial troubles within the existing Union. Why add to them? Americans would have to be satisfied for the moment with a role of tutelage in the hemisphere. Ultimately if inferior peoples failed to fulfill republican expectations, they risked being supplanted by the expanding, more dynamic populations of North America. With peace, the *Herald* became unedifyingly outspoken in sneering at its erstwhile heroes, the Mexican republicans who were "not up to the mark, not yet sufficiently civilized to control their own destinies. . .":

> They need policeing, and they shall have it; but they must have it of the right kind, and if we choose we can do it just as well as France. Our sympathies . . . are enlisted on the side of American governmental ideas and principles, and not purely and simply on that of the Mexican people, who are as dust on the scale . . . the population has deteriorated irretrievably through the process of miscegenation. . . .
>
> [August 26, 1865]

According to logic of this sort, Napoleon's cardinal sin was not the imposition of order on the Mexicans—"Marshal Bazaine and his soldiers . . . have done much good to Mexico, more, in fact, than all the native governments since the country became independent"—but that France went too far, and established a monarchy. Such comments indicate the difficulty, often unconscious, which Americans experienced in repudiating their European heritage for a philosophy more appropriate to a "good neighbor" foreign policy. Despite the shock caused by the "perfidy" of the powers to the United States during the civil war, Americans continued to share European racial and cultural values.

There were also diplomatic dangers in too rashly attempting to supplant French or British power in the continent by American. The *Herald*, again somersaulting, rehearsed the reasons for treating as gently as possible the "oldest ally" France. Napoleon would be wise to withdraw his minions from Mexico, for a renewed Franco-American friendship would counter British designs to embroil and weaken its major rivals. Annexation of neighboring territories, was thus, when analyzed, a deceptively simple program. In reality it was likely to impose unbearable strains domestically, and to close the ranks of America's enemies abroad.

The triumphant Union generals did not delve so deeply into the matter. Grant, Lew Wallace, and others favored a decisive strike against the French in Mexico. In March 1865, Grant and Wallace tried unsuccessfully to wean away from their allegiance General James E. Slaughter and Colonel John S. Ford, of the south's trans-Mississippi army, with the purpose of launching a joint expedition against Maximilian. Grant's posting of a powerful army of observation under Sheridan along the Rio Grande underlined the stark alternatives facing the French: they might evacuate under diplomatic pressure, or at the bayonet's point. (The presence of Sheridan's army, eager to invade, makes nonsense of claims that military exhaustion would have precluded American intervention. With Juárista assistance, Sheridan could justly expect to overwhelm opposition in quick style before French reinforcements arrived across the Atlantic.) While Republicans such as William M. Evarts, John A. Dix, and the Blairs were recklessly Francophobe, Seward and the Marquis de Montholon (now French minister in Washington) worked for a settlement. Seward blocked a provocative move, inspired by Grant, Romero, and General John M. Schofield and backed by Andrew Johnson and Stanton: Schofield was to take leave, cross the border into Mexico, and gather together an army of ex-Confederate and Union soldiers who had emigrated; men and materials would be funnelled across the Rio Grande to fight the French. Seward diverted Schofield to Paris as a special agent with instructions "to get your legs under Napoleon's mahogany and tell him he must get out of Mexico."[4] By the time Schofield arrived in December Napoleon had no need of further persuasion.

The anxiety of Juárez and his republicans to keep the dangerous Americans at bay is sometimes overlooked as a factor contributing

4. Van Deusen, *Seward*, pp. 489-490. Schofield never saw Napoleon, but interviewed government officials.

to a peaceful settlement. Juárez wanted to appear as the real savior of free Mexico, not a puppet brought in the baggage of a conquering army. His ambivalent attitude toward the great ally to the north was to become characteristic of Latin American nationalists. Juárez's aggressive independence would have been a massive stumbling block to any annexationist move in the United States. Even apart from the fact that the forces which prevented the consummation of the All-Mexico program twenty years before were still in existence, there would have been transparent hypocrisy in any attempt to shoulder aside the Juáristas. They had been portrayed for four years as archtypal nationalist heroes throwing off foreign colonial rule, as latter-day American revolutionaries. They repudiated *any* outside dictation, and the pure theory of American mission required the consent of the subject peoples in new acquisitions. The north, after all, had exhausted its invective against the French for imposing consent at the bayonet point in Mexico. Seward gave official assurances that his country desired no aggrandizement by conquest or by purchase of land or dominion. Rumors were thus scotched that Lower California or Sonoro would be bought up by the United States, and added to the national estate.

Lincoln's assassination, which evoked an extraordinary outburst of grief from world opinion, caused Maximilian especial depression. Lincoln had promised no more wars under his Presidency; Andrew Johnson might prove a creature of popular passion. The Emperor sent an agent, Felix Eloin, to see Napoleon and King Leopold of Belgium on a bootless quest for great power protection. After his round table audience at Puebla in June, Maximilian also sent Mariano Degollado to Washington with condolences and an offer of negotiations on border problems.[5] Johnson refused to receive Degollado, agent of a party which the United States officially regarded as in revolt against the sovereign authority of a friendly country.

The new President continued to give Seward his head at the State Department. Johnson sanctioned Seward's notice to the French of rising American impatience for an early end to the French occupation. Seward's formula for a settlement offered salve for French pride: America harbored no grudges, and Mexico alone prevented restoration of the ancient friendship between two nations. (There was intriguing talk in the north of rewarding French

5. Maximilian sent agents to influence the New York press, and even tried, without luck, to buy the *Herald* in September 1865 (Corti, p. 529).

compliance in Mexico by supporting French claims to the Rhineland at an international congress.) America, Seward said, had no ulterior motives of aggrandizement; after French withdrawal, America would abide the trial of Maximilian's monarchical experiment of which "the people of Mexico must ultimately be the arbiter;" the United States stood for nonintervention in the hemisphere as at large, and applied that rule to itself. But Seward had also made it abundantly obvious that his country preferred "a domestic and republican system of government" in Mexico, and did not intend the French to rule out the chance of armed American resistance to their Intervention. A private exchange of views between Seward and John Bigelow aptly illustrated this. Bigelow had succeeded Dayton as minister to France after Dayton's sudden death by a stroke in December 1864. On August 21, 1865, Bigelow said of the American people that "opposition to the extension of European influences in the Western Hemisphere is a sentiment which they cherish but not a policy for which they will fight." Seward administered a prompt rebuke. Bigelow and Seward were at one on the unstoppability of the American steamroller southward, and both saw it as a peaceful long-term process, a matter of migrants and economic penetration. But Seward assessed Bigelow's line as dangerously soft at a critical moment, and likely to encourage French braggadocio. Bigelow came under a cloud in America by making no secret of his belief that republicanism had enjoyed indifferent success in Latin America, and was not worth defending by a ruinously expensive armed campaign. He wrote to Seward:

> The Spanish race in our hemisphere will require for many years a much more centralized government than we can offer them under our present constitution, and, therefore, it is hardly worth our while, under pretext of defending republican institutions, to get ourselves into a war with one and perhaps several of the most powerful states of Europe. I doubt if there is a power in Europe that would formally sustain our pretensions under what is called 'Monroe doctrine' . . . The mere apprehension of such pretensions would impair our credit in Europe, postpone our reduction of tariff and check European emigration to America.[6]

Out of touch with American opinion, Bigelow believed that the French might trade withdrawal for an American guarantee to recognize Maximilian as soon as he proved self-sustaining.[7] A possible

6. Bigelow to Seward, August 21, 1865, q. Callahan, *American Foreign Policy in its Mexican Relations*, pp. 309-310.

7. Clapp, *Bigelow*, pp. 247-248.

formula involving simultaneous evacuation and recognition was arrived at between Bigelow and Drouyn. It was predictably squashed by Washington (November 1865).

Monographs have been written on the circumstances leading to the French evacuation of Mexico. What emerges is that Napoleon understood the minatory basis from which American pressure was unyieldingly applied, and was alarmed by it. That is why he tried, in November 1865, to arrange a mutual assistance pact with Britain, to be invoked if the United States tried aggression against either partner. It was not an irresistable proposition as far as London was concerned. The French were offering a highly dubious contribution to Canadian security in return for probable British embroilment in Mexico. Britain's rejection of the plan underlined the other key factor compelling Napoleon to cut his losses in Mexico: France's diplomatic isolation in Europe. At a time when forecasts of European conflagration were heard on all sides, the restoration of good relations between Paris and Washington, and the concentration of French troops where they were needed, in Europe, were obvious insurance policies for Napoleon.

There was, of course, nothing new about the intrusion of European considerations into the Mexican question. It had been, all along, one piece in a complex international mosaic. It would be no more extreme to contend that the abandonment of Maximilian had been ordained in 1863, with the failure of Napoleon's design for an Austrian alliance, than to declare that it was decreed by the looming Austro-Prussian war of 1866. The French decision to announce a staged withdrawal from Mexico was made *before* the Austro-Prussian feud had moved from the serious to acute stage. And in practice the withdrawal program differed little from that envisaged in the secret provisions of the treaty of Mirimar. On February 22, 1866, Napoleon publicly promised evacuation (the decision had probably been taken the previous November); on April 5 a dispatch to Montholon in Washington specified return of the army in three detachments (November 1866, March 1867, November 1867). Mirimar had proposed no more than a three year occupation (1863-1867).

Nevertheless it would be ludicrous to forget that Napoleon's retreat took place while Europe was enduring what A. J. P. Taylor calls "the lesser revision" of the old balance of power. The Prussian victory over Austria in 1866 paved the way for German unification; and the resultant cession of Venetia to Italy completed Italian unification. Napoleon, it is true, saw no immediate danger in a stronger Prussia (nor did London and St. Petersburg). He allowed the the war to occur because it assured Venetia to the Italians—his old obsession—and promised possible pickings on the Rhine. But he needed domestic unity, and peace with America, to exploit (even to cope with) a very uncertain situation. Hence elimination of the divisive and costly Mexican issue. As Blumenthal shows, Bismarck in 1865 worried that sudden resolution of Napoleon's American difficulties might dispose the Emperor to interfere in the German question. Diseased and depressed, the Emperor showed signs of being distinctly rattled over Mexico. Bismarck also feared French humiliation at American hands, for "Napoleon might seek to recover the prestige he lost in the New World by troubling the Old."[8] Prussian diplomacy hence aimed to keep France embroiled with America, maximizing the chances of French neutrality in any Austrian war. Whether Prussian intrigues had any effect is another matter.

The February promise to evacuate French troops followed intense pressure from the United States, leading to a near-crisis in Franco-American relations in the last months of 1865. Napoleon's bitterness derived from his inability to obtain a face-saving *quid pro quo* for French submission. He would have settled for an "amicable attitude" to Maximilian by the Americans; and he offered them economic concessions. But Washington refused to give official assurances of nonintervention. They were needless, went the argument; America had always been noninterventionist. Late in November Drouyn was flatly told that the United States "still regard the French effort to establish permanently a foreign and imperial government in Mexico as disallowable and impracticable." Drouyn bridled at this. Seward's language, according to Drouyn, "practically claims that the whole American continent belongs to the United States, and that governments and institutions there must correspond to your wishes . . . If you mean war why not say so frankly?" Bigelow was dutifully evasive in response, but riposted that the American people opposed "a government founded on our borders for the avowed purpose of limiting the diffusion of the Anglo-Saxon race on the American

8. Blumenthal, p. 176. For a perceptive analysis of the effects of European power politics, p. 175 and following. See also Corti (which shows Napoleon's real anxiety on Mexico and Prussia); C. A. Duniway "Reasons for the Withdrawal of France from Mexico," *American Historical Association Reports*, I (1902), pp. 315-328; Count Otto zu Stolberg-Wernigerode, *Germany and the United States during the Era of Bismarck* (trs. Reading, Pa., 1937; original, Berlin, 1928); Perkins, *Monroe Doctrine, 1826-1867*, pp. 515-518 takes exception to explanations based on European considerations.

continent." He reported that Drouyn spoke with warmth but "seemed to imply that, if we insisted, it would be the end of their Mexican experience. . . ."[9]

It seems that Napoleon, unbeknown to Drouyn, had already accepted the inevitable. In a long interview with Union General James Watson Webb (November 10), Napoleon declared his readiness to withdraw over a two year period.[10] An old acquaintance of the Emperor's, Webb had learned in a letter of 1863 that Napoleon was tormented by his Mexican albatross. Webb looked up Napoleon on his way home upon leave of absence from Brazil, where he had been Union ambassador. He later claimed that he had persuaded the Emperor to accept a timetable for evacuation; and he promised to sound President Johnson on the proposal, which left unresolved the question of Maximilian's recognition. (Napoleon, we know, was actively considering extracting more material consolations for a retreat—his ideas included selling Sonora to the United States, and securing, belatedly, American guarantees on the French debt in Mexico. These terms were suggested to Seward in January 1866, and turned down.) It is not known if Johnson's favorable reply was passed back to Napoleon by Webb; in any case the French had received abundant diplomatic indications that a genuinely peaceful settlement was on offer. But Seward knew henceforth that the game was won, and could pile on pressure for a swifter withdrawal.

It is now legend that Maximilian proved unable to hold Mexico without French troops, which were withdrawn ahead of schedule under the demands of the European crisis and American pressure. The American army of observation was conspicuously maintained on the Rio Grande during Maximilian's decline and fall before the Juáristas. Maximilian tried to enlist Habsburg help, in the form of regiments of Austrian volunteers raised for Mexican service, but was stymied by an unexpected American threat of war against Austria. Vienna backed down with nervous alacrity to prepare for the more imminent issue of war with Bismarck's Prussia.

---

9. Quoted, Callahan, *American Foreign Policy in its Mexican Relations*, pp. 310, 315 and following.

10. For Webb's unofficial diplomacy, Blumenthal, p. 177 and following; R. B. McCormack, "James Watson Webb and French Withdrawal from Mexico," *Hispanic American Hist. Review*, XXXI (1951), pp. 274-286. Webb alleged that Napoleon offered to sell Cayenne (in the West Indies) to the United States for 50 million francs, as part of his policy of liquidating the French colonial system. Webb, who wanted a string of coaling stations for the American navy, approved.

Maximilian's fall vindicated the view, asserted throughout the Civil War by the United States and the Latin American republics, that the imperial monarchy had been imposed against the will of the Mexican people. Maximilian's execution, at the hands of a republican firing squad on June 19, 1867, was a deliberate slap in the face by Juárez to Europe's monarchs. It was perhaps his harshest gesture of independence. Not only did he spurn appeals for clemency from the old powers of Europe, but even from Garibaldi, and the world's newest (perhaps only newly restored) great power, the United States. For Maximilian's release Seward was ready to join the Prussians and other European states in a pledge guaranteeing Mexican independence.

As an act of vengeance against Napoleon, the execution was incalculably successful: the "betrayal" of Maximilian (for which the Habsburgs never forgave Napoleon), the depressing futility of the entire Mexican escapade, became the scandal of the Second Empire. The grand design had become grand folly, and Bismarck (as he aspired) took the spoils. When Prussia crushed France in 1870, few North Americans lamented the Emperor's ruin. Prussia had earned credit for its pro-northern sympathy during the Civil War, and for contributing emigrants to the Union armies. But Napoleon III was remembered as one who had, with cynical disregard, placed in hazard the mythical Gallic alliance—and all for the silver of Sonora and the "white gold" of the Confederacy. Consistent with their civil war faith in the fundamental soundness of the French people, and their belief in the need for an international fraternity of democrats, Americans welcomed the Third Republic.

Chapter XIV

Verdicts

The restraint of the great powers during the American Civil War may have been pregnant for world history, but it was too clearly the product of contingency, cynical self-regard and moral hesitations to impress as a piece of generous and lofty statesmanship. And such was the contemporary view on both sides of the Atlantic. In retrospect the distractions of European power politics helped to save the Union. What had provided earlier administrations with the opportunity to extend American hegemony provided security for the Lincoln government in America's moment of weakness. The powers did not meddle because they were unable to subdue their rivalries or find a mutually acceptable basis for intervention. Reduced to essentials, the powers, in particular France, would not intervene without the cooperation of Britain, still the world's Number One nation. As has been always recognized, British nonintervention was the key to civil war diplomacy. Even British sanction for unilateral action by France or other countries—which was on occasions forthcoming—was inadequate: indeed to Napoleon III British coaxing was highly suspicious, a trick to get him involved in yet another eroding commitment and to weaken France in Europe. The time for a joint move by France and Britain, a serious and risky intervention, had probably passed by the time Poland exploded, and it became more remote as the European situation worsened over the vital "German Question." Napoleon spoke still of joint recognition of the south and titillated southern hopes, but to further his European policies he was willing to cut his losses in Mexico (a policy arrived at during, not after, the war) and to maneuver for northern friendship. War might conceivably still have come between the north and one of the powers, had the diplomats been clumsier, had questions involving national honor and face been pressed to extremes—for there was ill-will and in plenty on all sides—but war would have come against the European realpolitik interests of the participants.

Britain was certainly subject to these restraints. Despite its power, Britain was finding it difficult to have its say on Europe's future, partly because of its military weakness in Europe and partly because it had lost control of some key diplomatic pressure points. A war with the United States would have meant having no say at all in Europe, would have sacrificed its precious freedom of action on the major theater of international politics at a vital period of change. As it was, Britain's American distractions prevented it playing the role in Europe it might otherwise have essayed. Thus America was saved, as Horace Greeley hoped it would be, by "the unprincipled egotism that is the soul of European diplomacy." Fortunately for the Union, the Civil War coincided with the first major revision of the European power balance which had lasted since the Napoleonic wars.

It is not enough to argue that Britain stayed neutral because of the profits of neutrality: booty from munitions; the spoils of blockade-running; the monopoly of the Atlantic shipping trade through transfer of the American merchant marine to the British flag; the bonanza which wartime demand brought to a range of industries (offsetting cotton unemployment). Nor is it enough to urge the more vigorous proposition that intervention spelt war, and war spelt certain economic pains and only uncertain gains: the destruction of an integrated Atlantic economy, disruption of British maritime trade, economic unrest and social divisiveness at home, etc., for the distant attractions of a southern alliance, cotton and markets. (Had there been general awareness that the cotton famine was a largely artificial crisis, and one offering enticing opportunities for development of India's colonial economy, even the cotton thesis could have been weakened.) These were powerful deterrents to adventurism, particularly powerful at the height of the free trade era, but they were capable of being overwhelmed by considerations of strategy, national interest and imperial security. What is crucial to an understanding of British neutrality is the fact that the latter factors never unequivocally demanded war and disruption of America. Ambiguity at this level permitted economic, humanitarian, moral, and domestic political forces to exert their sway upon the American question.

Englishmen debated the prospects of a war with the north at length, but there was a consensus that it would be a difficult, expensive, and in certain circumstances, an unpopular war. There is no need to rehearse the warnings that were constantly made concerning the vulnerability of Canada to the Union army, of the far-flung and exposed British possessions to naval attack, of the British merchant marine to commerce-destroyers. Again the Union was lucky, for the Civil War coincided with a time of rapid modernization in naval technology, and the north's industrial strength would have enabled it to build an effective striking force, partly neutralizing British superiority in traditional ships, and forcing Britain in any war into an expensive naval program. As one informed writer saw it in 1863, American naval advances were likely to render obsolete the blueprint for maritime war which the Royal Navy had offered during the *Trent* affair:

> Before, and at the commencement of, the civil war now raging in America, English fleets could with impunity have ravaged the seaboard of America; and I believe that our North American squadron might have steamed up to New York and laid the city in ashes. These things, however, cannot now come to pass. Doubtless we possess four or five of the finest iron-plated ships in the world; but their powers of endurance when fighting against land fortifications have not as yet been tested. Nor are we quite certain that, after having been tossed about upon the turbulent Atlantic, large iron-plated ships would be in a fit condition to enter upon a contest with earthen or stone fortifications . . . neither country would think of sending wooden ships into an engagement when one hostile iron-clad might crack them into pieces like so many nutshells. . . our military operations must of necessity be on a very limited scale—confined, probably, to the defence of Canada, the West India Islands, and other of our possessions, such as British Columbia, Nova Scotia, &c., that are in proximity to the United States' territory. Whether we could successfully defend Canada against an American invading army is problematical; at all events, to attempt its defence would cost an enormous amount of money . . . British Columbia, Vancouver's Island, and other of our outlying colonial possessions, would of necessity succumb to any serious attack made upon them, most being utterly unprotected and unfortified, and merely garrisoned by a handful of British soldiers.
>
> Taking, then, all these circumstances into consideration, it must be made apparent to every thinking mind that England has really nothing to gain, but everything to lose, by a war with America, even hampered as the Federal Government is by a successful and triumphant rebellion.[1]

1. "Gracchus" in *Reynolds' Newspaper*, May 10, 1863. This is the view of a radical spokesman, but no lover of the north.

While others were more optimistic of British chances, the force of such arguments was appreciated realistically by the War Office and Admiralty.

What international objective could justify taking such a grisly gamble? Unfortunately the documents are elusive on this vital subject. It may well be that it was never thoroughly discussed by British policy-makers, either because it was ruled out as a live issue or because they followed a pragmatic course of meeting American problems as they arose from day to day amidst a welter of other demanding questions. Even when war was seriously contemplated, at the time of the *Trent*, preservation of national honor was the only cogent and consistent motive for hostilities urged by ministers. The cliché about England wanting a breakup of the Union for realpolitik reasons, to destroy a rival in the hemisphere, to pave the way for an expansion of British hegemony in the hemisphere, was much paraded by northerners during the war, and has been paraded by many writers since; but it is a mere speculation upon which to erect a weighty edifice.[2] One might assert, with greater plausibility given the record of Anglo-American relations in the latter 1850's, that the British ministry took account of an opposite view: that British interests better flourished in a stable hemisphere based upon United States power. A balkanized America could engender threats by a revanchist north against Canada, and a wave of Confederate imperialism to the south; while the hemisphere might become a cockpit of European rivalries, open to all sorts of fishing in troubled waters. Even Napoleon, who did not scruple when advantage was offered for French aggrandizement, saw danger as well as opportunity in any breakdown of American unity; for southern ambitions threatened any client state he might set up in Mexico, while the extinction of American maritime power deprived France of a counterweight to Britain. The British were already a giant imperial power, unenthusiastic about further territorial commitments and expense. If Napoleon stood (at least nominally) for revisionism of boundaries, Britain stood instinctively for a settled international order and minimal change in the balance of power.

---

2. Palmerston made some utterances to cabinet colleagues (Russell and probably Gladstone) on the gain to England of separation, but such sentiments were uncommonly rare from government members, and, in Palmerston's case, uttered in anger at Union navy high-handedness with British ships. Bell, *Palmerston*, p. 315. Wilbur Jones, in his study of the papers of prominent Conservatives, was unable to find any expression of desire for a permanent split of the Union. W. D. Jones, "British Conservatives and the American Civil War," *AHR*, LVIII (1953), pp. 535, 542.

Nor was the generation of men who controlled British destinies in the sixties cast in adventurous mould, willing to gamble for high but frighteningly uncertain stakes in America. For most of them it was a matter of keeping out of trouble and playing safe, balancing immediate neutral interests against long-term naval interests, preserving face against Yankee bluster but avoiding a "partisan" interference which would divide the English nation. The long-term problem for England must have seemed not how to exploit American weakness, but how best to face up to the international results of the rebellion's inevitable success. Whether desirable or not for Britain, separation was going to occur. The mediation suggestions of 1862, although also spurred on by humanitarianism and a supposed need for cotton, proposed accepting this inevitability. They by no means necessarily endorsed the strategic implications of an American breakup. Gladstone personified this ambiguity, wanting peace to rescue the remnants of American liberty but believing that a unified Republic best suited British interests. When the north insisted that the issue was still in doubt, and rejected mediation as intervention in favor of the south, the steam behind mediation dissipated. It evaporated completely as the war became chronic, and as parallel attempts by the powers to mediate in Poland crumbled because of irreconcilabilities between the participants. Harcourt saw to the heart of the matter when he catalogued the reprehensibilities in Russell's peace proposals. The implications of a settlement to the war had simply not been thought through. A scheme which was forcibly imposed upon the north, and which never came to grips with the issues dividing America (including slavery and states' rights), lacked moral validity. It would appear merely a pretext for sealing the fate of a rival power. And one which offered prospects of interminable jealousies between Britain and France, jostling for position in an American power vacuum, lacked statesmanship.

Britain ended the Civil War, as Lord Campbell had forseen, despised by both sides. Victor and vanquished complained inconsolably that Britain's neutrality had favored their opponent, an indication of the problem of neutrals in extended warfare. In war, powers demand from their friends sympathy, not calculated self-interest or cool correctness, and even less a detached appraisal of the issues at stake. The war illustrated the potential for emotional crisis embedded in the Atlantic connection. It showed the extent to which intimacy of cultural contact could exacerbate and complicate ordinary power relationships. France's expediency and notorious disposition to intervention, if safe, was not as deeply resented in the north as Britain's more circumspect behavior. Resentment would have been greater toward France, one suspects, if a republican regime had been in power. Ungenerosity from a Napoleonic autocracy was to be expected; from kith and kin it was unforgivable.

To regard the recrimination which marked Anglo-American relations in the postwar generation as a mere temporary misfortune, to be rectified with the Great Rapprochement of the 1890's, appears to me misguided. The war marked the end of a distinctive, and probably the most intimate, phase in Atlantic history. The war markedly accelerated a process of social and economic disengagement which was taking place inevitably as the result of American national maturation. Cultural and economic emancipation from the old metropolitan center were natural features of this transformation. But the war added immeasurably to the incubus of bitterness and rejection which Americans carried as an historical legacy. The war disrupted, brutally and almost beyond repair, the integrative bonds of the Atlantic connection, just as it tore asunder the fibers of the body politic in America itself. What has been perhaps insufficiently recognized is the rapidity with which the relationship was impoverished, and reduced to the stark essentials of power. Peace demanded a reconstruction of America's major foreign relationship as well as of American society. Both processes proved to be acrimonious, divisive, and ultimately disappointing.

Canada raised difficult questions concerning the nature and strength of American expansionism. The whole subject of American imperial concepts and forces during the Civil War and the following decade is in need of intensive monographic research. The fate of ideals of external expansion during a time of pathological internal development may well bring into relief the critical social values underlying the debate on American destiny, both in mid-century and later. At the moment, only generalizations may be hazarded. Here are some: There was a strong expansionist undercurrent in mid-century America, despite the distractions of the sectional debate—and they were literally distractions and an irrelevancy to those intoxicated by the broader vision—and it was not extinguished by the war. Rather, anger against the powers was channeled into demands for the evacuation of all European influence (except white North American republican) from the hemisphere. America's might, having been mobilized by the rebellion, would come into its own after the south's suppression. The arrogance of northern language (one might hypothesize) was sharpened by the primitive emotions of wartime; and was unrestrained by considerations of feasibility, because everybody except a dwindling band of "foreign war panaceaists" agreed that such vendettas and adventures were to be shelved until peace. Idealist arguments justified the conferring of republican independence upon peoples still enslaved by the imperial powers of Europe; and the hope was held out that such peoples might freely join the United States, the "citadel of freedom," on terms of equality with its present inhabitants. The ideological justification for expansion was presented the more forcibly because the war had reawakened a sense of America's missionary revolutionary role in world affairs. Although the idea was quickly abandoned after Appomattox, northerners spoke violently during hostilities of launching an international movement which would unite the submerged masses of the world in a democratic jihad against oligarchic oppression.

If this demonstrated American doctrinal egotism, the war produced full measure of less edifying self-centeredness. Greed for the possession of new economic resources and control of strategically placed trade routes and communications featured in discussions of hemispheric change. Ideas of white racism and global power considerations underpinned the debate. James Gordon Bennett's suggestion that Russia and the United States divide the world between them, Russia dominating Europe and Asia while the United States ruled the "Western World," was merely an extreme expression of "brute realist" sentiment.

Peace however brought the expanionist debate back to earth, and resurrected all the old national divisions on the subject. Conventionally the latter 1860's are regarded as antiexpansionist, and it is a measure of the failure of the annexationist school that neither Canada, Mexico, nor Cuba were harvested for America, as had been freely predicted in 1865. "Horace's thunder," as we have seen, was mysteriously dissipated. Traditional preferences re-emerged for American sponsorship of continental freedom without territorial acquisitions; for annexation only on the earnest request of colonial peoples; for American racial purity and thus the exclusion of racially-mixed states (e.g. Cuba and Santo Domingo); for concentration on the development of existing frontier lands. To these considerations must be added a profound emotional reaction throughout the nation against more wars. Top priority was given to the restoration of peace, and to the problems and politics of reconstruction. While expansionism was approved in the form of informal commercial "empire," expensive military adventures were anathematized as adding to a colossal war debt. As peace brought industrial dislocations and agricultural difficulties, the hallowed cry of government retrenchment became strong. Congressional opposition was powerful even to the purchase of strategically valuable bases such as the Danish West Indies, plausibly but unsuccessfully urged by Seward as a bargain at 7.5 million dollars. Even the purchase of Alaska, which admirably suited American geo-political and strategic interests, was pulled off by Seward only after some skillful Russian bribery of Congressmen. "Seward's Folly" was acquired, instructively, amidst general public indifference.

But to characterize the postwar years baldly as antiexpansionist is to oversimplify. There were apostles and theorists of empire aplenty, even if the public was less responsive than they wished; and their ideas were to bear fruit as war memories faded, economic conditions changed, and escape was desired from the aridities and corruptions of domestic politics. Seward's restrained case for acquiring strategically important outposts on trade routes vital to American interests—e.g., St. Thomas and San Domingo in the Caribbean, Hawaii on the way to Asian markets—might have succeeded in less bitter political times. Congressional opposition to Seward's projects was essentially a method to abash the hated Andrew Johnson rather than a considered judgment on empire. The emotive politics of Reconstruction were to cut across and confuse the issue of expansion in myriad ways during the Johnson and Grant administrations. Jealousy between executive and legislative killed Grant's Santo Domingo project as surely as suspicion of sordid speculators. The nation came close to intervention in the Cuban rebellion, but Grant and a strong force of Congressional warhawks encountered the restraining influence of Sumner's radicals, and the Federalist caution of Hamilton Fish at the State Department. The hostility of Congress to the lame duck Johnson government killed Seward's hasty efforts to reach rapprochement with Britain, when the Johnson-Clarendon convention was rejected by the Senate 54 to 1. There can be little doubt that in this case Congress prevented the administration stifling deep national resentment over the *Alabama* claims. The outcome opened the gates to a flood of expansionist designs upon Canada. Some of the rhetoric on the annexation of Canada was hot air, directed by parish-pump politicians at the Irish and other immigrants; but much of it was genuine. While the "cede Canada or fight" school was a small, vocal minority, the hope of acquiring Canada peacefully—perhaps in a deal over wartime claims—penetrated even to the State Department. Zach Chandler, senator for Michigan, was not talking practical politics when he declaimed:

> Great Britain owns a little land up north of us and I, Sir, am willing to consider this a first mortgage on the little debt that Great Britain owes. I do not want arbitration. I want to let it rest until the time comes to foreclose that mortgage. This North American continent belongs to us and ours it must be.[3]

But Chandler's "spread-eaglism," uncomplicated by sophisticated economic theorizing, had wide appeal. What confounded the annexationists, ultimately, was miscalculation concerning Canadian eagerness for achieving greatness within a mammoth republic. They had interpreted the Canadian Confederation movement as a symptom of the disintegration of the British connection, and as prelude to a Canadian stampede into the Union. Instead the Dominion became established fact, permanently confining the American homeland south of the 49th parallel. Alaska was left in frozen abeyance, the top arm of a pincer originally designed to squeeze the British from the lands of the Hudson Bay Company and the crown colony of British Columbia.

The legacy of the Civil War to European politics was curiously meager, especially so considering the mammoth events and intense debate which had occurred. Perhaps the war was simply too horrible to remember. Even the military lessons it flaunted to the world—the destructiveness of modern firepower, evoking the answer of defensive trench warfare and foretelling the horrors of World War I—were quickly forgotten as Prussia's campaigns against Austria in 1866 and France in 1870 illustrated new offensive patterns.[4] Politically, the triumph of the north gave only short-term impetus to democratic movements in Western Europe. Moreover that triumph was cruelly ambiguous.

The Civil War contributed to the passing of electoral reform in Britain in at least two ways: the outcome encouraged a climate of opinion conducive to change; while the war forged a fighting partnership between middle class and trade union radicalism on behalf of the north, an experience which smoothed the path for their cooperation in the campaign for the 1867 Reform Bill. The verdict of arms at Appomattox gave a crushing answer to those who claimed that transatlantic democracy was incapable of surviving

---

3. Quoted Doris W. Dashew, "Story of an Illusion: the Plan to Trade the *Alabama* Claims for Canada," *CWH*, XV, No. 4 (December, 1969), p. 338. See also LaFeber, *New Empire*, pp. 28-39; Van Alstyne, *Rising American Empire*, p. 176.

4. See Jay Luvaas, *The Military Legacy of the Civil War: The European Inheritance* (Chicago, 1959).

as a workable system. After Lincoln's apotheosis, it seemed capable even of producing heroic statesmen. Moreover Gladstone was not alone in his joy that the distressed cotton operatives had acted reliably and responsibly during the war. During the reform debates much was made of this point as an argument for conferring the vote upon the artisan and mechanic class. Nevertheless the major franchise changes wrought in 1867 were the product of complex forces: the legislation was shaped by political contingency and expediency, it was engineered by a parliamentary elite within a largely parliamentary context, and it owed its form to hierarchic reasonings rather than to democratic doctrine.[5] The second Reform Bill, like the first, aimed to preserve the balance of the constitution—and the predominance of the country's natural rulers—by permitting a limited infusion of healthy new blood into the political system. The vote might be safely extended to include steady workingmen, likely to be deferential and adhere to current social values. Disraeli's bill, he freely admitted, was a "bulwark against democracy" and would strengthen the exclusive character of Parliament by founding it "on a broad popular basis."[6] Population pressures and expanding industrialization rendered some such adjustment inevitable. The significance of American events was as one more sign that the world was going in much the same direction. In France, the victory of the north was more damaging to the existing regime, for it magnified the prestige of Napoleon's republican opponents, the men who were to come to power with the creation of the Third Republic.

In retrospect, however, the Civil War may be seen to have occasioned the last great liberal evangel on behalf of American democracy. The great rallying which accrued to the northern cause in the war's latter years was perhaps to prove less prophetic than the doubts and hesitations which beset liberal consciences in the opening phase. As America entered the age of Big Business and the robber barons, it became easier to interpret the Civil War as a success for capitalism, political centralism and force. Those were very appropriate themes for Europe in the Age of Bismarck.

---

5. F. B. Smith, *The Making of the Second Reform Bill* (Melbourne, 1966).

6. Smith, p. 233.

Suggestions for Further Reading

The list below emphasizes important recent writings and specialist articles. For a detailed critical bibliography, dealing particularly with primary sources, see: Norman Ferris, "Diplomacy," in Allan Nevins, et. al., eds., *Civil War Books: A Critical Bibliography* (Baton Rouge, 1967), I, pp. 241-278. Many of the works cited below have excellent bibliographies, while the journal *Civil War History* includes material on diplomacy in its annual "Bibliography of Civil War Articles." The footnotes to the present work constitute more detailed references.

E. D. Adams, *Great Britain and the American Civil War.* 2 vols. (New York, 1925), and F. L. Owsley, *King Cotton Diplomacy: Foreign Relations of the Confederate States of America* (Chicago, 1931; revised ed. by Harriet C. Owsley, 1959) dominated the field until recently. Written at the time of the "great rapprochement" between Britain and the U.S., Adams' work de-emphasizes the antagonisms which developed in Anglo-American relations during the Civil War; events are carefully recounted but are viewed from the meridian of London, Union diplomacy receiving little analysis. Owsley's monumental research in the Confederate archives will remain of permanent value, but southern partisanship and an imperfect awareness of European power politics limit the book's value.

Recent monographs which have spectacularly widened our knowledge of affairs include: Lynn M. Case and Warren F. Spencer, *The United States and France: Civil War Diplomacy* (Philadelphia, 1970), a massive treatment illuminating Napoleonic policy, Union and Confederate intrigues for French sympathy. The authors confirm the traditional view that French freedom of action on America was severely limited by the alliance with Britain. The omission of the

Mexican affair from the book imposes difficulty upon the reader seeking a broad view of French strategy. Frank J. Merli's *Great Britain and the Confederate Navy, 1861-1865* (Bloomington, London, 1970) now provides the best account of southern shipbuilding abroad. His portrayal of a jittery British ministry, beset by the traditional problems of a neutral power, and meshed in the web of circumstances, offending all parties, is more convincing than the image of a malevolent anti-Yankee nation which was generated at the time. Another side of the maritime war is conveyed in Stuart L. Bernath, *Squall Across the Atlantic: American Civil War Prize Cases and Diplomacy* (Berkeley and Los Angeles, 1970), showing that the Union Navy's efforts to stifle trade with the south were made at the serious risk of an Anglo-American war. Concern for national interest, on both sides of the Atlantic, caused a retreat from the brink.

There is still no definitive study of Union diplomacy, but the gap is partially filled by Glyndon G. Van Deusen's admirable, if highly compressed, biography, *William Henry Seward* (New York, O.U.P., 1967). Seward's role as a theorist of empire is discussed in Walter LaFeber, *The New Empire* (Ithaca, New York, 1963). Students may profitably consult the rich literature on Manifest Destiny and the expansionist impulse to gain deeper insight into both Union and Confederate foreign policy. Other writings on Seward and the Lincoln administration are listed in Van Deusen's bibliography. David Donald, ed., *Inside Lincoln's Cabinet: The Civil War Diaries of Salmon P. Chase* (New York, 1954) and H. K. Beale, ed., *Diary of Gideon Welles* (New York, 1960), are sometimes useful. David Donald, *Charles Sumner and the Rights of Man* (New York, 1970), exposes Sumner's efforts to undermine Seward and take his place. Allen Nevins's ample volumes on the Civil War contain well-researched chapters on foreign policy and international opinion. Jay Monaghan, *Diplomat in Carpet Slippers: Abraham Lincoln Deals with Foreign Affairs* (New York, 1945) is lightweight and exaggerates Lincoln's role. Martin B. Duberman, *Charles Francis Adams* (New York, 1961), Margaret Clapp, *Forgotten First Citizen: John Bigelow* (Boston, 1947) are competent, but not detailed, biographies of Union diplomats. Norman B. Ferris, *Tempestuous Mission, 1861-1862: The Early Diplomatic Career of Charles Francis Adams* (Unpub. Ph.D. thesis, Emory University, 1962) is a valuable pioneering study which deserves publication. See also N. B. Ferris, "An American Diplomatist Confronts Victorian Society," *History Today*, XV (August, 1965), pp. 550-558, and other articles. S. A. Wallace and F. E. Gillespie,

Journal of Benjamin Moran, 1857-1865 2 vols. (Chicago, 1948), is a delightfully informative record of people and events by Adams' waspish secretary of legation. John Bigelow, *Retrospections of an Active Life* (London, 1910); Brainerd Dyer, "Thomas H. Dudley," *CWH*, I (1955), pp. 401-413; La Fayette C. Baker, *The U.S. Secret Service in the Late War* (Philadelphia, c. 1889, Lost Cause Press microcards, 1957); R. D. Saltvig, *Charles Francis Adams and Special Missions to England, 1861-1865* (Washington, Unpub. M.A. thesis, 1959); A. E. Taylor, "Walker's Financial Mission to London on Behalf of the North, 1863-1864" *J. Econ. & Business H.*, III (1931), pp. 296-320; H. C. Owsley, "H. S. Sanford and Federal Surveillance Abroad" *MVHR*, XLVIII (1961), pp. 211-228; D. H. Maynard, "The Forbes-Aspinwall Mission" *MVHR*, XLV, No. 1 (June, 1958), pp. 67-89 provide information on Union agents, espionage and missions abroad. P. Van Doren Stern, *When the Guns Roared: World Aspects of the American Civil War* (New York, 1965), is mainly for the general reader.

Specialist articles on the *Trent* affair are listed in Chapters 5 and 6 of the present volume, but mention may be made here of: N. B. Ferris, "Lincoln and the *Trent* Affair," *Lincoln Herald*, LXIX (1967); V. H. Cohen, "Charles Sumner and the Trent Affair," *JSH*, XXII (1956), pp. 205-219; Gordon Harris Warren, *The Trent Affair, 1861-1862* (Unpub. Ph.D. thesis, Indiana, 1969), with a useful discussion of the literature.

Owsley's work, mentioned above, is still the main authority on Confederate diplomacy, but a refreshing short reappraisal is contained in Henry Blumenthal, "Confederate Diplomacy: Popular Notions and International Realities," *JSH*, XXXII (1966), pp. 159-167. James Morton Callahan, *Diplomatic History of the Southern Confederacy* (New York, 1901; repr. 1964) is dated, but puts southern aims within a proper hemispheric context. Robert D. Meade, *Judah P. Benjamin, Confederate Statesman* (New York, O.U.P., 1943) is a competent short biography of the south's best Secretary of State. R. W. Patrick, *Jefferson Davis and His Cabinet* (Louisiana State University Press, 1961) treats relations between Davis and Benjamin. Van Mitchel Smith, "British Business Relations with the Confederacy, 1861-1865" (Unpub. Ph.D. thesis, Texas, 1949) may be used in conjunction with Martin P. Claussen, "The U.S. and Great Britain, 1861-1865: Peace Factors in International Relations" (Unpub. Ph.D. thesis, Illinois, 1937), summarized in Claussen, "Peace Factors in Anglo-American Relations, 1861-1865" *MVHR*, XXVI (1940), pp. 511-522. That the south miscalculated the nature of conditions within the British cotton industry is revealed by Eugene A. Brady, "A Reconsideration of the Lancashire 'Cotton Famine'," *Agric. H.*, XXXVII (1963), pp. 156-162, which cites the existence of ample reserves of raw cotton in England and claims that Lancashire was suffering an overproduction crisis. For the controversy over the relative importance of southern cotton and northern wheat within the British economy, see account in Chapter 9 (pp. 259-261) and statistics in Robert H. Jones, "Long Live the King?", *Agric. H.*, XXXVII, No. 4 (Oct., 1963), pp. 166-171. Jones' assertion that the British did not worry about "King Corn" may be treated with caution. Confederate financing is considered in Richard Lester, "Confederate Finance and Purchasing in Great Britain During the American Civil War," (Unpub. Ph.D. thesis, Manchester, 1962). That the Erlanger loan, with a bad press from historians, elicited vital funds in 1863-1864 is contended by Judith F. Gentry, "A Confederate Success in Europe: The Erlanger Loan," *JSH*, XXXVI, No. 2 (May, 1970), pp. 157-188. There is supplementary material in C. S. Davis, *Colin J. McRae: Confederate Financial Agent* (Tuscaloosa, 1961); Charles P. Cullop, *Confederate Propaganda in Europe, 1861-1865* (University of Miami Press, 1969) and "Edwin de Leon, Jeff Davis's Propagandist," *CWH*, VIII, No. 4 (1962), pp. 386-400; Robert T. Smith, "The Confederate *Index* and the American Civil War," (Unpub. M.A. thesis, University of Washington, 1961); Louis M. Sears, *John Slidell* (Durham, 1925). Works on Civil War Mexico (see following discussion) provide a vital dimension on southern territorial ambitions, too often neglected by scholars.

The international wrangles which arose over the maritime war and Confederate attempts to build a navy abroad are skilfully studied in monographs by Merli and Bernath, mentioned above. Readers are urged to consult Merli's exhaustive critical bibliography for further references. On the Union blockade, see articles by Marcus W. Price in *Am. Neptune*, VIII (1948), pp. 196-237; XI (1951), pp. 262-290; XII (1952), pp. 229-238; XV (1955), pp. 97-131; proving that impressive numbers of small craft broke the blockade. John B. Heffernan, "The Blockade of the Southern Confederacy," *Smithsonian J. Hist.*, II, No. 4 (1967-1968) indicates that the blockade achieved its major strategic objectives. Richard S. West, Jr., *Mr. Lincoln's Navy* (New York, 1957) and Joseph T. Durkin, *Stephen R. Mallory: Confederate Navy Chief* (Chapel Hill, N.C., 1954) discuss the naval objectives of both sides. Confederate shipbuilding is dealt with in: Wilbur D. Jones, *The Confederate*

Rams at Birkenhead: A Chapter in Anglo-American Relations (Tuscaloosa, 1961), with intriguing insights into official thinking at the British Foreign Office and Admiralty; Douglas Maynard, "Union Efforts to Prevent the Escape of the *Alabama*," *MVHR*, XLI (1954), pp. 41-60 and "Plotting the Escape of the *Alabama*," *JSH*, XX (1954), pp. 197-209; Rupert C. Jarvis, "The *Alabama* and the Law," *Trans. Historic. Soc. Lancashire and Cheshire*, (1959), pp. 181-198, plausibly arguing that the British government was legally justified in not stopping the *Alabama*'s departure; D. Maynard, "The Confederacy's Super-*Alabama*," *CWH*, V, (1959), pp. 80-132, describing efforts to build the C.S.S. *Pampero*. D. Higginbotham, "A Raider Refuels: Diplomatic Repercussions," *CWH*, IV (1958), and Frank L. Owsley, Jr., *The C.S.S. Florida: Her Building and Operation* (Philadelphia, 1965) deal with one of the early rebel raiders. James D. Bulloch, *The Secret Service of the Confederate States in Europe or How the Confederate Cruisers Were Equipped*, 2 vols. (New York, 1883; repr. 1959) is a valuable original source, written by the south's greatest agent abroad. Britain's concern to maintain her long-term interests in strong belligerent rights at sea qualified her attitude to Union naval operations: see James P. Baxter, "Some British Opinions as to Neutral Rights, 1861-1865," *Am. J. Int. Law*, XXIII (1929), pp. 517-537, "The British Government & Neutral Rights, 1861-1865," and "Papers Relating to Belligerent and Neutral Rights, 1861-1865," *AHR*, XXXIV (1928), pp. 9-29, 77-91.

British diplomacy is surveyed generally in Kenneth Bourne, *The Foreign Policy of Victorian England, 1830-1902* (Clarendon Press, Oxford, 1970), while Bourne's *Britain and the Balance of Power in North America 1815-1908* (London, 1967) examines Britain's historic naval and military policies in that theater. The chapter on the *Trent* affair is essential reading on British strategy, giving London's blueprint for an all-out Anglo-American war. Britain's European and hemispheric diplomacy is often neglected in civil war studies: see A. J. P. Taylor, *The Struggle for Mastery in Europe* (Oxford, 1954, repr. since), and *The Trouble Makers: Dissent Over Foreign Policy: 1792-1939* (London, 1957), especially chapters 2, 3, on Cobden and Gladstone, for Britain in Europe; and Richard W. Van Alstyne's articles on Central America: e.g. "British Diplomacy and the Clayton-Bulwer Treaty, 1850-1860," *J. Mod. Hist.*, XI, No. 2, (June, 1939), pp. 149-183. Van Alstyne's *The Rising American Empire* (Oxford, 1960) gives a brilliant account of the clash of British and American imperialisms in the C19. H. C. F. Bell,

Lord Palmerston, 2 vols. (London, 1936) is probably still the best biography, with more detail on the civil war years than more recent works. Bell shows that Palmerston's reputation for showy aggressiveness was belied by his concern for pragmatic British interests. Donald Southgate, *The Most English Minister* (London, 1966), and Jasper Ridley, *Lord Palmerston* (London, 1970), although excellent studies, are not revealing on civil war diplomacy. Further reading on British politics and society may be obtained by consulting Geoffrey Best, *Mid-Victorian Britain, 1851-1875* (London, 1971).

An understanding of "Atlantic history," of the cultural, economic, and political links between Britons and Americans, is essential if the war's impact abroad is to be appreciated. Frank Thistlethwaite, *The Anglo-American Connection in the Early C19* (Philadelphia, 1959), and D. P. Crook, *American Democracy in English Politics, 1815-1850* (Clarendon Press, Oxford, 1965) may serve as guides to the ante-bellum years. J. Potter, "Atlantic Economy, 1815-1860, etc." in A. W. Coats and R. M. Robertson, eds. *Essays in American Economic History* (London, 1969) illustrates the strong economic bonds between industrial Britain and a developing northern economy. Such views (including Claussen, above) give much needed corrective to the southern-oriented emphasis upon cotton's "kingly" sway within Atlantic trade. Brady (above) reappraises the nature of the "cotton famine." See also: Amos Khasigian, "Economic Factors and British Neutrality, 1861-1865," *Historian*, XXV (1963), pp. 451-465.

Max Beloff, "Great Britain and the American Civil War," *History*, XXXVII (1952), pp. 40-48, and H. C. Allen, "Civil War, Reconstruction, and Great Britain," in H. Hyman ed., *Heard Round the World: The Impact Abroad of the Civil War* (New York, 1969), are provoking general essays. Wilbur D. Jones, "The British Conservatives and the American Civil War," *AHR*, LVIII (1953), pp. 527-543, is a fine study which illustrates the Tory heirarchy's disinclination to meddle in American affairs. Case studies of international crisis points include: N. B. Ferris, "The Prince Consort, the *Times* and the *Trent* Affair," *CWH*, VI (1960), pp. 152-157; J. Wheeler-Bennett, "The *Trent* Affair: How the Prince Consort Saved the U.S.," *Hist. Today*, XI, No. 12 (Dec., 1961), pp. 811-816 (includes rare archival extracts); Frank J. Merli and T. A. Wilson, "The British Cabinet and the Confederacy: Autumn, 1862," *Maryland Hist. Mag.*, LXV, No. 3. (Fall, 1970), pp. 239-262; E. W. Ellsworth, "Anglo-American Affairs in October of 1862,"

Lincoln Herald, LXVI, No. 2 (1964), pp. 89-96; K. J. Brauer, "British Mediation and the American Civil War: A Reconsideration," *JSH*, XXXVIII, pp. 49-64.

For the historiography of the vexed issue of British public sympathies during the Civil War, see Joseph M. Hernon, "British Sympathies in the American Civil War: a Reconsideration," *JSH*, XXXIII (1967), pp. 356-367, claiming that historians writing with hindsight of Federal victory exaggerated the influence of Union supporters in Britain during the war. D. Jordan and E. J. Pratt, *Europe and the American Civil War* (1931, repr. New York, 1969) helped to create the view that English bourgeois and nonconformist opinion was partisan for the north. Their array of evidence still commands respect. The most telling recent blow against the legend of proletarian support for a democratic north is struck by Mary L. Ellison, *Support for Secession: Lancashire and the American Civil War* (University of Chicago Press, 1973). Bradford leaned to the north, according to D. G. Wright, "Bradford and the American Civil War," *J. British Stud.*, VIII (May, 1969), pp. 69-85. Joseph M. Hernon, *Celts, Catholics and Copperheads: Ireland Views the American Civil War* (Ohio State University Press, 1968) shows that the slaughter of Irish-Americans caused progressive Irish disillusion with the north. Scots opinion is treated in Robert Botsford, *Scotland and the American Civil War* (Unpub. Ph.D. thesis, 1955, Edinburgh.) D. P. Crook, "Portents of War: English Opinion on Secession," *J. American Studies*, IV, No. 2 (Feb. 1971), pp. 163-179 shows how initial journalistic sympathy for the plight of the north was eroded by events (p. 163 for review of the literature). A. Whitridge, "British Liberals and the American Civil War," *History Today*, XII (Oct., 1962), pp. 688-695, illustrates the dilemmas the war posed for liberals, the theme also of C. Collyer, "Gladstone and the American Civil War" *Proc. Leeds Philosophical Soc.*, VI, part 8 (May, 1951), pp. 583-594. Royden Harrison, *Before the Socialists: Studies in Labour and Politics, 1861-1881* (London, 1965), Chapter 2 "British Labour and American Slavery," shows the early wartime influence of a small group of labor editors with southern sympathies. Sheldon Van Auken, "English Sympathy for the Southern Confederacy: The Glittering Illusion" (Unpub. D.Phil. thesis, Oxford, 1957) is dogmatically pro-Confederate, but assembles much useful material; he claims that nonintervention by Britain was a sign of complacent belief in the inevitability of rebel independence. Biographical works of relevance include: H. Ausubel, *John Bright: Victorian Reformer* (Wiley, New York, 1966); Donald Read, *Cobden and Bright: A*

Victorian Political Partnership (London, 1967); M. Churchman, "Bagehot and the American Civil War" in N. St. John-Stevas, ed., *Collected Works of Walter Bagehot*, (London, 1968), IV, pp. 179-194; see pp. 195-425 for Bagehot's articles on the war; J. O. Waller, "Thomas Carlyle and his Nutshell Iliad," *Bull. New York Pub. Libr.* LXIX, pp. 17-30; J. O. Waller, "Dickens and the Civil War," *Stud. Philol.*, LVII (1960), pp. 535-548; W. D. Jones, "Blyden, Gladstone and the Civil War," *J. Negro H.*, XLIX (1964), pp. 56-61; Elisabeth Wallace, *Goldwin Smith, Victorian Liberal* (Toronto, 1957); F. L. Bullard, "What Goldwin Smith did for Uncle Sam during the Civil War," *Lincoln Herald*, LII (Dec. 1950); J. Saville, *Ernest Jones, Chartist* (London, 1952); N. F. Adkins, "Thomas Hughes and the American Civil War, etc.," *J. Negro H.*, XVIII (1933), pp. 322-329; J. O. Waller, "Charles Kingsley and the American Civil War," *Stud. Philol.*, LX (1963), pp. 554-568; R. Greenleaf, "Marx and the St. James Hall Meeting," (with reply from R. Harrison) *Science and Society*, XXVIII, pp. 323-325; also Karl Marx and F. Engels, *The Civil War in the U.S.* (Citadel Press, 3rd ed. 1961); G. N. Ray, *Thackeray: the Age of Wisdom 1847-1863* (Oxford, 1958). W. M. Rosetti, "English Opinion of the American Civil War," *Atlantic Monthly*, XVII (Feb., 1866), pp. 129-149 is an interesting contemporary analysis. See also C. E. Shain, "English Novelists and the American Civil War," *Am. Quart.*, XIV (Fall, 1962), pp. 399-421, and Oscar Maurer, "Punch on Slavery and Civil War in America, 1841-1865," *Victorian Studies*, I (Sept., 1957), pp. 5-28.

Further reading on Franco-American relations may be located in the bibliography to Case and Spencer's authoritative account of the topic (above). Henry Blumenthal, *A Reappraisal of Franco-American Relations, 1830-1871* (Chapel Hill, N.C., 1959) is a brilliant short analysis, giving proper weight to European power politics. Daniel B. Carroll, *Henri Mercier and the American Civil War* (Princeton, 1971) is an excellent biography of the French minister in Washington. Carroll clears Mercier of the charge of excessive partisanship to the south. Serge Gavronsky, *The French Liberal Opposition and the American Civil War* (New York, 1968) traces how Napoleon's liberal critics reinforced their domestic program from principles enunciated by Lincoln. Harold Hyman ed., *Heard Around the World: The Impact Abroad of the Civil War* (New York, 1969), has essays upon Britain, France, Central Europe, Russia, Canada, and Latin America. Vatican diplomacy has attracted much attention: e.g. Anthony B. Lalli, S.X., and Thomas H. O'Connor, "Roman Views on the American Civil War," *Catholic*

Hist. Rev., LVII, No. 1 (April, 1971), pp. 21-41. See also Jordan and Pratt, (above). Albert A. Woldman, *Lincoln & the Russians* (New York, 1952); J. W. Wieczerzak, *A Polish Chapter in Civil War America* (New York, 1967); J. Kutolowski, "The Effect of the Polish Insurrection of 1863 on the American Civil War Diplomacy," *Historian*, XXVII, pp. 360-377, are informative. For the "Russian fleet myth" see writings listed in Wieczerzak, *ibid.*, pp. 177-178. See also H. I. Kushner, "The Russian Fleet and the American Civil War: Another View," *Historian*, XXXIV, pp. 633-649.

Canada and Mexico were important theatres in which international tensions were played out. Robin Winks, *Canada and the United States: the Civil War Years* (Baltimore, 1960) is a definitive study. K. Bourne, *Britain and the Balance of Power in North America, 1815-1908* (London, 1967) is vital for British defense policy. Alfred J. Hanna and Kathryn A. Hanna, *Napoleon III and Mexico: American Triumph Over Monarchy* (Chapel Hill, N.C., 1971) narrates the rise and fall of Napoleon's "Grand Design." Their exhaustive bibliography includes recent writings on Mexico and Latin America. Nancy Nichols Barker, "France, Austria, and the Mexican Venture, 1861-1864," *French Hist. Stud.*, III, No. 2 (Fall, 1963), pp. 224-245, fits Napoleon's Mexican intrigues into the mosaic of his Austrian-Italian strategies.

Index